D1286619

HENRY KISSINGER AND THE AMERICAN CENTURY

HENRY KISSINGER

and the AMERICAN CENTURY

JEREMI SURI

THE BELKNAP PRESS OF HARVARD UNIVERSITY PRESS

Cambridge, Massachusetts 2007

Printed in the United States of America

Library of Congress Cataloging-in-Publication Data
Suri, Jeremi.
Henry Kissinger and the American century / Jeremi Suri.
p. cm.
Includes bibliographical references and index.
ISBN-13: 978-0-674-02579-0 (alk. paper)
ISBN-10: 0-674-02579-2 (alk. paper)
1. Kissinger, Henry, 1923—Political and social views. 2. United States—Foreign relations—1969–1974. 3. United States—Foreign relations—1974–1977. 4. Cold War. 5. United States—Foreign relations—Philosophy. 6. Statesmen—United States—Biography. I. Title.

E840.8.K58S87 2007
327.730092—dc22 2007006648

Epigraph: Henry Kissinger, *White House Years* (Boston: Little, Brown, 1979), 54.

To Alison, Natalie, and Zachary—
the anchors of my world

Contents

Illustrations

The convictions that leaders have formed before reaching high office are the intellectual capital they will consume as long as they continue in office.

—*Henry Kissinger, 1979*

Introduction: The Making of the American Century

The Cold War was very good to the United States. Emerging from a debilitating economic depression and a bloody world war, American society quickly amassed more wealth and power than any peer in recent memory. Ordinary citizens consumed more cars, clothes, movies, and especially food than anyone could have imagined just a few years earlier. Ordinary citizens also conceived of themselves as global leaders—spreading a gospel of political reform and economic openness to "old" societies like Germany and Japan and "new" nations like India, Israel, and Vietnam. Wealth and power were not shared equitably within the United States, but even those groups subject to discrimination lived better than they had before. Although ethnic and racial minorities continued to experience violence and exclusion, they also benefited from unprecedented social mobility. The decades between the onset of the Second World War and the terrorist attacks of 11 September 2001 were a period of grand expectations and grand achievements. The United States became—as Henry Luce, the founder of *Time* magazine, predicted—"the dynamic center of ever-widening spheres of enterprise," the "training center of the skillful servants of mankind," the self-proclaimed global "Good Samaritan." This was the "American Century."[1]

This was also Henry Kissinger's century. His career tracked the transformations of this extraordinary period. His rise to power followed broader social and political currents that he could not control. His conceptualization of policy reflected the traumas and triumphs of his rise. Kissinger echoed Luce when he explained: "I believed in the moral significance of my adopted country. America, alone of the free countries, was strong enough to assure global security against the forces of tyranny. Only America had both the power and the decency to inspire other peoples who struggled for identity, for progress and dignity." Kissinger's words reflected his personal despair during the 1930s, "when the democracies faced the gravest danger," and his personal mission during the succeeding decades, when the nation towered as the "embodiment of mankind's hopes," including his own. Kissinger was a product of his times, a child of the American Century.[2]

Kissinger shaped the larger forces around him. His influence, however, was not traditional. It did not draw on the standard sinews of power in American society—electoral politics, business success, or elite-born families. Kissinger worked through the new sources and circumstances supporting the American Century. He was part of a pioneering generation that populated new military institutions built to destroy fascism and to occupy enemy territory, new academic programs designed for postwar challenges, new expert circles charged to formulate global grand strategy, and new policymaking bodies empowered to fight the Cold War. The growth of American power meant the distribution of influence among a broader range of U.S. actors. Kissinger contributed to the American Century, operating through the new power centers.

Observers generally view Kissinger as a larger-than-life figure—a hero or a villain, a savior or a war criminal. He was, in fact, none of these things. Kissinger did not transcend his times like some Olympian "great man." Instead, he adapted to changing circumstances and seized unpredicted opportunities as they arose. His career, like the American Century as a whole, was not inwardly driven. It was deeply affected—sometimes distorted—by external factors. These included military conflicts far from North America, the collapse of foreign societies, and the emergence of aggressive regimes. The American Century was a response to international transformations; it was a global century.

It was also a century of extremes. "Our paradoxes today," Luce wrote, "are bigger and better than ever. . . . We have poverty and starvation—but only in the midst of plenty. We have the biggest wars in the midst of the most widespread, the deepest and the most articulate hatred of war in all history. We have tyrannies and dictatorships—but only when democratic idealism, once regarded as the dubious eccentricity of a colonial nation, is the faith of a huge majority of the people of the world." For all the optimism implied by the phrase "American Century," these were also what

Kissinger identified as "tired times." Leaders had to reconcile limitless expectations with limited capabilities.[3]

This historical context mattered enormously. Kissinger responded to strong social and political pressures. He did not resist these pressures so much as he channeled them for what he regarded as useful purposes. He attempted to build upon them, rather than get embroiled in them. "Leadership," Kissinger explained, "is the art of bridging the gap between experience and vision. This is why most great statesmen were less distinguished by their detailed knowledge (though a certain minimum is indispensable) than by their instinctive grasp of historical currents."[4]

Kissinger led by instinct and experience, not a rigid model or an all-encompassing theory. This was Kissinger's genius as a strategist. He held to a series of core beliefs, but he was flexible in their application. He creatively adapted his thinking to changing circumstances. For all his titanic ambitions, he recognized the constraints on individual action. Kissinger did not

Henry Kissinger working on an airplane between meetings. Kissinger made his career through tireless international travel, extensive networking, and long hours of hard work. (Courtesy of National Archives, Washington, D.C.)

seek to design a new sea for his life's voyage. He sailed along the existing currents, tacking nimbly to catch the wind in his sails. He navigated through the tidal waves of Weimar democracy, Nazi Germany, Depression-era America, the Second World War, European reconstruction, the Cold War, Vietnam, and Watergate. He survived all these storms with the scars to show their lasting effects.

This book is not a traditional biography of Henry Kissinger or a standard history of Cold War America. It is a narrative of global change, a study of how social and political transformations across multiple societies created our contemporary world. Kissinger was directly connected to many of these transformations from his early days as a schoolboy through his years as a White House official. His life offers a window into the complex international vectors of the period. It is a natural focus for understanding the intersection of different, seemingly contradictory, developments. Kissinger's career is about the rise of fascism, the Holocaust, and democratic responses. It is also about ethnic identity, education, and social networking. His activities shed important light on state institutions and definitions of citizenship. His thinking exemplifies the role of ideas, memories, and prejudices in daily life. Kissinger was a German, a Jew, and an American. He was an idealist and a realist; an internationalist and a patriot. He was the mixture of familiar and exotic ingredients that made the American Century.

The main argument of this book is that we must understand the experiences of Henry Kissinger and American power as processes of *globalization*—the interpenetration of ideas, personalities, and institutions from diverse societies. Globalization revised what it meant to be a citizen, a leader, a democrat, and a person of faith. Globalization also redistributed power among nations and people. American political and cultural assumptions shaped the formation of postwar Europe, and they did so through young men like Henry Kissinger. European "Old World" perspectives, however, gained a greater hold on American society—also through young men like Henry Kissinger. Influence was unequal, but it was multidirectional and multidimensional. It involved the politics of elite officials and the daily lives of local citizens; it included refined learning and popular knowledge. Most fundamental, influence traveled in the words and actions of bridge figures—especially Kissinger—situated by attitude and experience between different societies, as well as between different groups within societies. Henry Kissinger was an agent of globalization, but his influence came from the social margins of a changing world, not from the traditional centers of "established" authority.

Many writers have commented, often critically, on Kissinger's qualities as a thinker and a policymaker. Few, however, have attempted to understand him in his global context. A focus on the details of Kissinger's White House decisionmaking, while valuable, has contributed to a narrow perspective. As one examines the endless documentary record of his daily activities—including shining examples of brilliance and dark moments of self-serving lies—the reader quickly loses the forest for the trees. Why did Kissinger pursue particular policies in Vietnam, China, and the third world? How did he conceive of power? What were his ultimate aims? What was his grand strategy? What is Kissinger's contemporary legacy?

The more we read, the more difficult it becomes to answer these questions. Kissinger's memoirs alone run to more than 3,500 pages. Historians have followed suit with their own hefty tomes. Although this book is based on a deep immersion in the documentary record (as well as numerous interviews with Kissinger and others), it is not a chronicle of actions. I focus not on what Kissinger did, but on *why* he did it. This approach involves also asking *how* Kissinger came to a position where he could do what he did—*why* so many people invested this German-Jewish immigrant with so much power.[5]

These are the crucial questions that we must answer if we are to make sense of our recent past and think intelligibly about our future. The intricate details of Kissinger's conversations with foreign leaders are, in fact, less important than how the nature of global power changed during his career. Interpretations of Kissinger that focus on his morally questionable deeds—and there was no shortage of these—lead us to conclusions that are too superficial. Of course the brutalities committed in Vietnam, Cambodia, Chile, and Angola during Kissinger's time in office deserve condemnation. Of course his policies in these areas frequently failed to limit, and sometimes exacerbated, local suffering. These are easy judgments, particularly for those writing about events with the benefit of hindsight.

Why did Kissinger adopt particular policies? Why did so many people go along? These are the tougher nuts to crack. These are the questions about motivation, perception, and circumstance that surround any serious analysis of behavior. These are the questions about meaning and purpose that linger long after the fires of prior wars have been extinguished.

Critics of Kissinger have often resorted to labels like "evil" and "war criminal." In attempting to explain why he acted as he did, and what that tells us about broader social and political changes, these labels are intellectually bankrupt. They assume a preexisting, almost genetic, explanation for misdeeds. They remove the causes of behavior from analysis, and they absolve everyone but the perpetrator from criticism. We can all feel better about ourselves if we can find Kissinger alone responsible for thousands of deaths. The rest of us have proven our moral fiber by condemning him.

This is much too simplistic. If only evil men and women committed bad deeds, then we could easily eliminate the bad apples from our basket of potential leaders. The fundamental issue is why good men and women com-

Henry Kissinger and Mao Zedong in November 1973. Kissinger had little expertise on Asia, but he saw China as a natural regional power that could work with the United States. Kissinger's thinking about an "opening" to China grew from his political and strategic considerations before he entered the Nixon administration. (© Bettmann / CORBIS)

mit bad deeds—why the "best and the brightest," in David Halberstam's memorable words, sometimes produce the worst results. Leaders must be accountable for outcomes, but outcomes alone do not explain the leaders' behavior or their character. We must avoid reading history as a simple moral tale, devoid of context and complexity. We must place the individual, even the most empowered individual, in his larger social and political setting.[6]

Good men made policy during the American Century, and Kissinger was one of them. Their accomplishments and failures were not genetic. They were rarely personal. Policy reflected ideas, pressures, and perceptions rooted in shared international experiences. The circumstances of the Cold War, and the common understandings of those circumstances, encouraged good men to make particular decisions—for better and for worse. They were not tools of their times, but they were powerful products of it. We can understand why men like Kissinger acted as they did only if we examine how they reacted to the hopes and fears of their era. They formed their convictions, as Kissinger admits, before they entered office—in the crucible of common and disorienting experiences. The American Century grew from a few key formative moments and the shifts they elicited in dominant views of power.

Democratic Weakness

The American Century began with the collapse of Weimar democracy. Germany in the 1920s was one of the most vibrant, sophisticated, and diverse societies. It boasted the best minds of the era—Thomas Mann, Martin Heidegger, Theodor Adorno, Bertolt Brecht, and Albert Einstein, among many others. It also had a wealth of political parties—social democrats, conservatives, centrists, communists, and national socialists—representing a broad spectrum of opinion throughout the country. Weimar Germany was at the center of Western civilization and the democratic hopes of the twentieth century. In comparison, the United States was still a backwater.

The rise to power, with little resistance, of a genocidal Nazi regime exposed the hollowness of these hopes. Sophisticated citizens supported hatred and violence. Good democrats failed to resist brutal dictatorship. Foreign societies pledged to humane principles of government—including

Great Britain, France, and the United States—failed to act against the Nazi onslaught until something more than their principles was at stake.

Witnessing these events firsthand, Henry Kissinger could only conclude that democracies were weak and ineffective at combating destructive enemies. They were too slow to act, too divided to mount a strong defense, and too idealistic to make tough decisions about the use of force. This was the central "lesson" of appeasement—the appeasement of the Nazi party within the Weimar system, the appeasement of Nazi Germany within the international system. Democracies needed decisive leaders, and they needed protections against themselves. The solution was not to jettison democracy as a whole, but to build space for charismatic, forward-looking, undemocratic decisionmaking in government. This was precisely the route that Great Britain and the United States took, under the leadership of Winston Churchill and Franklin Roosevelt, when they finally went to war with fascism. This was precisely the model of heroic politics for Kissinger and many others of his generation.

The United States was a savior—a "haven," as Kissinger put it—not because it was a democracy, but because it possessed enormous power that it was willing to deploy, however belatedly, for the defense of humanity and Western civilization. Although American society was filled with prejudice, violence, and injustice, it valued basic freedoms that fascism denied. For Kissinger and many other Europeans, the United States was a necessary protector, not an idealistic beacon. It had a mandate to destroy dangerous threats, not to remake the world in its image.[7]

Countless citizens of Europe, Asia, and other parts of the world looked to America for refuge and encouraged its influence in their societies against worse alternatives. This was the consensual basis for the American Century. One might even call it the foreign "invitation" for an American Century. Kissinger certainly thought in these terms. In the years around the Second World War, the United States expanded its reach in response to local pressures and often against its own contrary inclinations. This was not an empire designed in Washington.[8]

It also was not an empire of democracy. The primary urge for American expansion was protection—physical protection, protection of basic freedoms, and protection of an imperiled Western civilization. Too much democracy, on the model of Weimar democracy, was the problem, not the solution. Many observers feared that in countries like Germany, Japan, and

Italy democracy would bring communists and other enemies to power. The United States took the global lead to prevent this occurrence. It frequently sacrificed democracy abroad and at home to combat perceived threats. This was a reaction to the apparent weakness of democracy, evident in the collapse of Weimar Germany and the rise of Nazi power. It was a source of the skepticism about democracy, and the desire to curb its excesses through firm leadership, that underpinned policymaking in the Cold War.[9]

The American Century reflected a turn away from democratic idealism and a turn toward the "realism" of strong, authoritative "statesmen." This shift reflected the influence of actors at the social and political margins of power, particularly citizens in societies threatened or overrun by fascism. Although it heightened U.S. global power, this "realism" challenged assumptions about good governance. It set a new tone for American relations with foreign countries, as well as for political behavior within the United States. The language of democracy proliferated, but the practice of democracy narrowed.

Henry Kissinger with Egypt's Foreign Minister Ismail Fahmy in August 1975. Kissinger's "shuttle diplomacy" transformed the Middle East and set the trajectory for contemporary politics in the region. Kissinger's Jewish background was an ever-present issue in his negotiations. (Courtesy of David Hume Kennerly / Getty Images)

Kissinger came of age with a generation that defined growing American power in terms that challenged bedrock democratic beliefs. Calling for the United States to "temper its missionary spirit," Kissinger emphasized the limits on ideals in the American Century. On the basis of his own personal experience in Weimar Germany, he warned: "Righteousness is the parent of fanaticism and intolerance."[10]

Jewish Cosmopolitanism

The American Century was not a democratic century, but it was a Jewish century. Many people, including Kissinger, are uncomfortable with this statement, but it is nonetheless true. With remarkable speed and breadth, Jews moved from the margins to the centers of global power. In the United States and other countries before the 1930s only a very small number of Jews attended elite universities, directed public corporations, or made government policy. These walls of Jewish exclusion crumbled in the decades after the horrors of the Holocaust and the Second World War. By the 1960s Jews had achieved extraordinary success in mainstream society, with a powerful presence in universities, corporations, and government offices. They continued to face prejudice and exclusion, but Jews were prominent players in the American Century.[11]

Henry Kissinger was part of this story. His career reflected major shifts in popular attitudes and professional needs that not only allowed Jewish mobility, but often encouraged it for instrumental purposes. Kissinger's German Jewish identity limited his opportunities for becoming a doctor in the U.S. Army, but it facilitated his ascent into counterintelligence, his return to Germany in American uniform, and his assumption of high-level occupation duties. Desperate to manage the vast territory it held in Europe at the end of the Second World War, the Army privileged Kissinger's German-language skills and his knowledge of European society. Despite his own short time in the United States, Kissinger's Jewish background ensured that he would not sympathize with the Nazi enemy.

This pattern of combined exclusion and privilege continued throughout Kissinger's career. He gained admission to Harvard University after the Second World War, when American higher education sought to accommodate military veterans and showcase the openness of a free society. Students like Kissinger displayed the country's commitment to "Judeo-

Christian" values, in contrast to the anti-Semitism of Nazi Germany and the atheism of the Soviet Union. Jews became symbols for the creation of more worldly, open, and policy-relevant universities. The U.S. government underwrote this effort through the G.I. Bill and new infusions of funding to private and public institutions.

Kissinger, however, was never a "Harvard man." He and other Jews of his generation lived separate lives from other students. They did not have access to the elite social clubs, and they were not fully accepted among their peers. Instead, they gravitated to fields—including international affairs—where they had skills and experiences valued by powerful academic figures on campus, as well as by policymakers in Washington. Jewish immigrants like Kissinger had knowledge of foreign societies that the United States needed as it prepared for a wider global presence. They had foreign networks that could help build American influence overseas. Most significant, they felt a deep commitment to assuring American power as a necessary bulwark against the violence and hatred they had experienced in their native lands. Jewish immigrants were cosmopolitans and patriots at the same time—an essential combination for successful policy in the Cold War.

Kissinger and other Jews rose through tradition-bound institutions because their attributes as "outsiders" were valued by specific "insiders." They gained enormous power through informal channels of influence—including new programs at universities, new international exchanges sponsored by various governments, new links between the campus and the White House, and new policymaking bodies. Influence, however, did not buy acceptance. For all his fame and power, Kissinger remained an outsider to mainstream American society. He and other Jews depended on personal patronage from non-Jews, and they remained targets of anti-Semitic suspicion, often from the very men who promoted them.

Kissinger's career captured the mix of Jewish privilege and exclusion that characterized the American Century. His German Jewish background was essential for his rise to power, but it detracted from his public legitimacy. It gave him an aura of sophistication and cosmopolitanism that policymakers embraced. It also made it much more difficult for him to escape the distrust of ordinary citizens. He was a fascinating figure, but he was a shadow figure. He was the consummate globalist, but he did not fit the common image of a mainstream American leader. Kissinger was acutely aware of this ambivalence. He sought to assert his American manhood by staging photographs with some of the nation's best-known feminine celebrities. This maneuver, however, only highlighted the social awkwardness of a German Jewish "sex symbol" in the American Century. Kissinger's ethnic identity increased and diminished his power at the same time.[12]

His Jewish background is a topic Kissinger does not discuss in public. He is hardly unique in his reticence. Nonetheless, this book will demonstrate how the "interlocking economic, political, and cultural conditions of Diaspora Jewry"—and various reactions to these conditions—deeply affected his career. Kissinger's Jewish background did not determine his policies, but it did shape his opportunities and his choices. It helped to define his hopes and his fears. Most significant, it influenced his understanding of power and its appropriate uses. The American Century was about much more than struggles over Jewish identity, but Kissinger's life shows the centrality of this topic to global change.[13]

I want to be clear: this is not an argument about some kind of international Jewish conspiracy. That is absolute nonsense. It is also offensive. My argument is that the contested and transformed social status of Jews is

Kissinger's ceaseless travels and negotiations drew a mix of admiration and derision. This cartoon from 7 December 1976 captures some of the public ambivalence about Kissinger. The wording also refers to Kissinger's Jewish background. (As published in the *Chicago Sun-Times*. Cartoon by John Fischetti.)

crucial to understanding Kissinger's career, international politics, and the history of the last eight decades. We need to find the language for discussing the relationship between Jewish identity and international power. Kissinger never did this. I hope to end this silence.

Foreign Policy

What does this discussion of the American Century, democratic weakness, and Jewish identity mean for foreign policy? How did it affect diplomatic decisionmaking?

Kissinger provides an answer. He admits that policymakers, including himself, depended on the "convictions" they acquired before they entered office. "Any statesman," he writes, "is in part the prisoner of necessity. He is confronted with an environment he did not create, and is shaped by a personal history he can no longer change. It is an illusion to believe that leaders gain in profundity while they gain experience." Referring to his own frantic schedule in office, Kissinger recounts: "There is little time for leaders to reflect. They are locked in an endless battle in which the urgent constantly gains on the important. The public life of every political figure is a continual struggle to rescue an element of choice from the pressure of circumstance."[14]

Foreign policy is dominated by discussions of interests, threats, and capabilities. Big ideas rarely get direct attention because decisionmakers are so focused on day-to-day pressures. The ways in which leaders interpret and respond to daily events, however, are deeply conditioned by their basic assumptions, their core values. Ideas do not determine interests, threats, and capabilities, but they have enormous influence. American anticommunism, for example, was surely strengthened (and perhaps overmilitarized) by ideological assumptions about the inhumanity and aggression of Soviet-style regimes. This was not a proposition subject to proof. It was a belief shared by many citizens, born of a common set of experiences. It was an assumption that preceded and framed daily policy decisions.[15]

Kissinger was no different from other policymakers. He brought deeply held ideas into office. If anything, he had a more fully formed strategic vision than many of his counterparts, and he was determined to implement it. Like most people's, Kissinger's assumptions about the world came from formative experiences in his life before he entered office. If we are to understand his policies, we must understand these experiences and the ideas they produced. If we are to understand why he acted as he did, we must understand where he came from. Kissinger's life context is necessary policy context.[16]

Despite numerous claims about his moral failings, Kissinger firmly believed that he acted within the bounds of a strong "moral compass." And of course he did. All policy involves moral calculation. Interrogating the sources and meaning of Kissinger's moral compass provides a foundation for analyzing his motives and purpose. It also sheds light on the ethical atmosphere of the time—the deeper values buried within the American Century.[17]

For all his distinctive characteristics, Kissinger is one of us—a product of the remarkable social and political transformations since the 1930s. He is an immigrant who achieved great success in postwar America. He is a thinker who embraced revolutionary changes in society, but also remained attached to traditional ideas about Western civilization. He is an internationalist who continued to emphasize the importance of national loyalty and state power. Most of all, Kissinger is a man of passion who sought to do good in the world by making tough choices—"helping my adopted country heal its wounds, preserve its faith, and thus enable it to rededicate itself to the great tasks of construction that were awaiting it."[18]

Having witnessed the violent "collapse" of a society filled with morally self-righteous figures, Kissinger defined his career as a response. He was "impatient with people who thought that all they needed to do was make a profound proclamation that made them feel good." "I mean," Kissinger elaborated, "I had seen evil in the world, and I knew it was there, and I knew that there are some things you have to fight for, and that you can't insist that everything be to some ideal construction you have made." This was the central "lesson" of the 1930s that guided millions of citizens through the Cold War. It continues to influence foreign policy.[19]

Perhaps Kissinger was too impatient with moral proclamations about democracy and human rights. Perhaps he was too quick to fight, too confident in his own judgment about acceptable deviations from ethical strictures. This is the accusation that haunts Kissinger and the American Century. When I asked Kissinger where he would draw the line between necessary and excessive moral compromise—just and unjust deviations from principle—he did not have a clear answer:

Author: What are your core moral principles—the principles you would not violate?

Kissinger: I am not prepared to share that yet.[20]

Kissinger is a man struggling with this question. He entered politics for moral reasons, and he worked feverishly to make the world a better place. His actions, however, did not always contribute to a world of greater freedom and justice. Frequently, the opposite was the case. Like all of us, Kissinger confronts the realization that good intentions often produce bad results. He contends with his own complicity in unintended consequences.

Henry Luce encouraged the United States to become a global "Good Samaritan" in the American Century. Americans generally strove to play this role. Sometimes they succeeded, and sometimes they failed. Kissinger's career captures this contradictory experience. It points to the difficulties of coordinating power with goodness. It reminds us that instead of simple slogans, we need more engagement with the hard work of political compromise.

ONE | *Democracy and Its Discontents*

"The fateful question for the human species," Sigmund Freud wrote in 1930, is whether civilization can master the "human instinct of aggression and self-destruction. . . . Men have gained control over the forces of nature to such an extent that with their help they would have no difficulty in exterminating one another to the last man. They know this, and hence comes a large part of their current unrest, their unhappiness, and their mood of anxiety."[1]

Freud was hardly alone in his premonitions of disaster at a time when the world had entered a severe economic depression and fascist demagogues were preparing to seize power across Europe. The decade since the end of the First World War had witnessed a remarkable expansion in *both* democracy and violence. This was especially the case in Germany. Under the February 1919 constitution signed in the town of Weimar, Germany had a vibrant political system of multiple parties, a directly elected president and legislature (the Reichstag), and even a bill of rights guaranteeing equal freedoms. German society in the 1920s was a mecca for experimental literature, arts, and life styles. With the dissolution of the imperial regime at the end of the First World War, Germany had become one of the most democratic societies in European history.

Hand-in-hand with democracy, Weimar Germany became a site of pervasive violence. Paramilitary groups operated throughout the country, often engaging in street battles and attacks upon political figures. The Nazis were only one of many parties to maintain their own militia for the purposes of intimidating enemies, bullying citizens, and, on occasion, attempting to seize government power. Paramilitary groups also used rhetoric designed to incite violence. Through newspapers, beer hall meetings, and public speeches, they encouraged citizens to embrace extreme racism, xenophobia, and anti-Semitism. Demagogues used the democratic process to call for the murder of the alleged internal enemies who had "stabbed Germany in the back" during the First World War.

Democracy in Weimar Germany allowed a culture of violence to flourish. Freud recognized this when he wrote of the "aggression" and "self-destruction" that challenged contemporary civilization. His analysis also anticipated the Nazi seizure of power in 1933, through a combination of elections, political maneuvering, and violence. The Nazi party rejected basic democratic assumptions of individual freedom, but it exploited democratic protections for dissent to build a base of public support. This was not only a German story, as Freud recognized. Throughout continental western Europe after the First World War, fascist parties emerged as powerful forces within the most civilized and democratic societies—Italy, Republican Spain, France, Austria, and Germany. These violent threats to democracy were, paradoxically, creatures of democracy.[2]

Historians have complicated this assessment of the Nazi rise to power, but the association between Weimar democracy and fascist violence remains strong in the minds of many, especially those who remember the horrors of the 1930s. Hannah Arendt, a refugee from Nazi Germany, famously argued that the breakdown in the old aristocratic order in Europe, and the emergence of an atomized "classless society," allowed for violent "totalitarian" regimes to acquire mass support. "Totalitarian movements," Arendt wrote, "use and abuse democratic freedoms in order to abolish them." Theodor Adorno, also a refugee from Nazi terror, was highly critical of Arendt's writings, but he concurred with her assessment of violence in mass society. In the shadow of the Second World War, Adorno contributed to a landmark study that deciphered an "authoritarian personality" lurking beneath the rhetoric of individual freedom in the United States and other countries—an inclination to repression and violence among citizens that undermined democracy from within.[3]

A deep apprehension about democratic weakness accompanied this fear of democratic violence. Democracies, according to this view, often enable extremism and prevent effective government responses. This was also a lesson that many observers internalized from the experience of the 1930s.

Confronted with consistent aggression from the fascist powers in Europe and Asia, the more powerful democratic states—especially Great Britain, France, and the United States—failed to respond. Fascist leaders were remarkably open about their long-term expansionist aims, but democratic societies were unwilling to use necessary force. Focused on their internal needs, distrustful of the military, and fearful of fighting another world war so soon after the cataclysm of 1914–1918, they capitulated to fascist aggression through a weak-kneed policy of appeasement. Japan seized Manchuria without serious sanction. Italy attacked Ethiopia in complete disregard for the League of Nations. Germany remilitarized the Rhineland, persecuted its own Jewish population, and seized first the Sudeten region and then all of Czechoslovakia without any military resistance from the major democratic states. It is not surprising that on the eve of the Second World War Hitler viewed Great Britain and the United States as cowardly societies.

As with accounts of the Nazi rise to power, historians have complicated this assessment of appeasement. Surely, France, Great Britain, and the United States confronted many limitations on their ability to deploy military force in the context of economic depression and internal unrest. Nonetheless, the glaring fact for men and women who lived through this period was the absence of any effective democratic response to fascism until it was too late for the millions who suffered. Nazi Germany's neighboring states could have defanged the regime without too much difficulty in the mid-1930s, when the nation still commanded limited economic and military resources. Instead, democratic citizens chose the path of least resistance, assuming postures of moral righteousness in the nonuse of force and hoping, without any evidentiary basis, that their adversaries would moderate themselves if only they received kind treatment. Winston Churchill spoke for much of the generation that witnessed appeasement's failure when he recounted "how the malice of the wicked was reinforced by the weakness of the virtuous; how the structure and habits of democratic states, unless they are welded into larger organisms, lack those elements of persistence and conviction which can alone give security to humble masses."[4]

Despite the skepticism about democracy evident in these comments, the leading American foreign-policymakers after the Second World War were Churchillian in aspiration, and often in rhetoric as well. Churchill's warnings about the perils of appeasement and democratic weakness in the face of determined enemies provided a framework through which Cold War presidents and their advisors analyzed foreign threats. Instead of tolerating the perceived aggression of an adversary—especially the Soviet Union—in faraway places, American leaders acted to bolster U.S. capabilities and to deter the enemy with shows of strength. Maintaining what one historian describes as a "preponderance of power" across modes of force and regions of conflict would prohibit communist expansion before the threat grew beyond manageable proportions.[5]

This was the essence of containment—holding the line against enemy advances through actions that rejected both appeasement and a headlong rush to war. George Kennan, one of the most influential architects of U.S. containment doctrine, famously articulated this approach when he called for a commitment to "confront the Russians with unalterable counterforce at every point where they show signs of encroaching upon the interest of a peaceful and stable world." Contrasting "intelligent long-range policies" with the "momentary whims of democratic opinion," Kennan counseled "patient but firm and vigilant containment of Russian expansive tendencies." Containing communism, in the eyes of Kennan and America's other leading Cold War strategists, would require "moral and political leadership" that extended beyond the normal "indecision" and "disunity" of democracy.[6]

The nature of containment, and the judgment of democracy implied by this doctrine, contributed to an unprecedented centralization of power in institutions like the Department of Defense, the Central Intelligence Agency, and the Office of the President after the Second World War. The United States did not become a "garrison state," but the institutions of political and military power extended far beyond the democratic limits assumed by earlier generations of citizens. Never before did the U.S. maintain such a large permanent war-fighting capability in peacetime. Never before did American society devote itself on such a scale to permanent international commitments of military force and economic aid. This strategic transformation constituted, according to one historian, a "revolution" in the structure and assumptions of American democracy.[7]

Henry Kissinger's career was a product of this revolution. From the perspective of 1930, no figure was less likely to rise to the top of American society. From the perspective of the twenty-first century, no figure appeared more firmly rooted in the upper echelons of power. Understanding this transformation in Kissinger's status reveals how fundamentally the structures and assumptions of international authority changed from the demise of Weimar Germany through the Cold War. In an era that made democracy the touchstone of political legitimacy, pervasive distrust of democracy anchored the professional maturation of Kissinger and many of those around him.

Kissinger's biographers consistently criticize their subject for being out of touch with a common American democratic sensibility. There is certainly some truth to this claim. Kissinger, however, was not unique in this characteristic. Placed within his historical context, it becomes clear that his profound misgivings about democratic influences on society and foreign policy were, in fact, quite common. The experiences of Weimar Germany's collapse, the Nazi rise to power, and the Second World War convinced an entire generation of observers, including Henry Kissinger, that democracy had a very dark side.[8]

Politicization of the citizen body contributed to instability and violence at home. It also motivated inaction and cowardice when confronting foreign threats. Forced into exile by the failures of Weimar democracy, and witnesses to the flaccid nature of democratic responses to fascism during the 1930s, young men and women of Kissinger's milieu could not help but search for some alternative to mass politics. This was more than just an intellectual issue; it was a matter of deep emotion for people violently uprooted from their homes and threatened with death while their neighbors passively looked away. Where was the democratic resistance to Hitler? It was sparse and ineffective within the "civilized" world. Freud anticipated this when he described the aggression and self-destruction that underpinned modern societies. Kissinger and his generation never forgot this painful lesson.

A Bavarian Jewish Background

When Nazi officials began to track the Kissinger family in the early 1930s for eventual elimination, they noted that Louis Kissinger, Henry's father, was of "Bavarian" citizenship. They recorded the same citizenship for Henry and his younger brother, Walter. A Bavarian political identity did not, of course, preclude German loyalty, but it did indicate an important set of historical peculiarities. The Nazis described many of the citizens they observed, including Jews, as "Germans." They made a special effort to single out Jewish families like the Kissingers as "Bavarian."[9]

The Nazis recognized something obvious, but generally forgotten by historians of the twentieth and twenty-first centuries. Bavaria's long history of independence and its frequent antagonism with other major German states, particularly Prussia, had a lasting impact on political and social development in this central European region. After 1800 the kingdom of Bavaria expanded its territorial holdings as part of Napoleon's imposed reorganization of the German states. King Max Joseph allied himself with France, and benefited accordingly. The expansion of his kingdom involved the acquisition of territories heavily populated by Orthodox Jews. A more centralized Bavarian monarchy implemented new laws for civil equality, but it also maintained strict restrictions on Jewish mobility. The new Bavarian state was a mix of Enlightenment and anti-Enlightenment ideals. It navigated between French and Prussian influences.[10]

Bavarian political uniqueness, especially with regard to Jews, became particularly pronounced during the nineteenth century. Like many of its

Kissinger's parents celebrating the Jewish holiday of Purim with friends in Fürth, Germany, 1930. Last row, second from left: Louis Kissinger. Second row, first from right: Paula Kissinger. (Courtesy of Miriam Kühnberg)

counterparts, the state pursued a series of rapid "modernization" programs, but the major reforms differed in important ways from those instituted in the rest of what became a single Germany. These historical particularities had a lingering influence on Henry Kissinger, especially as he witnessed the collapse of Weimar democracy and the rise of Nazi power in his youth.

Efforts to create an urban industrial economy, a standardized educational system, and an efficient system of bureaucratic administration—all touchstones of modernity in the nineteenth century—followed in Bavaria from the actions of a highly centralized monarchical government. In 1813 Maximilian I signed a "Jewish Edict" that gave this small and repressed minority a new status for the purposes of strengthening the economy and bringing social stability to his state. The edict continued to restrict Jewish residence and marriage rights, and it was filled with limitations on religious observance. It did, however, grant Jews standing as Bavarian citizens, subject to protections from the monarchy. In place of their previous legal status as foreigners, the Jewish Edict made this minority population a legitimate part of a modernizing society.[11]

Maximilian II, ruling Bavaria during the turbulent revolutions of 1848, prohibited the implementation of reforms for more representative and democratic governance throughout the kingdom. He did, however, seek to expand the legal protections for Jewish citizens. The legislation written by Maximilian II's government promised Jewish emancipation from residential, marriage, and other legal restrictions. It would, at least in theory, guarantee Jews full legal equality before German law. This initiative reflected the efforts of the monarch to improve Bavaria's foreign image and to strengthen the region's economy, which was partially dependent on Jewish traders. Maximilian II and his advisors used their considerable power to force the lower house of the Bavarian parliament to endorse unprecedented freedoms for Jewish citizens.[12]

Jewish emancipation was imposed from above by a centralized and absolutist Bavarian monarch. It followed the will of an authoritarian leader. Citizens, in contrast, expressed their opinions through widespread and often violent resistance to expanded Jewish rights. Grassroots activism ran strongly in the direction of anti-Semitism. Avenues for democratic expressions of popular opinion—especially political clubs and daily newspapers—

became highways of hatred and intolerance. As one historian explains, "democratic forms were used for non-democratic purposes."[13]

Much of the resistance to Jewish emancipation came from apparently liberal groups that had pushed, especially in 1848, for democratic openings in Bavarian society. In 1849 and 1850 more than 1,700 local organizations petitioned the government to reject Jewish emancipation. These organizations included many of the "democratic clubs" that had formed in earlier years to advocate general political reforms. Only three communities, including Kissinger's future hometown of Fürth, petitioned in support of emancipation. The municipal council in the village of Hirschau was more representative of common Bavarian beliefs:

> Although as Christians we have the duty to extend our love also to our Israelite brethren and intend to exercise that duty to its full extent, we find ourselves nevertheless compelled by the equally sacred duty of self-preservation to protest most energetically against the emancipation of the Jews. . . . we consider the proposal to grant equality absurd because in many of the circumstances of civil life, for example, in the observance of religious holidays, in marriages, and so on, they [Jews] can under no conditions ever be part of our community.[14]

Popular opinion and democratic activism in Bavaria forced the government of Maximilian II to rescind its promises of Jewish emancipation. Opposition throughout the kingdom created a powerful backlash that undermined progressive authoritarian reforms. Among the thousands of grassroots activists at the time, very few individuals and organizations stepped forward to defend Jewish rights. The governing elites of Bavaria were a crucial and ultimately ineffective brake on the spread of mass intolerance. The majority of citizens probably did not wish any harm to the Jewish population, but they were apathetic, and sometimes explicitly supportive of anti-Semitic social movements, long before Adolf Hitler came on the scene.[15]

Bavarian Jews like Louis Kissinger and his son Henry were certainly aware of this history. They could see its effects around them everyday in the residential and recreational isolation that continued to characterize the Jewish community in the region, even after the First World War. They had also witnessed enough popular manipulations of anti-Semitic sentiment to know that democratic activism could not be trusted to bring tolerance and progressive reform. Quite the contrary: popular opinion in Bavaria had frequently motivated expressions of hatred and violence. This was the case even in relatively tolerant cities like the Kissingers' own Fürth.

For Bavarian Jews faith in democracy did not come easily. As a very small religious and cultural minority, they had a lot to lose from governance by popular opinion. At the same time, they had also long suffered under the yoke of intolerant authoritarian regimes. This situation created a dilemma with few simple solutions. The Kissinger family appears to have reacted as one might have expected: they eschewed Marxist-inspired movements that promised liberation through the empowerment of the masses. They similarly refrained from joining any of the countless rightist parties in early twentieth-century Germany that advocated a return to absolutist government.[16]

Henry Kissinger grew up in a household that, like many contemporary Bavarian Jewish families, generally avoided politics. Louis Kissinger appears to have favored conservative nationalists who promised to improve life for all German citizens through strong and effective leadership rather than reliance on mass action. Henry remembers that his father voted for the Center (Zentrum) party, which emphasized civil equality and rejected both socialist collectivism and liberal individualism. The Center pledged to preserve authority and tradition, infusing politics with a strong moral impulse. It sought to build an enlightened antirevolutionary government with wise leaders. This vision drew extensive Jewish and Catholic support in Bavaria, as well as in other parts of Germany. It survived the onslaught of Nazism and the Second World War to become the basis, after 1945, for Christian Democracy in West Germany and the powerful leadership of Konrad Adenauer.[17]

Conservative nationalism differed markedly from the democratic idealism and distrust of centralized government so common throughout Europe during the early twentieth century. In the history of Bavarian Jewish emancipation, centralized government policies were more progressive than democratic opinions. Reformers around the globe looked to "the people" for positive change, but the peculiarities of Bavaria created a strong bias against popular rule. One should not be surprised to find that a young man coming out of this milieu focused his intellectual energies on the actions of governing elites, not those of grassroots activists. For Henry Kissinger, progress was born in the palaces of the most powerful statesmen, not among the rowdy rabble in the street. Circumstances in Weimar Germany furthered this sensibility, just as they offered new opportunities for economic and social advancement.

The Weimar Experience

Kissinger began his life as a witness to democracy's brightest hopes and its darkest despairs. Born on 27 May 1923 to a respected teacher, Louis Kissinger, and the daughter of a prosperous merchant family, Paula Kissinger (née Stern), he grew up in a culturally dynamic and relatively wealthy German community. Kissinger's hometown of Fürth, located just west of Nuremberg in the relatively flat Middle Franconia section of Bavaria, was a trading hub for farmers and small-scale industry. The town had a modest population of about 70,000 residents at the time of Kissinger's birth, 2,500 of whom, including the Kissingers, were Jewish. In a setting that was almost 75 percent Protestant, the small Jewish community had seven synagogues. Like the population of Fürth as a whole, the town Jews had strong ties through family, religion, and trade to rural Jews, as well as to those residing in larger urban settings, particularly Nuremberg and Munich.[18]

Fürth was, in many ways, a model of democratic politics at work during the Weimar years. From 1920 to 1932 more than 80 percent of the town's population voted in each election for the Reichstag, a higher proportion than elsewhere in Bavaria or in Germany as a whole, not to mention other Western countries. At least four different parties—some representing the extreme right, some the extreme left—received more than 5 percent of the vote in each election. Although the Social Democratic party (SPD) was the largest political organization in Fürth until 1932, it never dominated the town the way single parties did in the United States at the time. Even when support for the Nazi party grew across Germany in 1932, the SPD and other parties (including the Communist KPD) continued to draw competitive voter totals. Citizens of Fürth—Protestant, Catholic, and Jewish; male and female—actively participated in politics. Democracy nurtured a truly diverse and representative spectrum of opinions.[19]

Kissinger recalls that his family was part of the comfortable "middle class" during his early years. Neither elite nor impoverished, they had access to education, modest financial resources, and high culture. Louis and

Paula Kissinger had every reason to expect that their two sons, Henry and Walter, would live even more comfortable and respectable lives. Daily life in Fürth was democratic in its promise (and reality for a time) of social mobility—even for Jews. Long after his forced exile from the city, Louis Kissinger recalled that it provided him with the "happiest years of my professional career." Growing up in Fürth during the 1920s, the Kissinger children probably had better social prospects than their counterparts in Paris, London, or even New York.[20]

Religious groups generally lived separately from one another, but Fürth was integrated in its professional and recreational spheres. The Kissingers belonged to the Orthodox Neuschul synagogue, and Henry recalls that his father was "strictly observant." Louis Kissinger, however, taught at secular schools, where the vast majority of students were non-Jewish, until he was prohibited from doing so by the Nuremberg Laws of 1935. Similarly, Henry and Walter Kissinger attended secular state schools for their early education. This division between private religiosity and public identification with German culture was typical for upwardly mobile Jewish families in Fürth and other cities. The Kissinger children received instruction in Goethe at their state school and the Talmud within family and synagogue circles.[21]

The Kissingers were never fully assimilated into German society; they lived in Jewish neighborhoods, belonged to Jewish religious and recreational groups, and socialized predominantly with other Orthodox Jews. The Kissingers and their counterparts nonetheless conceived of themselves as Germans in their national, professional, and cultural identity. They were German Jews inhabiting a social space that was neither entirely Jewish nor fully German. This in-between position for German Jews was a source of insecurity, but it was also largely accepted, and even respected, in mainstream Weimar society. Despite pervasive anti-Semitism, Jewish voices were overrepresented in the German public culture of the time. German Jewish uniqueness often translated into recognized cultural creativity.[22]

Henry Kissinger's recollection of his middle-class upbringing reflects the combined aspirations and limitations of his German Jewish youth. He could never be one of the *Volk,* rooted deep in the soil of German society. Nor could he ever reach the status of the *Junker* elite, with their familial connections to large landed estates and the aristocratic honors of military service. This outsider status was reinforced by Louis Kissinger's exclusion from military service during the First World War. The Kissingers were a patriotic German family, but they lacked the markers of identity that defined belonging in the mixed milieu of inherited aristocracy and mass nationalism during the early twentieth century.[23]

Confronted with the exclusions derived from their ethnic background, upwardly mobile Jews defined their German identity in terms of culture, not blood. Historian George Mosse, himself a German Jew, writes that families like the Kissingers "reached for *Bildung* in order to integrate themselves into German society." *Bildung,* roughly translated as "inward cultivation," implied a connection with the best and most beautiful mani-

Neuschul, the Orthodox Jewish synagogue attended by the Kissinger family in Fürth, Germany, circa 1935. (Courtesy of Sammlung Vizethum, Stadtarchiv Fürth)

festations of German culture. Instead of defining identity by inherited characteristics, this concept of the learned and well-rounded person attached belonging to a set of timeless ideas accessible to all citizens who strove to improve themselves. The imagined world of *Bildung* was a community of cultivated intellects acting for enlightened self-interest and the welfare of the German people.[24]

Aspirations to *Bildung* were the lodestar for Henry Kissinger's early upbringing, and they colored his mature identity as a scholar and policymaker. Louis Kissinger's salary was by no means large, but it allowed for the acquisition of materials that placed the family in dialogue with the elements of high German culture that marked citizens, including Jews, as people of stature and respectability. The small apartment at 5 Marienstrasse, where the family resided from 1925 through the fall of 1938, included a wealth of books from the German literary classics and a piano on which to learn the finer forms of music. These were common nourishment for the worldview of the aspiring middle class, seeking an assured place for itself within Weimar society. *Bildung* was an elitist framework for defining values and belonging, but it was also democratic in allowing for participation based on study and intellect, not on lineage. *Bildung* promised that culturally attuned citizens could transcend their contemporary circumstances.[25]

The literary classics and the piano in the Kissinger household were all indications that this family, like its neighbors, sought to transcend the confinements of early twentieth-century Fürth. They perceived themselves to be in dialogue with the cultural values articulated by Goethe, Schiller, and Wagner. These were the great ideas that made good German citizens, even of Orthodox Jews. As a teacher and a proud inheritor of Germany's best traditions, Louis Kissinger passed these values on to his children, providing what his famous son later remembered as the "family's moral compass."[26]

When he does talk about his childhood, Henry Kissinger emphasizes soccer rather than study, but there is no doubt that the home and intellectual community where he came of age placed great emphasis on cultural self-improvement rather than youthful pleasures. German society encouraged this approach to life, and the experience of interwar democracy in Fürth made the basic elements of *Bildung*—attention to cultural tradition and a striving for connection with the great ideas of the past—central to the worldview of individuals who were both upwardly mobile and insecure in their standing within German society. *Bildung* was an anchor not just for learning, but also for belonging among the Kissingers and other Jewish families.

Kissinger's first major intellectual work is a clear manifestation of the profound influence this German cultural background had on his thinking. Less than twelve years after his family fled Fürth, and less than four years after he completed his military service in the U.S. Army, Kissinger wrote a truly extraordinary undergraduate thesis at Harvard University, "The Meaning of History." Unreadable in sections, and obscure in others, this 388-page document (perhaps the longest undergraduate thesis ever written at Harvard) reproduces the peculiarly German intellectual climate of the early twentieth century. In structure, argument, and scope it reflects a striving for self-improvement through a deep engagement with the most distinguished thinkers of the past. Focusing in particular on the philosophy of history in the writings of Oswald Spengler, Arnold Toynbee, and Immanuel Kant, the text ranges much further afield to meditate on Homer, Virgil, Dante, Milton, Spinoza, Goethe, Rousseau, Hegel, Dostoyevsky, and many others. Kissinger could not possibly have read all of these au-

Henry Kissinger (right) with childhood friend Heinz (Menachem) Lion in Germany, 1937. (Courtesy of Miriam Kühnberg)

thors during the brief period he attended Harvard. Nor could he have digested these works during active military duty in the Second World War. The conceptualization of his thesis and the dialogue with classical literature on which he drew came, at least in part, from his German education in Fürth.

The thesis makes an extended argument about the necessity of *Bildung* for a free society. This is most evident in the concluding section, titled "Freedom and Necessity Reconciled—A Clue from Poetry." "Poetry," Kissinger writes, "is truer than history for it exhibits the spirituality with which man meets the inexorability of events."

> . . . action derives from an inward necessity, from the personal in the conception of the environment, from the unique in the apprehension of phenomena. Consequently, objective necessity can never guide conduct, and any activity reveals a personality. Reason can help us understand the world in which we live. Rational analysis can assist us in developing institutions which make an inward experience possible. But nothing can relieve man from his ultimate responsibility, from giving his own meaning to life, from elevating himself above necessity by the sanction he ascribes to the organic immanence of existence.

Echoing the giants of the German literary canon, the twenty-seven-year-old Kissinger concluded that "ultimate liberation derives from within us, from an experience both personal and essentially incommunicable."[27]

Kissinger focused his thesis on the relationship between culture and freedom—one of the central issues for German thinkers in the early twentieth century. He argued that the ideas, practices, and institutions of a particular time provide the only foundations for expressions of human value. Freedom for Kissinger is not a manifestation of individual autonomy or even individual rights (this phrase is largely absent from his thesis), but instead a distillation of a society's inherited wisdom and a creative application for human betterment. Cultures rise and inevitably fall as their collective wisdom peaks, and then reaches a dead end, soon surpassed by another emergent culture. Freedom is about the "recognition of limits," "which man transcends by infusing it with his spirituality." Kissinger defines spirituality in secular and psychological terms, to mean the inner emotions and strivings of the human soul, the "mystical" longings of humanity for meaning beyond immediate material pleasures:

> Freedom is not a definitional quantity, but an inner experience of life as a process of deciding meaningful alternatives. This, it must be repeated, does not mean unlimited choice. Everybody is a product of an age, a nation, and environment. . . . No culture has yet been permanent, no striving completely fulfilled. It is not given to man to choose his age, or to the statesman the condition of his time. But the form taken by the particular period, the meaning given to life is the task of each generation. Man can find the sanction for his actions only within himself.[28]

This somewhat tortured meditation on the relationship between culture and freedom implies an intellectual skepticism about democracy as an inherent political value. Buried in a long footnote in his thesis is the assertion: "If a man has no transcendental experience of freedom . . . an argument about democracy becomes a discussion of the efficiency of economic systems." Democracy without transcendent culture is empty and unfree. Cultural achievement, for Kissinger, must come before democracy. *Bildung* provides the framework for freedom.[29]

Like other thinkers who came of age in Weimar Germany, Kissinger saw culture as the fount of political and social value. He and his family gained stature and freedom in society through neither wealth nor aristocratic loyalties. Their mobility reflected an asserted personal connection with the inherited values of German culture, the assumed touchstones of greatness that passed from one generation to another and were accessible through education in the broadest possible sense.

Democracy allowed for access to *Bildung,* but it also devalued the cultural wellsprings that Kissinger and many of his generation venerated. Weimar society, like its other democratic counterparts, nurtured a plethora of avant-garde activities that explicitly challenged cultural tradition. The plays of Bertolt Brecht, for example, inverted assumptions about the good, the beautiful, and the righteous, leading viewers to question the basic boundaries of cultural authority. Similarly, the atonal music of Arnold Schoenberg re-attuned ears to accept a new grammar for melody and rhythm in their lives. These expressions of cultural radicalism had their analogues in politics, especially among the parties of the far left. Political radicalism threatened to explode the cultural ballasts that middle-class German Jews like the Kissingers clung to in Weimar society. Freud and Spengler were only two of many authors who saw cultural decline in the innovations of a more democratic public square.[30]

Of more immediate significance, Weimar democracy permitted the most violent and destructive groups, particularly the Nazis, to terrorize those who most deeply valued German cultural traditions. Inherited German values and contemporary democratic institutions proved remarkably weak at defending themselves against internal assault. Skilled demagogues, particularly Adolf Hitler, bastardized complex ideas and subverted elaborate political institutions by appealing to the base emotions of a defeated and insecure people. The emotional instability of a sophisticated democracy, and its susceptibility to simplistic manipulations of inherited thought, remained a staple of Kissinger's thinking long after he had personally heard the Führer's oratory. "Demagogic skill," Kissinger remembered, "catapulted Hitler to the leadership of Germany and remained his stock in trade throughout his career."

> With the instincts of an outcast and an unerring eye for psychological weaknesses, he shunted his adversaries from disadvantage to disadvantage, until they were thoroughly demoralized and ready to acquiesce to his domination. . . . The essence of demagoguery resides in the ability to distill emotion and frustration into a single moment. Gratifying that moment and achieving a mesmeric, nearly sensual relationship with his entourage and the public at large became Hitler's specialties.[31]

Demagoguery of this kind exploited democracy. Hitler and other Nazi leaders recognized that they could make their extremist vision respectable by combining it with a thin veneer *Bildung*. They framed their calls for militant nationalism and racial purity not as a revolutionary program, but instead as a return to a unique German cultural essence. The Nazis, as a consequence, did not depict themselves as a party, but instead as an organic movement rising from the inherited values of German culture. Through modern technology and organization, the Nazis promised to resurrect the imagined civilization of greatness and purity described by Goethe, Wagner, and other cultural icons. The Nazis would construct a "Third Reich"—a third empire, a third Rome—built on backward-looking ideas of spirit, righteousness, and race. Their program was one of cultural revitalization in the face of alleged repression and decline.[32]

A society that valued cultural sophistication was, paradoxically, susceptible to cultural extremism in an environment filled with political uncertainty. The "psychological weaknesses" Kissinger identified derived from the factionalized partisanship of Weimar Germany and from the inability of any government to pursue a coherent and effective set of policies after the late 1920s. Worldwide economic depression combined with a disunited political system to make true statesmanship nearly impossible. Mass "emotion" and "frustration" opened the door for a "mesmeric" figure who could offer simple cultural solutions to deep structural problems.[33]

Kissinger's assessment of democratic demagoguery reflected specific experiences of the Jewish community in Fürth during the Weimar years. For all the prospects that this city offered for middle-class Jewish mobility, it also floated precariously amidst a sea of intolerance. The Franconia region of Bavaria, in which Fürth was located, possessed one of the most virulently anti-Semitic populations in all of Germany. This circumstance was, in part, a reaction to the fact that the majority of Bavaria's Jews lived in this area, making their presence more of a perceived threat to non-Jewish residents. Franconian Jews lacked adequate numbers for democratic political clout, but their economic and cultural presence was sufficient to draw popular animosity.

Public figures exploited the combined prosperity and vulnerability of Jewish communities to mobilize citizens. One of the region's foremost historians points to the ways in which local extremists, especially within the clergy, mixed anti-Semitic prejudice with religious zealotry:

> Synagogue arson, the desecration of cemeteries, attacks on Jewish property, the hanging of effigies, and other outrages were prompted not only by economic rivalry or social envy, but reflected, too, still existent religious antagonism of Christian towards Jew. Allegations of ritual murders or well poisonings and the ancient slur attached to the "crucifiers of Christ" or "murderers of Christ"—sentiments sometimes inflamed by comments of Catholic priests or Protestant pastors—all occasioned isolated outbreaks of violence against Jews throughout the nineteenth century.

Jews were not only an economic threat, but also a population that, despite their self-conscious attachment to *Bildung*, undermined the cultural hegemony of Christian beliefs. Demagogues drew on a large repertoire of religious intolerance to enlist Christianity in their anti-Semitic attacks.[34]

The Kissingers' neighbors generally were not vicious Jew-killers, but they carried a common cultural prejudice against Jews that, when provoked, triggered exclusion, harassment, and sometimes violence. Although the majority of the citizens in Franconia did not participate in anti-Jewish attacks, they also refrained from any strong action to prosecute or condemn extremists. In the years after the First World War, public attacks on Jews increased in the region just as new professional opportunities for Jews were opening. Demagogic figures, including Hitler, merged cultural prejudices with more virulent assertions of Jewish racial inferiority and treachery against the German nation. This rhetoric garnered support from groups of citizens, particularly in Kissinger's Franconia, who resented the achievements of Jewish families.[35]

Even successful and respected Jews lived precarious lives, susceptible to threats from demagogues who played upon public prejudice. Raffael Mibberlin, a prominent physician, explains that a small cohort of anti-Semitic extremists used public denunciations of Jewish professionals to threaten their safety and to intimidate their potential clients. Mibberlin recounts how, following a denunciation of him in the anti-Semitic press, loyal patients apologized: "Now, doctor, I can no longer visit your practice." The patients confessed disagreement with anti-Semitic slurs, but also fear of public harassment for associating with a condemned citizen. Mibberlin benefited from opportunities to become a doctor in Weimar Germany, but he also suffered from the inherent precariousness of his professional stature as a German Jew.[36]

Louis Kissinger and his son Henry could hardly have avoided a similar sense of precariousness. They lived in close proximity to one of the most notorious and effective anti-Semitic demagogues of the Weimar period—Julius Streicher. From the neighboring city of Nuremberg, Streicher commanded a private militia of thugs who terrorized Jews throughout the region. The fact that Fürth was only minutes by train from Nuremberg rendered Streicher an ever-present threat to Kissinger's community. He published a newspaper, *Der Stürmer,* that used the freedom of the Weimar press to spread vicious and provocative calumny about German Jews throughout Bavaria, and Germany as whole. It was, for example, Streicher's *Der Stürmer* that jeopardized Raffael Mibberlin's medical practice, without legitimate cause.[37]

Beginning with its first issue in April 1923 (one month before Henry Kissinger's birth), *Der Stürmer* published a steady stream of salacious, disgusting, and baseless articles about Jewish sexual defilement of German women, abuse of German workers, and corruption of German neighbors. The articles contained graphic language that accused Jews of criminal, heartless, and animalistic behavior. They also included emotionally manipulative cartoons contrasting clean-cut Germans with apelike Jews to incite even the most casual newspaper reader. Published weekly, with an average circulation of about 13,000, *Der Stürmer* expounded hatred of Jews as a call to arms in Nuremberg, Fürth, and all of Germany. After early 1927 most issues of the newspaper proclaimed on the front page, in large bold print: "The Jews are our misfortune!"[38]

Streicher played upon the fundamental weaknesses of Weimar democracy: anti-Semitic prejudices, protections for extremists who exploited these prejudices, and the unwillingness of citizens to take concerted action against groups committed to undermining democracy. As a lingering presence, Streicher contributed to a growing culture of intolerance and violence, particularly during the years of economic depression after 1929. Long before the Nazis came to power, *Der Stürmer* circulated as an ever-present cudgel to wield against the Jewish population. One observer explains: "Never before or since was there a newspaper that so crudely proclaimed racial hatred to so many people."[39]

Streicher also made it possible for the Nazis to become a political force, with extensive organizational roots and a small core of committed followers, in Fürth and surrounding areas. Despite frequent tensions between Streicher and Hitler, the two men coordinated their activities to maximize Nazi support. Their collaboration included planning mass rallies, fabricating news stories, and undermining potential challengers on the left and the right. Although the Nazi party never enrolled more than 200 official members in Kissinger's hometown before 1930, thanks to Streicher it had widespread recognition and a strong street presence, including a contingent of "shock troops" (the Sturmabteilung, or SA) that Hitler had personally ordered to Fürth.[40]

Living in the shadow of Streicher's rabid anti-Semitism, the Kissingers were certainly aware of his hate-filled activities. He was a bully who circulated around Nuremberg during the late 1920s and early 1930s. Henry Kissinger's childhood friend Menachem Lion recalls the fear that swept through the Jewish community of Fürth, particularly when Streicher and the Nazis held public meetings. Lion remembers that Jewish families, including his own and the Kissingers, stayed at home as much as possible.

Streicher's followers frequently harassed and beat Jews they encountered on city streets.[41]

The local Jewish press focused on Streicher and his threat to respectable families. On 1 December 1929, for instance, the widely read *Nürnberg-Fürther Israelitischer Gemeindeblatt* published a detailed exposé on the anti-Semitism provoked by *Der Stürmer.* The article closed with a call for Jews to "demand an acknowledgment of our rights in this embattled position." Alarmist accounts of growing threats and the need for legal redress appeared frequently in Jewish newspapers.[42]

Before the Nazis came to power in 1933, Streicher threatened the survival of Jews in Nuremberg and Fürth. Menachem Lion explains that even as a boy living in Fürth he recognized that his fate was affected by Streicher's hooliganism. Henry Kissinger surely shared his friend's insight. During his career, Kissinger would reserve special animosity for dictators who operated with the zealotry and violence he remembered from Streicher. Kissinger's views of fascist and communist extremism, embodied most clearly by the figures of Hitler and Stalin, were filtered through his early years in Fürth.[43]

Even more significant than Streicher's presence in Weimar Germany was the absence of effective resistance against his hate-filled demagoguery. The historian Fritz Stern, who also came of age in Germany at this time, comments on how rarely one witnessed acts of "civil courage"—how rarely people challenged unjust authorities. Stern and Kissinger saw the failure of learned, wealthy, and well-informed Jewish citizens to organize practical political alternatives against the rising anti-Semitism in their midst. Despite all the attention given to Streicher in the Jewish press, leaders of the Jewish community remained essentially unpolitical. Confronted with hatred and violence, Jews turned inward, arguing that a more united and religiously devout community would outlast its adversaries.[44]

Jewish newspapers published numerous articles calling upon readers to renew their spirituality and, simultaneously, prove to society at large that they were good Germans. As late as December 1933, nine months after the Nazi seizure of power, the *Nürnberg-Fürther Israelitischer Gemeindeblatt* printed a front-page article by a prominent rabbi explaining that the future safety of the Jewish community required redoubled efforts at German "assimilation." In the face of Nazi political manipulations and acts of terror, the rabbi returned to *Bildung:* A "good German spiritual life—that is true assimilation." *Das Jüdische Echo,* published by the leading Zionist group in

Bavaria, had a plan for Jewish immigration to Palestine, but for those who stayed in Germany it, too, counseled assimilation, not resistance.[45]

One must be careful not to blame the Jews of Fürth for their tragic fate. Nonetheless, the lack of resistance to Streicher and Nazi extremism, especially in this particular Jewish community, is striking. Jews had limited capabilities, but they possessed wealth, professional standing, and organizational resources through their religious and social institutions. The inability of the Jewish population to mobilize against extremists, even when the overriding threat was clearly acknowledged, revealed a fundamental limit in the possibilities of democratic activism. Not only were Germans generally passive in the face of Nazi terror; the very targets of terror failed to take defensive action. The Jews of Fürth were not deluded, but they were unwilling to face reality and to act accordingly. They lacked effective leaders, and they lacked a sense of collective purpose. Their reaction to Streicher and Nazism devolved to a pathetic and self-defeating appeasement. "Assimilation" in 1930s Germany was a defeatist attempt to mollify hateful enemies.[46]

The most consistent strain in Kissinger's writings, throughout his career, is a definition of leadership—what he often calls "statesmanship"—as the exact opposite of the German Jewish passivity he witnessed in the 1930s. His assessment of the great leaders in history has always rested on the presumption that democratic citizens are not capable of recognizing and responding to grave threats in the midst; they need powerful figures who can cajole them to act in concerted and effective ways before it is too late. This was the conclusion Kissinger drew from his early study of Prince Clemens von Metternich and Viscount Castlereagh, the "masters" of Europe in the early nineteenth century:

> The statesman is therefore like one of the heroes in classical drama who has had a vision of the future but who cannot transmit it directly to his fellow-men and who cannot validate its "truth." Nations learn only by experience; they "know" only when it is too late to act. But statesmen must act *as if* their intuition were already experience, as if their aspiration were truth. . . . The statesman must therefore be an educator; he must bridge the gap between a people's experience and his vision, between a nation's tradition and its future.[47]

Kissinger used almost exactly the same words in his assessments of Otto von Bismarck, Winston Churchill, Mao Zedong, and Charles de Gaulle.

All these men, in Kissinger's estimation, resisted overwhelming popular opposition and created new possibilities for those around them. All these men were heroic in vision and effectiveness. Of Bismarck, in particular, he wrote: "The real distinction is between those who adapt their purposes to reality and those who seek to mold reality in the light of their purposes. Bismarck—as all revolutionaries—belonged to the latter group. . . . Bismarck sought his opportunities in the present; he drew his inspiration from a vision of the future."[48]

There were few heroic leaders in Fürth, in Weimar Germany, or in interwar Europe as a whole. Kissinger wrote of the need for leadership as a very young man, and he came back to this exact topic in the final volume of his memoirs, published more than forty years later:

> The ultimate task of a leader is to take his society from where it is to where it has never been. But this requires a willingness to travel on the difficult road between a nation's experience and its destiny. He is bound to be alone at least part of the way until his society's experience catches up with its possibilities. . . . A leader unwilling to risk solitary acts will doom himself and his society to stagnation—witness the democratic leaders of Europe between the two world wars. This is why courage is probably the most important single attribute of a successful leader.[49]

Looking across his experiences in Weimar Germany and his subsequent career, Kissinger concludes that "normal electoral processes" will not alone produce true statesmen. In modern democracies, he laments: "Leaders rise to eminence by exploiting and manipulating the mood of the moment. They define their aims by consulting focus groups rather than following their own perceptions. They view the future as a projection forward of the familiar."[50]

The leaders of the nation and of the Jewish community in Weimar Germany were not statesmen, by Kissinger's definition. They comfortably extolled familiar prejudices and forms of behavior to a mass audience. Men of courage and vision did not emerge from the state's democratic architecture. Courage and vision required nurturing in separate, nondemocratic quarters.

Democracy, from Kissinger's earliest years in Fürth, gave succor to violence, demagoguery, and cowardice. Like Freud, Kissinger recognized that society required something more—leaders who could mobilize and inspire for positive purposes. Kissinger would struggle throughout the rest of his life to associate with leaders of this kind. He would also strive to act and represent himself in this heroic mold.

Internal Exile in Nazi Germany

Louis Kissinger was not a heroic figure. In all his son's writings on leadership, he never mentions his father in this context as a model or even as an inspiration. This is a telling silence. Instead, Henry Kissinger describes his father as a victim—a man trapped within circumstances he could not control. This is a marked contrast from Henry Kissinger's refusal to describe himself in these terms. The father represents the tragic plight of good German Jews, alienated from their cultural homeland and maladjusted to a new country; the son embodies the generation of the Second World War, with roots in two societies but also exiled from both in certain ways.

Louis Kissinger's alienation from German society began almost immediately after the Nazi accession to power in March 1933. In the autumn of that year he was suspended from his teaching post at the city girls' school in Fürth. With the passage of the anti-Jewish Nuremberg Laws in 1935, Louis officially lost his job and his professional status in German society. After 1935 this respected teacher who had taught in secular state schools for more than two decades could find work only in Jewish religious schools. The "happiest years" of his professional career were now over.[51]

The Kissinger family and the Jewish community as a whole continued to function in the early Nazi years. German Jews adjusted to the growing restrictions on their freedom and their stricter isolation from mainstream society. Nazi authorities in Fürth initiated a boycott of Jewish businesses within one month of taking power, constraining the sources of income for Jewish families. The Nazi economic boycott in Fürth was more immediate and further-reaching than in most other parts of Germany. Some consumers and businesspeople ignored the boycott, but it took crippling effect with little resistance. Anti-Semitic extremism was now more than the project of Streicher and his thugs; it was government policy.[52]

Enforced isolation extended to recreation as well. Jewish children could not play with non-Jews in Fürth and surrounding communities. Out of necessity, Henry Kissinger joined the local branch of the national Bar-Kochba sport association, a Zionist organization that encouraged displays of Jewish strength and self-sufficiency. The Kissinger family did not share the Zionist principles of the organization, but they had few alternatives if they wanted their son to enjoy recreational opportunities under Nazi rule. Henry Kissinger's mother, Paula, later recalled that her son's exclusion from the activities of non-Jewish Germans was very hurtful at the time. For Kissinger's childhood friend Menachem Lion, the experience of Jewish isolation has been a "trauma for me ever since."[53]

Under Nazi rule, Jewish citizens—young and old—experienced enforced exile within their own country. The secular public identity that Orthodox

Henry Kissinger and his younger brother, Walter, in the 1930s. (© Bettmann / CORBIS)

Jews like Louis Kissinger had nurtured over decades was shattered. The bright, shining promises of mobility and respectability disappeared beneath a storm cloud of anti-Semitic extremism. The institutions and habits of democratic tolerance evaporated quickly, and were replaced by multiplying manifestations of mass hatred. Louis Kissinger was only one of many proud German Jews to find himself in a state of shock at the nightmare that had now convulsed him and his family. He had been emasculated by events he barely understood.[54]

Violence, fear, and physical suffering accompanied internal exile, particularly for Jewish citizens in the Middle Franconia region. On 25 March 1934 a mob of more than 1,000 citizens rioted against the small Jewish population in the village of Gunzenhausen, less than forty miles from Fürth. Large groups of residents attacked the businesses, homes, and personal property of the town's 184 Jews, proclaiming that "the Jews must go!" The mob dragged thirty-five Jewish residents of Gunzenhausen to the town prison and beat them brutally. Two Jews died, one from a hanging, another from five fatal knife wounds. Mobs of local men and women cheered the violence. Local authorities did nothing to stop the frenzy. In the aftermath, the ringleaders of the riot received only symbolic prison sentences of less than a year.[55]

The "quasi medieval pogrom" in Gunzenhausen was "the worst expression of anti-Jewish violence in the whole of Bavaria" before the nationwide attacks of Kristallnacht, 9–10 November 1938. The proximity of this violence to Fürth meant that families like the Kissingers felt the peril. The outward veneer of German civilization and lawfulness had proven paper thin when faced with Nazi-inspired violence against Jewish citizens. Self-preservation required an inward focus, a form of self-isolation. Personal insecurity and suspicion about the intentions of one's neighbors were unavoidable and, in fact, well founded in these circumstances.[56]

In his early teens at the time, Henry Kissinger recounts that he accepted the internal exile of his life as a matter of course. It was, he remembers, "much harder on my parents than it was on me." Anti-Semitic violence in Fürth before 1938 was rare, and the Jewish community was very close-knit. "It was unpleasant but not violent in those days," Kissinger recalls. The unpleasantness created by popular hatred and intimidation did, however, take its toll: "Hitler Youth kids could beat you up in the street, but that too wasn't all that frequent, and so it was an uncomfortable existence, but when you are my age . . . the age I then was, it was not an unhappy existence." Kissinger could remember the joys of youth in Fürth, but the dark presence of nameless "Hitler Youth kids" and extreme acts of violence in nearby towns must have made moments of happiness feel precarious.[57]

This precariousness resulted in direct physical suffering for some of Kissinger's closest relatives, especially his maternal grandparents. Falk and Fanny Stern lived in one of the most impressive houses at the center of the village of Leutershausen, about fifty miles from Fürth. Like many rural Orthodox Jews, Falk Stern was a cattle merchant. He had inherited the business from his grandfather, and by the early twentieth century the family had acquired considerable wealth and public respectability among the predominantly Protestant population in the area. Henry Kissinger frequently visited his grandparents, enjoying the comfort and seclusion of their home. Despite the pervasive Nazi sentiment in Leutershausen, the

A Nazi rally, like the kind that Kissinger witnessed as a young man in Germany. This photo comes from a November 1937 march in Munich, including Adolf Hitler and Hermann Goering, commemorating the failed Nazi attempt to seize power in 1923. (© Hulton-Deutsch Collection / CORBIS)

Sterns had the means to insulate their family from anti-Semitic threats in a way that was not possible in the more crowded neighborhoods of Fürth.[58]

Even wealth and status, however, could not hold the popular tide of violence at bay. The anti-Semitic frenzy in Leutershausen reached such a height that local Nazis did not wait for the national party's call for what became the Kristallnacht pogrom against Jews. On Sunday evening, 16 October 1938—three weeks before Kristallnacht—local residents vandalized the village's synagogue and broke the windows of homes belonging to Jews, including Falk and Fanny Stern. A young visitor to the Stern household at the time recounts the shock and anguish felt by Kissinger's grandfather. He reacted to the attacks with a determination to abandon his house and business in Leutershausen immediately. This prosperous German cattle merchant fled to Fürth, where he became an internal exile from his home, and died seven months later, at least in part from the personal stress of recent events. The Nazis deported Fanny Stern to Izbica, Poland, a holding location for the nearby Belzec extermination camp. She never returned.[59]

Living his first ten years in Weimar Germany, Henry Kissinger had witnessed the weakness of democracy. His five teenage years under Nazi rule revealed the potential for popular and extreme violence within civilized society. The pogroms in Gunzenhausen and Leutershausen, as well as the "Hitler Youth kids" on the streets of Fürth, displayed the dangerous dynamics of mass action. The crowds that rampaged against Jews did not follow direct orders from the Nazi leadership. Instead they took politics and social change into their own hands, acting in the spirit of what they perceived as a larger Nazi program. This kind of popular, grassroots politics was a particular Nazi talent, and it frightened Kissinger when he experienced it in the 1930s and throughout his later career.[60]

In Germany, and later in the United States, Kissinger developed a profound sense that he was an outsider not only because he was a Jew, but also because he could not trust the crowd. He became a permanent exile, always suspicious of the enemies he knew were lurking among his neighbors. The popular violence of the Nazi years inspired a drive for self-protection and toughness among a generation that witnessed how easily good citizens could join a murderous mob. Kissinger became hardened against idealistic rhetoric that neglected the "realistic" importance of extensive armed force and preparations to use it. Kissinger's position on this issue connected him with other observers at the time, but it placed him profoundly out of step with American citizens' hopes for a respite from war. Life in Nazi Germany taught Kissinger that violence is a permanent part of international and domestic politics.

Foreign Exile in New York City

Henry Kissinger, his brother, Walter, and his parents had already fled Germany, on 20 August 1938, before the tragic events in Leutershausen. Like so many other refugees, they relied on the sponsorship of a cousin in the United States. After a brief stop in London, the family entered New York City in early September. They rented a small apartment in the Washington Heights neighborhood, located on the hilly and narrow northern tip of Manhattan Island, closer to the Bronx than to the commercial heart of the city. The family's new dwelling was much more cramped than the home they had fled in Fürth. Kissinger remembers that he had "no privacy," "no closet for myself." Visiting this apartment sixty years later, he "couldn't believe that I ever lived there."[61]

Washington Heights was not mainstream New York City. Kissinger arrived in the United States without any knowledge of English, but this fact did not matter very much in an area dominated by German Jewish immigrants, most of whom conversed, read, and wrote in German. If anything, Washington Heights resembled Fürth more than it did other sections of New York. In early 1940 the neighborhood was home to 20,000 German and mostly Jewish refugees. They were not the majority in the area, but they had a distinctive, growing, and concentrated social presence. The German Jews also had strong internal bonds, derived largely from their common ties to southern Germany, and to small towns like Fürth in particular. This was a community that looked and acted in ways recognizable to a young man reared in Middle Franconia. In this sense, Kissinger is surely accurate when he recounts that adjustment to his new home was not traumatic: "All these books say I suffered . . . not true, nonsense."[62]

As was the case in Fürth under the Nazis, Kissinger's father suffered the worst dislocation. He had lost not only his profession and his social standing; he had also lost his traditional paternal authority. Like many other immigrant men, Louis Kissinger found himself inhabiting a new country whose culture and economy he could not understand. He no longer enjoyed the traditional German anchors of public respectability—through work, *Bildung,* and neighborhood—that allowed him to play the role of family educator and mediator with the outside world. Louis' reflections on his "happiest years" in Fürth surely reflect a longing for the standing and authority he lost irretrievably with emigration. Henry Kissinger does not comment directly on his father's diminished family role, but he does admit that the inability to find work in New York was "very demoralizing." Kissinger's memoirs also include a reprint of a letter from his father, indicating a combination of depression and self-pity: "I know the different conditions in this country which gave a man of my age so little hope for future life made it impossible for me to be a guide for you both [Henry and his brother, Walter] as I would have been in normal times. But I subordinated all my personal decisions to your future."[63]

Kissinger's mother, Paula, took up domestic housecleaning and food catering to support the family in Washington Heights. Henry found employment in a brush-cleaning factory, and his brother Walter also began working outside the home soon after coming to America. The entire family faced difficult adjustments, and Louis was the most isolated. He had gone from the public face of the family to its most alienated and troubled member.

This is a somewhat typical immigrant story, but it highlights the absence of assimilation during Kissinger's early years in the United States. The family did not fit neatly into a new American milieu. It remained strongly tied to a German Jewish community, and it was self-consciously unmoored from the larger society around it. Louis' unemployment and demoralization made this latter condition most troubling. The family's first years in the United States marked a period of continued exile, now within a small neighborhood in an unknown and frequently hostile foreign land. Violence against Jews was far rarer in the United States than in Nazi Germany, but the Kissingers' new country of residence was pervaded by anti-Semitic hostility, in addition to general prejudices against recent immigrants, even within the Jewish community.[64]

The Kissingers were living a continuation of the anxious, precarious, and isolated lives they had led in Nazi Germany. They remained outside mainstream society. They lacked security and stability. Most significant, the Kissingers received little direct benefit from America's democratic political institutions and culture. Henry and his family were far removed from American democracy in their small Washington Heights apartment, their menial jobs, and their other daily travails. If anything, the individualistic and entrepreneurial nature of American society made it harder for a *Bildung*-infused German patriarch like Louis Kissinger to find his way.

The relatively free American marketplace of ideas constituted an overwhelming cacophony for non-English-speakers, and it allowed for a festering of anti-Semitic slanders. The most widely read German-language newspaper in Washington Heights, *Aufbau,* acknowledged the dangers of anti-Semitic democracy in a 1940 article titled "Awake, America." Quoting the words of New York Senator James M. Mead, *Aufbau* warned:

> We must war against intolerance and bigotry and misunderstanding here in America. . . . our most serious enemy will not be the parachutist, nor the aeroplane-bomber, nor any of the other terrifying implements of modern war. If we are made vulnerable to assault, it will be because we have failed to strengthen, to solidify, and to adequately provide the defenses of tolerance, of neighborliness, and of good will among our own people.

The same issue of *Aufbau* included a call for recognition of Jewish rights and accomplishments from émigré author Thomas Mann. As in Weimar Germany, democracy was neither an adequate defense against anti-Semitism nor an effective source of belonging.[65]

The Kissingers turned to what was perhaps the institution in Washington Heights most removed from mainstream American democracy: Orthodox Judaism. In a community with at least five Orthodox Jewish synagogues, as well as various Conservative and Reformed alternatives, they joined the most traditional, strict, and self-contained congregation. K'hal Adath Jeshurun did not reject mainstream American society, but it opposed public Jewish political movements like Zionism. As was the case for Kissinger's Jewish congregation in Fürth, this synagogue encouraged the members of its community to establish secular professional lives even while adhering closely to Jewish religious law. Congregants were to strive for public acceptance as good citizens, but to maintain a distinct and separate communal identity as Orthodox Jews.

The emphasis of K'hal Adath Jeshurun on a separate Jewish identity was serious. It was, in fact, the only congregation in Washington Heights to recreate a self-contained German "organic community" *(kehilla).* This included a day school, a youth organization (Agudath Israel), a rabbinical court, group medical insurance, and other services. The congregation later added a ritual bath, a social hall, an elementary yeshiva, and an advanced yeshiva (Beth Medrash). K'hal Adath Jeshurun was a relatively small, exclusive, homogeneous, and hierarchically ordered institution. For the Kissingers, it provided their primary source of social connection in the United States. Speaking of her attachment to this traditional Orthodox community fifty years later, Paula Kissinger explained: "This is where I belong; here within the German Jewish community with my many friends. Here is my Synagogue; here is my Rabbi."[66]

Henry Kissinger would drift away from K'hal Adath Jeshurun in his adult life, but one cannot escape the centrality of this institution to his first years in the United States. This was the site for his initial acquaintance with America. He attended George Washington High School and completed a year of undergraduate work, at night, at the City College Business School. These were also important experiences for Kissinger, but they did not provide the intensity, the family anchoring, or the sense of belonging that came through daily participation in the Orthodox German Jewish community. As in Fürth, this was the only space where the family could find temporary freedom from anti-Semitism and the anxieties derived from cultural dislocation.[67]

The K'hal Adath Jeshurun Synagogue constituted the spiritual and social home for the Kissinger family. They were in the United States, but not of the United States. They were living in a democracy but conducting their primary social relationships within a separated and hierarchical milieu. Most significant, they were organizing their lives around their religious congregation rather than around their civic community. Turning sixteen in May 1939, Henry Kissinger experienced his new American home as a foreign continuation of his internal exile under the Nazis. Immigration to the United States saved Henry and his family, but it did not give them a strong connection to America's democratic culture and politics. If anything, the winds of democracy that swirled around Washington Heights only reinforced anxieties about belonging, driving the Kissingers to embrace the Orthodox Jewish community, which was self-consciously undemocratic.

Immigration reinforced Henry Kissinger's now deeply rooted discomfort with mass democracy. He shared this reaction with many other German Jews who had endured the collapse of Weimar, suffered under the Nazis, and then fled across the Atlantic. The "permanent exiles" of the 1930s would soon create a new trajectory for American society, public policy, and global politics.[68]

Memory, Emotion, and Politics

Henry Kissinger has repeatedly denied that the anti-Semitism, violence, and dislocation of his early years had any effect on his later development. He has condemned those who seek to understand his career and his policies through the prism of a traumatic childhood: "I was not consciously unhappy. I was not so acutely aware of what was going on. For children, those things are not that serious. It is fashionable now to explain everything psychoanalytically, but let me tell you, the political persecutions of my childhood are not what control my life."[69]

Kissinger, of course, has a point. A focus on his early experiences too easily descends into a linear explanation of his policies that discounts the sophistication of his later thinking, his change over time, and his frequent echoing of opinions accepted by more respected personalities. In addition, Kissinger is hypersensitive to the frequent accusations that he represents an "immigrant," "un-American," "Jewish" point of view. These slanders imply a static and treacherous identity, rooted in his early life. They help to explain Kissinger's unwillingness to open the subject of his childhood. During a 2004 visit to his hometown of Fürth, he was visibly torn between the emotional connection he quite obviously feels to the place of his youth and his desire to separate himself from the traumas and associations of that past. When asked directly how his experiences in Fürth affected his later life, he did not deny the relevance of his early years. Instead he defensively responded: "You know I will not answer that question." His brother then began to address the same query, but Kissinger cut him off with the warning: "You have given Herr Suri some good material."[70]

Kissinger defines himself as a "statesman" who has served "the country that gave my family refuge in America's traditional quest for a world in which the weak are secure and the just free." This is the America of Horatio Alger—of mobility, assimilation, freedom, and prosperity. This is not the America that Kissinger experienced in his initial immigrant years, but it is the one he wishes to embrace. He conceives of himself as part of a "melting pot" that transformed diverse immigrant peoples into a single secular culture over the course of the twentieth century. From this perspective, origins matter much less than later experiences.[71]

Beyond the denial of traumatic memory, this point of view neglects the emotional content of political judgments—including Kissinger's honorable and publicly espoused patriotism. If Freud overemphasized the role of feeling in human behavior, self-styled "realists" like Henry Kissinger have gone too far in denying its presence in policymaking. Kissinger's career development was not determined in any irrevocable way by his early experiences. His basic understanding of social and political change, however, was deeply inflected by assumptions and prejudices born of the crises he witnessed at an early age. These years did not give him anything like a cohesive political philosophy, but they made it difficult for Kissinger to feel confident in the resilience of democratic institutions when confronted by extreme internal and external threats. Despite his rejection of Freud's psychoanalysis, the young German Jewish boy in Fürth observed the same "human instinct of aggression and self-destruction" in his civilized neighbors that Freud described in Vienna. In early twentieth-century Europe, mass democracy contributed to violence, hatred, and suffering. The experience of mass democracy left emotional scars on survivors.[72]

The 1930s raised troubling questions for advocates of populist politics. Anxieties about democracy were based on rational observation. They were also rooted in the reactions of individuals personally touched by the violence and deprivation of the period. How could you remain a believer in the prosperity of democratic capitalism when the most advanced capitalist states descended into economic depression? How could you maintain faith in the peace-loving and humanistic values associated with democracy when the people supported extreme militarism? How could you assert that a world of democratic states will be stable and peaceful when the democratic states were unwilling to protect stability and peace against obvious offenders? Some people offered rational arguments in defense of democratic idealism, but the emotional content of contemporary experience ran in the opposite direction.

Men like Henry Kissinger did not oppose democracy. Democracy appeared as the only viable route to modernization for societies invested in individual rights, economic growth, and popular participation. Kissinger cherished the opportunities that democracy (both in Weimar Germany and midcentury America) offered his family, but he developed a deep foreboding about what he called the "fragility of societies, and the fragility of achievement." Fritz Stern spoke for Kissinger, himself, and many others when he explained: "Though I lived in National Socialist Germany for only five years, that brief period saddled me with the burning question that I have spent my professional life trying to answer: why and how did the universal potential for evil become an actuality in Germany?"[73]

Kissinger is obsessed with this question and with the actions leaders must take to control and destroy evil. His words on this subject are intensely emotional. Kissinger recounts that the years around the Second World War

> affected my ideas about global issues importantly. For one thing, you know, it made me impatient with people who thought that all they needed to do was make a profound proclamation that made them feel good. I mean, I had seen evil in the world, and I knew it was there, and I knew that there are some things you have to fight for, and that you can't insist that everything be to some ideal construction you have made.[74]

Democratic rhetoric sounded good, but it played poorly in the dirty world of politics. Kissinger was part of an international generation that experienced this truism. He lived a precarious life as a German citizen and as an American immigrant. In neither society was he fully accepted in the national community; in both societies he struggled as an exile. During Kissinger's first eighteen years, democratic institutions provided at least as much succor to Freudian self-destruction as to social justice.

The "Americanization" of Henry Kissinger, much of his generation, and parts of the global landscape came in the crucible of the Second World War and the immediate postwar years. In this period Americanization was not primarily about democratization. It marked a decisive international turn toward militarized, hierarchical politics. Kissinger sensed this shift and benefited from it. He was not exceptional in his thinking. Quite the contrary: his consciousness of democratic fragility was the new conventional wisdom across Europe and the United States. Kissinger's career embodied an emerging consensus ("the Cold War consensus") that democracy needed new sources of protection from its own weaknesses.

Kissinger played the role of neither Metternich nor Bismarck. He was one of countless young, cosmopolitan men to emerge from the Second

World War with Churchillian aspirations to use military force, diplomatic maneuvering, and firm domestic leadership to assure that "the malice of the wicked" was never again "reinforced by the weakness of the virtuous." Or, as George Kennan put it in his warnings about the Soviet Union after 1945:

> Much depends on [the] health and vigor of our own society. . . . This is the point at which domestic and foreign policies meet. Every courageous and incisive measure to solve internal problems of our own society, to improve self-confidence, discipline, morale, and [the] community spirit of our own people, is a diplomatic victory over Moscow worth a thousand diplomatic notes and joint communiqués.

George Kennan and Henry Kissinger would later disagree on many issues, but both sought to harness the power of democracy while containing its self-destructive elements.[75]

TWO | *Transatlantic Ties*

The tree of America has long and strong roots stretching across the Atlantic. The sixteenth- and seventeenth-century colonies created on the North American continent, and their encounters with Indian peoples, grew from the expansion of European empires. The ideas about individual liberty and just government that have dominated American political thought since before the Revolution reflect a long-standing dialogue among thinkers on both sides of the Atlantic. The American economy has also consistently depended on trade, labor, and technology traveling over this ocean. Most often neglected, the very definition of what it means to be an American has involved a continuous but ever-changing mix of European and non-European ethnic identities. Free and forced immigrants defined the nation. American history is transatlantic history.[1]

The years after 1941 epitomize the transatlantic contours of the American experience. They stand out as the period when the interpenetration of societies on both sides of this ocean deepened beyond earlier proportions. President Franklin Roosevelt anticipated this development when he spoke in December 1940 of the European resistance to Nazi invasions as the "front lines" of "democracy's fight against world conquest." Calling for a mobilization of American resources to support Europe's defense, Roosevelt announced that "we must be the great arsenal of democracy" in "the defense of our civilization." The latter phrase denoted a political, economic, and cultural connection between the United States and Europe that extended beyond defeating Nazi brutality. At the end of 1940 Roosevelt asserted that the societies on both sides of the Atlantic shared a common fate. Although his "arsenal of democracy" address discussed the military challenges in the Pacific as well as the Atlantic, the president did not assert the same bond with the Asian lands ravaged by Japan. Roosevelt sensed that the war against Hitler would forge a powerful, new, and unique transatlantic identity.[2]

In the aftermath of the Japanese attack on Pearl Harbor and America's entry into the Second World War, the United States tied its destiny to the future of Europe as never before. President Woodrow Wilson had intervened in an earlier war across the Atlantic to assure that the world was made "safe for democracy," but now Roosevelt led the nation into a crusade that would expend far more American blood and treasure to eliminate an evil force from the heart of Europe. The American president would accept nothing short of "unconditional surrender": "We will have no truck with Fascism in any way, in any shape or manner. We will permit no vestige of Fascism to remain." Freedom in Europe was necessary for freedom in the United States. Long before the German surrender in May 1945, virtually all observers recognized that postwar relations across the Atlantic would be more intimate than ever before. Fighting at such cost to save the continent, Americans could not retreat to their traditional aloofness from European affairs.[3]

The Second World War deepened transatlantic ties beyond security, economics, and family lineage. A pervasive sense of shared mission emerged from the personal intimacy forged in war between citizens—soldier and civilian alike—from the United States, Great Britain, France, Italy, Belgium, the Netherlands, and eventually Germany and other nations. The pressures of the war created new bonds of friendship, symbolized most dramatically by the close relationship cultivated between Winston Churchill and Franklin Roosevelt. Armed occupation of foreign territories in Europe also provided a context for fraternization between military personnel and local civilians, including in many cases marriage. Americans not only grew more familiar with Europe; they came to identify with the people on the continent as they had not before. In a sense, the war and its immediate aftermath reversed pretensions to "independence" from Europe dating back to before the American Revolution. Even former skeptics of U.S. intervention overseas, particularly Michigan senator Arthur Vandenberg, embraced American *interdependence* across the Atlantic. The Second World War erased the oceanic divide between the "Old World" and the "New World";

there was now only "one world" connected by a body of water that bridged societies more interdependent than ever before.[4]

Secretary of State George Marshall spoke of one transatlantic world in these terms when he famously called upon the American people to restore "the confidence of the European people in the economic future of their own countries and of Europe as a whole." "The role of this country," Marshall explained in June 1947, "should consist of friendly aid in the drafting of a European program and of later support of such a program so far as it may be practical for us to do so. The program should be a joint one, agreed to by a number, if not all, European nations." The Marshall Plan—formally the "European Recovery Program"—created the initial framework for European-wide cooperation, it solidified a transatlantic liberal capitalist order, and it provided an astronomical $13 billion in reconstruction capital to west European societies, including the former fascist countries of Germany and Italy.[5]

This was the largest single foreign-aid commitment that the United States has ever made. For a people still reeling from the combined deprivations of depression and war, a transfer of treasure on this scale reflected much more than cold calculation. Americans across the political spectrum felt that they were contributing to the sustenance of their own values, their own culture, their own civilization. The prosperity of the United States depended on transatlantic prosperity not only for economic purposes, but for reasons of basic legitimacy as well. In the aftermath of the Second World War, a degenerate Europe threatened to bolster fascist, communist, and other challengers to American liberal capitalism. This dark prospect could undermine the material basis of the American system and discredit its moral claims. George Kennan hammered home this point in June 1947, describing the ominous future for the United States without European recovery: "Today we Americans stand as a lonely, threatened power on the field of world history. Our friends have worn themselves out and have sacrificed their substance in the common cause. Beyond them—beyond the circle of those who share our tongue and our traditions—we face a world which is at the worst hostile and at best resentful."[6]

Just as the Atlantic Ocean no longer insulated the United States from the ravages of war, it no longer separated the political identities on both sides of the water. Kennan's "common cause" coalesced around antifascism in the Second World War, and it extended to anticommunism after 1945.

Within this emerging geopolitical environment, west Europeans often squabbled over the details of Marshall Plan aid, but they almost uniformly accepted American assistance with gratitude and an enthusiastic nod to transatlantic interdependence. A new culture of cooperation on both of sides of the Atlantic defined the "good" side in the early Cold War.[7]

Henry Kissinger's socialization as an American and his early career advancement occurred within this transatlantic framework. His accomplishments are, in fact, unimaginable in any other setting. Without the collapse of the old order in Europe and the rise of fascism, the Kissinger family would not have emigrated across the Atlantic. Without American entrance into the Second World War and Franklin Roosevelt's antifascist crusade, the young German Orthodox Jewish émigré would not have gained access to powerful American institutions. Most significant, without the new emphasis given to transatlantic ties, few people would have paid any attention to Kissinger's ideas about foreign policy. Although he frequently wrote about the "great men" of the nineteenth century—Metternich and Bismarck, in particular—Kissinger's self-conception and his professional career were direct results of the new transatlantic community formed in the crucible of the twentieth century's bloodiest war. Kissinger had no grand plan for his future when he arrived in America, and America had no grand plan for him. He was, in words he would quote from Bismarck, struggling like other refugees to "listen to the footsteps of God, get hold of the hem of His cloak, and walk with Him a few steps of the way."[8]

Kissinger acknowledged the interplay of circumstance, luck, and opportunism implied by Bismarck's insight. "My life," he admitted decades after he arrived in America, "has been so unusual, and has depended on so many accidents that I couldn't control." He did not transcend his surroundings or bring a "strange" sensibility to them. Quite the contrary: Kissinger was a child of his times. His genius was not his originality, but his ability to recognize the changed circumstances around him and take advantage of them. This is exactly how Kissinger defines politics and diplomacy, again with reference to his hero Bismarck: "The charge of opportunism . . . begs the key issue of statesmanship. Anyone wishing to affect events must be opportunist to some extent. The real distinction is between those who adapt their purposes to reality and those who seek to mold reality in the light of their purposes. . . . Bismarck sought his opportunities in the present; he drew his inspiration from a vision of the future."[9]

The transatlantic intimacy of the mid-twentieth century provided Kissinger with his key opportunities and the core of his vision. Unlike the generation of their fathers—fully formed in Germany and emasculated in exile—youthful refugees like Henry Kissinger managed to negotiate a position of empowerment as transatlantic translators. In addition to their obvious language skills, they became bridge figures, capable of addressing the basic, often unstated, assumptions of multiple societies through their mixed cultural identity. They were the men "in the field" who managed relations, conveyed messages, and negotiated differences. They constituted the wartime diaspora that knitted together separated territories.

This diaspora had a strong Jewish quality in its composition and its assumed social role. As an excluded cultural and religious community, Jews had long been the familiar strangers carrying capital, goods, and ideas across borders. For survival in a hostile world, Jews had developed local knowledge of multiple societies that did not allow them full standing. The image of the Hebrew peddler was a prejudicial stereotype, but it was also a reflection of the social marginality that Jews turned, by necessity, into a professional niche. The struggle against fascism and the Cold War promoted the peddling of capital, goods, and ideas—through the Marshall Plan and other programs—across the Atlantic. As never before, leaders on both sides of the ocean needed young men to connect their societies. They sought out "good Jews" as advisors and diplomats.[10]

Age, circumstance, talent, and luck made Kissinger into one of these "good Jews." Torn between Fürth and Washington Heights, he emerged during the Second World War as a promising transatlantic bridge figure, filling a growing need in the global struggle. He quickly assumed this role as a young Army counterintelligence officer charged with locating former Nazis and assisting American forces in their endeavors to transform German society. Contrary to assumptions that national identity is formed within the landscape of the nation, Kissinger's Americanization came through his training for a return to Europe and his activities as a German émigré-turned-occupier. Kissinger's self-conception as an American was not imagined or invented, but instead forged through the war and its aftermath. The lived experience of transatlantic movement, within a highly militarized setting, came to define American identity for Kissinger, and of course for many other "good Jews" who found similar belonging at the time. The Second World War broadened the geographic definition of American identity, and it raised the profile of transatlantic connections within the nation's most powerful institutions.[11]

In the years after 1945, Kissinger's transatlantic experiences marked him not only as an American patriot, but also as someone who deserved special promotion in policy circles. He had highly valued transatlantic knowledge and connections. Within fifteen years of his immigration to the United States (before he turned thirty), Kissinger had already overseen American occupation of two sizable German towns, lectured Army officers on international affairs, briefed the White House on the future of Germany, and advised the State Department on fighting communist aggression in Asia. He did all of this without any claim to authority beyond his transatlantic credentials. In each of these cases, and later in his career, Kissinger asserted a unique ability to translate the interests of various societies into a coherent global vision. Even as a very young man, he drew on the history of European diplomacy, in particular, to advise Americans about managing their interests abroad and anticipating inevitable tragedies in the course of legitimate foreign-policymaking. Kissinger clearly saw himself as a young cosmopolitan sage speaking to an innocent nation.[12]

Many observers respected Kissinger's transatlantic wisdom, but, like other émigrés, he still was not fully accepted in elite American intellectual and social circles. For all the attention he received, he remained an outsider. In this sense, his German Jewish background was both an asset and an encumbrance. The new transatlantic relationship of the mid-twentieth century set the heights and the limits of Kissinger's career. It was much more than a strategic concept and a marker of national belonging. It was the foundation for his personal identity.

Becoming American

The Second World War wrenched Henry Kissinger from his few places of comfort in a foreign land. Drafted into the U.S. Army in early 1943, he lived apart for the first time from his family, the Orthodox Jewish community, and fellow Germans. This was a difficult transition for the twenty-year-old émigré. He later admitted that "living as a Jew under the Nazis, then as a refugee in America, and then as a private in the Army isn't exactly an experience that builds confidence."[13]

Kissinger received his basic training in the Deep South—Spartanburg,

South Carolina. Camp Croft was more than 700 miles from Washington Heights and worlds away in its social composition. The white male draftees came from different parts of the country, and very few were German or Jewish. Many were from small midwestern towns—people Kissinger would later refer to as "heartland Americans." This was by far the most diverse group of young men Kissinger had ever encountered in such an intimate setting. It was, he remembered, "a tremendous education for me."[14]

The intensity of basic training erased the boundaries between public secularism and private religiosity that had defined Kissinger's experiences as an Orthodox Jew in Fürth and Washington Heights. Daily activities—including drilling, mess hall meals, and recreation—forced him to depart from the basic life rhythm his family had preserved even through the ordeal of immigration. The Army did not respect the Jewish sabbath or the sanctity of Jewish holidays. It explicitly broke the family- and synagogue-centered community that structured Orthodox life. At a most basic level, Army mess halls did not accommodate religious strictures. Formerly kosher Jewish boys found themselves "eating ham for Uncle Sam."[15]

Food represented a small manifestation of a larger social transformation. Orthodox Jews, like other religious minorities, immediately shed many of the obvious markers of their difference from mainstream society. They were integrated into a common identity, defined in part by the homogeneity of Army life. Everyone followed the same daily rituals, wore the same uniforms, and ate the same mess hall offerings. Basic training created a close community of diverse draftees. In an authoritarian setting, it forged a common American man from the sons of distinct ethnic neighborhoods and religious traditions.

As was the case in other countries, during the mid-twentieth century the military became the school of the nation. Kissinger and his counterparts recognized this fact. Despite his homesickness, Kissinger recalls, "The significant thing about the army is that it made me feel like an American." "It was an Americanization process," he continues. "It was the first time I was not with German Jewish people. I gained confidence in the army." Kissinger's brother, Walter, who also served in the Army, explains that the military "opened a new world for us, one that our parents couldn't share or understand."[16]

This experience altered more than just personal identity. The Army gave recent immigrants a new standing in American society; it made them legal citizens. Kissinger was "naturalized" in March 1943, within six weeks of his drafting. Sixty years later, this moment still had profound meaning for him. Repressing memories of rampant anti-Semitism in places like Camp Croft, he asserted: "I was never made to feel like a foreigner. . . . I actually thought I had lost my accent when I was in the Army." Anyone who has listened to Kissinger recognizes that this is a willful exaggeration, especially when one considers that this young German Jewish draftee received his basic training surrounded by southerners and Dixie culture. The Army experience did not erase prejudices and insecurities, but it created a new foundation for exiles to claim belonging in American society.[17]

Jewish soldiers occupied a contradictory position in the war effort. The U.S. government gave them unprecedented access to the legal and institutional demarcations of citizenship. They were fighting for "their country" in a common struggle against fascism. Jews, however, remained marked by their difference from mainstream society. Despite the homogenizing experience of boot camp, they continued to look, sound, and behave distinctively. If anything, the mobilization of young men from across the country meant that the small minority of Jews in a place like Camp Croft numbered more than the total Jewish community in most towns, excluding New York City. For all the efforts to forge a common American in war, Jews still stood out.

Five hundred fifty thousand Jews served in the U.S. military during the war. As a whole, they became more conscious of their dual American and Jewish identities. Similarly, non-Jews gained a greater appreciation for the Jewish contribution to the United States and the distinctness of this community. Fighting in large numbers alongside one another, those who had never met a Jew before could no longer deny their legitimate existence. At the same time, the distinctiveness of Jewish culture and religion—experienced through prayer, diet, and speech—was also highlighted from boot camp to the battlefield. As one historian explains: "The history of World War II as experienced by American Jews in the armed forces is one of difference amid similarity, of exclusion amid integration, of transfiguration amid routine, of triumph amid catastrophe."[18]

Prominent Americans recognized these contradictions and worked hard to address them through the construction of a government-sponsored "Judeo-Christian" sensibility. In 1942 one of Henry Kissinger's future mentors at Harvard, Carl Friedrich, famously called for the defense of an imperiled

"Judeo-Christian world culture—a culture that is still struggling to build its 'universal state.'" Friedrich, himself a non-Jew, went on to link stable democracy to "Judeo-Christian ethics." According to this analysis, anti-Semitism, particularly in its extreme Nazi form, undermined civilization and democracy by denying the "individual and collective participation of the Jews in the building of the future." Defense of Christianity required a defense of Jewish ideas and individuals.[19]

Friedrich's analysis had the virtue of integrating Jews into the struggle against fascism and, later, communism. It appealed to what one scholar

Henry Kissinger in U.S. Army uniform, 1945. Kissinger returned to Germany during the Second World War. He exercised important local influence in the American occupation and reconstruction of his native country. (Courtesy of National Archives, Washington, D.C.)

calls a "common faith for a united democratic front." This common faith emphasized individual rights, monotheism, and a sense that Americans were a "chosen" people. Beyond an appeal to values, the Judeo-Christian rhetoric provided a strong justification for bringing Jews and non-Jews together in the close confines of boot camp. The war against Nazi Germany became a struggle to coordinate faiths in the interest of defeating a demonic foe.[20]

Friedrich and others grounded their appeals to a Judeo-Christian tradition in universalistic terms. They envisioned the creation of a single world government with common values to guide behavior. For Friedrich this required a "reawakening of the ethical and religious convictions of mankind. The great universal religions which share a recognition of the dignity of man will discover a common foundation in the ethical standards of a new humanism. Such a universal basis may readily be shared by the Jewish people, whose great prophets first raised the cry for a universal religion."[21]

This Judeo-Christian vision presumed the formation of a strong transatlantic identity. The "great universal religions" to which Friedrich and others referred were Christianity and Judaism—the most prominent faiths on both sides of the Atlantic, and the belief systems most contested in the Second World War. The term "Judeo-Christian" clearly excluded Islam, Buddhism, Hinduism, and other prominent faiths rooted outside the transatlantic area. Émigré intellectuals like Friedrich made the case for a Judeo-Christian sensibility because it reflected their own dual footing in European and American societies. Younger immigrants like Kissinger benefited from the new opportunities it opened for Jews, but not for other groups, within mainstream institutions.[22]

The construction of a transatlantic Judeo-Christian identity legitimized, and in fact mandated, increased Jewish participation in universities, corporations, and especially the military. It made Jews "white" by outlawing many of the anti-Semitic assumptions about race and ethnicity that had largely excluded them from circles of economic, intellectual, and military power. The U.S. government had previously used the term "Hebrew" to identify racial difference. Under a Judeo-Christian rubric, "Jew" became the accepted term, emphasizing a fluid culture rather than a primordial race. Jews were to be distinctive but integrated participants in a "multinational" alternative to fascism, communism, and traditional rivalries among European states.[23]

The assertion of a Judeo-Christian sensibility connected poor immigrants from Washington Heights with other white Americans as they jointly struggled through boot camp in the Deep South. They now shared a common faith and a common mission to eliminate fascism. American military authorities enforced the adoption of Judeo-Christian assumptions to create a more integrated and more effective fighting force. They also used these assumptions to justify total warfare against an enemy with whom, they claimed, Western civilization could not coexist spiritually. The U.S. military set itself apart from Nazi Germany by asserting that it protected Judeo-Christian values and rejected anti-Semitic threats to a pluralistic democratic creed. The Army and other branches of service officially outlawed anti-Semitism, defining it as a prejudice that would aid the enemy.[24]

The U.S. military was particularly effective in its efforts to build an interfaith basis for Judeo-Christian cooperation. In February 1943, the same month that Kissinger arrived at Camp Croft, the Army began integrating the training and duties of Protestant, Catholic, and Jewish military chaplains. It soon became standard practice for the integrated chaplains to lead joint religious services. Rabbis entered the Army as chaplains in unprecedented numbers, and they now addressed non-Jews at nondenominational gatherings. The Army encouraged rabbis to serve the religious needs of observant Jews and also to lead ecumenical celebrations of Jewish holidays, including Passover, for Jews and non-Jews alike. Rabbis accompanied Protestant and Catholic ministers at funerals for unknown soldiers; chaplains from the three faiths offered prayers in English, Latin, and Hebrew. In combat and in death, the military asserted a common Judeo-Christian heritage.[25]

Some soldiers viewed these interfaith activities as a superficial approach to religion, eliding significant differences among and within the three faiths. This was a legitimate objection, especially when one considers the instrumental purposes behind the policy. The U.S. military's efforts to implement a Judeo-Christian form of religious expression, however, had profound effects. The interfaith services preserved Jewish distinctness, but they also included Jews in a shared identity that was closed to other minority groups. They created an open, ecumenical model of religious practice, and they connected it with a global American mission. Most often overlooked, the Judeo-Christian military creed fostered a sense of close transatlantic interdependence. If the Protestant, Catholic, and Jewish faiths constituted the basis for civilization and democracy, their preservation in western Europe, as well as in North America, was crucial. The destruction of Judeo-Christian roots across the Atlantic would isolate and ultimately degrade their more recent flowering in the United States. Judeo-Christian civilization was self-consciously transatlantic in its primary dimensions.

As *Bildung* in Weimar Germany provided Jews with a touchstone for asserting their belonging, so did the Judeo-Christian framework in the United States after 1941. Espoused in the barracks at Camp Croft and other facilities, it offered standing in American society through a public secularization of faith. In place of ritual, community, and tradition, Jews would become American by defining religion in terms of civic virtues—including individualism, social mobility, and support for state institutions. Praying for success in war and prosperity in victory put religion to the service of these ends. It also nationalized the transatlantic qualities of the Jewish experience, giving young immigrants an opportunity to convert their foreign background into a mechanism for claiming domestic belonging.

Like many other Orthodox Jews, Kissinger departed from religious stricture in the Army, but he never rejected Judaism. The adoption of a secular Jewish identity was his entrée into a Judeo-Christian culture under construction during the Second World War. This is what he means when he refers to his own "Americanization" in the military. Kissinger defines American identity as a civic religion that is consistent with many elements of Jewish thought. It emphasizes "motivation over structure" and "extols the image of a universal man living by universal maxims, regardless of the past, of geography, or of other immutable circumstance." Kissinger observes, somewhat critically, that Americans tend to place faith above analysis. He contends, however, that the nation's "refusal to be bound by history and the insistence on the perpetual possibility for renewal confer a great dignity, even beauty, on the American way of life."[26]

A sense of God-given American mission anchors Kissinger's connection to his adopted country. This mission not only fits with a secularized version of the Jewish religion; it mandates some religious expression of faith. For Americans who came of age at midcentury, national identity implied belief in a Judeo-Christian God. Just as there was little space for Orthodox Judaism in mainstream society, there was also no room for atheism, polytheism, and other departures from transatlantic assumptions about religious faith. The crucible of war molded a new American man from a mix of secularism, Judeo-Christian religion, and immigrant cosmopolitanism. Henry Kissinger's journey from Washington Heights to Camp Croft marked the midcentury transformation of both Judaism and American identity in a transatlantic context.[27]

The African Americans serving in segregated military units, populating the community around Camp Croft, and participating in the war effort as a whole did not benefit directly from the expanding definition of American identity. Judeo-Christian values folded Jews into a definition of "white" society that continued to exclude on the basis of race. Transatlantic definitions of civilization contributed to inherited prejudices against descendants from African and other non-European ancestries. The European societies with which the United States closely collaborated had long-standing colonial empires, built upon "Orientalist" assumptions of black inferiority. In some sense, Judeo-Christian identity emerged from a shared desire to differentiate a European (and American) "us" from a non-European "them."[28]

This exclusion meant that racism conditioned the broadened religious definition of American identity. Young Jewish men like Kissinger gained new professional opportunities, but their African American counterparts did not. Even more significant, as upwardly mobile Jews forged deeper interpersonal relations with white non-Jews in places like Camp Croft, they simultaneously distanced themselves from African Americans. Historians often overlook these facts. Henry Kissinger was only one of many draftees to move rapidly from a self-contained German Jewish community into an expansive Judeo-Christian culture. He made this life-changing journey absent any serious relationships with the African Americans all around him. Kissinger's career reflected the institutionalized racial segregation that accompanied ethnic diversification at midcentury. Even when these circumstances changed in later decades, he would remain personally cut off from nonwhite communities in the United States. Like many others from his generation, Kissinger's maturation as a cosmopolitan American included gaping ignorance about the African American population. Not surprisingly, he would manifest frequent insensitivity toward the aspirations and difficulties of racial minorities.[29]

In contrasting Jewish mobility with African American repression around 1945, one should not overstate the degree of Jewish inclusion in mainstream society. The Second World War discredited public articulations of anti-Semitism, but it did not eliminate more subtle expressions of prejudice. In particular, Jews like Kissinger who found new professional doors open for their advancement also confronted continued restrictions. Exponents of a common Judeo-Christian faith rejected the full assimilation of various religions into a single form. Jews would become more deeply connected to Christian civilization, but they would not be completely of it. Although they would contribute to defeating fascism and building a peaceful world, Jews would make their contributions from the margins, not the center, of society. Even in Carl Friedrich's writing, a Judeo-Christian tradition assumed the predominance of Christianity.[30]

Kissinger surely felt the exclusionary side of Judeo-Christian culture even as he benefited from its openings. Despite his claim that he was "never made to feel like a foreigner" in the Army, those who knew Kissinger at the time recall how he suffered from occasional anti-Semitic epithets and sometime government-sanctioned exclusion. The most noteworthy case of official prejudice occurred when Kissinger applied to train as an Army doctor. Despite a superior record in Army courses and a reputation for intellectual brilliance within his unit, he was not allowed to pursue this route. The Army had quotas limiting the number of Jews accepted for training as physicians. Kissinger suffered from more limited opportunities than his non-Jewish counterparts, and perhaps also from a prejudice against what one author describes as a demeanor that was "not yet Americanized for Army evaluators." The Army was more comfortable sending Jews into the grime of infantry life than into the white-coated world of medicine.[31]

Throughout his time in the Army and his later career, there is little evidence that Kissinger was ever accepted in mainstream social circles. People generally respected his capabilities and his hard work, but they rarely perceived him as one of "them." When he became a celebrity, Kissinger would remain a curiosity rather than an established member of the jet-setting crowd. With his deep voice, his Germanic features, and his bookish disposition, Kissinger always stood out. He used humor to soften this awkwardness, but his self-deprecating wit only highlighted the fact that he did not seem to belong.

Kissinger's personality—particularly his abrasiveness, self-centeredness, and excessive ambition—account for much of his social isolation. These qualities reinforced the stigma that a young German Jewish man could not escape in the Army and in American society at large, no matter what he did. Although Kissinger's background gave him some insider standing as the definition of American identity broadened during the Second World War, his obvious German Jewish qualities made him a perpetual outsider. He could never become fully accepted within the American mainstream in the way that an American-born figure like Robert McNamara could. He could never escape the accusation that he really did not understand America. Most significant, he could never establish the sense of personal security in the United States that came naturally to many others from different backgrounds.[32]

The transatlantic contours of American identity, forged in the armed forces at war, allowed men like Kissinger a basis for national belonging that would soon translate into professional mobility. The same transatlantic qualities, however, would leave Kissinger and others with a nagging sense of rootlessness in American society. This observation, more than anything else, explains why Kissinger refuses to discuss his early years. They remain a source of profound insecurity.[33]

Returning to Germany

German Jewish immigrants to the United States found themselves in a contradictory position. The Nazi regime had forced them into a painful exile, but they could never escape their ties to Germany. "Try as I might to erase my six years under the Nazis from my mind," one of Kissinger's contemporaries, Peter Gay, writes, "my past would not let me alone." Another contemporary, George Mosse, explains:

> my acceptance of myself was set within the constant awareness of a past which refused to go away, and indeed I did not try to transform or overcome the vivid feeling that I was a survivor. The Holocaust was never very far from my mind; I could easily have perished with my fellow Jews. I suppose that I am a member of the Holocaust generation and have constantly tried to understand an event too monstrous to contemplate.[34]

Gay and Mosse were prominent members of the German Jewish diaspora who attained respectability as bridge figures between the United States and Europe. Youthful immigrants in the late 1930s, they studied and wrote about subjects that were somewhat distant from their country of birth. Over the course of their careers, however, they circled back to Germany, writing vivid accounts of the collapse of Weimar, the rise of Nazism, and the mass murder of Jews. Gay and Mosse translated the ideas, the hopes, and the tragedies of German society into compelling narratives that Americans could understand. They influenced thousands of students who heard them lecture and read their books. They lived in exile from their country of birth, but their success in exile depended on their continued attachment to the society that rejected them.[35]

The same is true for Henry Kissinger. Despite his pretensions to a transcendent "statesmanship," his worldview and his career path have embodied a strong connection to the land from which he fled. Kissinger was not only an immigrant from Germany; he was also an active contributor to the occupation and reconstruction of the country. Like Gay and Mosse, Kissinger built his career on his ability to translate German society for Americans. His Americanization did not erase, but in many ways heightened, his ties to his country of birth. "I was in the army of occupation," Kissinger recalls, "and I have been emotionally and practically connected with Germany all of my life, but primarily from the time of occupation onward."[36]

The military defeat of the Nazi regime and the postwar presence of American forces in Europe transformed Kissinger from a refugee into a ruler. His comments indicate that he sees these roles as distinct, but they were, of course, interwoven in the experience of Americanized German Jews. Serving in the 84th Infantry Division of the U.S. Army during the last months of 1944, Kissinger was assigned to Division Intelligence because of his German language skills. He soon moved into the Counterintelligence Corps, charged with apprehending Nazis, extracting information from them, and managing the occupation of the nation. The tables had turned very quickly. The exile returned to his native land, empowered to punish those who had banished him.

This was not an accidental assignment. William Donovan, the head of the Office of Strategic Services (the OSS, precursor to the Central Intelligence Agency), pressured the Army and other American military institutions to promote German Jewish émigrés. He recognized their potential contributions to the analysis and eventual occupation of German society. In April 1943 Donovan wrote to the Army's assistant chief of staff endorsing the recruitment of these "specially qualified personnel" into intelligence activities. German Jews had the knowledge and experience to identify Nazis, anticipate their actions, and apprehend them. The Army could trust

German Jews in these roles because of their obvious antipathy to the Nazi regime. Kissinger echoes the attitude of many German Jewish exiles when he recounts: "I welcomed the opportunity to fight against the Germans, and that's about as far as it went." He could not "feel hatred towards all of the Germans," because he remained one of them. He did, however, feel a personal mission in extricating Nazism from this society.[37]

By some accounts, nearly half of all American military personnel working on the close study of German society were refugees, like Kissinger. They formed what one former German Jewish intelligence officer calls the "backbone" of U.S. activities in this area. They were the guides, translators, and interpreters for the bulky American military, treading on unknown terrain. The German Jewish intelligence officers calibrated the general aims of the U.S. government with local knowledge of the enemy society. Kissinger recounts how he matched the American goal of denazification with his instinct for the "German sense of hierarchy." Instead of organizing large police roundups of suspected figures, he operated through personal interactions and social networks to find Nazis. He appealed to the sense of duty among German citizens, to their deference to laws requiring that people turn themselves in for misdeeds.[38]

Decades later, Kissinger enjoyed recounting how he manipulated German habits for American purposes. In 1945 he posted signs in occupied areas requesting job applications from men with "police experience." When an applicant arrived at Kissinger's office, "I asked him what he had been doing, and he said, *Staats polizei* [state police]. I then asked him in a joking manner, *Geheim Staats Polizei* [Gestapo]? And he said yes. So I locked him up." The story does not end there. Kissinger manipulated German obedience to help uncover Nazis in hiding: the self-identified Gestapo agent "volunteered to prove his good faith, and I told him to find his colleagues. He found them. I locked up more Gestapo than the entire rest of the U.S. Army."[39]

Kissinger surely exaggerates his omniscience and the gullibility of the Gestapo, but his recollections capture the vital role played by young American soldiers who could knowledgeably adapt Washington's aims to the German social context. The troubled experience of American occupations in other lands, where bridge figures like Kissinger were noticeably absent, reinforces the value of refugees as returning rulers in their former societies. Exiles can penetrate their old communities while faithfully serving the aims of their new nation. Kissinger's rapid promotion in the Army indicates that American policymakers recognized and exploited this dynamic.

His position as an intelligence officer working within the army of occupation, rather than in the more elitist OSS, reflected the unique niche that his generation of German Jews came to play in the Second World War. Despite Donovan's calls for the recruitment of more German Jews, the OSS was a gentlemen's club of intellectuals and blue-blooded adventurers—"half cops-and-robbers and half faculty meeting," in the words of one observer. Founded in June 1942, the OSS quickly grew into a semi-independent intelligence empire, employing hundreds of men for intercepting communications, manipulating public opinion, organizing covert action, and producing basic research and analysis about the enemy. The research and analysis section, in particular, comprised an all-star collection of the greatest scholarly minds in the humanities and social sciences, including William Langer, Sherman Kent, Charles Kindleberger, and Arthur Schlesinger Jr. Émigré intellectuals—Franz Neumann, Hajo Holborn, Felix Gilbert, and Herbert Marcuse, among many others—also contributed to the analysis of German society. Many of the refugee intellectuals were Jewish, but they all came to the OSS as distinguished thinkers with prestigious academic pedigrees and gentlemanly affectations. This was a very clubby community.[40]

A young, undistinguished, and relatively uneducated refugee like Kissinger had no place in the OSS. He was an outsider from the circles of power and influence represented by this new institution. Kissinger's route to intelligence work ran through Army basic training, field combat, and the difficulties of managing the daily occupation of German territory. He did not fight the war in words from a distance. He served on the front lines and took on a special role because of his relative marginality in two societies. Through the Counterintelligence Corps Kissinger attained a position of privilege, and he gained access to personalities and institutions that would propel his career forward, but he never overcame his outsider status. He was never an OSS man, never a gentleman spy. Although German Jewish exiles returned to their native country with previously unimagined power, they retained their "in-between" identity. Their authority was fragile.[41]

This observation explains, in part, why Kissinger has repeatedly emphasized the limits, rather than the achievements, of the occupying forces in Germany. They ruled a defeated country, but they lacked the legitimacy and resources to govern without local assistance. Army counterintelligence work combined apprehending former Nazis with inducing other former Nazis to help run things. Soldiers managing the occupation quickly realized they could not establish rigid demarcations about political acceptability; they had to negotiate, coexist, and cooperate with people they found morally abhorrent. Occupation politics were dirty, pragmatic, and filled with compromises. Not surprisingly, these characteristics would run through the diplomacy Kissinger practiced during his later career. He recognized that the world was filled with choices among lesser evils, and he became "impatient with people who thought that all they needed to do was make a profound proclamation that made them feel good." Getting things done—rebuilding a society, protecting basic freedoms, and assuring general security—required imperfect, sometimes distasteful, decisions.[42]

In this context of moral ambiguity, Kissinger showed sympathy, even compassion, for Germans who had worked with the Nazis for self-preservation and now found their lives torn asunder. "It is hard to explain this," he recounts. "I found it very depressing to arrest people, and have weeping wives. . . . these were people who had party positions, they had not necessarily done anything that I knew about." Other members of the Army who accompanied Kissinger into Germany commented on his lack of vengeance toward the German people. Ralph Farris, who served with Kissinger, attests that he was "always a very even-handed gentleman" when questioning suspected Nazis. Farris remembers that Kissinger would criticize other Jewish soldiers who did not contain their anger in similar situations: "I remember one occasion when some of these refugees [in the Army] were being a little abusive to a civilian couple. The couple weren't under investigation; they were just being asked for information. Henry began yelling at the questioners thusly: 'You lived here under the Nazis—you know how abusive they were! Now how can you turn around and abuse these people the same way?'"[43]

Despite the suffering of his family and his new loyalty to the United States, Kissinger continued to feel connected to German society. This connection was not only a consequence of his personal history, but also a reflection of his contemporary placement within the U.S. military, the Army intelligence apparatus, and the emerging transatlantic community. He knew very well that he would not have attained promotion to the Counterintelligence Corps and the right to return to Germany without his ability to bridge societies on both sides of the Atlantic. This was the fundamental characteristic that identified him as "specially qualified," though still not acceptable to the OSS club. The massive expansion of American military activities and the monumental burden of occupying the center of the European continent heightened attention to Kissinger's German social characteristics and their utility for Americans. His linguistic and cultural cosmopolitanism made him an outcast in Nazi Germany, but these same qualities offered limited access to power in the transatlantic context of the Second World War. Like Gay, Mosse, and many other German Jewish exiles, Kissinger's professional mobility after 1945 grew from the exact sources of his personal displacement the decade before.

Paradoxically, vengeance against non-Jewish Germans for their anti-Semitic brutality threatened to undermine the advancement of German Jews in the United States. If one condemned all "ordinary" Germans, intimate knowledge of their society would have little utility. Plans for general retribution required little of the local knowledge and policy calibration that German Jews provided.

Transatlantic partnership, in contrast, reinforced the niche that Kissinger and others came to occupy in the Second World War. German-American cooperation privileged refugees, especially young Army intelligence officers, with recent experience in both societies. To rebuild and coordinate across the Atlantic, policymakers needed detailed analyses of local conditions and informed assessments of popular attitudes. These required understanding and even empathizing with German citizens who had contributed to Nazi rule. Kissinger's compassion for the regime's "little people" reflected the needs of the U.S. government and the promise of German Jewish transatlantic mobility. Cooperating with anti-Semites—both in Germany and in the United States– became an important part of Kissinger's postwar career.

German Occupation

The American troops who entered German territory in the spring of 1945 did not have a clear plan for occupying and rebuilding what Kissinger described as a "totally smashed" country. After months of intense fighting, they were stretched thin by the large and densely populated terrain that they now had to cover. They were battle-hardened soldiers, not administrators prepared to help citizens confronting serious shortages of food, energy, and shelter. Many of the young Americans entering Germany, including Kissinger, had never even managed their own lives without parental or military supervision. This was hardly an ideal cohort for remaking German society.[44]

The American occupation helped democratize part of a nation that had lived under Nazi rule for more than twelve years, but it accomplished this through pragmatic, ad hoc, and sometimes contradictory actions. This was not a smooth process. It involved many setbacks and changes of course. Denazification, for example, was never pursued consistently within U.S.-administered areas. The breakup of dominant German business groups—"decartelization"—also occurred in partial fits and starts under American supervision. Despite these inconsistencies, the occupation brought Americans and West Germans together in a common effort to ensure peace and security. This was, in Kissinger's recollection, the shared "moral dedication" that solidified transatlantic ties so soon after the war, and made it possible for inexperienced American soldiers to cooperate effectively with established local figures.[45]

Kissinger was one of the many young soldiers who quickly found himself commanding enormous local responsibility. In March 1945 the Army appointed this twenty-one-year-old the military administrator of the city of Krefeld—a community with nearly 200,000 residents, located along the Rhine River, close to the Dutch border. When American forces arrived in Krefeld, the "city was full of people now hiding in basements and bunkers." Kissinger's superiors did not view him as the ideal choice for overseeing this area, but he had impressed them with his administrative skills, his political seriousness, and his knowledge of German society. As in the past, his German Jewish background helped. It assured that he had the requisite language skills to communicate with the local population, but also a religious and ethnic identity that would prevent him from becoming too beholden to them. Most significant, from his limited activities in Army intelligence, Kissinger had convinced those around him that he could operate effectively in uncertain settings, among antagonistic groups. This attribute was particularly evident when Kissinger famously crossed enemy lines, posing as a German civilian, to interrogate Nazi soldiers in April 1945. He received a Bronze Star for his courage and acumen.[46]

As military administrator of Krefeld, Kissinger did not institute any major political or social reforms. He worked to improve the daily functioning of local services by finding competent officials and empowering them to do their jobs. Kissinger delegated the management of technical matters—including waterworks and food distribution—to city authorities. He used the resources of the American military to assure order. Kissinger supported the denazification and democratization of Krefeld, but he believed that these processes could take shape only after the restoration of basic services. German citizens, not American military personnel, would provide the leadership for political transformation. The U.S. Army could not, in his view, implant needed social changes; these had to grow from the people themselves, engaging in a slow process of education and reform.[47]

Kissinger also confronted firsthand evidence of cowardice and cruelty in Krefeld. Saul Padover, an Army intelligence officer who arrived in Krefeld only days before Kissinger, recounts in his memoir that the citizens of the city showed no signs of serious resistance to Nazi authority, even when it became clear (in early 1945) that the war was lost. They were not zealots, just individuals who accepted the dominant politics of the moment. When the Americans took control of Krefeld, the citizens quickly switched sides, offering obsequious deference to their new rulers. There was nothing particularly German about the behavior of the people Kissinger encountered; they were simply living ordinary lives. Political courage had to come from leaders, domestic and foreign, who transcended local circumstances.[48]

The cruelty that accompanied ordinariness appeared in the callousness of Krefeld's citizens toward the millions of Jews and other individuals murdered during the war. Cruelty, however, was not a German monopoly. The American soldiers who liberated the city brought their own hatred, self-indulgence, and violence to civilians. Padover recounts the horrors of American behavior that he and Kissinger witnessed: "After a battle soldiers of every country are pretty much the same, and the warriors of Democracy were no more virtuous than the troops of Communism were reported to be. Soon the German population was quite scared, and we ourselves . . . did not feel safe either." Wholesome American soldiers, freed from battlefield constraints, became ruffians of the worst sort. They drank to excess, vandalized property, beat local men, and raped countless women. The anger of the women who now suffered in liberation, as they had under Nazi rule, burst on to the streets of Krefeld: "It was difficult to walk down the streets during the day without being stopped by civilians, mostly women, who wanted to know whether we spoke German. Saying *Ja,* meant being surrounded by clamorous and complaining crowds. Once a group of scared women asked whether they were obliged to open their doors at night when American soldiers knocked; many women had regretfully done so."[49]

As military administrator of the city, Kissinger had to contend with two populations—the German citizens and the American soldiers—that exhibited the same degenerate group behaviors he had witnessed in Weimar Germany. Cruelty and cowardice appeared to be common human attributes. Krefeld needed order from above, safeguards against uncontrolled violence, and figures who would guide the people toward self-governance. Kissinger responded by deploying force to prevent continued acts of local cruelty and by establishing working relations with local authorities to create strong incentives for friendly cooperation rather than conflict. Kissinger, the U.S. Army, and eventually a new German government exercised firm control, in alliance with chosen allies. Their definition of legitimate authority would sound paternalist, even imperialist, to a later generation of observers. For Kissinger and others who experienced Weimar, the Second World War, and the early postwar years, however, this approach was unavoidable. In Krefeld and elsewhere, Americans and Germans began a process of constructing political authority against a common fear of both international and domestic violence.

One of Kissinger's closest Army confidants and mentors recounts his astonishment "at the way this twenty-one-year-old did the job": "In just two or three days, the government was again working, in a splendid fashion. Henry had planned things wonderfully. This was a prodigy. He had a fabulous innate sense of finding his way out of the most difficult situations. Here this little Kissinger had set up in three days a working municipal government in a large city where everything had been run by the Nazis just two days before."[50]

Kissinger applied a similar approach to the town of Bensheim and the Bergstrasse County *(Kreis),* located in southwestern Germany, near the confluence of the Rhine and Neckar Rivers. This area was about 110 miles west of his former hometown of Fürth. Although Bensheim had only about 17,000 residents, its environs were densely populated. The nearby city of Heidelberg, a center both for commerce and for American soldiers stationed in Germany, gave the region particular importance. Following his apparent success in overseeing the occupation of Krefeld, in June 1945 the

U.S. Army appointed Kissinger the military administrator of Bensheim and the larger community.

Now a sergeant and the commandant of the newly created 970th Counterintelligence Corps detachment, Kissinger was "the absolute ruler of Bensheim." The local secretary he hired remembers: "He was completely self-assured, and he exuded so much authority that even his American friends would never dare to put their feet on the desk in his office." Kissinger seized a well-appointed villa outside Bensheim and a fancy Mercedes car for his tours around the area, further contributing to his image as an imperial figure. Stories of his affairs with German women and his lavish dinner parties quickly began to swirl. Jerry Bechhofer, an Army officer who visited Kissinger at the time, recounts: "He really enjoyed the trappings of authority."[51]

As in Krefeld, Kissinger used his authority to arrest Nazi officials, but

American soldiers enter Bensheim, Germany, in late March 1945. Kissinger served for ten months as the military administrator for reconstruction in Bensheim and the surrounding area. (© CORBIS)

also to assure order and the restoration of basic services. He hosted social gatherings at his villa to build close working relationships with the town mayor, the former police chief, and others who could help rebuild the region. He emphasized practical solutions to common problems, rather than large ideological projects like democratization. Although Kissinger made his presence felt throughout Bensheim, he delegated day-to-day work to knowledgeable local people. Under Kissinger's leadership, the U.S. Army took an active but restrained role in reconstruction. It offered general guidance, allowing (and even encouraging) local flexibility in implementation. The overstretched nature of American resources, the lack of preparation, and the general recognition of the limitations on military power meant that U.S. soldiers did not dominate everyday life in occupied Germany.[52]

Reflecting on his experiences in Krefeld and Bensheim sixty years later, Kissinger explained that he was acutely aware that Germany, like all other defeated states, had to be rebuilt from within. He understood the inherited complexities of the society, and he distrusted uninformed idealists who sought to purify the land in one fell swoop. Democratic reform required years of slow social and cultural change in a community accustomed to hierarchy and authoritarianism. In this context the American penchant for rapid and total solutions—exemplified by calls for "unconditional surrender" during the war—would elicit only failure and disillusionment. Just as the United States could not immediately eliminate anti-Semitism from society, it also could not immediately institute liberty. An exile returning to his native land, Kissinger saw his role in 1945 as defeating fascism, restoring order, and empowering local figures who could gradually guide Germany to a freer future. This endeavor was not about high-minded proclamations. It required compromise and choices among lesser evils. Once the United States identified reliable local authorities, Kissinger argued, it had to "let history take its course."[53]

The fatalism of this comment is striking, and indeed alien to common American assumptions about the possibilities of reform. Kissinger's return to Germany during the Second World War highlighted for him both the destructive potential of modern society and the limits of social change. The defeated German population of 1945 was not strikingly different in its cultural attitudes from the German population of the Nazi years. The habits of mind from Weimar were also alive in the citizens of Krefeld, Bensheim, and other communities. The relative stagnation of social attitudes, in fact, allowed Kissinger and other German Jews to assist the U.S. Army in anticipating local behavior. Postwar politics in this context was not about transformation. It focused for Kissinger and many of his contemporaries on leadership—identifying and empowering local figures who would repress violent threats and carefully guide their citizens toward expanded but regulated democracy. "A leader," Kissinger later wrote, "does not deserve the name unless he is willing to stand alone. He cannot content himself simply with registering prevailing attitudes. He must build opinion, not merely exploit it." In Germany at the end of the Second World War, and across the globe during the next half-century, Kissinger and his Cold War contemporaries sought leaders who would build what they perceived as an orderly path to democracy while history took its somewhat inevitable course.[54]

German Leadership

The experience of exiled German Jews occupying their former land inspired a search for leaders who could guide their people to a better future. German citizens needed protection against external enemies, especially the Soviet Union, which had already shown a disposition to dominate postwar central Europe. They also needed protection from their own internal pathologies, as witnessed in the militarism and hatred that preceded two world wars. Kissinger was only one of many observers to recognize that Germany required a new political orientation, aided by the United States but directed from within. Only in those terms could a new Germany rise with legitimacy and popular consensus. In addition, the extensive demands on U.S. resources at the end of the war meant that American leaders and citizens were neither willing nor able to establish anything like a permanent occupation. Washington wanted reliable German allies in place soon.[55]

Surveying the cowered populations of Krefeld, Bensheim, and other devastated communities, American observers looked for effective father figures to guide German citizens through the postwar chaos and uncertainty. This search, of course, posed a grave problem because most fathers had also been Nazis. The challenge centered on locating personalities whose wisdom transcended Nazism, personalities who drew on deeper and more respected German traditions of social and political order. This became a process of recovering the "good" German qualities that had survived the onslaught of Nazi evils.

Kissinger was immediately taken with this vision, embodied most flamboyantly by Fritz Kraemer, a private, soon promoted to lieutenant, in the U.S. Army. Kraemer was an obsessive German conservative who devoted his life to the recovery of core human values lost in the rush to modernity. He also dressed and behaved as if he were still living in a previous century. He wore a monocle, was partial to riding boots, and spoke in a ponderous, aristocratic tone. A non-Jew who believed that the Nazis were destroying the inner German spirit, Kraemer voluntarily emigrated in 1933, eventually arriving in the United States in 1939. He enlisted in the Army after the Pearl Harbor attack and very quickly found a unique niche for himself in military intelligence. Kraemer became famous for his lectures to soldiers about the fundamental purposes behind the Second World War and the degenerate nature of Nazi society. Kissinger remembers hearing one of these sermonlike presentations in 1944, before he traveled with his unit to the battlefields across the Atlantic: "The subject was the moral and political stakes of the war . . . Kraemer spoke with passion, erudition, and overwhelming force, as if he were addressing each member of the regiment individually. For the first time in my life—and perhaps the only one—at least I can recall no other such occurrence—I wrote to a speaker how much he had moved me. A few days later Kraemer came to where my company was training."[56]

The two men established a personal bond that lasted for thirty years, exceeding in depth and longevity any of Kissinger's other relationships outside his immediate family. Kissinger recounts: "We were both refugees from Germany. I by necessity, Kraemer by choice. He was thirty-six years of age; I nineteen. He had two Ph.D. degrees [in economics and law]. I had two years of night college in accounting. . . . Out of this encounter grew a relationship that changed my life."[57]

Kraemer helped Kissinger to procure a promotion into the Counterintelligence Corps. His greatest influence, however, was on the young soldier's evolving worldview. Kraemer articulated a vision of politics as a moral calling, in which leaders protected basic human freedoms and nurtured respect for the accumulated wisdom of Western civilization. This was, in some ways, a Platonic ideal that defined human dignity according to a transcendent set of values. It also drew explicitly on the German tradition of *Bildung*. Almost sixty years after their first meeting, Kissinger paid homage to the moral inspiration he received from his conservative German mentor:

> Kraemer dedicated his life to fighting against the triumph of the expedient over the principled. "Intellectuals," Kraemer once said, "have always preached that everything is relative and that there are no absolute values. . . . The result is spiritual emptiness. Everything is possible and therefore nothing is." "The worst thing about a loss of faith is not the fact that someone has stopped believing but that they are ready to believe anything."[58]

The basic values of Western civilization—individualism, rule of law, respect for property, and deference to a monotheistic ("Judeo-Christian") deity—underpinned the faith that Kraemer and Kissinger came to share. This faith, like democracy itself, was fragile. It reflected the accumulated wisdom of society, but it did not emerge organically. Kraemer emphasized both the natural passivity of human beings and their tendency toward escapism. Wisdom and creativity, according to this logic, required discipline and forced commitment. Most high-minded rhetoric about democracy and social justice, he argued, masked self-indulgence and thoughtlessness. In one of his typically long-winded didactic letters to Kissinger after the war, Kraemer applied this criticism to intellectuals as much as to ordinary citizens:

> Glued to our executive desks we compile searching analytical studies, profound policy reviews and ever so clever articles, but we do know so very well that history is not really made by pen or printers' ink. Oh yes, we can rationalize what we are doing, most beautifully. Are not our memoranda and think pieces very important weapons in the struggle for the minds of other men? Yet, we are mercilessly aware of the fact that, in truth, men will adopt the bold and imaginative policies we want them to adopt, not because their brains are convinced by conclusive arguments, but because their hearts are moved. And here we sit . . . not risking our precious existence to propagate a new faith, but arguing in the manner of lawyers and college professors. Studiously we cling to a dehydrated style, eliminating from our outpourings every last vestige of emotionalism.[59]

Looking back on their experience in the U.S. Army, Kraemer revealingly commented to Kissinger: "The days of the war, when we were but privates, were such good days, because our conscience, then, was at rest." The war was an authentic moment for the realization of human will and reason. Young men like Kissinger worked with deep emotion to defeat evil and reorder a society. For Kraemer, this was the kind of principled action, rather than just talk, that leaders had to embody. They had to transcend the temptations of their moment and reach back to preserve a set of inherited cultural values. They had to educate their citizens for a nobler purpose. Kraemer self-righteously modeled this behavior in his dress, demeanor, and declamation. He inspired Kissinger and others to seek out "great men" who could do the same in postwar Germany. A romantic spiritual transcendence, rather than solid democratic credentials, became the key criterion for defining authority after the Nazi darkness.[60]

Kraemer and Kissinger were particularly influential in disseminating this vision among American occupation officials. In April 1946 the Army transferred Kissinger from Bensheim to the U.S. military's European Command Intelligence School, located in the picturesque town of Oberammergau, amidst the Alpine landscape of southern Bavaria. Oberammergau was strategically situated near the region's most famous castles, some of the most notorious Nazi redoubts, and the Austrian border. Kissinger joined Kraemer in this post, where both served as instructors educating allied soldiers about German society.[61]

Teaching a course on "the structure of the Nazi state" to men with little knowledge of the society they occupied, Kissinger served once again as a crucial transatlantic bridge figure. Kraemer was the dominant thinker at the school, but his younger colleague most meaningfully translated concerns about inherited values, political order, and local leadership to soldiers. Dick Van Osten, another instructor at the school, recounts Kissinger's effectiveness: "He had this ability to convey information that could be very confusing in an intelligent and simple way. He was young but he was already a very impressive guy to me. . . . He was short on the podium, but easy to listen to." Henry Rosovsky, an Army corporal and later dean of arts and sciences at Harvard University, remembers that Kissinger was incredibly knowledgeable and authoritative as a lecturer—intellectually mature beyond his years. "If I close my eyes," Rosovsky explains sixty years later, "I can still hear that voice."[62]

Kissinger was only twenty-three years old at the time, he did not have a college degree, yet he was lecturing older and better-educated Army officers about German society. In late May 1946 he officially left the U.S. Army and rejoined the European Command Intelligence School as a civilian instructor, earning $10,000 (a generous sum at the time) for a year of teaching. Although this unique situation reflected Kissinger's exceptional personal abilities, it also grew from his connections to Fritz Kraemer and the U.S. military's search for people who could interpret German society for Americans, and vice versa. Kissinger's German Jewish background and his experiences in Krefeld and Bensheim were definite assets. The Army, and the U.S. government in general, were also partial to Kraemer's argument about the need for "great men" to restore the values of Western civilization in occupied territory. The European Command Intelligence School trained allied soldiers to support this endeavor. It also encouraged the promotion of Germans who would be particularly effective in establishing political order and a Western defense against communist adversaries.

In this context, Oberammergau was more than just a military occupation site. Its proximity to numerous Nazi mountain hideouts made it a primary location for apprehending influential elements of Hitler's regime. Not all the captured Nazis were punished. Through its base of operations in the area, Army counterintelligence orchestrated the defection of certain valuable individuals to the United States, where they became part of the nation's evolving postwar defense forces. The most famous of these defections in the vicinity of Oberammergau included Wernher von Braun, the leading figure in Nazi Germany's rocket program (particularly the "V-2"). With the assistance of Army counterintelligence, von Braun and other prominent German rocket scientists became active contributors to American missile programs during the next two decades. Kraemer and Kissinger were not directly involved in the defection of the Nazi officials, but they surely knew of these activities and justified them in the name of building effective postwar authority rather than pursuing short-term democratic justice.[63]

The figure who did the most to establish postwar authority in the western half of Germany was Konrad Adenauer, the first chancellor of the Federal Republic. In the eyes of Kissinger and many others, he was the strong father (or grandfather) figure destined to guide the German people out of their recent nightmares. Kissinger maintained a deep reverence for Adenauer from the days following the Second World War through the last years of the twentieth century, after the chancellor was long dead. This monumental postwar German was a manifestation of the inner spirit, the sense of tradition, and the personal strength that Kraemer advocated in a "great man" who would lead a new Germany. Kissinger was only one of many Americans who took this image of leadership to heart and saw it embodied so powerfully in the chancellor. Observers were drawn to Adenauer not only for what he did, but for what he appeared to represent. He would provide a tradition-bound ballast for Germany and the transatlantic community as a whole, during a period of extreme social and political turbulence. He would build effective postwar authority that avoided the excesses of both Nazi fascism and Weimar democracy.

In 1945 Adenauer was a relic from the conservative politics of a pre-Nazi past. Born in 1876, he came of age in the Catholic community of the Rhineland, around the cosmopolitan city of Cologne and the smaller town of Bonn. He attended one of Wilhelmine Germany's tradition-bound universities, in Freiburg, where he was active in the student fraternity life that

Konrad Adenauer, the father of West German politics after the Second World War, 1957. Kissinger greatly admired Adenauer's commitment to strong leadership, transatlantic partnership, and Christian democracy. (© Karl Schnürrer / dpa / Corbis)

groomed men for elite society. After a short career as a lawyer, he entered politics, becoming a prominent national figure in the Center party, which had strong Catholic roots but also appealed to an upwardly mobile professional class, including Louis Kissinger. Both Adenauer and the Kissinger family were drawn to conservative Center politics, which emphasized civic equality, political stability, and cooperative relations with west European societies.[64]

Adenauer served as mayor of Cologne from 1917 through 1933, when the Nazi regime forced him from office. During this long tenure he worked to strengthen inherited ties between the residents of the city and their French neighbors across the Rhine. This was what many Rhinelanders viewed as the natural west European and larger transatlantic geography for German society. Adenauer's biographers have emphasized his long-standing affinity for a westward-facing Germany and his disdain for the Prussian influences centered around Berlin. Cooperation across the Rhine promised, in Adenauer's eyes, to preserve the entrepreneurial and Catholic character of German culture in Cologne, in contrast to the militaristic and Protestant influences he perceived from areas farther east. Bavaria, Kissinger's home region, had a special place in Adenauer's worldview because it shared, with the Rhineland, a large Catholic population and a discomfort with Prussian domination in Germany. Like the Rhineland, Bavaria's geography also made it an area poised between societies. This circumstance explains, in part, why Kissinger's ancestors and many other Orthodox Jews migrated to the region in the eighteenth and nineteenth centuries. The Rhineland and Bavaria, not Berlin, were at the heart of Adenauer's vision of a modern, civilized Germany. As mayor of Cologne and as an internal exile under the Nazis, Adenauer defined politics as a moral calling, rooted in the protection of Western civilization. The nation needed, according to this view, firm political leadership against the degenerate tendencies within its own borders. In this sense, Adenauer's ideas formed an identical match with those of Fritz Kraemer and young Kissinger. Despite their differences in age, they had in fact much in common.[65]

Adenauer's conservatism, his extensive political experience, and his freedom from any Nazi taint made him an ideal candidate for Americans seeking a "great man" to lead postwar Germany. His conservatism and stubbornness had alienated the British occupation authorities in Cologne during the early months after the war, but American policymakers would turn to Adenauer in later years for political guidance. His image of self-discipline, his cautious approach to policy, and his unmistakable commitment to "good" German values fitted closely with the leadership hopes articulated by Kraemer, Kissinger, and many others. The American occupation, one historian explains, "discriminated against both Left and Right extremes in a halting yet continuing attempt to bring stable, moderate democracy to postwar Germany." Strong prejudices against the fractured politics of Weimar, the disorder of places like Krefeld and Bensheim after the war, and the emerging Soviet threat prepared the way for Adenauer's rise to eminence in American judgments.[66]

Under Adenauer's authority, a new political party—the Christian Democratic Union (CDU)—came to dominate the politics of western Germany with explicit American support. This alliance between the CDU and U.S. occupation officials was more than a marriage of convenience. It manifested a shared commitment to controlled social change through an inclusive political ideology—"Judeo-Christian" thought in the United States, "Christian Democracy" in Germany—that nurtured consensus among diverse religious groups. Occupation officials did not want to separate religious faith from politics; they wanted to make it a source of unity, stability, and progress behind a strong fatherly figure. Adenauer repeatedly came back to this point when he emphasized the importance of building national and transatlantic society around faith, embodied by firm leaders rather than the materialism of daily life. Once again, the echoes of Fritz Kraemer in Adenauer's politics are striking.[67]

Henry Kissinger did not meet Adenauer until 1959, and he had little influence on the formation of American policy toward the CDU and Germany before that time. His memories and judgments of Adenauer, however, reflect the degree to which he and other observers came to see the German chancellor as an indispensable "great man" in the creation of a new Germany, a new Europe, and a new transatlantic identity. Kissinger describes Adenauer as "the greatest German statesman since Bismarck." His extensive reflections on the two German leaders emphasize their similar abilities to mediate between extremes, to impart their firmness of will on society, and to transcend immediate pressures in favor of a broader vision of Western civilization. The last characteristic, for Kissinger, derived from their religious devotion: "God provided the mechanism to transcend the transitoriness of the human scale." Their strength of purpose "derived more from faith than from analysis." Each man had "gone through the school of his country's convulsions and possessed an extraordinary intuition for the trends of his period."[68]

Adenauer was not an intellectual, but a romantic hero for Kissinger: "Possessed of the granitelike features of a Roman emperor, Adenauer also had the high cheekbones and slightly slanted eyes which suggested the hint of some Hun conqueror who might have trekked across the Rhineland in the previous millennium." He gave his country "the courage to face an uncertain future." Kissinger sees a certain destiny in this: "it seemed as if his entire life had been a preparation for the responsibility of restoring self-respect to his occupied, demoralized, and divided society."[69]

As the father of the postwar Federal Republic of Germany—built on the parts of the country occupied by American, British, and French forces in 1945—Adenauer reconstituted the people of Krefeld, Bensheim, and other communities as a nation bound to the central moral tenets of the West. These values were the "good" German traditions of the Rhineland before the Second World War: entrepreneurship, civility, and individual freedom. They not only ran against the extremes of Weimar democracy and Nazi fascism; they also contradicted the state intrusiveness of Soviet communism. For Kissinger and many other Americans, Adenauer became the German prophet who recognized the perils of an uncommitted Germany. He forged a state in the western half of his nation that found security, stability, and freedom through transatlantic institutions, particularly the North Atlantic Treaty Organization (NATO), founded in 1949:

> Adenauer's response to the chaos of the immediate postwar world was that a divided, occupied country severed from its historic roots required a steady policy if it were to regain some control over its future. Adenauer refused to be diverted from this course by nostalgia for the past, or by the traditional German love-hate relationship with Russia. He opted unconditionally for the West, even at the price of postponing German unity.[70]

Adenauer was, in many ways, the German father figure Kissinger and other occupation officials searched for. His power was mutually constituted in interactions between the Americans and the Germans. His chancellorship, and the Federal Republic as a whole in its early years, was a child of dual parentage. Kissinger is only one of many observers to note that the Americans could not have "reeducated" the Germans without Adenauer.

At the same time, Kissinger also joined a large group of Americans and Germans who made careers for themselves after the Second World War working to assure Adenauer the transatlantic support he needed for his mission. NATO, early efforts at West European integration, and the close U.S.-West German relationship that developed during the Cold War were a continuation of the project for reconstructing Germany and the transatlantic community, begun before the first American soldiers reached places like Krefeld and Bensheim.[71]

Between 1959 and 1967 Kissinger and Adenauer met seven times for intense discussions about the issues that occupied their waking hours: German politics, transatlantic cooperation, and Soviet threats. The fact that the chancellor met so frequently with Kissinger, then an academic without an official policy position, is extraordinary in itself. Their discussions reveal a common anxiety about internal weaknesses within their countries, and a shared desire to imbue cooperation between their governments with a moral weight that would make any alternative unthinkable. This was a relationship based not on strategic analysis, but on a recognition that their two careers and the societies formed around them after the Second World War embodied an emerging transatlantic identity. The rise of Kissinger and Adenauer as figures of importance in the postwar world was a manifestation of this identity at work. Although it penetrated deeply throughout the United States and western Europe, the new partnership across the ocean was, at its core, driven by a generation of leaders who experienced the occupation of Germany firsthand.[72]

The challenges of the early Cold War that brought Kissinger and Adenauer together focused on strengthening transatlantic ties to thwart enemies at home and abroad. Adenauer built the institutions of the Federal Republic with this mission in mind. Returning to the United States in 1947, now a decorated twenty-four-year-old war hero, Kissinger quickly rose through the most influential transatlantic institutions in the United States. Henry Kissinger's Cold War career was both a product and a producer of a transatlantic world.

Internationalizing American Society, Narrowing American Power

Henry Kissinger's socialization as an American and a foreign-policy expert occurred in a militarized, transatlantic setting. His rapid maturation from a

German Jewish émigré into an American soldier, an occupation administrator, and a respected lecturer—all before the tender age of twenty-five—reflected broader international transformations. People at the time recognized his extraordinary talents, as did Kissinger himself. He most crucially benefited, however, from historical circumstances that placed a premium on his capabilities. Henry Kissinger was not a self-made man; he was made by the Second World War.

The fight against fascism created a unique niche in American society for young men like Kissinger who had their feet (and minds) in two worlds. German Jews, in particular, became crucial translators for American officials seeking to understand, destroy, and reconstruct central Europe. They acquired respected status within powerful U.S. institutions, played an influential role in the occupation of Germany, and helped define the postwar order. German Jews moved from Washington Heights to Washington, D.C. Having left Germany as refugees, they returned, less than a decade later, as rulers.

The pressures and promises of the Second World War internationalized American society. Foreign influences had always played an important role in the United States, but now they came to dominate key American institutions. The U.S. Army and the new intelligence agencies recruited Jews and other traditional outsiders for their cosmopolitanism. "Establishment" circles of influential thinkers solicited opinions from formerly ignored figures who did not share traditional American assumptions about democracy and social order or a stereotypical white Anglo-Saxon Protestant (WASP) family background. Paradoxically, the war empowered elitism in the mobilization of national resources, but it also broadened the elite in the pursuit of diverse knowledge and skills. Talented and hard-working Jews like Kissinger benefited enormously from the combination of increased power and diversity in the U.S. Army and other militarized institutions. The Second World War provided Kissinger and his counterparts with remarkable political and social mobility.

The internationalization of American society and the newfound mobility that it offered for many outsider groups created a self-consciously transatlantic American identity. Americans now defined their security synonymously with the security of western Europe. They thought explicitly in terms of a common Western "Judeo-Christian" civilization. Most significant, the daily operation of politics and society on both sides of the Atlantic grew deeply intermingled. American voices became ubiquitous in West

Germany, France, Britain, and Italy. European figures, from Churchill to Einstein, became icons of postwar America. Many scholars have examined the expansion of U.S. cultural influence in the second half of the twentieth century (the "Coca-colonization" of the world), but they often neglect the ways in which the workings of transatlantic politics and society constructed the foundation for what became a rich bidirectional flow of ideas. Culture followed the networks emerging around men like Kissinger. His mobility into mainstream American society solidified the new bridges of influence spanning the vast ocean of historical separation.[73]

Transatlantic ties meant a new transatlantic set of political and social assumptions. The internationalization of American society loosened the hold of "exceptionalist" ideas about democracy, individualism, and social justice in the United States. At the same time, common American beliefs on these and other topics gained new currency in Europe. A transatlantic dialogue took shape, emphasizing rational government under strong leaders, civilized community based on a nondenominational religious faith, and moderation between populist and authoritarian extremes—what Arthur Schlesinger Jr. called the "vital center." Soviet-supported communism emerged as an overriding threat because it explicitly challenged the leadership, faith, and moderation at the core of transatlantic thought. Stalwart in his call for a return to Germany's civilized traditions and his rejection of communist alternatives, Konrad Adenauer embodied the postwar constellation of transatlantic values. Fritz Kraemer, Henry Kissinger, and others espoused these beliefs to both American and European listeners. Kissinger's status as a transatlantic translator of words and ideas during the war assured that he was perfectly positioned to continue this role after 1945.[74]

An institutional and ideological narrowing also accompanied the openings of the Cold War. German Jews gained some insider status in intellectual and policy circles, but they remained outsiders in many ways. They could not escape their Jewish and German associations, no matter how hard they tried. They could not assimilate. In fact it was the very German Jewish background of men like Kissinger that gave them the opportunity and aspiration to pursue a more "normal" American existence. This was never possible. German Jews took on enormous responsibilities in war and peace, but they never became fully accepted members of a now transatlantic elite. Kissinger could enter the Counterintelligence Corps in the U.S. Army, but he faced barriers to becoming a military physician. After the war, he could gain special admittance to Harvard University, but the social clubs that shaped lifelong business and political prospects were closed to him. Among intellectual and policy insiders, Kissinger remained an outsider.

This position, within the elite but never of the elite, was a troubling consequence of the mid-twentieth century's transatlantic contours. Although Jewish men gained some access to power and influence, dominant ideas and institutions systematically disempowered women and other minorities. Under the paternalistic assumptions of a muscular, courageous, and romantic leadership, the model transatlantic figure was an educator and a disciplinarian, a powerful father figure who could guide his people to cultural maturation and protect them from harmful influences. Jewish men like Kissinger had to play to this image of toughness and hyperrationality, regardless of emotional and moral motivations. Women, with few exceptions, could not conform to this image.[75]

African Americans, Asian Americans, Chicanos, and other non-European minorities suffered from the priorities of a transatlantic worldview. These groups had long encountered virulent racism within the United States. The sacrifices made by minorities in the Second World War provided a new spur for civil rights reform, but the war also strengthened presumptions about comparative geographic importance. European Jews had knowledge and experiences valued in a transatlantic worldview; they gained access to influence accordingly. Non-European groups did not have highly valued knowledge and experiences; they lost allies among European minorities and found themselves consistently excluded from powerful institutions.

The geographic biases of a transatlantic worldview had foreign-policy implications as well. Fighting a truly global war, the U.S. government greatly expanded its expertise on various non-European regions of the world. This expertise became the basis for the flowering of "area studies" in universities after 1945. American leaders, however, paid little heed to abundant local knowledge of "third world" societies; they remained fixated on European priorities. U.S. policy extended its geographic reach during the early postwar years, but it narrowed its range of geographic priorities. The United States was a global superpower with a transatlantic worldview.

The American experience in Vietnam is, of course, the best-known and perhaps most tragic example of this phenomenon. American policymakers underwrote and later replaced French colonial authority in opposition to the counsel of area experts within the U.S. government. The decision to intervene in Vietnam, as elsewhere in the third world, reflected concerns about European security, in this case the stability of postwar France. The United States became a colonial power in Southeast Asia not because of colonial interests in the area, but because of anxieties about what decolonization would mean for European security. The French and other allies exploited these American concerns for their own purposes.[76]

Transatlantic priorities distorted American policies in Vietnam and other areas. Dominant ideas and institutions privileged European regional experience and disempowered third world expertise. Kissinger and other experts on Europe gained unprecedented influence over U.S. policy. Area specialists from many other regions often found themselves facing the same barriers to influence that afflicted women and non-European minorities.

The transatlantic ties forged in the crucible of the Second World War clearly had contradictory effects. Kissinger's experiences during the war and his postwar career manifest these traits. The most virulent public attacks on transatlantic assumptions coincided with the period two decades after the war, when Kissinger was closest to the center of the dominant policymaking institutions. Those groups largely excluded from political influence on both sides of the Atlantic—non-European minorities, women, and third world experts—mobilized in large numbers against the troubling manifestations of transatlantic policy, especially in Vietnam. The limitations of a transatlantic worldview had, in fact, become most evident at its moment of maximum power. Many transatlantic elites also came to share this point of view. In this context, Kissinger found once again that the sources of his influence were also the sources of his exclusion. Working through dominant transatlantic institutions, he became a policy insider; the attacks on these institutions made him an intellectual outsider.

Much of the continuing controversy surrounding Kissinger is an extended debate over the appropriate place for a transatlantic worldview within a more multicultural American identity. Kissinger recognizes this dynamic, and condemns the "intellectual class" for superficially moralizing about politics and neglecting the moral content of his own perspective.[77] The transatlantic ties of the mid-twentieth century were indeed a moral response to the collapse of Weimar Germany, the war against fascism, and the threat of communism. These ties were strong and enduring, but they remained dependent on a common moral framework. Shifting philosophical and emotional points of view have inevitably challenged inherited transatlantic values. In this sense, attacks on Kissinger are attacks on a generation formed from the experiences and lessons of the Second World War.

THREE | *The Cold War University*

Henry Kissinger has many enemies, but none attracts more attention from him than what he calls the "intellectual class." "I feel sorry for policymakers today," Kissinger comments with an implied reference to himself; "intellectuals condemn [them] without understanding." Harkening back to a more favorable historical moment in his mind, he explains: "When I was a young professor, we used to have Saturday afternoon seminars" where scholars examined tough policy issues, sympathizing with the difficulties facing officials. The people attending these seminars often criticized policy, Kissinger admits, but they concentrated on formulating constructive and respectful advice, not morally self-righteous condemnations. Intellectuals saw themselves as public servants rather than academic critics.[1]

Kissinger's comments drip with irony. He was, and in many ways remains, a central member of the "intellectual class." He returned to the United States from Germany in 1947 with three assets on which he would build his career: his military experience, his familiarity with German society, and his powerful mind. He did not have access to an influential social network or an official policymaking position. These would come only later. Kissinger harnessed his personal assets to build a name for himself among scholars and politicians. Through prolific writings and tireless program-building he became a recognized figure, and from this position he crossed into government service. Ideas and words transformed the twenty-four-year-old German Jewish immigrant into a public presence. For Kissinger, intellectual activities were an avenue to political power, not a counterweight.

In the aftermath of the Second World War, Kissinger benefited from a crucial transformation in the American intellectual environment. The mobilization of society for a global conflict, and the creation of a transatlantic "Judeo-Christian" identity, opened academic institutions to German Jews, who had generally been marginalized in the past. Kissinger's insights into military affairs and German society received unprecedented attention among intellectuals (and their government sponsors), pursuing policy-relevant scholarship as they had not before. Kissinger's knowledge held great currency after 1945. Other equally gifted thinkers, from more privileged backgrounds, did not possess similarly privileged knowledge.

The Cold War University

Harvard University, the most distinguished American academic institution in the mid-twentieth century, stood at the center of this process. More than any of its Ivy League counterparts, it embraced the new personalities and the new knowledge of the postwar world. Harvard's president, James Conant, redefined the university's mission in these terms, creating intellectual space for men like Kissinger. Prewar Harvard had been cosmopolitan in its range, but provincial in its general disdain for immigrant identities and practical knowledge. Postwar Harvard remained exclusive in its social prejudices, but it recognized the enormous financial and political incentives attached to policy-relevant instruction and research. Although other institutions—particularly the Massachusetts Institute of Technology and Stanford University—received more direct funding from policymakers, Harvard moved most effectively into a position of direct policy influence.[2]

This intellectual and institutional transformation from traditional scholarly detachment to contemporary political empowerment created the "Cold War University." It operated more as an extension of government than as an independent academy. When American military servicemen returned from the Second World War, universities integrated them back into society through expanded enrollments, orchestrated socialization, and professional training. Government regulations, particularly related to national security secrets and foreign threats, set the tone for life on campus. Most significant, federal financing directed research into new areas, discouraging it in others. Universities not only cooperated with government authorities;

they now depended on them. The same was true in reverse. Federal attention to universities reflected perceived postwar necessity.[3]

Anxieties about Soviet expansionism and a perpetual state of foreign-policy crisis made the Cold War an ever-present reality on campus after 1945. In this sense, universities never demobilized from wartime footing, but instead continued to enlist more bodies and resources for defeating a threatening enemy. Classroom instruction, especially in the humanities, focused on instilling values of democratic citizenship that would steel students against treacherous ideas and prepare them to fight for their "unique heritage." This was the moment of enforced "consensus" in American self-analysis.[4]

Working directly with government officials, universities created special "area study" programs that investigated topics of pressing national security concern. They encouraged an unprecedented investment in linguistic and analytical skills needed for permanent foreign-policy vigilance. The Russian Research Center, founded at Harvard in 1948, was the first and most prominent of these new university institutes. It provided a home where former members of the U.S. Office of Strategic Services (OSS) could continue their intensive analysis of Soviet behavior, connecting the knowledge available on the university campus with the policy access offered in Washington. It became a model for what one scholar-turned-policymaker praised as the "high measure of interpenetration between universities with area programs and the information-gathering agencies of the government."[5]

The Russian Research Center and its proliferating counterparts contributed to the development of a scholarly field, "Sovietology," that dominated the study of the Soviet Union within both America's growing universities and its expanding intelligence agencies. Many influential figures, particularly George Kennan, moved with relative ease between the two communities. Sovietology was much more than just the study of the contemporary Soviet Union; it involved the formulation of theories designed to explain current policy and predict future threats to U.S. interests. In a manner similar to government intelligence analysts, university scholars monitored Soviet thinking as revealed in émigré interviews, newspapers, and public events. The intentional blurring of the lines between academic and policy analysis, as well as scholarship and national defense, constituted the Cold War University.

Henry Kissinger was never a member of the Russian Research Center, but the intellectual and institutional shifts that it embodied were at the root of his professional maturation. If Fürth defined his German Jewish identity, and the U.S. Army defined his American citizenship, Harvard as the dominant Cold War University defined his intellectual persona. Kissinger rose within a setting of intensive scholarly analysis designed to provide immediate policy payoffs for the postwar world and the emerging American struggle against the Soviet Union. The Saturday afternoon seminars that Kissinger frequently attended made him a prominent intellectual and, soon, a man with the attention of presidents. The abnormal Cold War merging of intellectual and policy worlds was, for Kissinger and many of his generation, all that they knew. They took it for granted as the appropriate mode for organizing knowledge.

When Kissinger condemns the contemporary "intellectual class" for its turn against this relationship, he is not criticizing intellectual aspirations. He still, in fact, thinks of himself in these terms. Instead, Kissinger is condemning the loss of intimacy between scholars and practitioners that proved so fruitful in his career. For foreign-affairs specialists of Kissinger's generation, the estrangement of intellectuals from government officials has cut power from its roots in knowledge, producing episodic and shallow policies. This is what Kissinger laments most of all.[6]

The postwar transformation of intellectual life in the United States empowered this poor German Jewish immigrant. Beginning in the late 1960s, the slow undoing of this transformation empowered his critics. To understand the evolution of society after the defeat of fascism, and the emergence of a new contested world order, one must look inside the Cold War University.[7]

Jewish Mobility

After decades of exclusion, Jews emerged as central actors in universities and policy communities following the Second World War. Although they remained dependent upon powerful non-Jewish patrons, they played a fundamental role in reshaping established institutions like Harvard and the White House. As they bridged societies across the Atlantic, Jews also built the crucial inroads that integrated scholars with practitioners. They were not the face of power, but they came to occupy key positions of influence behind the scenes and between traditional sites of authority. They were the connective tissue of Cold War society.

This was not an entirely new role for Jews. In earlier centuries they had occupied similar positions of influence at the intersection of politics and society. Absolutist monarchs, particularly in seventeenth- and eighteenth-century central Europe, turned to "Court Jews" to raise money for the crown and thus limit the power of the landed elite. "The absolute ruler," according to one scholar, "made use of the Court Jew as a tool to destroy the feudal and patrimonial forces of the Middle Ages which stood in his way. He used the Court Jew as a collaborator and as an advisor in his program for establishing a modern mercantilist economy and a unified, centralized state." The Court Jew was a powerful, but largely isolated, member of the absolutist court, drawing on social networks outside the nobility and dependent on the protection of the monarch.[8]

With the rise of the bureaucratic nation-state in Europe during the nineteenth century, the "State Jew" succeeded the Court Jew. France, in particular, relied on French-educated Jews as bulwarks of the republic. They attained positions of authority within the administrative institutions of the state that emphasized meritocracy, especially through nationwide examinations. As civil servants, magistrates, generals, and government ministers they defended the republic against the political extremes on the left and the right. They were State Jews because they played a critical role in managing the basic functions of the state, protecting its principles, and defending it against attack. State Jews hinged their fate on the survival and prosperity of the state. They were, one historian writes, "truly impassioned by their new roles in public service. They gave their hearts and souls to their jobs, stripping off their former costumes to take on the noble livery of grave and responsible state dignitaries. They intended to serve with all their might this emancipatory, rationalist Republic that was so concerned with progress." The hijacking of the republican state by fascist forces in the early twentieth century destroyed this vision and those who clung most closely to it.[9]

The Cold War University became the incubator for a hybrid of the Court Jew and the State Jew—what we might tentatively call the "policy Jew." As in early modern Europe, policymakers after 1945 looked for new resources outside traditional political circles to contend with the challenges of occupying, rebuilding, and defending postwar society. In the United States presidents turned to intellectual experts who could mobilize knowledge about science, economics, and foreign policy for national purpose. The overriding concern with international affairs that drove this search for expertise placed a premium on the cosmopolitanism of Jews. Like Court Jews, the educated German Jews of the postwar years could draw on networks of knowledge and experience, particularly in Europe, that mainstream Americans did not possess.[10]

The Cold War University was an ideal institution for mobilizing intellectual expertise. By definition, it identified and ranked individuals with particular knowledge and skills. It also operated as the closest analogue to an absolutist court in the modern world. This was especially the case at a self-consciously elite university like Harvard. Deans and professors had very few limits on their power. They allocated resources and privileges with little oversight. Their junior colleagues and students were almost completely dependent on their patronage and goodwill. Most important, they could select talented individuals for rapid advancement with few bureaucratic hindrances. Professors made and unmade careers with monarchical whim.

This academic absolutism served the expert needs of the policy community. Faculty became talent scouts for government. They commanded devotional loyalty from their students, and they moved chosen individuals on a "fast track" into the policy world. Instead of compelling their protégés to pursue the slow, step-by-step climb through an orderly hierarchy that state bureaucracy usually requires, academic patrons pushed their favorites quickly to the top. This was the route that many ambitious and talented Jews followed after the Second World War, including Walt Rostow, Daniel Ellsberg, and, of course, Henry Kissinger.

Assembling around Harvard, these young, talented Jews identified themselves as defenders of the United States against extremes at home and abroad. For all their intellectual expertise they pursued research explicitly designed to serve practical and immediate government purposes, in the process protecting a liberal capitalist world order. This was the overriding ethos of the Cold War University. It rewarded, in status and resources, figures who developed applied policy knowledge. It also encouraged a mix of specific expertise and broad familiarity with international affairs. Cold War intellectuals would examine the intricacies of science and society, but they would also connect their studies with common problemsolving. They would serve as experts and generalists at the same time, just as they would simultaneously operate as scholars and policymakers.

The state was more than just a central focus of study; it was a fundamental source of self-protection. The continued presence of anti-Semitism after the Second World War, even within the Cold War University, compelled upwardly mobile Jewish intellectuals to look to government for personal security. Their production of policy-relevant knowledge served two purposes: it promoted the continued pursuit of enlightened government initiatives, and it assured that powerful non-Jews recognized the importance of Jewish figures. Useful scholarship bolstered national and personal security—these were one and the same. Traditional scholarly detachment risked national diversion and personal vulnerability. The privileged status that some Jews attained within the Cold War University, and within society at large, remained precarious. They felt constant pressure to reaffirm their utility.

Henry Kissinger's career embodies the hopes and limits of postwar Jewish mobility. The Cold War University provided him with the patronage necessary to transcend his Orthodox German Jewish background to some extent. From a very early age, he became an active contributor to broad discussions about government policy among a remarkably cosmopolitan and elite network of people. He occupied a niche as an intellectual expert who contributed general knowledge about the world to policymakers. This was an unelected role that crossed political parties and subverted traditional bureaucracies. It involved frequent collaboration with policymakers but preserved Kissinger's status and freedom as an intellectual. It promised new ideas for meeting the challenges of a new era, but it depended on the continued patronage of tradition-bound elites. Most significant, Kissinger's social position defined American success in the Cold War as a necessary foundation for personal achievement and belonging. His mobility hinged on the perceived value of his suggestions for policy.

Kissinger's career drew on a series of inherited assumptions about the place of Jews in society. This historical background helped to define his public persona and the controversies surrounding it. Kissinger's Jewishness conditioned his relationships with prominent postwar figures. Although it did not determine his ideas and actions, his Jewishness influenced the questions he asked, the personal networks he formed, and the paths he followed. If he were not a German Jew, Kissinger would have lived a very different life. His experiences reflected the intersection of the Cold War and Jewish mobility in the post-1945 world.[11]

These two phenomena transformed Harvard. The institution pursued new avenues for policy influence, and it promoted selected individuals from traditionally excluded groups, particularly German Jews. These activities made Kissinger's career possible. They also influenced its direction. Despite his criticisms of the "intellectual class," Kissinger was a product of the Cold War University and its reconstitution of knowledge—as well as ethnic identity—in society.

Harvard before the Second World War

"When I got to Harvard," Dr. Albert Cohen remembers, "I thought that the university would be full of very intelligent, unprejudiced people. It was obvious, the very day I got there, that this was not the case." Cohen grew up in a poor neighborhood less than two miles from Harvard. Attending the university in the mid-1930s provided a "door up and out" of the ghetto for the young man who later became a respected pediatrician. Among the more progressive institutions in the Ivy League, Harvard accepted a small group of unprivileged (mostly local) students each year, but they were still the exception, not the rule:

> I came in with a bunch of people who were commuters. Other students made snide comments about people who commuted, from whence they came, and what their origins were. On the other side, there was the "Gold Coast." I was taken aback by the fact that there were guys who actually did not buy their clothes in stores, that they waited for a custom-tailor, for a custom-booter, and they had their shirts made to order. That they had people who brought them their car every day and took the car back at night; they lived in clubs and they toured Europe every summer. This was so far away from my childhood—coming from a poverty-stricken area of East Cambridge and thrust into this kind of environment. I was totally ill at ease. I was totally maladroit in this environment.[12]

Arthur Schlesinger Jr. matriculated in the same class as Cohen, but he was much better prepared for Harvard. He had attended elite schools,

Cambridge Latin and Exeter, and his father was a prominent member of the faculty. Schlesinger was not wealthy, but he fitted in with the gentlemanly ethos of the university's social life in the 1930s. He recalls weekend jaunts to the Berkshires, courting trips to Wellesley College, and ceremonial lunches at the Signet Society—"it served the best luncheons in Cambridge, prided itself, sometimes justifiably, on the quality of its table talk and laid hold of visiting dignitaries, like H. G. Wells, for special parties." This was the real Harvard; poor commuters like Cohen could attend the university, but they were not invited to lunch.[13]

Looking back, Schlesinger shares Cohen's wonder at the combination of cosmopolitanism and provincialism at Harvard. A small college in the mid-nineteenth century, it became a world-class university with the rapid growth of a renowned faculty, extensive research facilities, a rigorous curriculum, and, most important, an unmatched base of wealthy contributors. By the 1930s even uneducated observers like Cohen's parents recognized that Harvard laid claim to be "the greatest school in the world." Foreign dignitaries and celebrities who visited the United States frequently stopped at Harvard to mark their intellectual status and join the likes of Schlesinger in conversation. Cambridge became the central American salon for the chattering classes.[14]

Beneath the surface, however, Harvard was still an insular community. Schlesinger remembers: "The Great Depression was all around us, but for me, at least, it seems to have been largely a succession of offstage noises. Harvard was a cocoon." The gentile habits that encouraged condescension toward outsiders like Cohen also contributed to a general apathy about the world beyond the university. Harvard prided itself on standing apart from the corruptions of ordinary politics, business, and society. Much like Boston, just across the Charles River, it was to be a "city on a hill," a cloistered world of privilege, a temple of learning and gentlemanly grooming. Harvard was not a hothouse for new policy ideas in a moment of world crisis.[15]

At the university's tercentenary celebration in 1936 its distaste for contemporary political and social engagement was evident, amidst the parade of distinguished intellectual voices. The triumphal institutional history commissioned for the occasion described an "Olympian age" with hardly any reference to the deep poverty, social dislocation, and political extremism that dominated daily life in Boston, throughout the United States, and across the globe. Harvard was above it all. What mattered most was that the university had, despite external pressures, preserved "the ancient 'collegiate way of living.'"[16]

The Harvard community displayed disdain for its most prominent graduate at the time, President Franklin Delano Roosevelt, whose New Deal policies rejected this callously detached worldview. When the university reluctantly invited the president to speak at the tercentenary convocation, the hostility to his populist and experimental politics pervaded the campus. Faculty, students, and alumni spoke of Roosevelt with contempt. The organizers of the tercentenary sought to curtail the president's speaking time and prohibit his reference to policy issues. Influencing the White House was not on the agenda for this glamorous showcase of Harvard's accomplishments. Cambridge was a long way from Washington, D.C., and the university sought to maximize the independence reinforced by distance. Harvard, like its counterparts in New Haven and Princeton, sheltered itself from the society around its gates.[17]

Making the Cold War University

The Second World War did not undermine elitism at Harvard, but it opened the university to unprecedented policy influences. Despite its jealously guarded independence, Harvard became a direct contributor to the war effort and a rich recipient of government funding. Breaking with tradition, President James Conant called upon the university to take its "appointed place in the vast national effort." The march of fascism across Europe and Asia, and the Japanese attack on Pearl Harbor, changed the moral calculus for an institution that claimed ethical superiority from political detachment. Now the greatest university felt compelled to prove its greatness in battle, hand-in-hand with President Roosevelt. At the baccalaureate ceremony for the Harvard Class of 1942, Conant was explicit about this shift in purpose:

> You who now graduate from Harvard enter, as it were, into a band of chosen men who have shared a certain experience. You have served your apprenticeship during the years of youth in contact with a great and living tradition based on the cultural inheritance of our civilization. From this experience provided for you by organized society you have derived

> benefits which will endure throughout your life. Recognizing the peculiar obligation placed upon you by these benefits received, you together with all members of the fellowship of educated men go forth now to place your talents at the disposal of your country. To many generations the fulfillment of the obligation never takes the form of a clear-cut call for action. . . . But to you of the Class of 1942, immediately upon graduation, and for a few years still earlier, the country has turned for special service. For a time the imperious demands of a nation fighting a desperate war must transcend all else.[18]

Only six years removed from its "Olympian" moment of self-congratulation, Harvard no longer stood apart from the turmoil beyond its gates. Conant embodied the university's rapid shift into contemporary politics. Unlike all his predecessors, he transformed the presidency of Harvard into a job that included a vast government policymaking portfolio. During the Second World War, Conant helped the White House set procedures for national military conscription, organize defense collaboration with Great Britain, and deploy the first atomic weapons. His government work, like the university's, only expanded after 1945.

Harvard and other institutions of higher learning partnered with the government in preparing young officers for command. With the precipitous decline in the available civilian student population during the war, Army and Navy personnel, enrolled in intensive math and science courses, came to dominate the campus. Responding to military needs, the university revised the academic calendar and the admissions requirements for undergraduate and graduate programs. Harvard was now officially supporting the war, and its operating revenue depended as never before on government compensation for its efforts.[19]

Similarly, research at Harvard became a creature of war priorities and government financing. The university received a windfall of $31 million in defense-related grants for major projects on computation, radar, and napalm. Prominent scientists, including Conant, worked with the secret Manhattan Project. Many distinguished scholars in the humanities and social sciences took up positions in the newly formed OSS, where they applied their linguistic and analytical skills to preparing military operations against the nation's enemies. Harvard was now so deeply integrated in the war effort that it became difficult to distinguish where the authority of the government ended and that of the university began.[20]

By 1945 Harvard was no longer the insular community that Albert Cohen and Arthur Schlesinger Jr. had experienced less than a decade earlier. Social condescension and Signet Society lunches remained a staple of university life, but Harvard had personal, financial, and intellectual ties to government policy that it could not renounce. It had taken on a new mission as an international defender of American national interests. Most significant, its prestige was bound to the fate of U.S. foreign policy as never before. If Americans failed to build a better international order and prevent another world war, the efforts of Harvard men would appear ineffective.

A great university could not tolerate such a verdict. The Second World War and its aftermath redefined Harvard as a policy institution, with a strong stake in formulating and defending American global strategy. The university accepted a "new position of responsibility in the community of the world." "Together," the *Alumni Bulletin* explained, the "university and war-wrought scholar are coming out of the tower to meet the world face to face." The college embraced what one of its most distinguished professors and government policy advisors called a "dual existence."[21]

This is the Harvard Henry Kissinger entered in 1947. His presence in a large class of war veterans, many of whom did not come from privileged backgrounds, symbolized the university's broadening social base and its direct connection to American military policy. During the immediate postwar years undergraduate enrollments grew by more than 50 percent from the years before Pearl Harbor. Men returning from war accounted for more than half of this ballooning population, with an average age of twenty-three. (Kissinger was twenty-four when he entered Harvard.) In contrast to Cohen and Schlesinger, postwar undergraduates were older, more worldly, and more serious about putting their education to practical use. Conant called the veterans "the most mature and promising students Harvard has ever had." Although they often lacked the social and educational pedigrees of their predecessors, they demonstrated what one dean called "capacity and character, the qualities likely to provide informed and responsible leadership in a community."[22]

The shared sacrifice of the war, and the common commitment to preventing its recurrence, grounded university life in contemporary politics. Conant encouraged this attitude, instituting curricular reforms that emphasized "general education" for effective citizenship. This move was an extension of his wartime efforts to make instruction integral to the defense of national interests. "The primary concern of American education today," Conant wrote, "is not the development of the appreciation of the 'good life' in young gentlemen born to the purple. . . . Our purpose is to cultivate in the largest possible number of our future citizens an appreciation of both the responsibilities and the benefits which come to them because they are Americans and are free." Accordingly, courses in the social sciences, particularly government, grew in popularity. Kissinger joined a crowd of fellow veterans when he attended classes on politics.[23]

The postwar emphasis on government and citizenship rather than on social finishing encouraged greater acceptance for recent immigrants, especially talented Jews. The enforced "Judeo-Christian" sensibility of the war effort carried into the university, affirming the contributions of Jewish veterans and instilling self-confidence in them to participate more fully in campus life. Sherman Starr, a Jewish student who began his studies before Pearl Harbor and finished after the close of hostilities, recounts:

Kissinger's yearbook photo from Harvard University, 1950. Kissinger was part of a large cohort of Jewish immigrants who entered Ivy League institutions after the Second World War. He experienced rapid professional mobility in this new environment, but he also remained an outsider among traditional elites. (Courtesy of Harvard University Yearbook Publications)

"When I got back to Harvard after the war, the whole atmosphere was changed. It was totally different. The grand motif of ecumenism was a great leveler."[24]

Admissions records confirm Starr's assessment. The returning veterans were "the most diverse student body" in the university's history to that time. Jews were a rising group, constituting 17 percent of the university's enrollments in 1947, increasing to 25 percent of the student body in 1952. Anti-Semitism still colored university life, as evidenced in the admissions preference accorded to wealthy preparatory school graduates and in the exclusion of Jews from elite social clubs. The growing presence of Jews at Harvard, however, gave them a much greater claim to belonging, both as full members of the academic community and as figures making important contributions to contemporary society. Henry Rosovsky, a graduate student in the late 1940s and later a dean at the university, recounts: "for our generation, being Jewish was not an issue."[25]

This assertion is not quite true. Jewish identity remained clearly marked at Harvard, as it did in American society as a whole, but it no longer elicited the same rigid exclusions as a decade earlier. Harvard broke new ground in bridging the worlds of scholarship and policy, and it also forged ahead faster than any of its counterparts in building a "Judeo-Christian" community. The university sought out selected Jewish veterans like Kissinger who displayed both intellectual brilliance and strength of character. As it carefully preserved what Provost Paul Buck called a "balance" between different traditions on the campus, Harvard opened limited space for formerly marginalized groups. The university proclaimed, with some justification, that in this respect it was more progressive than its competitors. Yale and Princeton were slower to recognize the intellectual and political advantages of admitting a more diverse student body.[26]

"Judeo-Christian" inclusiveness, as practiced at Harvard, was Cold War policy. The U.S. government transformed universities into settings for the socialization of former soldiers through professional training and intellectual enrichment. The Servicemen's Readjustment Act of 1944 (popularly known as the G.I. Bill) provided unprecedented federal financing for the education of more than 2 million veterans. As a consequence, Harvard and its counterparts—public and private institutions alike—broadened their enrollments, hired new faculty, changed admissions standards, offered new courses, and, most significant, rejected many traditional forms of exclusion. The G.I. Bill did not officially force universities to expand so rapidly, but it placed enormous pressure on them to do so, especially in the context of their growing dependence on federal financing.

Despite Conant's support for cooperation between colleges and government, even he bridled at the interference from Washington. He lamented that the G.I. Bill failed "to distinguish between those who can profit most by advanced education and those who cannot." Disregarding Conant's reservations, the federal government used financial and political pressures to force the doors of the university opened to a more diverse population than would otherwise have had a chance at admission. Without the G.I. Bill, men like Kissinger would have returned home with much narrower educational and professional prospects.[27]

This bold intrusion into university administration reflected much more than a sense of obligation to men who had taken up arms in defense of their country. President Franklin Roosevelt was determined to avoid the debilitating domestic difficulties that accompanied the return of veterans from the First World War, and the weakening of America's international position that followed from that ordeal. During the 1920s and 1930s Roosevelt witnessed the disorder and sometime radicalism that followed from the unemployment and impoverishment of so many former servicemen. The G.I. Bill—which included provisions for unemployment benefits and for home, farm, and business mortgages, as well as education—prevented a replay of these conditions. Extending the most generous elements of the New Deal to veterans, it guaranteed them a foundation for personal empowerment. Universities, in particular, would give young men returning from the front the knowledge to succeed in society, as well as a stake in the continued stability and strength of the nation.

One professor at Harvard confirmed the success of this strategy when he observed that the veterans given unprecedented access to his university "don't want to tear everything down; they want to make the existing system work better." President Roosevelt recognized that demobilized soldiers often become a restive and even radical force in domestic society. Admission to universities would counteract this tendency, enlisting the nation's intellectual resources to build a peaceful and stable Cold War consensus. In a remarkable exercise of federal fiat, the G.I. Bill made higher education, even at Harvard, a servant of political order. As students, veterans received strong incentives to work *within* existing institutions. This was particularly the case for Jewish veterans, who recognized their dependence on federal policies for institutional and social mobility.[28]

Throughout their lives, Kissinger and many of his counterparts would accept the legitimacy of existing American institutions as axiomatic. They would define patriotism as a commitment to improving them from the inside. This was the attitude encouraged by the Cold War University, particularly for those traditional outsider groups given new access by government authority. They became a "civic generation" with a strong commitment to mainstream politics and federally regulated social change.[29]

As in Germany and the United States before 1945, progressive change appeared to come from the top down, when social and political elites (whose members included James Conant and Franklin Roosevelt) collaborated to improve the living conditions of citizens. This is exactly how Kissinger narrates his career. He benefited from the continued access, support, and encouragement offered by elite men and institutions. He does not perceive himself as receiving the same assistance from the critics of elitism, including many intellectuals.[30]

After the Second World War the dominant American institutions remained prejudiced and imperfect, but they offered the most promising anchor for an ambitious and talented immigrant like Kissinger. Anticommunism, in this context, grew not only from a well-founded fear of Soviet expansionism after the Second World War, but also from a perception that Marxist-inspired thought called for the destruction of the very American institutions—the army, the government, and the universities—that traditional outsiders could cling to as stepping-stones toward inclusion. Kissinger and many of his counterparts defined communism as both a foreign threat and a domestic vulnerability. Like fascism in Weimar Germany, communist-inspired ideas in the United States promised rapid change that would, in practice, destroy the most effective vehicles of reform. Communism was a false prophecy. Patriotism and progress, for Kissinger, required firm government-led resistance.

As in the U.S. Army, the position of German Jews within the university was fraught with contradictions that profoundly shaped the Cold War world. The opening of higher education, under government pressure, had major limitations. Women did not benefit from the G.I. Bill because they were generally excluded from recognized military service and admission to many universities. African American veterans confronted the same racist restrictions that had been in place before and during the war. Despite their military service, informal quotas and adherence to racial segregation (even in northern states) meant that predominantly white colleges like Harvard remained largely closed to African Americans. The G.I. Bill increased access to universities, but it intentionally allowed local politicians and administrators to enforce racial exclusions. The Cold War University was, at least in the first decade after 1945, a white male institution.[31]

Jewish veterans like Kissinger had a place in the Cold War University that women and African Americans did not. This circumstance further reinforced the emerging tendency to view Jews as "white" citizens, particularly those with a German attachment that provided valued knowledge after 1945. Continuing a process that began in the U.S. military during the Second World War, young Jewish men, who might otherwise have felt a sympathetic connection to African Americans as a fellow minority, began to identify more closely with the dominant social groups that continued to condescend toward them, but at least now offered limited access to power. Instead of finding empowerment in minority solidarity, many Jews who benefited from the G.I. Bill devoted their energies to moving through dominant institutions. Kissinger and others began careers at Harvard that would involve minimal contact with African Americans. The Cold War University segregated not only whites from blacks, but also Jews from fellow minorities.[32]

Over the next half-century, this social bifurcation contributed to growing divergences in wealth and judgments about America's place in the world. At Harvard, Kissinger and his counterparts transformed themselves from immigrants into prosperous defenders of Cold War America. Many African American veterans condemned the racism and inequality embedded in the very institutions Kissinger defended. The mix of inclusion and exclusion within the Cold War University contributed to lasting divisions in perceptions of public policy. Throughout his career, Henry Kissinger would have difficulty understanding African American criticisms of the United States, and he would become a favored target for the anger of those minorities left behind by the postwar opening of society. These divisions followed from the transformation of intellectual life after the Second World War.[33]

Social Outsider, Cold War Insider

Kissinger and other Jews at Harvard gained "insider" access to knowledge and power in the United States, but they remained "outsiders" from the traditional elements of social life that survived the Second World War. They continued to live between worlds in a way that profoundly shaped their activities. Jews felt pressure, in Henry Rosovsky's words, to be "totally unselfconscious" about their religious and cultural background. Anthony Lewis, the future *New York Times* columnist who graduated from Harvard in 1948, confirmed this point: "There was a sense of uneasiness about Jewishness, in Boston and at Harvard, and I suppose blending into the mass felt safer. I know from older generations that Jews at Harvard were far less accepted, less secure, before World War II. But the immediate post-war generation was not wholly at ease, or so I have to say." Kissinger recalls similar feelings of insecurity when he arrived at Harvard: "I was completely unsure of myself. I had gotten out of the Army and I felt like an immigrant again. When I went into the Army I was a refugee, and when I got out I was an immigrant."[34]

In the autumn of 1947, when Kissinger matriculated at Harvard, the university segregated the living quarters of immigrants and Jews from those of the rest of the student population. Jews were Harvard insiders and outcasts at the same time. During his freshman year, Kissinger resided in the overcrowded Claverly Hall on Mt. Auburn Street, with two other Jewish roommates. Although he endeavored to avoid any explicit references to his religious background, and declined participation in Jewish groups on campus, fellow students remember that Kissinger did not fit in with any part of the student community. He remained an immigrant, out of place in his surroundings. His feigned indifference to his own past alienated him from fellow Jews, who found him cold and distant; his inescapable German Jewish appearance, accent, and seriousness prevented him from fitting in with the mainstream Harvard boys. Arthur Gilman, one of Kissinger's roommates, remembers that he was "really a loner." Herbert Englehardt, who lived downstairs from Kissinger, describes a young man who was an outcast among his peers: "He was deadly serious all the time. He never liked to chase after women. His famous wit and nuance were not in evidence when he was an undergraduate. He had no judgment, no feel for what was happening around him, no empathy for people he was with. He was clumsy, socially awkward, I guess a little shy. Basically he was a very limited person."[35]

Kissinger, in the words of one writer, "made no lasting friendships with the other students." This difficulty with social intimacy plagued him throughout his career, from Harvard to the White House. With very few exceptions, Kissinger found it hard to let his guard down, to share his inner hopes and fears with others. His intensity and overweening ambition left little space for relaxed personal relations. His insecurity expressed itself in a jarring self-centeredness that was already in evidence during his undergraduate days. Most significant, his suspicions encouraged in him a secrecy and deviousness that frequently produced the very enemies he dreaded. These are all personality traits that Kissinger's fellow students recognized at the end of the Second World War, but they were also reactions to his concentrated experiences of exile, immigration, and war at such an early age. They were, in some sense, a response to his predicament as a German Jew, caught between societies.[36]

Within the Cold War University, these socially alienating qualities attracted the attention of powerful people. Like his superiors in the U.S. Army, members of the Harvard faculty quickly recognized that Kissinger's seriousness accompanied a remarkably powerful mind, capable of digesting enormous amounts of information, formulating compelling arguments, and applying complex propositions to practical problems. Kissinger's experiences as an exile and a military occupation official melded this intellectual firepower to a very pragmatic sensibility; he had learned through personal ordeal that the selective adaptation of ideas, rather than academic consistency, was the basis for successful action. Kissinger's intimate knowledge of German society and his deep understanding of its culture, meant that he could offer valued insights on pressing issues of concern. In a class of students that was far more mature and experienced than its prewar counterparts, Kissinger stood out for his unpolished sophistication. His social alienation confirmed stereotypes about German Jews, but his intellect embodied all the best suppositions associated with his ethnic-religious group—analytical brilliance, ceaseless work, and attachment to *Bildung*.

William Yandell Elliott, a professor in Harvard's government department with close ties to the American Cold War policy community, saw particular value in Kissinger's personal and intellectual qualities. This was a student who could escape the allegedly shallow popular attitudes about power, and work effectively to build firm alternatives. Elliott famously warned that the United States confronted a "struggle of national survival" with the end of the Second World War and the opening of a new contest for dominance with the Soviet Union. In words that resonated with George Kennan, Paul Nitze, and other foreign-policy planners in Washington, he asserted that traditional habits of decentralized democratic governance were a source of weakness in a time when the country needed

William Elliott, Kissinger's mentor at Harvard. Elliott helped Kissinger to found the famous International Seminar that catapulted Kissinger to the attention of international and domestic elites. (Courtesy of Royden Dixon, Library of Congress Prints and Photographs Division)

strong centralized leadership. It was necessary, Elliott advised, to "cut off some of the fatty tissue of small town, courthouse, city hall politics, with the accompanying waste and inefficiency." In place of the gentrified civic culture that preceded the war, Elliott demanded the kind of seriousness, intensity, and firmness of personal will exhibited by men like Kissinger.[37]

Elliott echoed Fritz Kraemer when he described "the most elementary lesson of history: No power retains friends which is too weak to defend itself in will or in war potential." Cowardice, wishful thinking, and bureaucratic divisions had encouraged Americans to disregard this simple proposition before Pearl Harbor, according to Elliott. He contended that the United States faced similar perils in its emerging relationship with the Soviet Union. A critic of the pragmatic political philosophy that he believed encouraged Americans to seek negotiated compromises for most disputes, Elliott demanded that his countrymen show firm moral purpose and a steadfast willingness to adopt forceful measures against adversaries. Criticizing what he viewed as excessive American acceptance of Soviet expansion in Europe and Asia, Elliot lamented that "psychologically we have lost far more through weakness than we shall ever get through placating timid allies." Peace and prosperity were not organic conditions, as many American pragmatists assumed. They had to "be won, that is, through strength."[38]

Elliott looked to Kissinger, as Kraemer had earlier, because he recognized in him a deep intellectual and instinctive appreciation for transcendent leadership. At a time when impersonal "scientific" approaches to human behavior (emphasizing social structure and economic calculation) were achieving academic popularity, Elliott believed that Kissinger offered a promising antidote. This grave young man had a feeling for the power of ideas and the role of "great men" in history. As early as 1948, when Kissinger had spent little more than a year at Harvard, Elliott identified him as "a combination of Kant and Spinoza."[39]

Hyperbole aside, Elliott's comment captures his respect for the depth of Kissinger's thought and his exultation in its connection to a combined German (Kant) and Jewish (Spinoza) tradition. Nothing could be further removed from the pragmatism that informed much of American political and social scientific thought at the time. "You are left completely incapable of understanding what the realities of modern politics are," Elliott preached to students like Kissinger, by "expecting a rule of law where there is no common sense of right." Appealing to the affirmations of the divine and the "self-will" associated with the classical ideals of *Bildung,* Elliott demanded grand acts of politics that corrected "the great mistake of liberalism": the assumption "that there was [an] automatic character about the rights of people without an affirmation of values or a dedication to duty." International society, according to this argument, needed more than just methods of compromise; it called for an "orientation of will" that would create through politics a "common bond" for humanity on the model of a "great novelist, a great musician, [or] a great artist." Citizens in the Cold War craved inspiration and even a touch of divinity, according to Elliott. Only leadership inspired by an inner moral purpose could create a better world.[40]

Elliott encouraged Kissinger to study the philosophical roots of moral leadership and to define a place for it in contemporary politics. Addressing both academics and government officials, he called for new mechanisms to bring analysis of timeless needs, rather than just immediate tactical demands, to bear on policy. Intellectuals trained both to appreciate the wellsprings of Western civilization and to apply their knowledge to present conditions would "furnish that long-range view of national security policy that has to take into account, above all, balance and importance for the essentials." The "essentials" were the moral and historical needs of society. The new Harvard men of the Cold War would articulate and fulfill them. Their work would connect the classroom and the White House, scholarship and policy advising. This was the Cold War University in action.[41]

Under Elliott's tutelage, Kissinger studied political philosophy and organized programs at Harvard for improving American foreign policy. The two activities were interrelated. They were, according to Elliott, part of a determined effort aimed at "mobilizing our educational resources" to preempt foreign adversaries, particularly the Soviet Union.[42]

Kissinger's undergraduate thesis examined the challenge of societal decline and the need for transcendent leadership, as articulated in the philosophical writings of Oswald Spengler, Arnold Toynbee, and Immanuel Kant. Finishing his thesis around the outbreak of the Korean War in June 1950, Kissinger affirmed Elliott's critique of mechanistic approaches to politics: "It does not suffice to show logically deduced theorems, as an absolute test of validity. There must also exist a relation to the pervasiveness of an inward experience which transcends phenomenal reality." Standard American approaches to liberalism, according to Kissinger, pursued compromise at the cost of value; they neglected existential threats to Western civilization (Spengler), creative solutions to pressing problems (Toynbee), and the moral absolutes of the human condition (Kant). More than reacting to external daily pressures, Kissinger's thesis called for "active recognition" of deeper human limits, perils, and possibilities.[43]

A version of this argument reached high-level government ears. Contributing to a series of memos that William Elliott sent to Paul Nitze, then the chairman of the Policy Planning Staff in the State Department, Kissinger used similar language to assess contemporary international affairs:

> All the statements about "settlements," "conferences" and "negotiations" imply that the present crisis [around the Korean peninsula] reflects a misunderstanding, or perhaps a grievance of a specific nature, to be resolved by reasonable men in a spirit of compromise. The stark fact of the situation is, however, that Soviet expansionism is directed *against our existence, not against our policies.* Any concession therefore would become merely a springboard for new sallies.[44]

The Korean War, according to this analysis, was a struggle not over territory alone, but over fundamental values. Common assumptions that communist containment focused primarily on resisting Soviet aggression at distant geographic points exposed a "fundamental timidity and at times superficiality of conception" among Americans. Not yet thirty years of age, Kissinger called for a more determined effort to defeat the Soviet Union by seizing the initiative, articulating broader purposes, and fighting to American strengths—that is, choosing the sights of specific conflict, rather than reacting to Soviet-sponsored incursions in Korea and elsewhere. The United States would assert power and purpose through a firm display of national will:

> A line should be clearly defined, any transgression of which would mean a major war, *though not necessarily at the point where the Soviet move occurs.* This would have the advantage of (1) clarifying our position and reducing the danger of the world sliding into war through a series of bluffs and (2) allowing the United States to choose the theater of conflict for maximum Soviet disadvantage. At present the Soviet Union is in a position to determine both the battlefield and the extent of its commitment.[45]

Conceiving of the Cold War as a "total" conflict that required both philosophical and military transcendence of local crises, Kissinger and Elliott worked to make Harvard a center for formulating a holistic "strategic concept" to guide policy. Doing this would involve interdisciplinary research. It would bridge the worlds of scholarship and politics. Most significant, it would nurture an elite core of young leaders who combined knowledge with vision, moral fortitude with political acumen. Elliott created a mini-school for leaders of this kind at Harvard, and Kissinger provided both the legwork and the intellectual energy for this endeavor. As in Krefeld and Bensheim, he showed a remarkable capacity for both consistency and adaptation.[46]

Like Kissinger's mentors in later years (Nelson Rockefeller and Richard Nixon in particular), Elliott relied on his protégé for managing complex projects and personalities. As a graduate student in the early 1950s, Kissinger was the effective director of various foreign-policy programs at Harvard, but he remained dependent on Elliott's continued patronage and support. Kissinger worked the back rooms while Elliott presided in public. This was the position that Kissinger assumed and mastered from Cambridge to the White House. He made himself indispensable to powerful people, but he remained an outsider among his peers. If anything, the seriousness of mind and work that attracted men like Elliott to Kissinger only reinforced the common stereotypes of hidden Jewish control, and even conspiracy.

The *Harvard Crimson* revealingly parodied Kissinger as "Owly Vowly," the lurking figure who "spoke very distinctly, authoritatively, and with a slight German accent." He identified problems that were "as yet theoretical and not practical," and he took it upon himself to guide higher governing authorities. Kissinger was indeed a new kind of Harvard man, who exercised unprecedented influence but also suffered from traditional prejudice. He was owlish, or so the writers at the *Harvard Crimson* thought, because of his ubiquity and inscrutability.[47]

Kissinger's consistent role throughout his career as a shadow advisor to mainstream figures reflected the architecture of intellectual transformation and ethnic condescension within the emerging Cold War University. Beginning in his days as a student, Kissinger worked to articulate international policies that reached beyond the crisis of the moment and his own position of privileged marginality. His invocation of universal political principles from "great men" philosophers and diplomats manifested a common search for transcendence among ambitious thinkers, particularly Jews, who continued to feel the sting of stereotyped group identification. Kissinger sought timeless truths in historical personalities who defied the social divisions that he confronted.[48]

Cold War Networks

Kissinger's position as a Cold War insider and social outsider at Harvard manifested itself in the new programs that he and Elliott built during the 1950s. They shunned the traditional paths for academic recognition through scholarly specialization and disciplinary politics. Instead, they focused on leveraging the prestige of Harvard and the public salience of the Cold War to pursue activities that would create a new audience. They sought to reach young leaders abroad and at home, imparting their ideas about transcendent moral purpose and strategic vision. In this endeavor, they contributed to the creation of new Cold War networks of association. Like the transatlantic collaborations that characterized the years after 1945, these successor groupings self-consciously bridged the worlds of scholarship and policy, professors and politicians.

The new networks were more than just collections of like-minded individuals. They self-consciously served as extensions of the Cold War University, mobilizing an international range of intellectual talent for policy purposes. Cold War networks meditated upon, and often obsessed about, the challenges posed by communist expansion through military and subversive means. Even more, they focused on the perceived difficulties of maintaining moral authority for the use of anticommunist force in democratic societies. Kissinger was only one of countless observers to conclude, from the experience of the 1930s, that free societies lacked the necessary unity and resolve to combat external threats without effective leadership and sometime coercion.

Leadership would come from an international collection of young, intelligent, and "tough-minded" elites who actively shared ideas and strategies. They constituted a culture of Cold War politics that emphasized the values and security of Western civilization. Working through government institutions, transnational organizations, and special university-based projects, they collaborated in addressing common foreign and domestic challenges to anticommunist authority.

The famous "International Seminar" at Harvard was one of the first and most influential centers for Cold War network formation. In the fall of 1950, now a first-year Ph.D. student in government, Kissinger helped conceive and manage the seminar, operating out of the Harvard Summer School with little oversight. In a typed memorandum to William Elliott, the twenty-seven-year-old Kissinger laid out an ambitious intellectual and policy agenda, embodying the emerging imperatives of the Cold War University:

> the program can constitute a spiritual link between a segment of the foreign youth and the U.S. Among a generation for which, both in Europe and Asia, war has come to be a normal state and power the only criterion of political decision, cynicism and indeed nihilism is obviously rampant. In the groping for certainty in a world, in which American material aid represents frequently only an alleviation of misery and can therefore never supply the ultimate answer, the greater humanity of the American principles does not always suffice to swing the spiritual balance in favor of the U.S. The determination of the Communists, their show of interest in the souls of the young generation, constitutes a powerful appeal. It is primarily in the spiritual field that American stock is lowest in overseas countries due to a combination of Nazi and Communist propaganda which pictures the U.S. as bloated, materialistic, and culturally barbarian.

A new program to bring young and rising foreign figures to Harvard would, Kissinger explained, help "create nuclei of understanding of the true values of a democracy and of spiritual resistance to Communism. If the summer at Harvard becomes an experience, not just a course of study, one could expect that contact among former students might be maintained, with possible technical assistance by the Summer School. A basis for international understanding would thus be created among groups of promising young individuals." On the American side, Kissinger called for the selection of a "committee of inwardly alive, interested U.S. students," who would serve as colleagues for the visitors.[49]

The "international understanding" that Kissinger sought had two overriding components. First, it emphasized the importance of democracy with strong leaders, rather than communism or mass rule. Following from the central argument in his undergraduate thesis, the exchange program focused on a small cohort of elites who would articulate common principles and direct their societies to embrace them through political action and personal example. Leaders would share a philosophically informed understanding of the perils of communism, and they would work together to develop policies that affirmed the deeper wellsprings of transatlantic civilization. The course outline that Kissinger compiled in early 1951 highlighted the perceived threats: "nihilism," "bureaucratization," "distrust of government," and "isolationism," among others. The exchange program sought to "assist in counteracting these tendencies" by reaffirming the bedrock reasons for defending individualism, private property, and the liberal-democratic state against their internal and foreign critics. Interpersonal connections and cultural consensus would, Kissinger argued, provide a basis for strong and steadfast anticommunist policy.[50]

Second, the exchange program targeted societies where American strategic and ideological interests came together—France, Italy, Austria, and West Germany. Finland and Yugoslavia, two countries with strong American ties but situated close to Soviet authority, also received particular attention. For these areas, building intellectual consensus was an extension of the Second World War and the years of reconstruction. Kissinger initially excluded Great Britain, the Scandinavian countries, and Switzerland because they had a "firm democratic tradition." The other European societies needed assistance in developing the institutions and habits that would support stable anticommunist democracy, cooperation with the United States, and joint defense efforts. The exchange program would cultivate leaders who recognized these values and could implement them effectively. In a sense, Kissinger used the connections between transatlantic intellectual elites to continue the work that he and other military officials had undertaken in Krefeld, Bensheim, and numerous other locales during the mid-1940s.[51]

In less than a year, Kissinger turned the exchange program concept into a functioning International Seminar. Elliott, recognizing Kissinger's administrative acumen, made him director of the program despite his graduate-student status. Twenty European participants spent the summer of 1951 in the sweltering Cambridge heat as the first seminar class. Over the next eighteen years, the program expanded the number of participants and their countries of origin to include students from Asia, Africa, and Latin America. The International Seminar, however, retained its transatlantic focus, in terms of both ideology and geography. These characteristics grew from the nature of the Cold War University and Kissinger himself, who directed the

Kissinger in 1957. After receiving his doctorate in 1954, Kissinger held a variety of influential but nonpermanent positions at Harvard, the Rockefeller Brothers Fund, and the Council on Foreign Relations in New York. He attained a permanent faculty position at Harvard in 1959. (© Bettmann / CORBIS)

program each summer until 1965 and again in 1967. The International Seminar did not endeavor to encourage cultural diversity. It aimed to reinforce inherited Western values behind American-inspired leadership.[52]

Harvard did not provide extensive funding for this ambitious project. Dean of Arts and Sciences McGeorge Bundy strongly encouraged Elliott's efforts to make the university more policy-relevant, but he also recognized the existence of external financial sources. Pointing to the government purposes served by the International Seminar, Bundy explained that "since it was undertaken initially at the suggestion of outside groups, we have not been in the position of underwriting it in a direct way from our own resources." Bundy described the program to build a transatlantic community of Cold War elites as a "special undertaking in the public interest": "It was on this ground that we were persuaded in the first instance to take it on."[53]

During its first years the International Seminar received funding from philanthropic foundations that worked closely with the U.S. government to support the spread of American culture, especially in Europe. In 1956, for example, the project procured a three-year grant totaling $90,000 from the Ford Foundation. This sizable award came with few strings attached. It aimed, in the language Elliott employed in his funding application, to ensure the continuation of "a unique high level experiment that has certainly paid off in precisely the terms that we hoped it would: not only in improving the understanding and the attitude of cultural leaders from a good many parts of the world where we badly need friends, but also in working out friendships between a very unique group which continue in their own countries and in regional and often even broader areas of what we loosely call the free world."[54]

This was precisely the language of "psychological strategists," including Kissinger, employed by various arms of the U.S. government in the 1950s. They sought to mobilize civil society for an American-led transatlantic community and anticommunist resistance. This process involved the use of public media and established institutions, especially universities. It also relied on the appearance of independent grassroots activism, designed to highlight democracy in action. The psychological appeal of American influence would grow out of the evidence that people voluntarily embraced it. Kissinger called this the "predominant aspect of the new diplomacy," embodied in projects like the International Seminar. For this reason, he and Elliott emphasized the public philanthropic sources of funding for Harvard's activities. A democratic and altruistic commitment to anticommunism constituted the central image of the "free world."[55]

Nonprofit foundations committed to American Cold War purposes furnished crucial financial and cultural capital for the International Seminar and related projects. Between 1953 and 1959 the Ford Foundation provided $1 million in grants for national security programs to Harvard. It made similar contributions to MIT, Princeton, the University of Chicago, the University of Illinois, and the University of Wisconsin as well. The Carnegie Corporation made grants totaling almost $1.5 million to a similar list of schools. The Rockefeller Foundation did the same, supporting Cold War research and training at Harvard and Princeton, as well as the Council on Foreign Relations and the Brookings Institution. These grants built "the basis for virtually every university program in the field." They also provided the sustenance and prestige for people like Henry Kissinger to prosper in the Cold War University.[56]

If the growth of federal authority in the Second World War broke down the barriers between the college campus and the government agency, the expansion of postwar philanthropic grants fueled a reorganization of intellectual life around Cold War research and training. Foundation funding was the bridge between the needs of government and the intellectual talent at universities. It supported new, policy-relevant research, it encouraged the promotion of specific scholars in both university and government settings, and it created spaces for collaboration among thinkers from various disciplines and societies. This was the model of the Russian Research Center broadened in geographic and policy range. It promoted the appearance of intellectual freedom and objectivity by relying on nongovernment money rather than federal fiat. Communist authority was centralized and totalitarian; democratic capitalist life was decentralized and pluralistic. Foundation funding served the assumptions of a free society, with limited government, and it contributed to policy needs, with limited costs. People like Kissinger, directing the International Seminar, worked for the university, philanthropies, and the federal government simultaneously. This was Cold War politics in action.[57]

Philanthropies were not simple extensions of government authority. They did not always follow Washington's lead, and they frequently pursued initiatives—arms control, for example—that national leaders neglected. Like many other citizens of the United States and western Europe, foundation leaders felt a sincere commitment to anticommunism, and they supported the construction of a common international Cold War culture that they associated with freedom and democracy. Government agencies did not create this sentiment. Instead they worked, often behind the scenes, to channel it in specific directions. The Central Intelligence Agency (CIA), in particular, played an influential role in building the ideological and psychological grounding for American policy through foundation-sponsored programs. The CIA did not control foundation decisions, but it encouraged philanthropies to support chosen projects, and it often funneled its own money through them. Just as the boundaries between the university and federal authority blurred, so did the lines between independent foundations and government agencies.[58]

The International Seminar, with its potential to reach a broad group of global opinion-leaders, immediately attracted CIA and foundation attention. The agency provided the seed money to turn Kissinger's concept into a functioning program, and it bankrolled the seminar's expanding annual budget. In the early 1950s this included more than $20,000 supplied by the CIA for travel and other expenses. During the decade the CIA provided the International Seminar with far more extensive financing through various front organizations, including the Farfield Foundation and a group called the Friends of the Middle East. Kissinger's project joined a growing web of academic programs around the world dependent on U.S. intelligence agencies, as well as philanthropic foundations, for their basic sustenance.[59]

The International Seminar was not, however, a creature of the CIA or its other sponsors. The program followed the initial conceptualization outlined by Kissinger in 1950, emphasizing political consensus and moral leadership in the face of communist threats. It embodied the basic assumptions about democratic weakness and transatlantic identity that Kissinger and many others had internalized from the experience of the Second World War. U.S. intelligence agencies certainly monitored the seminar, and they helped in the identification of foreign participants, but there is no evidence that they ever forced revisions in the structure and substance of the project. They did not have to. The Cold War University nurtured an emphasis on America's new role as the defender of Western civilization and the leader of a transatlantic postwar world. Henry Kissinger and other ambitious individuals, dependent on the Cold War University, were firmly attached to this ideological outlook and the cooperation it entailed with U.S. intelligence agencies.

Procuring support from foundations and the CIA, the International Seminar built a remarkably broad and powerful network of Cold War leaders. The roster of participants constitutes one of the most influential groups of international figures who came of age in the 1950s. The list includes Japanese prime minister Yasuhiro Nakasone, Belgian prime minister Leo Tindemans, Turkish prime minister Bulent Ecevit, Malaysian prime minister Mahathir bin Mohamad, Israeli deputy prime minister Yigal Allon, and Congo's ambassador to the United Nations Thomas Kanza, among many others. Those attending went on to influential nongovernment positions as corporate directors, public intellectuals, and publishers. This network of elites was worldwide in scope but concentrated on western Europe and Japan. It was almost entirely male, and drawn not from traditional aristocracies, but from the upwardly mobile, highly educated, and cosmopolitan generation that rose to prominence in each society after the Second World War. This was Kissinger's cohort of newly empowered policy actors on a global stage.

As the director of the International Seminar, Kissinger was at the center of this emerging network. He had more direct and sustained contact with each attendee than anyone else in the program. One former participant, Siegfried Unseld, who later worked as a prominent publisher in Germany, remarks that through the program he became "one of the Henry Kissinger boys." The two continued to exchange letters and to meet occasionally decades after Unseld's 1955 trip to Harvard. With Unseld and other International Seminar participants, Kissinger constructed an international range of lifelong associates who shared similar concerns and general goodwill toward one another. The International Seminar did not "Americanize" its visitors, nor did it "Europeanize" the hosts. The discussions and personal interactions created a self-contained group of Cold War elites who forged a collective identity as intellectual practitioners and protectors of civilization in a threatening world.[60]

Kissinger's prominent membership in this community and his access to valuable information about America's Cold War allies gave him newfound prestige in the United States. More established and more powerful figures found themselves turning to young Kissinger for insight about leaders and developments overseas. Thomas Schelling, a highly regarded economist and foreign-policy specialist (and later a Nobel Prize winner), recounts: "Once my wife and I were going to Greece for a summer holiday. I mentioned it in passing to Henry. He gave me the name of a contact there. He [the Greek contact] was an extremely influential person. He provided us with a car and a driver; I think he even paid for our boat ticket to visit some islands. A year later the same man invited me back to lecture and got me an interview with the royal family."[61]

Schelling later disparaged Kissinger's exploitation of the International Seminar's contacts as self-serving: an attempt "to make Henry known to great people around the world."[62] This assessment is undoubtedly valid for a man of Kissinger's driving ambitions, but Schelling's comment neglects the high value placed on Kissinger's international connections in a Cold War setting. American leaders saw themselves engaged in a worldwide struggle against communism that exceeded the nation's traditional range of foreign interactions. Though the United States had long engaged in global trade, its accumulated knowledge of distant societies—outside western Europe, North Asia, and Latin America—was very limited. This was one consequence of not having a large colonial empire. Prominent American figures, including economist John Kenneth Galbraith and strategic theorist Bernard Brodie, recognized this fact, and they pushed for a broadening of American relations with opinion-makers in the wider world. Kissinger's contacts through the International Seminar, though still Europe-centered, offered a welcome expansion of American knowledge in the struggle against communist adversaries.[63]

As was the case in the Army and his first years at Harvard, Kissinger's Cold War cosmopolitanism made him a valued figure. Prominent Americans—including Eleanor Roosevelt, Reinhold Niebuhr, Christian Herter, Arthur Schlesinger Jr., and William F. Buckley Jr.—made time in their schedules for appearances at the International Seminar, often repeatedly, because they recognized the importance of building a broader overseas network for U.S. foreign policy. Kissinger's facility for cultivating diverse but like-minded foreign elites opened new avenues for action through alliances and mutual understandings. Kissinger constructed interpersonal relationships that allowed policymakers to see developments through non-American eyes and to adjust accordingly.

Throughout his career, Kissinger would use his nearly unparalleled international network to convert foreign access to domestic influence. The two were mutually reinforcing. Meetings with prominent Cold War allies, or potential allies, drew attention from American policymakers. Kissinger frequently circulated "confidential" reports on his foreign audiences for this purpose. His periodic meetings with American leaders to discuss international contacts, in turn, contributed to Kissinger's prominence overseas. Every time a newspaper reporter discussed one of his conversations with a high-ranking State Department or Pentagon official, or even the president, he became a more desired guest in foreign chancelleries. More than almost any other person, Kissinger turned the Cold War obsession with international influence to his advantage.[64]

By the late 1950s, this recent immigrant had emerged as more than just an international bridge figure; he was now a consummate network-builder, operating on a nearly worldwide scale. Kissinger's diplomatic activities from the early days of the International Seminar through his years in Washington focused, almost obsessively, on managing interpersonal connections between global elites. Describing the "nature of statesmanship" in his dissertation, Kissinger pointed to the importance of persuasion and consensus in his praise of the early nineteenth century's dominant foreign-policymakers, Castlereagh and Metternich:

> it is not sufficient to judge the statesman by his conceptions alone, for unlike the philosopher he must implement his vision. . . . His instrument is diplomacy, the art of relating states to each other by agreement rather than by the exercise of force, by the representation of a ground of action which reconciles particular aspirations with a general consensus. Because diplomacy depends on persuasion and not imposition, it presupposes a determinate framework, either through an agreement on a legitimizing principle or, theoretically, through an identical interpretation of power-relationships, although the latter is in practice the most difficult to attain. The achievements of Castlereagh and Metternich were due in no small measure to their extraordinary ability as diplomats.[65]

According to Kissinger's analysis these two men achieved dominance by managing the interpersonal relations among European monarchs, under whom they served. They set the terms for discussion, orchestrated alliances, and, most important, brought potential adversaries together through frequent and carefully planned conferences. Metternich, in particular, was a cunning politician who manipulated the relations of his superiors and his counterparts. Kissinger approvingly quotes the Austrian statesman's boast: "Everybody wants something without having any idea how to obtain it and the really intriguing aspect of the situation is that nobody quite knows how to achieve what he desires. But because I know what I want and what others *are capable of,* I am completely prepared." This is the diplomat par excellence, omniscient in his understanding of others and his control over their relations.[66]

Kissinger played a similar, though less masterful, role among Cold War elites, negotiating new relationships for distant figures. Like Metternich, he maintained a broad network of diverse contacts, within which he acted as a central broker for various discussions and deals. Kissinger worked on behalf of patrons in multiple, sometimes antagonistic, communities. He gained stature and influence from his continual efforts to bring powerful people together, under his direction. Prominent figures in the 1950s found themselves responding to initiatives from "this man Kissinger," about whom they knew little, but who seemed to know a lot about them and their needs.[67]

Within a decade after the end of the Second World War, Kissinger had used the International Seminar and other activities inside the Cold War University to bore deep into the ranks of the American social and political elite. He had extended correspondence and frequent meetings with, among many others, Dean Acheson, Bernard Brodie, John F. Kennedy, Henry Cabot Lodge Jr., Nelson Rockefeller, and Arthur Schlesinger Jr. As these men came through the Signet Society and other elite clubs, they also visited with Kissinger. He offered them access to the kinds of international conversations that even the most distinguished salons could not match. The "establishment" remained powerful, but it was now too insular for the needs of its members. Kissinger would help internationalize the American elite, while respecting—even fortifying—its exclusivity. He was a useful outsider.

Serving diverse communities without full membership in any, Kissinger filled a vital foreign-policy need. He also attracted the resentment frequently directed at individuals, particularly Jews, in this position. Thomas Schelling's scorn of Kissinger's ambitious networking, repeated by numerous writers, treats his behavior as something unnatural and immoral. Kissinger's actions, however, reflected the demands of his time, and the comparative contributions he could make as a cosmopolitan figure. Metternich was the preeminent network-builder of the early nineteenth century. In the post-1945 world, German Jewish immigrants constructed powerful international networks—promoted within the Cold War University, supported by philanthropic capital, and enlisted for government purposes.[68]

Cold War Patriotism

The expansion of the American state fueled the transformation of domestic institutions and the mobility of Jews within them. Behind Kissinger's growing Cold War network stood the U.S. government as a protector and sponsor. Patronage, of course, does not come for free. In return, Kissinger and other privileged Jews recognized that their efforts must serve the asserted national interests of the state and, even more important, affirm the sanctity of the American system. These duties were particularly crucial at a time when communist competitors challenged the moral claims of the U.S. government. Patriotism, for Kissinger and many other recent immigrants, meant more than just citizenship. It called for explicit displays of fealty to the basic purposes and policies of the American state. "Having found a haven from Nazi tyranny in the United States," Kissinger later wrote, "I had personally experienced what our nation meant to the rest of the world, especially to the persecuted and disadvantaged." This sentiment would guide his consistent determination to serve the American government, even when its actions deviated from what many considered justifiable behavior.[69]

In the context of growing public intolerance toward dissent during the early 1950s—the period of "McCarthyism" in the United States—Kissinger cooperated with government-sponsored surveillance and prosecution of alleged communist sympathizers. On 10 July 1953 he telephoned the Boston Division of the Federal Bureau of Investigation (FBI) to report on the distribution of an alarming flyer among International Seminar participants. Kissinger uncovered this material when, in apparent violation of federal law, he opened someone else's mail. The flyer criticized the American atomic bomb project and the broader military policies of the country. It called upon readers to "resolve that life must be dedicated to peaceful endeavor."[70]

The text of this allegedly incriminating flier appears innocuous to later readers. Some might find it silly. But during a time of heightened Cold

War fears and paranoia about internal "subversives," it stirred grave concern. This was especially true for an ambitious young immigrant like Kissinger, who was anxious about both communist threats and his own acceptance in American society. Regardless of evidence, if the government or elements of the public came to believe that the International Seminar was a home for communist sympathizers, the program would die. Accusations of this kind would also close off many of the academic and policymaking opportunities that Kissinger, then only a graduate student, sought for his professional advancement.

Kissinger broke the law in opening another person's mail. He violated the trust of the International Seminar participants (and staff) by reporting to the FBI. Kissinger, however, did what one would expect from almost anyone in his time and place. He acted according to his definition of Cold War patriotism, placing the demands of the state above other ethical scruples. Instead of risking even unfounded allegations of communist subversion within the International Seminar, Kissinger turned a potentially damaging document into a mechanism for proving his loyalty and his value as a bridge figure between government and academia, as well as the United States and other societies.[71]

In a time of excessive fear and frequent attacks on those perceived to be "un-American," especially Jews, Kissinger sought security by working closely with national authorities. The U.S. government, not the defenders of civil liberties, had provided him with protection, mobility, and status since his immigration in 1938. His instinct was clearly to reinforce this bond and the policy purposes of the International Seminar, rather than risk exile again. He went out of his way to identify himself as a friend of the government: "an individual who is strongly sympathetic to the FBI." He also made himself a valuable contributor to government, providing additional information and establishing a link to the intelligence agencies as a "confidential source."[72]

As director of the International Seminar at the tender age of thirty, Kissinger benefited from privileges accorded intellectuals with policy-relevant knowledge, cosmopolitan credentials, and a firm commitment to the asserted values of transatlantic society. This was, however, a very precarious position in the early 1950s, when fear and intolerance also made these qualities a potential vice, a potential marker of "un-American" sympathies. Like Jewish figures in earlier centuries, Kissinger felt strong pressure to prove his belonging by identifying with the dominant political power in a time of crisis. His sycophantic displays of loyalty during the McCarthy years and at other points in his career fit a pattern that one historian identifies as "the persistent gravitation of Jewish political allegiances in the diaspora toward central authority." Insecurity and ambition encouraged conformity with government elites.[73]

The "Saturday afternoon seminars" about contemporary policy at Harvard were not extracurricular additions to Kissinger's academic activities. They served to define him as an intellectual. His study of early nineteenth-century great-power diplomacy in his dissertation, his founding of the International Seminar, his teachings as a professor of government, and his numerous publications on nuclear strategy all centered on strengthening the Cold War state. He emphasized this overriding theme in the introduction to his dissertation, where he stipulated: "I have chosen for my topic the period between 1812 and 1822, partly, I am frank to say, because its problems seem to me analogous to those of our day." Kissinger emphasized the practical lessons of scholarship for the survival of the state: "societies exist in time more than in space. At any given moment a state is but a collection of individuals. . . . But it achieves identity through the consciousness of a common history. This is the only 'experience' nations have, their only possibility of learning for themselves. History is the memory of states."[74]

For Kissinger diplomatic history was useful as an instrument for contemporary policymaking. The state—in this case the U.S. government—was the inspiration and the intended consumer of his work. "To be sure," he warned, "states tend to be forgetful. It is not often that nations learn from the past, even rarer that they draw the correct conclusions from it." Kissinger and other intellectuals in the Cold War University would work to assure that the young and naïve American state remembered the correct history: "each generation is permitted only one effort of abstraction; it can attempt only one interpretation and a single experiment, for it is its own subject. This is the challenge of history and its tragedy; it is the shape 'destiny' assumes on the earth. And its solution, even its recognition, is perhaps the most difficult task of statesmanship."[75]

States were Kissinger's subject, and "statesmen" applied scholarship to strengthen their governments. Ordinary citizens were almost completely absent from this vision. They did not make history, nor did they contribute to policy. They were subsumed within the state, as faceless "Austrians,"

"Russians," and "Americans" who depended on the statesman for their overall well-being. National governments, and their leaders, served as the only real repositories of value for Kissinger.

The Center for International Affairs

This statist approach to intellectual inquiry made Kissinger not only an ideal director for the International Seminar, but also a major agent in the creation of new research institutes designed to deepen cooperation between the government and the university. The most important of these bodies at Harvard was the Center for International Affairs (CFIA). Founded in 1958, it aimed to "combine basic research in foreign affairs with advanced study by experienced individuals."

> Free from the pressures of day-to-day concerns, the Center should be able to provide an environment fostering sustained and systematic analysis of fundamental issues. The joint participation of scholars and mature practitioners should have two-sided benefits. It should make the research more penetrating and significant. At the same time, a period of such work, offering the stimulation of other first-rate minds and opportunity for reflection, should enable the practitioners to deepen their understanding and broaden their perspective.[76]

After eight years of Cold War network-building through the International Seminar, the CFIA provided a larger institutional anchor for similar and expanded activities. The new center emphasized sustained connections between academics and policymakers, as well as figures from a variety of important Cold War states. The initial patrons of the International Seminar, McGeorge Bundy and William Elliott, supported the CFIA because it too fostered "relations among the officials of different nations which would facilitate franker and more useful discussions in their later careers." Through fellowships, conferences, seminars, and sponsored travel the center provided "advanced training of mature personnel." More than just discussions, the CFIA offered a laboratory for Cold War policy learning.[77]

Following the model of Kissinger's smaller project, it avoided case-specific research. Instead, the CFIA emphasized process—bringing people together, nurturing discussion, and building consensus. In addition, the center focused on values and overarching concepts rather than on particular policies. It was designed as a hothouse for collaborative "big think": "The pressure of the more immediate crises tends to divert energy and attention from more basic issues. One result is that policy making must often start with premises which are unexplored for lack of time or staff to analyze them. Such basic or long-range issues are often especially well-suited to outside study." The CFIA aimed to "attract people with the requisite training and skills" for common deliberation on fundamental foreign policy concerns.[78]

Kissinger was not the prime mover behind the creation of the CFIA, but his direction of the International Seminar provided the basic framework for this new center. Although many prominent people later derided his activities, Kissinger had authored a model for network-building that Harvard adopted and expanded. Thomas Schelling, in fact, joined the CFIA and contributed to the very activities that he criticized. While the Russian Research Center housed a somewhat secret pipeline from the OSS to Harvard, and the International Seminar placed the college at the center of an internationalizing policy elite, the CFIA created a direct channel between Cambridge and Washington:

> The Government and international agencies frequently need qualified people to perform specific tasks for limited periods as consultants, members of delegations and other special assignments. By experience and their work at the Center the permanent faculty should be well equipped for such short-term assignments. The aim would be to staff and organize the Center so that members could be made available for such purposes on relatively short notice as a regular part of its activities. Such a plan will help to meet an urgent public need and also serve as a stimulus for members of the Center.[79]

This language could not more thoroughly contradict the "Olympian" presumptions of scholarly detachment that motivated Harvard's leading lights, only twenty years earlier, to reject most associations with Washington. By the late 1950s the outward-looking Cold War University hammered the final nails in the coffin of its smaller, self-contained predecessor. Cosmopolitan networks of policy intellectuals, including Jews, supplanted the provincial fraternities of blue-blooded WASP thinkers that Arthur Schlesinger Jr. remembered from his days as a student.

Kissinger's rise and the institutionalization of his efforts through the

CFIA marked this sea-change. After completing his Ph.D. in 1954 he remained at Harvard—with brief periods of leave at the Council of Foreign Relations in New York—as a manager for various programs, especially his International Seminar. He was not a member of the faculty, but the importance of international network-building to the university made him a valued figure on campus. Two decades earlier he would have joined the large ranks of unemployed and forgotten academics. In the mid-1950s, however, external funding and Cold War pressures for policy-relevant knowledge gave an entrepreneurial Ph.D. without a faculty position access to resources and influence. Power within the Cold War University spread beyond traditional academic structures.

In addition to directing the International Seminar, Kissinger worked with the "Defense Studies Program," created in 1954 as a project that brought military officials and political decisionmakers together for consultations. It also trained talented civilians for military policymaking. Kissinger participated in the seminars sponsored through the program, he helped to arrange visitors, and he brought its activities—as well as his own—to the attention of influential people. The Defense Studies Program, like the International Seminar, employed Kissinger as a network-builder. He had enormous access to elites, but he remained excluded from faculty standing. This complex status, once again, magnified his contradictory position—Cold War insider, but social outsider.[80]

Kissinger continued in this role throughout his career at Harvard. With the creation of the CFIA he finally gained lecturer status, and then a tenured faculty position in 1959. He was also appointed associate director of the new center, working with Robert Bowie, the chosen director and former assistant secretary of state for policy planning. Even with tenure, however, Kissinger remained distinct from traditional professors. He spent very limited time in his home department, Government, operating primarily from his office at the CFIA. Students remember him as an effective teacher, but also as someone who was frequently absent for trips to visit policymakers in Washington or foreign capitals. Although he was a professor at Harvard, Kissinger was never an integral part of the institution. He remained a valuable bridge figure, who inspired a combination of awe and suspicion from his academic colleagues.[81]

Kissinger's distance from the traditional elements of Harvard reflected the tensions within the Cold War University, and within American society as a whole. The German Jewish émigré's efforts to build international recognition subverted, and in many ways flouted, established professional hierarchies. He wrote an intelligent dissertation and published a few articles from it, but he did not conform to the main research trends among academic scholars of political science and history. He performed extensive administrative duties, but they were not focused on his academic department, Harvard students, or even the college. Most significant, Kissinger appealed to powerful individuals at the university—particularly William Elliott and McGeorge Bundy—but he showed little regard for the interests and con-

Students stroll through Harvard Yard in the late 1950s. The university's student body was overwhelmingly white. Students and faculty had very little daily contact with nonwhite minorities. (Courtesy of Harvard University Archives, call no. HUP-SF Student Life, 264)

cerns of less prominent, middling figures, including those on the faculty. He did not, in this sense, play traditional academic politics.

By background Kissinger was excluded from this genteel world; by personality he excluded himself. As was the case with so many other ambitious Jews in American universities at this time, his politics looked to a broader national and international landscape that was more open and progressive than the inherited architecture of academic authority. Kissinger harbored many driving ambitions at a very young age, but becoming a traditional department chairman, a college dean, or even a president never attracted his serious interest, nor were these conceivable options. Although his administrative positions—director of the International Seminar, director of the Defense Studies Program, and associate director of the Center for International Affairs—held public significance, they were marginal to the university's internal hierarchy. Despite all his extraordinary accomplishments at such an early age, Kissinger was never a "Harvard man."

For a cosmopolitan figure like Kissinger, the Cold War University opened more doors in government than in higher academic administration. His career was born at the intersection between scholarship and government, and he matured with all the privileges and prejudices that accompanied this position. Until the late 1960s, Harvard University provided Kissinger with the necessary resources for personal advancement in policy circles. From his days as a student through his years on the faculty, this was the focus of his energies. Kissinger was, in this sense, made by the Cold War.

Knowledge and Power

In its self-contained campus design, its emphasis on scholarly credentials, and its guarantee of lifetime tenured employment, the modern university conceives of itself as a haven for disinterested knowledge production. Unlike the "real world" of business and politics, scholars research, discuss, and analyze issues without external interference—at least in theory. Most observers recognize that this is more an ideal than a reality, but they nonetheless cling to the image of disinterested knowledge as the distinctive source of a university's special status. Proponents and critics share a belief that professors are separated from the experiences of the average citizen—for better and for worse.[82]

Contrary to this image of free-floating thinkers, Kissinger's activities at

Harvard reveal that the production of knowledge served specific policy purposes in the Cold War University. The intellectual community he entered after his military service privileged cosmopolitanism, policy relevance, and patriotism. These qualities attracted financial support from the federal government (and philanthropies), they served an emerging international network of leaders, and they affirmed America's position in its struggle against communist adversaries. This was not a conspiracy. The Cold War transformed intellectual life in at least three mutually reinforcing ways.

First, the virtual takeover of American universities by the federal government during the Second World War created lasting institutional dependence on Washington. Through the G.I. Bill, increased research funding, a growing regulatory apparatus, and informal pressures the government created strong incentives for universities to orient their postwar research toward American foreign-policy purposes. The Cold War University became a policy institution. It thrived on new programs, like Harvard's International Seminar and the Center for International Affairs, that nurtured networks of influence across societies, and within government.

Second, the huge presence of war veterans and recent immigrants on university campuses after 1945 contributed to new social pressures for academic attention to contemporary international concerns—particularly the reconstruction of western Europe and the containment of communist threats. Prior historians have neglected the social origins of the Cold War University and the link between cosmopolitanism and anticommunism. Immigrants and veterans like Kissinger did not need encouragement to enlist their knowledge in the service of the state. This inclination grew from their self-understanding as young men who had "seen evil" and believed they could combat its recurrence only by bolstering democratic government through the best ideas, the best policies, and the best men. Knowledge devoted to any other purpose was wasted and potentially self-defeating. For Kissinger, in particular, the political apathy of Weimar intellectuals was a potent warning against disinterested, ivory-tower knowledge in a Cold War world.[83]

Third, and perhaps most revealing, Jews played a crucial role in making knowledge policy-relevant. This was especially the case for Kissinger and other German émigrés who assumed positions in the Cold War University as newly privileged bridge figures, bringing an international group of elites together to consult and coordinate. Traditionally excluded from the power centers on campus and in Washington, Kissinger's cohort could now do what others could not. They had the language skills and cultural familiarity with foreign societies necessary for nurturing effective contacts. They were serious—perhaps obsessive—in their willingness to take on inordinate amounts of work, including both sophisticated research and tedious organizational tasks. They were dependent on powerful patrons, including government officials, whom they served loyally. Most significant, these Jews understood and embraced the core values of Western "civilization" *(Bildung)* that underpinned America's asserted Cold War stature.

Defeating the Soviet Union was, in this view, much more than an endeavor in defending U.S. strategic interests. It was a world-historical struggle to protect an imperfect but free society—one that gave Jews an opportunity to escape fascist extermination. Reflecting on Metternich in this context, Kissinger praised "the ideal of 'excellence'" that, according to his account, brought unity to much of Europe during the nineteenth century. A steadfast defense of basic freedoms against communist subversion would do the same for a broader transatlantic community in the Cold War.[84]

Excellence for Kissinger was not about particular policies, but about general principles, including mobility, meritocracy, and leadership. During his years at Harvard he both expounded and embodied these ideas. The university, the U.S. government, and foreign leaders articulated their own support of these principles through their promotion of Kissinger. He thus became a very useful symbol as well as an agent for the aspirations of Cold War culture. This observation explains, at least in part, the fascination with Kissinger among diverse groups of elites at such an early stage in his career.

His fame reflected not just what he did, but who he was. Although he denies its relevance, Kissinger's background as a German Jewish immigrant is crucial to understanding his career, particularly at Harvard. His knowledge of Germany and his experiences as a Jew endowed him with uniquely valued skills in the Cold War University. Recognizing this, Kissinger used his ethnic assets effectively to promote his beliefs and himself. He did not defend common German Jewish stereotypes, but he certainly benefited from them.

As was the case with many Jewish figures in earlier decades, the privileges accorded particular Jews after 1945 were double-edged. Exclusion and resentment accompanied favoritism. The Cold War University made

Kissinger an insider and an outsider. For all his access to powerful people, he was never fully accepted as someone who belonged in the Signet Society, at the faculty club, or in the White House. Although he performed the tasks that traditional elites needed accomplished, he remained a target of suspicion and derision throughout his career. Men like McGeorge Bundy and Thomas Schelling would at the same time encourage and condemn Kissinger's cultivation of international leaders. They would promote his talents while they insulted his person. In this sense postwar privileges reinforced inherited prejudices. Kissinger confronted the same extremes of opinion that had burdened his historical predecessors.[85]

Knowledge was power and prejudice for Kissinger. He built his career on leveraging his intellectual skills for political influence. Kissinger's success reflected his sharp mind, his hard work, and, most important, his ability to address pressing policy challenges. Kissinger's knowledge had particular power in the context of the Cold War. His knowledge also made him a controversial figure from a very early age.

Kissinger's condemnations of the "intellectual class" are not intended to discredit intellectuals. He is, after all, one himself. His remarks are instead a criticism of how knowledge is constructed at the dawn of the twenty-first century. In the early decades of the Cold War, knowledge and policy were mutually constitutive, and perhaps too interdependent. Fifty years later the pendulum has swung to the opposite extreme: knowledge and policy are mutually antagonistic—frequently openly hostile—in academic circles. Professors and politicians rarely talk to each other anymore.

The lost "Saturday afternoon seminars" of Kissinger's career at Harvard point to the intense specialization and isolation of intellectual life since that time. The implications of this transformation are debatable. It is, however, difficult to imagine a career similar to Kissinger's in the twenty-first century. For all his talents and ambitions, his rise was dependent on a unique alliance of knowledge and power. Kissinger's activities as a scholar and policymaker reflected his tireless efforts to put ideas into action. He was, and remains, a Cold War public intellectual.

FOUR | *A Strategy of Limits*

"Atomic war means national suicide. The ultimate delusion of the atomic era is the notion that national suicide is a feasible means of defense." "How apparently sensible and sane men could drift into such beliefs," journalist I. F. Stone commented, "will astound future historians, if there are any." As the race to develop more destructive nuclear weapons with greater range escalated during the 1950s, Stone warned: "war clouds are gathering which could mean the end of our species. The Russians and the Americans resemble two huge herds moving toward possible conflict, too closely packed to struggle successfully against their fate. The helplessness of human kind is the dominant feature of the planetary landscape as the crisis approaches."[1]

Stone was a radical, but he was also an acute observer of society. His comments captured the pervasive public fear about the emerging nuclear age. With the proliferation of thermonuclear weapons and intercontinental delivery vehicles by the United States and the Soviet Union, security depended on the threat of total destruction. Each of the superpowers prepared for nuclear war in the hope that such preparations would deter both sides from initiating hostilities. The horrific prospect of another world war induced diplomatic caution. It also made citizens anxious about their future. The Cold War was not an abstract phenomenon; it created a personal sense of peril.[2]

Despite the psychological strains on citizens and leaders, the balance of terror proved remarkably stable. Washington and Moscow consistently avoided direct military confrontations that could cross the nuclear threshold. Strategic stalemate, however, created a series of recurring dilemmas: How could leaders respond to minor forms of aggression by nuclear-armed adversaries? Was the threat of nuclear annihilation appropriate and effective when the area of dispute was, say, Korea or Vietnam? Also, how could nuclear weapons serve political purposes beyond deterrence? How could they nurture democratic resilience and alliance solidarity when they required a centralization of military power and overwhelming dominance by a handful of states?

These questions animated an influential group of men who emerged during the 1950s as experts on strategy. Situated within the Cold War University and other institutions (particularly the RAND Corporation), operating at the intersection of academia and government, they combined sophisticated scholarly analysis with practical policy applications. They quickly formed a tight-knit community—located largely, but not entirely in the United States—that emphasized shared attention to the deployment of nuclear forces, frequent interactions with government figures, and a sense of intellectual superiority. These were the smartest young thinkers tackling the most difficult global problems. They read each other's work intensively, agreeing on the basic parameters for nuclear deterrence while debating the details of force structure, signaling, and war planning. The dialogue about these archaic but crucial issues was the stuff of "nuclear strategy."

The new field combined traditional insights about warfare and society with novel approaches, including operations research, advanced mathematics, political psychology, and game theory. Nuclear strategists were, in this sense, specialists and generalists at the same time. They focused their work on a discrete set of issues, but they drew conspicuously—sometimes superficially—on multiple modes of analysis. They wrote for both a self-contained community of scholars and an audience of informed nonexpert policymakers. In addition to their privileged knowledge and access to government, the nuclear strategists commanded enormous prestige because of the sense of urgency underpinning their work. Few citizens read their writings carefully, but many knew who they were. Public fear made nuclear strategists the oracles of the Cold War. They were prophets who promised to master the dilemmas of the age and resolve them in accordance with American interests. Wizards of the modern world, they would transform the weapons of ultimate destruction into a sustainable peace.[3]

Henry Kissinger was one of the wizards. His entrée into the community of strategists reflected his determination, from his earliest years at Harvard, to devise alternatives to the "helplessness" that I. F. Stone so poignantly predicted. Like many others, Kissinger believed that the proliferation of nuclear weapons contributed to heightened dangers in war and increased rigidity in peace. When confronted with serious challenges short of full-scale war, citizens would have a tendency to think in terms of nuclear retaliation or nothing-at-all. With such extreme options, politicians would frequently err on the side of conflict avoidance, as Kissinger had personally witnessed during the 1930s, in a prenuclear era of "total war." For the German Jewish émigré, saving democracy from the treachery of its adversaries and the weakness of its own constituents required self-conscious efforts to "rescue an element of choice from the pressure of circumstance": "How to strive for both peace and justice, for an end of war that does not lead to tyranny, for a commitment to justice that does not produce cataclysm—to find this balance is the perpetual task of the statesman in the nuclear age."[4]

Leaders—including politicians, nuclear strategists, and policy advisors—had to create avenues for forceful action that were neither suicidal nor

Kissinger's last seminar at Harvard before he joined the Nixon administration, 16 December 1968. (Courtesy of AP / Wide World Photos)

complaisant. They needed courage and creativity in this endeavor. Kissinger joined other strategists in decades of struggle to find effective uses for the "absolute weapon" as a symbol, a threat, and a source of destruction. Nuclear strategy involved the careful manipulation of horrific power for the needs of civilization. As Kissinger wrote in one of his earliest reflections on the topic: "the U.S. nuclear arsenal is no better than the willingness to use it . . . if we do not wish to doom ourselves to impotence in the atomic stalemate or near-stalemate just around the corner, it may be well to develop alternative programs."[5]

These lines, written only months after Kissinger's thirty-first birthday and the completion of his doctorate, became the touchstone for his career as a strategist and a policymaker. With remarkable consistency, he returned to this premise in all his writings and actions. Many other strategists disagreed with the "alternative programs" that Kissinger proposed, but most shared his concern about making this huge and expensive arsenal usable. Thomas Schelling, one of Kissinger's colleagues at Harvard, chillingly observed:

> The power to hurt is nothing new in warfare, but for the United States modern technology has drastically enhanced the strategic importance of pure, unconstructive, unacquisitive pain and damage, whether used against us or in our own defense. This in turn enhances the importance of war and threats of war as techniques of influence, not of destruction; of coercion and deterrence, not of conquest and defense; of bargaining and intimidation.

Schelling echoed Kissinger when he concluded: "Military strategy, whether we like it or not, has become the diplomacy of violence."[6]

Kissinger did not advocate nuclear warfare, but he refused to accept a passive faith that the existence of these weapons would intimidate enemies. Quite the contrary: they might encourage adversaries to challenge American interests, confident that the White House would not risk nuclear armageddon in response. As a graduate student, Kissinger explained communist aggression during the Korean War in these precise terms. He later attributed French and American setbacks in Vietnam to a similar strategic weakness. "The capacity to destroy," Kissinger explained, "proved difficult to translate into a plausible threat even against countries with no capacity for retaliation."[7]

Kissinger's work as a scholar and policymaker was all about navigating this difficult translation—making the American nuclear arsenal credible as a threat to enemies, acceptable as a source of security for allies, and useful as diplomatic leverage for political leaders. His extensive writings about these issues made him a respected member of the strategy community. As early as 1955, Bernard Brodie, one of the pioneering figures in the field, commented that he and the recent Harvard Ph.D. were "kindred spirits." Years before, Kissinger's powerful mind, his ability to master wide-ranging materials, and his seemingly boundless energy had drawn the attention of William Elliott at Harvard. These same qualities encouraged Brodie and other strategists to take him seriously as well. Confirming Elliott's judgment, Brodie referred to Kissinger as a "brilliant, incisive, and courageous" observer. Although they disagreed on many points, Brodie frequently joined a chorus of praise for Kissinger's "novel and penetrating" insights.[8]

These accolades, as well as strongly dissenting appraisals, made Kissinger a prominent public figure by the 1960s. He wrote numerous articles and books—more than any other strategist at the time—for both specialist and general audiences. Many readers, including I. F. Stone, found Kissinger's public explanations of nuclear posturing irresponsible. Others, especially the movie producer Stanley Kubrick, depicted him as an evil genius—"Dr. Strangelove." If anything, these attacks contributed to Kissinger's fame. After obtaining his doctorate in 1954 he quickly became a recognized expert, who garnered extensive public attention for his attempts—brilliant in the eyes of some, diabolical in the eyes of others—to master the new technologies of war. He was a legitimate, if not fully representative, face of nuclear strategy.[9]

Kissinger's public presence also reflected his ability to bridge different communities. More than anyone else, he brought the new transatlantic elites together with the new strategic wizards. He merged his position in new Cold War networks—centered on Harvard's International Seminar and the Center for International Affairs—with his contacts to Brodie, Schelling, and other leading nuclear experts. Kissinger acted as a conceptual synthesizer. He combined a cosmopolitan vision of Western civilization (embodied by the transatlantic elites) with a deep commitment to the calibration of power for foreign-policy needs (the work of the strategic wizards.) Strategy was not only a matter of leveraging weapons for policy, according to Kissinger; it reaffirmed inherited values. In this context, Kissinger concluded his first book on nuclear weapons with a philosophical rumination on the role of the heroic leader who can "bridge the gap between a society's experience and his vision, between its tradition and its future." Effective strategy would strengthen the moral fiber of civilization and empower enlightened leaders. It would restore confidence in the purposes of the state.[10]

This affirmation of state power opened many doors for Kissinger. Presidents—including Dwight D. Eisenhower, John F. Kennedy, Richard Nixon, and Gerald Ford—displayed a strong interest in Kissinger's proposals for innovative diplomatic and military initiatives. He was in a unique position to combine expertise on the emerging Cold War system with intimate knowledge of nuclear weapons. He could address both the political challenges of the period and the military possibilities of the nuclear age. In the words of President Eisenhower, his writings were "interesting and worth reading."[11]

By the late 1950s Kissinger had become not only a bridge figure but also a "grand strategist," helping to formulate a general framework for American policy that employed the new technologies of destruction for broader anticommunist purposes. Kissinger's approach followed what other analysts defined as the appropriate role for high-level strategy: it sought to "anticipate the trials of war, and by anticipation to seek where possible to increase one's advantage without unduly jeopardizing the maintenance of peace or the pursuit of other values." Kissinger contributed to an emerging Cold War grand strategy that provided a "genuine analytical method" for assessing international capabilities and applying them to local challenges and opportunities. Although he did not offer extensive regional expertise outside of Europe, he furnished valued assistance integrating specific conflicts around the world into a coherent vision. He helped draw a map for leaders to make sense of global complexity.[12]

This was Kissinger's supreme genius: his ability to connect diverse phenomena and to formulate practical political options. His grand strategy proved remarkably useful for policymakers, including himself, in a Cold War landscape shrouded by the balance of nuclear terror. It also deepened the blind spots in American interactions with a rapidly changing world. Kissinger's ideas contributed to both the bright successes and the dark failures of the United States in the Cold War. As a strategist and a policymaker, this man of such great intellectual promise became a tragic figure of his times.

Limits

Kissinger was obsessed with limits. His first three articles on nuclear strategy—published in 1955, the year after he completed his dissertation—criticized the U.S. government for seeking "total solutions" in its struggle against the Soviet Union. American military and economic capabilities were globally predominant and growing rapidly in the early Cold War years, but they were also insufficient for ensuring peace. Quite the contrary: an emphasis upon building American strength created a bias to postpone compromises until a future moment, when the United States would presumably be better prepared for combat with its adversaries. "Peace through strength," in these terms, meant containment today and negotiation only in the future. This was, to some degree, the traditional logic of American policy within the Western Hemisphere since the Civil War, and in Europe and Asia since 1941. The U.S. avoided compromises with adversaries, building strength to force desired change on its own terms.[13]

Unilateralism worked well when American territory was generally safe from direct threats. Protected by wide oceans and blessed with abundant resources, the nation could stand aloof from its adversaries until it embarked on an overwhelming deployment of force: "A power favored by geography or by a great material superiority, as we have been through most of our history, can afford to let a threat take unambiguous shape before it engages in war." This was exactly how the United States had approached the Second World War. The nation initially hesitated to enter the conflict, but then achieved victory by "outproducing" its adversaries. International power came from national "superiority in resources and technology." The "American Way of War" carried on into the Cold War as policymakers "assumed that the chief task was to bring about a certain level of military strength and that this depended almost entirely on United States policy and United States pressure."[14]

In a world of thermonuclear capabilities Americans had to abandon their unilateral strategic posture. The "destructiveness and speed of modern weapons," Kissinger observed, "have ended our traditional invulnerability, and the polarization of power in the world has reduced our traditional margin of safety." This was the fundamental "dilemma of American security" that motivated the work of the emerging nuclear strategists. Distance and preponderant power no longer ensured survival. A weaker enemy, particularly the Soviet Union, had access to technologies that could inflict irreparable damage on the United States. As a consequence, Americans had to recognize, as they had not before, the limits of their power. Kissinger called for an unmasking of "the illusion that there are 'purely' military answers to the problems of our security and that policy ends where strategy begins." The "luxury of such an approach," he contended, "ended with our atomic monopoly. Henceforth our problem will be one long familiar to less favored nations: how to relate the desirable to the possible and above all how to live with possible catastrophe."[15]

The constraints imposed by a thermonuclear world rendered the traditional extremes of war and peace almost meaningless. Total war, launched in retaliation for or anticipation of Soviet aggression, would be an act of suicide, much "more terrible than the conditions it seeks to allay. . . . It would not be an act of policy but of desperation." A renunciation of war and a determined pursuit of peace, however, would be equally disastrous in the face of what Kissinger perceived as an expansionist Soviet adversary. Drawing on his own memories of Nazi aggression and the feeble appeasement by the Western allies, he warned: "No idea has been more pernicious than that peace can be aimed at directly, as an end in itself where tensions suddenly disappear." Kissinger called this a "residue of our age of optimism" that preceded the Second World War: "Whenever peace—considered as the avoidance of war—becomes the only objective of a power or group of powers, the international system is at the mercy of its most ruthless member." A nuclear stalemate that enabled local Soviet advances could, in the long run, prove as damaging to American security as a nuclear war.[16]

The limits of U.S. power required cautious calculation, rather than militant idealism. Although Americans had never possessed the capability to remake the world on their own terms, through most of their history they had been able to pursue this naïve mission with minimal harm to themselves. Like so many of his contemporaries, Kissinger joined a chorus of writers who criticized former President Woodrow Wilson for advocating a vision of global democracy that simultaneously overextended the nation's commitment to international change and diminished its willingness to make necessary compromises with allies and adversaries. When Wilson's zealous idealism failed to produce promised results, according to Kissinger, the American people sought to protect the purity of their principles by isolating themselves from a corrupt world. This was the insular self-righteousness that accompanied the utopianism of John Winthrop's "City on a Hill." It contributed to another cataclysm after Wilson's death. Americans survived the perils of false prophecy, but only at great cost. In a thermonuclear world, Wilson's folly might induce irrevocable destruction.[17]

Kissinger's analysis expanded beyond nuclear technologies and the context of twentieth-century wars. He turned to the philosophers—Spengler, Toynbee, Kant, and others—whom he had examined in his student writings. Nuclear weapons were not the problem; they were symptomatic of broader limitations on freedom. Meditating upon the cruelty and destruction he had witnessed as a young man in Germany, Kissinger painted a dark picture of the human condition: "Life is suffering, birth involves death. Transitoriness is the fate of existence. No civilization has yet been permanent, no longing completely fulfilled. This is necessity, the fatedness of history, the dilemma of mortality."[18]

Praising the "conservative" policies of Metternich as an alternative to Wilson's idealism, Kissinger argued that "the most fundamental problem of politics" was "not the control of wickedness, but the limitation of righteousness."

> To "punish" the wicked is a relatively easy matter because it is a simple expression of public morality. To restrain the exercise of righteous power is more difficult because it asserts that right exists in time as well as in space; that volition, however noble, is limited by forces transcending the will; that the achievement of self-restraint is the ultimate challenge of the social order. Metternich dealt with this problem by asserting that excess in any direction was disruptive of society. The individual will was contingent because man was an aspect of forces transcending him.[19]

Kissinger's words contained a clear theological reference, common to Judaism and Christianity, about frailty under God. He wrote in almost biblical terms about the "feeling of humility" and the "inward reconciliation" that came from reverence to a higher power. God reminded humans of their moral purposes and their limitations. A religious sensibility gave meaning to politics and diplomacy. It was essential for determining the means and ends of strategy. In his analyses of Metternich and Bismarck, Kissinger explained that they used their religious faith to articulate a collective vision and to restrain excesses in pursuing that vision. For Bismarck "God provided the mechanism to transcend the transitoriness of the human scale." Freedom and national greatness came not from unregulated behavior, but from self-limiting actions. As in Orthodox Jewish teachings, to deny oneself was to find deeper spiritual meaning.[20]

The Wilsonian urge to purify society was a dangerous departure from this credo because it assumed that human beings had limitless possibilities for change and accomplishment, under earthly guidance. It was a false pride that followed a strain of American thought predicting a peaceful "end to history" when the nation's ideas and institutions carried to all corners of the globe. Even as an undergraduate, Kissinger, like many other émigrés to the United States, would have none of this missionary zeal. Despite their utopian promises, modern technology and bureaucracy appeared to deepen the "suffering and transitoriness" of contemporary life. For Kissinger these were "tired times," when the "generation of Buchenwald and the Siberian labor-camps can not talk with the same optimism as its fathers." Citizens in the mid-twentieth century had little reason to expect a better future.[21]

Effective policy required a "recognition by man of his limits." Even the most powerful state with the most impressive weapons could not change the world on its own terms. Leaders, therefore, had to accept an imperfect landscape with "boundaries to one's striving." This meant tolerance, cooperation, and even conciliation with adversaries. It also required compromise solutions to dangerous problems: "all of life," Kissinger wrote, "is not a chase after the images, the hopes, the completeness that elude us today." Individuals and states gave meaning to history by making difficult choices among bad alternatives. Fellow German émigré and Cold War strategist Hans Morgenthau articulated the same point: "To choose the least evil among several expedient actions is moral judgment."[22]

Kissinger abhorred the prospect of nuclear war, but the limits on American power made it necessary to contend with these weapons. They were a central part of the international system after the Second World War, and they were unlikely to disappear anytime soon. Nuclear weapons permanently restricted U.S. foreign-policy aims, forcing the nation to accept its own mortality. Americans had lacked what Kissinger called a "tragic experience" in their international relations, but now they would have to confront just such a possibility.[23]

Kissinger's premonition echoed the perspective of other prominent thinkers at the time, including the historian C. Vann Woodward and the theologian Reinhold Niebuhr. They perceived an abrupt end to the nation's innocence in a context of Cold War conflict and nuclear rivalry. Woodward called for a rethinking of the "national faith in unlimited progress, in the efficacy of material means, in the importance of mass and speed, the worship of success, and the belief in the invincibility of American arms." The United States no longer benefited from what Woodward called "free security"; it was no longer "an innocent nation in a wicked world." Americans had to come to grips with the need for a more cautious use of their resources and a less categorical imposition of their ideas on the world. Doing this required not only new policies that recognized limits, but also a reinterpretation of national identity that accepted the imperfection, contradiction, and "guilt of wielding power." Like Kissinger, Woodward saw the thermonuclear age as a period ending the United States' "exceptional" relationship with history. The burdens of middle age had replaced the freedoms of youth.[24]

Reinhold Niebuhr, more than any other figure, gave public voice to this changing view of power and identity. Like Kissinger and Woodward, he meditated on the aging of America since the development of the atomic bomb. A "strong America," Niebuhr wrote, "is less completely master of its own destiny than was a comparatively weak America, rocking in the cradle of its continental security and serene in infant innocence. The same strength which has extended our power beyond a continent has also interwoven our destiny with the destiny of many peoples and brought us into a vast web of history in which other wills, running in oblique and contrasting directions to our own, inevitably hinder what we most fervently desire. We cannot simply have our way, not even when we believe our way to have the 'happiness of mankind' as its promise."[25]

Niebuhr condemned the advocates of total war and the proponents of a permanent peace. Both groups sought complete solutions that were beyond human capabilities. Similarly, he criticized supporters of technical fixes, including many of the nuclear strategists, who presumed that intellect and rationality could address conflicts born from basic worldviews—especially the Cold War conflict between liberalism and communism. Niebuhr joined William Elliott in attacking American culture, as well as that of its adversaries, for devaluing moral purpose in politics. Drawing from the same German intellectual traditions *(Bildung)* as Kissinger, Niebuhr called for leaders to undertake the righteous use of force (including nuclear weapons) against enemies with a firm recognition of their own flaws. Threats required courageous action, but they also demanded a humble consciousness of limits. The warriors of the right were not the prophets of a new Messiah; they were sinning humans struggling to survive and choose the lesser of various evils. Despite the achievements of modern civilization, Niebuhr sermonized, leaders could strive for only short and incremental improvements in society, not for revolutionary utopias. The achievements of the statesman could come only from a recognition of his transitory powers—the fact that even the blessed American nation was impermanent, that "man must die in the end."[26]

Niebuhr's and Woodward's chastened America was also Kissinger's Cold War America. These men shared not only a common perspective on the thermonuclear world; they articulated an expansive but delicate international role for the United States. The nation now had to make the tough choices and consistent sacrifices that it had largely avoided in the past. High-minded principles of freedom and justice needed alteration in their application. Attitudes of superiority required revision to take account of interdependence and vulnerability. Most significant, grand expectations about revolutionizing the world called for a sobering reassessment. Americans had to confront their limits.

As a precocious undergraduate Kissinger had, like Woodward and Niebuhr, meditated on limits, employing the same metaphor of aging. He described the painful realization of narrowing options as lost "youth": "In the life of every person there comes a point when he realizes that out of all the seemingly limitless possibilities of his youth he has in fact become one actuality. No longer is life a broad plain with forests and mountains beckoning all-around." Almost thirty years later, at the conclusion of his formal service in the White House, Kissinger returned to this precise reflection:

> In the life of nations, as of human beings, a point is often reached when the seemingly limitless possibilities of youth suddenly narrow and one must come to grips with the fact that not every option is open any longer.

> This insight can inspire a new creative impetus, less innocent perhaps than the naïve exuberance of earlier years, but more complex and ultimately more permanent. The process of coming to grips with one's limits is never easy.[27]

Across his career, all of Kissinger's ideas about foreign policy begin and end with a focus on the limits of American power. Like other strategists, he sought to maximize the utility of modern weapons without jeopardizing the nation's security. In Kissinger's case this endeavor involved more than just a technical analysis of policy; it also involved a philosophical rumination on the nature of American aspirations in a dangerous world. Although Kissinger's thinking was not unique, it was incisive, and at times quite profound. It combined a deep reading of German intellectual traditions with attention to contemporary challenges. It merged a religious consciousness of human fallibility with a historical sensibility about the need for creative action. Most significant, Kissinger's thought denied an inevitable path to American greatness, although it demanded American leadership as the best of available alternatives. For Kissinger the United States was far from God, but closer than any of its Cold War counterparts.[28]

Critic of Containment

Citizens who believed they had a special, if still distant, relationship with God could not settle for what Kissinger called the "paralysis" of a thermonuclear stalemate. He argued for a new strategy emphasizing creative initiatives, rather than reliance on massive retaliation against enemy threats: "Simply because we are strongest in strategic striking power, we cannot base all our plans on the assumption that war, if it comes, will be inevitably all-out. We must strive for a strategic doctrine which gives our diplomacy the greatest freedom of action and which addresses itself to the question of whether the nuclear age presents only risks, or whether it does not also offer opportunities."[29]

Freedom of action would come, according to Kissinger, from an effort to "bring our power into balance with the issues for which we are most likely to have to contend." This meant an emphasis on proportionality—the ability to calibrate force to serve specific and limited purposes. The large thermonuclear armaments that the United States had developed for an all-out war were blunt and cumbersome. They promised wide-scale destruction but offered few alternatives. They were "total war" weapons designed to deter a direct attack on the nation or its closest allies. The American arsenal of the 1950s emphasized intimidation through "overkill" rather than discrete force. It neglected "capacities for local defense."[30]

The technical nature of thermonuclear weapons was not, however, the main source of U.S. rigidity. The fundamental problems, Kissinger wrote, emanated from failures of strategy. Throughout his career, Kissinger criticized American containment policy for refusing to mix limited force and energetic diplomacy more effectively. As early as December 1950, when he had just finished his undergraduate thesis at Harvard, he explained that the reactive nature of U.S. policy (its "fundamental timidity") and the reliance on massive nuclear retaliation as a deterrent (its "superficiality of conception") ceded the initiative to the Soviet Union. In territories outside western Europe, especially in Korea and Vietnam, Moscow chose the "points of involvement for maximum United States discomfort, leading to a fragmentation of our forces and their committal in strategically unproductive areas." Washington commanded overall strategic superiority, but it fought from positions of comparative weakness. Policymakers reacted to Soviet moves rather than fighting on their own terms.[31]

This extension of conflict into various regions outside Europe (what Kissinger and other strategists called the "grey areas") exposed the limits of American capabilities. "The very tentativeness of our reactions," Kissinger wrote, convinced the Soviets that they could continue their local aggression without any serious risk of "major war with the United States." The all-or-nothing quality of American forces made them unimpressive as potential responses to aggression outside Europe.[32]

The inflexibility of Washington's military doctrine, according to Kissinger, created grave shortcomings in deterrence, as evidenced by the Soviet- and Chinese-sponsored attack on South Korea in June 1950. Thermonuclear forces were not credible as weapons of retaliation in this context. Neither America's adversaries nor most of its allies believed that it would risk its own destruction in a nuclear exchange with the Soviet Union to protect Seoul, Taipei, or even Tokyo. The structure of American forces and the doctrines governing their use left few alternatives to mutual suicide or conventional desperation, as the early weeks of the Korean War demonstrated.[33]

In response to communist aggression in Asia, Secretary of State Dean Acheson called for developing regional "situations of strength" to intimidate and, when necessary, retaliate against enemy aggression. Kissinger argued that this policy was a recipe for overextension and passivity: "It did not deal with the question of how the position of strength was to be demonstrated in the absence of a direct attack on us or on our allies. It did not supply a doctrine for translating our power into policy except as a response to Soviet initiative." Acheson's containment strategy would continue to let Moscow set the terms of conflict and spread U.S. forces thin across the globe, requiring them to fight at their weakest points. "By attempting to achieve situations of strength at each point around the Soviet periphery," Kissinger explained, "we in effect allow the Soviet General Staff to deploy our forces and to lure our Armed Forces into endless adventures." This was precisely the trap that Kissinger believed the United States was falling into throughout Asia during the 1950s and 1960s.[34]

Containment also contributed to what Kissinger described as the "irresponsibility" of allies and the "psychological" weakness of citizens living in democracies. More than anything else, these concerns dominated his thinking throughout his career. The tendencies toward the extremes of war and appeasement within the Western world were, for Kissinger, more threatening than the inherent qualities of Soviet power. Seared by the experience of Weimar Germany, he and many other strategists feared that liberal democracy would collapse when confronted by its external adversaries. "It should not be forgotten," Kissinger inveighed, "that the defense of the Free World is a problem not only of power but of will."[35]

Containment undermined collective will because it promised all-or-nothing. In the case of enemy aggression, the United States would either initiate major war or it would accept a *fait accompli.* Neither prospect looked favorable to western Europeans, who could expect that they would bear the brunt of the fighting or suffer under the yoke of Soviet tyranny. Kissinger feared that this strategic no-win situation would breed hopelessness, alienation, and defeatism—the very qualities that doomed democracy in the 1930s. It would "sap the vitality" of alliances and domestic politics: "either our Allies will feel that any military effort on their part is unnecessary, or they may be led to the conviction that peace is preferable to war almost at any price." Only a more flexible policy, mixing military threats with promising diplomatic moves, could ensure what Kissinger called a favorable "psychological climate" for consistent, effective, and limited actions by the societies allied against communism.[36]

In his writings as a scholar and his activities as a policymaker, Kissinger advocated the integration of diverse armed forces with coordinated diplomatic overtures toward the Soviet Union. He called for the creation of more extensive indigenous military capabilities, particularly in West Germany and Japan, which could "assume the major burden" of their "ground defense" and provide additional retaliatory options against enemy aggression, short of full-scale nuclear war. He also supported the creation of an American force that mixed heavy destructive power with speed and maneuverability—"a compact, highly mobile U.S. strategic reserve, within striking distance of Soviet vital centers." Formed "in conjunction with our British allies" and trained for fighting with high-technology weapons on enemy terrain, this flexible U.S. retaliatory force would "be stationed in the Middle East, not close enough to the Soviet border to constitute an overt threat, but at a distance sufficient to allow rapid concentration in case of war." It would provide the United States with a credible threat against Soviet territory, which Washington could brandish in a moment of crisis without risking thermonuclear war.[37]

Kissinger also advocated the development of small nuclear weapons for tactical battlefield use and for strategic strikes against enemy territory. Nations would deploy them to display a readiness for conflict, short of full-scale annihilation. In war, they would allow undermanned American and west European armies to inflict extensive but controlled damage on larger communist forces. Small nuclear weapons would create a "spectrum of capabilities with which to resist Soviet challenges." Instead of having to threaten massive nuclear retaliation in response to attacks on West Berlin or Taiwan, the United States would calibrate its weapons to respond with strong but limited force. The enemy would suffer serious damage but could disengage without unleashing irreparable consequences. Limited nuclear war would provide new military alternatives and opportunities for control over the escalation of conflict. Kissinger called it a necessary "complement" to threats of massive retaliation.[38]

A limited nuclear conflict, with radioactive mushroom clouds rising above battlefields and cities, was a frightening prospect, but Kissinger argued that preparation for this possibility had important strategic value. It would make deterrence more credible when adversaries could threaten to destroy the United States in response to an American retaliatory strike. Small nuclear weapons empowered local defense without an inevitable widening of conflict. American leaders would not have to choose immediately between jeopardizing their own territory on behalf of West Berlin or ceding that city for fear of reprisals against the United States. Washington would have a basis for firmness in Europe and Asia that did not necessarily imperil the United States. "Limited war," Kissinger wrote, "represents the only means for preventing the Soviet bloc, at an acceptable cost, from overrunning the peripheral areas of Eurasia." It would allow "the smallest amount of force consistent with achieving the objective" of deterrence and defense.[39]

Applying Thomas Schelling's insights about war as a method of international bargaining, Kissinger argued that small nuclear weapons would prove politically valuable in negotiations with adversaries. Full-scale nuclear war was an all-or-nothing proposition; it left no room for compromise. Once the conflagration began, there would be no turning back. In contrast, a calibrated strategy of directed, proportional, and controlled deployments of nuclear force would allow for deliberation, trade-offs, and conciliation in the midst of conflict. Force and diplomacy would go hand in hand. Nuclear weapons would be used to inflict specific damage on an adversary, in hopes of encouraging a favorable settlement, not total annihilation. In this sense, small nuclear capabilities would serve as bargaining chips that a skilled leader could use for eliciting concessions. Limited nuclear war would make nuclear weapons a more usable commodity. Military conflict between the superpowers would become more rational and survivable.[40]

Kissinger's argument sought to return warfare to its normal role as an extension of politics by other means. Preoccupation with thermonuclear annihilation had distorted American assumptions, creating an obsessive focus on "pure" and unrestrained nuclear conflict. Wars were rarely fought in these totalizing terms. Even the Second World War had witnessed restrictions on the deployment of gas and other chemicals in conflict. The belligerents, including Nazi Germany, observed certain limits. Facing communist aggression on many fronts, the United States had to prepare itself for the use of its most powerful weapons for discrete and finite purposes. Limited war, Kissinger explained, "is fought for specific political objectives which, by their very existence, tend to establish a relationship between the force employed and the goal to be attained. It reflects an attempt to *affect* the opponent's will, not to *crush* it, to make the conditions to be imposed seem more attractive than continued resistance, to strive for specific goals and not for complete annihilation." In these terms, limited war created leverage to achieve important political aims and to avoid a descent into more horrific conflict. It was a terrible but still lesser evil, according to Kissinger, than the alternatives presented by containment.[41]

This discussion of limited nuclear warfare sparked immediate controversy. Kissinger's 1957 book, *Nuclear Weapons and Foreign Policy,* became a national bestseller and the most widely read text on American strategy at the time. Many prominent reviewers, including Bernard Brodie and Reinhold Niebuhr, praised his analysis. Brodie called it "the best that has thus far appeared in the field of United States national security policy." Niebuhr observed: "No book in recent years promises to be so influential in recasting traditional thinking about war and peace in a nuclear age." He lent his moral prestige to Kissinger's discussion of small nuclear weapons: "We must be ready to fight limited wars in terms of our objectives and to win them with the appropriate weapons. This circumspect and wise analysis of possibilities and probabilities makes more sense than anything which has come to our notice in recent times."[42]

Critics contended that Kissinger overstated the ability of policymakers to control nuclear war. Once a state introduced these weapons in a conflict, preventing escalation would prove difficult. Thomas Schelling observed that although the distinction between nuclear and nonnuclear capabilities was clear, it was more difficult to set a boundary between small and large weapons, between limited and full-scale forces. Future wars, Schelling predicted, would involve greater resort to nuclear destruction, not less, after these weapons entered battle on even the most restricted scale. Schelling's argument, echoed by other writers, convinced most policymakers to reject Kissinger's strategy. Even small nuclear weapons were too dangerous for limited battlefield use.[43]

Kissinger backed down on his claims about limited war, but he continued to argue for small nuclear capabilities. During the 1960s the stockpile of American battlefield ("tactical") nuclear weapons in Europe increased by more than 50 percent. The British military, in particular, showed a keen interest in using these small warheads to create a more credible and secure deterrent against Soviet incursions. Kissinger remained dissatisfied with

Washington's excessive reliance on a doctrine of massive nuclear retaliation. Throughout his career, he sought to make nuclear weapons more usable for discrete military objectives and general political purposes. He departed from conventional wisdom in his endeavors to give "our diplomacy the greatest freedom of action" through nuclear maneuvers.[44]

Kissinger envisioned a strategic reserve that included small American nuclear weapons and extensive allied capabilities. This arsenal would increase U.S. policy options by widening the geographic and destructive avenues for response to enemy aggression. Washington would develop the ability to fight on its own terms at reduced cost and risk. In contrast to massive retaliation, "the graduated employment of force would enable us to escape the vicious circle in which we find ourselves paralyzed by the implications of our own weapons technology." Effective management of evolving threats required the "ability to meet the whole spectrum of possible challenges" in adjustable, rather than mechanistic, ways. This was the task of dynamic leadership. "Given the power of modern weapons," Kissinger wrote, "it should be the task of our strategic doctrine to create alternatives less cataclysmic than a thermonuclear holocaust."[45]

Nurturing a more flexible arsenal of forces would restore "fluidity" to the international system and better serve American interests through "actions short of total war." Many others made similar arguments during the 1950s. Kissinger's thinking was not unique, but it reflected a sophisticated calculation of means and ends by a scholar who had only just acquired serious academic credentials. Very early in his career, Kissinger formulated a strategy for creating initiative amidst pervasive limitations. He gave new meaning to Cold War policy, and many observers recognized his important contributions.[46]

None other than President Dwight Eisenhower, recommending Kissinger's early work on *Nuclear Weapons and Foreign Policy* to his assistants, commented: "the author directs his arguments to some general or popular conceptions and misconceptions, and, as I say, I think you will find interesting and worth reading at least this much of the book." Eisenhower, like many other readers, did not agree with all of Kissinger's ideas. The young German Jewish immigrant did not offer silver-bullet solutions to the Cold War, but his strategic analysis was provocative and influential nonetheless.[47]

Kissinger maintained his early views on Cold War strategy twenty-five years later. In his memoirs he wrote:

> containment treated power and diplomacy as two distinct elements or phases of policy. It aimed at an ultimate negotiation but supplied no guide to the content of those negotiations. It implied that strength was self-evident and that once negotiations started their content would also be self-evident. It did not answer the question of how the situation of strength was to be demonstrated in the absence of a direct attack on us or on our allies. Nor did it make clear what would happen after we had achieved a position of strength if our adversary, instead of negotiating, concentrated on eroding it or turning our flank.[48]

Negotiations

Rejecting the assumption of Acheson and others that absolute strength must precede negotiation, Kissinger argued that new overtures to the Soviet Union should accompany new weapons. Washington would diversify its force and diplomacy at the same time. A more flexible military posture would allow the United States to take the initiative in manipulating threats and encouraging Soviet cooperation on American terms. "The flexibility of our diplomacy," Kissinger counseled, "will increase as our military alternatives multiply." U.S. leaders could use the movement of force as a symbolic contribution to superpower negotiations, creating more concrete incentives for cooperation from adversaries, more convincing evidence of determination to protect allies, and more compelling reason for hope among ordinary people living in a thermonuclear age. Diplomacy, in this sense, would involve a mix of pressure and encouragement, sticks and carrots.[49]

Kissinger criticized the practitioners of containment policy for failing to use negotiations creatively. He contended throughout his career that they had missed opportunities to seek a beneficial settlement with the Soviet Union and prove their goodwill. Even if the Kremlin failed to accept American overtures, Kissinger contended that offers for strategic compromise would place the Kremlin on the defensive and allow Washington more leverage with allies and citizens. Writing to the White House in the aftermath of President Eisenhower's July 1955 summit with Soviet leader Nikita Khrushchev in Geneva, he called for more meetings: "There is no doubt that the desire for peace is the predominant trend in the public opinion of all the countries of the world including the Soviet Bloc. It is the attitude which must be used to legitimize any U.S. policy." Although the United States had to prepare for Soviet intransigence, Kissinger argued that it must also keep "the door open to a real accommodation." If Moscow proved unwilling to pursue a diplomatic peace, "the failure of negotiation can be used as the basis for increasing the pressures on the Soviet Bloc" and building a "motive for Soviet conciliation."[50]

Superpower summitry acknowledged both the limits and the possibilities of American power, according to Kissinger. Negotiations displayed a commitment to compromise, and they placed the onus for a positive response on the communist states. This was an argument about strategic interest and the "psychological dimension" of the Cold War. It was a call for building consensus through diplomacy rather than through force and threat alone. It marked the moment, yet again, for the statesman to imagine a new future for his people.[51]

In these terms, Kissinger continually called upon American leaders to propose a settlement for Soviet-American tensions, particularly in Europe. A "grand bargain" would involve a permanent division of the continent into a transatlantic community governed by a common "Western" identity, and an "Eastern" counterpart dominated by Russian influences. These were two separate worlds that Kissinger believed could live peacefully side by side. Metternich and Bismarck had recognized this potential, and they had mixed diplomacy and force to manage the two Europes. They had also worked with a multiplicity of intermediary states—including Belgium, Italy, and Austria-Hungary—to create a fluid ("multipolar") system so that the gains of one side did not necessarily result in losses for the other. Napoleon and Hitler had failed to recognize the wisdom of this approach; they had reached for continental dominance, and inspired unity only in resistance to their ambitions.[52]

To the surprise of many people, Kissinger joined Cold War revisionists in their criticism of the United States for dismissing diplomacy and accommodation in favor of toughness and threats. As early as 1955 he questioned the categorical anti-Soviet positions adopted by many American policymakers. He argued that it "should have been the task of the United States to expose Soviet inconsistencies" through tactical engagement rather than blunt opposition. "Instead," he lamented, "we pursued a policy of half-measures: our tone was sufficiently intransigent to lend color to the Soviet peace offensive, but our actions were not sufficiently so to induce Soviet hesitations." The United States talked tough and emphasized rigid military options that damaged both the nation's stature and its security.[53]

From a position of maximum relative strength at the end of the Second World War, Kissinger contended that American leaders should have been more active and creative; they should have developed more effective military uses for their weapons, short of thermonuclear annihilation; and they should have formulated proposals for accommodation with the Soviet Union, carefully pursuing more open relations. He looked to British prime minister Winston Churchill and American journalist Walter Lippmann as advocates of a firm anticommunist position that also entailed negotiations. Both Churchill and Lippmann criticized the passivity of containment—its tendency to encourage diplomatic inaction as the major powers added to their arsenals. Kissinger quoted Churchill's call in the early years of the Cold War for a combination of strength and compromise: "No one in his senses can believe that we have a limitless period of time before us. We ought to bring matters to a head and make a final settlement. We ought not to go jogging along improvident, incompetent, waiting for something to turn up, by which I mean waiting for something bad for us to turn up."[54]

The task of diplomacy was to provide options beyond war and destruction. It would work in conjunction with armed force, but not as a substitute for or a prisoner of military doctrine. Negotiations with allies and adversaries were the key to strategy, the mechanism for making nuclear and conventional weapons useful in obtaining desired ends—especially peace and prosperity in western Europe. "This has never been more true," Kissinger wrote, "than at present, when the available power and manner of its employment so largely delimit the available alternatives."[55]

Throughout his career, Kissinger pointed to missed opportunities, when the United States failed to pursue negotiations with the Soviet Union for a peaceful settlement in Europe. He began with the immediate aftermath of the Second World War: "Our military and diplomatic position was never more favorable than at the *very beginning* of the containment policy in the late 1940s. That was the time to attempt a serious discussion on the future of Europe. We lost our opportunity." The United States failed to recognize that it had maximum leverage, and that its power would only face greater limits in the future. Echoing Churchill, Kissinger believed that American leaders should have offered Josef Stalin a proposal for a stable division of Europe into two separate spheres, with some protections for movement and freedom. This arrangement would have served the interests of western Europe and the United States, it would have acknowledged the limits on American power, and it would have allowed Washington to play a more active role in defining the structure of postwar Europe. The United States could have taken the initiative through negotiations and forced the Soviet Union to react.[56]

A second missed opportunity, according to Kissinger, occurred during the Korean War. He argued that throughout the conflict the United States failed to coordinate its use of military maneuvers with its diplomacy. After American-led United Nations forces landed at Inchon Harbor, on 15 September 1950, the war temporarily turned against the communist states, but President Harry Truman chose not to negotiate, pushing for the total defeat of the enemy. His decision reflected general American sentiment that favored seeking the unconditional surrender of adversaries, without negotiations. Truman overstated U.S. capabilities and underestimated the determination of the communist states supporting North Korea, particularly the People's Republic of China. Before the disaster of Chinese intervention, "when we were in the strongest military position," Kissinger observed, the president should have proposed a negotiated settlement to the war on terms favorable to Washington.

After the war turned against the United States again, and the Truman administration began to seek an exit from the fighting, the White House fell prey to the opposite extreme in its thinking, according to Kissinger. Instead of threatening to escalate the war as a way of inducing conciliation in its enemies, Washington "ceased military operations except of a purely defensive nature," Kissinger explained. After Inchon, Truman was too categorical in his rejection of negotiations; after the Chinese intervention, he was too weak in his pursuit of negotiations. In both instances Kissinger argued that Washington suffered from an inability to match force and diplomacy in pursuit of a favorable settlement. The United States did not create effective incentives for an acceptable conclusion to hostilities. As a result of seeking "total solutions" through force or negotiations alone, it produced a stalemate that remained in place on the Korean peninsula for more than fifty years. Throughout this period, Kissinger lamented the missed opportunities for a political agreement among the belligerents.[57]

He also looked to the months around the death of Josef Stalin, in March 1953, as a neglected chance for overtures toward a new leadership in Moscow. Kissinger argued that American proposals for negotiation, coupled with continued displays of military force, would have placed pressure on a new Kremlin chief to accept more conciliatory policies in Europe and other regions, especially in light of the June 1953 worker uprisings across East Germany. Kissinger criticized American policymakers for failing to call a new four-power summit involving the United States, the Soviet Union, Great Britain, and France. At such a meeting, Washington could have taken the initiative by proposing an agreement on German unity and peaceful interactions between the two halves of the continent. Kissinger regretted that containment's emphasis on military strength and its avoidance of diplomatic compromise encouraged American passivity during a crucial moment of Soviet vulnerability:

> we are still suffering from our mistakes of omission in 1953. It can never be proved, of course, that a bolder policy then could have reversed the strategic situation. The advocates of inaction always have the advantage in debate, that the risks of an alternative course of action are certain while its benefits remain conjectural. But if ever there was a moment when it might have been possible to drive a wedge between the Soviet Union and its satellites, or to reduce the Soviet sphere, that time was after the death of Stalin—unless we wish to admit that the United States can under no circumstances affect Soviet measures.[58]

Kissinger differed from the most respected practitioners of containment policy—including Dean Acheson and Dwight Eisenhower—who counseled for patience and threats of massive force to combat communist adversaries. These men assumed that time was on the side of the United States, that Washington could wait for a more promising moment to negotiate. Kissinger fundamentally disagreed. He believed that America's strength, in relation to its communist counterparts, was in decline. Americans "never fully understood that while our absolute power was growing, our *relative* position was bound to decline as the Soviet Union recovered from World War II." Returning to his undergraduate work on Spengler and Toynbee, Kissinger reflected on how the United States, flush from victory against fascism, had grown out of its youthful self-perception of omnipotence and now entered a middle age of limits and early decay. The proliferation of nuclear weapons, the spread of communist revolutions (especially in Asia), and the weakening morale of democratic citizens were causes *and* symptoms of this process: "History knows no resting places and no plateaus. All societies of which history informs us went through periods of decline; most of them eventually collapsed."[59]

Decline was inevitable, but not irreversible—at least temporarily. A powerful leader could formulate policies to transform limits into strengths. This task required well-timed and creative uses of diplomacy. The statesman, according to Kissinger, would use superior skill and intuition to "struggle against transitoriness. . . . He may know that history is the foe of permanence; but no leader is entitled to resignation. He owes it to his people to strive, to create, and to resist the decay that bests all human institutions."[60]

Kissinger argued that Washington needed bold initiatives. Coordinating more effective uses of military force (including nuclear weapons) with creative diplomatic overtures, the United States could protect Western civilization. Settlement proposals at points of conflict would put the Soviet Union on the defensive and reassure citizens of Washington's desire for peace. Echoing Churchill and Lippmann, as well as Woodward and Niebuhr, this was a strategy of initiative and limits. It rejected the more passive and unilateral aims of containment. "The challenge," Kissinger wrote in the aftermath of the Cuban Missile Crisis, "is to couple the prudence, calculation, and skill of a government of experts with an act of imagination that encompasses the opportunities before us."[61]

Alternative Imaginings

Kissinger's call for imagination drew the attention of prominent individuals—Democrats and Republicans, Americans and west Europeans. By the late 1950s fears of thermonuclear destruction, frustrations with diplomatic stalemate, and the emergence of vocal Cold War critics in Western and various third-world states created a pervasive hunger for new ideas. Kissinger filled this demand for many groups. Arthur Schlesinger Jr., seeking to formulate a more effective Democratic foreign policy, promoted Kissinger's ideas to the Council on Foreign Relations and its influential journal, *Foreign Affairs*. At the opposite end of the political spectrum, Henry Cabot Lodge Jr.—the former Republican senator from Massachusetts and a prominent party figure—called White House attention to Kissinger's "clear-headed, profound, and constructive" proposals. The West German Foreign Ministry shared the interest in Kissinger exhibited by both Democrats and Republicans, devoting special attention to analyzing his writings and cultivating him as an ally. Kissinger's ideas traveled remarkably far and wide because they addressed central Cold War concerns.[62]

Kissinger was not only an advocate of strategic imagination; he, in fact, filled the imagination of many interested observers. His cosmopolitanism, his connections through the Cold War University, and his iconoclastic contributions to strategy allowed him, once again, to become a valued figure in a changing international environment. He remained socially excluded from elite circles, but his serious and eccentric search for policy alternatives provided establishment figures like John F. Kennedy and Nelson Rockefeller with useful material. Kissinger was the perfect outsider for insiders who wanted to transform conventional Cold War wisdom from within.

As a German Jewish immigrant, it also seemed appropriate for Kissinger to do the grunt work—asking tough questions, investigating politically rancorous subjects, and organizing study projects—that gentile elites often found distasteful. This role persisted from the Cold War University to the White House. In both settings, and in all places in between, Kissinger depended on the patronage of powerful non-Jews. He served their ambitions. He provided intellectual leadership, but he also performed menial administrative duties. Although Kissinger gained name recognition, he largely worked behind the scenes—behind more acceptable public faces. He acted, yet again, as an imaginative and exotic bridge figure, a respected strategist situated on the margins of elite foreign-policy institutions.

Nelson Rockefeller, the scion of one of America's wealthiest families and a man with political ambitions, made extensive use of Kissinger. In 1955 Rockefeller served as President Eisenhower's special assistant for psychological warfare, charged with formulating new diplomatic initiatives that would highlight U.S. desires for peace, encourage anticommunist sentiment, and increase pressure on the Soviet Union to sign agreements on American terms. Thermonuclear stalemate was unacceptable to Rockefeller and many other observers. With the growth of Soviet arsenals and the spread of Moscow's propaganda, the United States was too often on the strategic and political defensive. For the next decade and a half, Rockefeller devoted his time and fortune to uncovering creative ideas for capturing the initiative in the Cold War. Soon after beginning this endeavor within the Eisenhower administration, he set up his own independent "Special Studies" project to pursue alternatives to containment. This would become Rockefeller's platform in his failed bids for the presidency in 1964 and 1968. Kissinger supplied both the ideas and the organizational labor for these campaigns.[63]

The two men first met in August 1955, when Rockefeller invited Kissinger to join a group he assembled, following the superpower summit in Geneva, to formulate a new Cold War strategy. Like Schlesinger, Lodge, and many others, Rockefeller saw the creative potential in this young scholar's early publications and work through the International Seminar. Kissinger had energy, cogent ideas, and an ability to connect with various constituencies. These were exactly the qualities that Rockefeller demanded. He recounted how "tremendously impressed" he was with Kissinger in their initial encounter: "He had the capacity to mobilize all the facts and arguments and to give both sides. And he was a conceptual thinker—he thought in broad terms." Unlike other intellectuals, who tended toward abstraction, Kissinger was both a strategist and a network-builder. "He was a man with ideas and he was willing to take the responsibility for organizing them," Rockefeller recalled. "He understood exactly what I wanted to do in the study. And he could take right ahold—he knew who to get to write the papers, who were the people, and if he didn't know them he knew how to get to who knew, in this field, who were the best people in the country."[64]

Kissinger's youth, talent, and creativity immediately attracted Rockefeller. The German Jewish immigrant's eccentricity added to his appeal. "You see," Rockefeller explained, "Henry was always slightly offbeat, I guess, in college. He wasn't the straight academician in the sense of traditional positions, he was an offbeat guy. And therefore he would be a little bit outside the club—or whatever they called it." Rockefeller believed that the "super-brains in academia" were too narrow and too conventional. He wanted offbeat thinking for new directions in Cold War policy. He wanted to enlist an outsider in reshaping the world of insiders.[65]

The wealthy politician recognized that he could draw on the intellectual and administrative firepower of the recent Ph.D. As he promoted Kissinger in policy circles, he also made this young man dependent on his support for resources, status, and future advancement. This relationship would ensure that Kissinger's work primarily served Rockefeller's purposes, at least in the short run. Although Kissinger gained a lot from this arrangement, he became the servant of a wealthy patron—at least until the late 1960s. Kissinger's access to power was now tied to Rockefeller's political success. Like the aristocrats of Europe in prior centuries, the elite figure privileged an exceptional Jew to serve his needs. Both men benefited, but the status of the servant remained uncertain and contested. Kissinger's activities as "Rockefeller's man" would invite both praise and derision. Kissinger's policy proposals would simultaneously challenge Cold War orthodoxies about containment and ennoble assumptions about elite rule. He had to criticize the foreign-policy establishment and at the same time empower one of its pillars.

Kissinger played many roles as Nelson Rockefeller's foreign policy advisor, speech writer, and campaign aide. He also served as the intellectual agenda-setter and daily administrator for the various "Special Studies" projects organized under the auspices of the Rockefeller Brothers Fund. (Courtesy of Carl Mydans / Time & Life Pictures / Getty Images)

Kissinger accomplished this delicate feat by defining a strategy of "dynamic conservatism" that escaped the confines of containment but also preserved the guiding values of civilization. Rockefeller, as an American Bismarck, would formulate international compromises with adversaries and allies that nurtured the peace, prosperity, and general freedoms of Western society. He would mix threats of force, both conventional and nuclear, with diplomatic overtures to open opportunities for controlled international change. Marrying new technologies to inherited state structures, dynamic conservatism would show "how tradition can buttress progress." Returning once again to his early writings on *Bildung* and his criticisms of technical solutions to the problems of humanity, Kissinger explained that Rockefeller should use this approach to oppose the common Cold War

Rockefeller and Kissinger developed a close personal rapport, but their relationship remained an unequal one. Rockefeller was an heir to wealth and prestige; Kissinger was an intellectual and a political climber. This unequal status persisted even after Kissinger became an international celebrity in the 1970s. (Courtesy of Rockefeller Archive Center, Pocantico Hills, N.Y.)

"tendencies of reducing man to a manipulable quality." Dynamic conservatism would "enhance the dignity of the individual" against the pressures of a world pervaded with thermonuclear dangers, godless materialism, and stultifying bureaucracy. As a charismatic leader, Rockefeller would renew the inherited anchors of life value through creative adaptations. This was the foundational architecture for Kissinger's thinking dating back to his undergraduate years, and it guided his work for Rockefeller, and later for Richard Nixon.[66]

Both containment and Kissinger's strategy were conservative efforts to combat the spread of communist influence and preserve inherited values. The key difference was in the dynamism that Kissinger advocated as a means to this end. Through an outpouring of scholarly articles, political speeches, and correspondence, he formulated a series of initiatives that departed from conventional strategic wisdom. The iconoclasm of these proposals made them particularly appealing to Rockefeller. They promised an alternative to Cold War stalemate, and they differentiated this politician from his counterparts.

Offbeat ideas from the German Jewish immigrant gave the wealthy scion a visionary, and maybe even a charismatic, profile. This was the image employed so successfully by President John F. Kennedy. Like the New Frontiersmen around Kennedy, Kissinger formulated a strategy to make Rockefeller appear as "the only national leader with the courage and moral credit to carry out the hard, perhaps even thankless, measures which will then be required to assure our survival." Kissinger and Rockefeller hoped that they could capture growing public discontent with the Cold War in the 1960s, most evident among "young people, seeking meaning for their lives; the type of middle-class person now living in suburbs; and indeed all those concerned with national and international affairs." An alternative to containment could make Rockefeller into a Republican Kennedy.[67]

A Federalist Foreign Policy

Kissinger articulated his strategic vision most clearly in a series of lectures he wrote for Rockefeller to deliver at Harvard in February 1962. The Cold War University was the perfect place to announce new policy ideas. Speaking as the governor of New York State, as an aspiring presidential candidate, and as an advocate of foreign-policy reform, Rockefeller began with the invocation that "nothing less than the historic concept of the free individual's worth and dignity, defined and attested by the whole Judeo-Christian tradition, is at stake in our world."

> The basic belief that these lectures will finally state is the urgent, historic necessity summoning Americans of this generation to match the founders of this nation in their political creativity, boldness, and vision. The Founding Fathers devised a structure of order for a nation within which free men could work and prosper in peace. We are required to help build such a framework for freedom not merely for a nation but for the free world of which we are an integral part. And we are called to do this with far greater speed, I believe, than many of us realize or admit.[68]

The parallels with Kennedy's rhetoric about generational peril and responsibility were intentional. Instead of the unlimited potential implied by a New Frontier, however, Kissinger tempered Rockefeller's language with attention to the limits on American capabilities. Gesturing toward the remarkable accomplishments of the United States during the New Deal and the Second World War, Rockefeller reminded his audience: "All the triumphs of our own national life still do not assure even our national security in the world we live in. We see, then, that all the monuments of the past are matched—in number and in greatness—by the menaces of the present." These words echoed Kissinger's warnings against "total solutions" and an "end to history."[69]

The "federal idea," defined as a "balance of strengths" between different sovereign bodies "operating within a framework of laws and principles," promised to provide opportunities for enhancing American security while recognizing limits. "It encourages," Rockefeller explained, "innovation and inventiveness—governed by principle, and guided by purpose. It assures responsiveness more thoughtful than mere reflex—and liberty that does not lapse toward anarchy. In short, it seeks to hold the delicately precarious balance between freedom and order upon which depend decisively the liberty, peace, and prosperity of the individual." Federalism was an alternative to anarchy on one hand and imperial domination on the other. It implied a basic consensus on rules, with freedom for competition, and even conflict, within safe boundaries.[70]

On an international scale, federalism assured basic cooperation among allies and adversaries in the pursuit of peace. At the same time, it affirmed a diversity of cultures, ideologies, and political systems. Instead of seeking to contain communism until it crumbled, a federalist approach integrated communism and other political organizations into a larger structure of relations. This was not only the American model for the Western Hemisphere; it had been Bismarck's approach to security among the German states, and within Europe as a whole. The German leader had recognized, Kissinger wrote, that peace did not come from universal claims of authority, but instead from coordination among diverse sovereigns—from managed relations between adversarial states.[71]

The United Nations or some other international body could not manage the federalist world that Kissinger imagined. Institutions of this kind provided technical and bureaucratic fixes for tasks that required deeper understanding and more imaginative leadership. Federalism, in this sense, was not about creating a world forum or a global government, but instead about nurturing a cooperative ethos through adjustments of force and inspiring direction. The enlightened statesman had to work within the system of states, crafting principles and alignments that also transformed this system. This was "dynamic conservatism" in action. The protector of the nation, on Bismarck's model, was also a prophet of historical change. In describing this vision to Rockefeller, Kissinger returned once again to his ponderous language about leadership and limits: "A people often learns only by experience; it 'knows' only when it is too late to act. But a leader must act as if his aspirations were already reality."[72]

For Kissinger, a federalist foreign policy meant an acceptance of limits on unilateral power, a commitment to negotiations, and a creative search for mutual gains among adversaries. It was about balancing promises and threats, carrots and sticks. It affirmed the power and legitimacy of the largest states, but it also encouraged political activities that cut across nations—especially within the Cold War networks that Kissinger nurtured through the International Seminar and other endeavors. Most significant, a federalist foreign policy hinged on the imaginative work of select leaders in the dominant countries. They would build the framework for global cooperation and shared authority. They would "create their own reality."[73]

Kissinger meant what he said. His federalist strategy had three primary components, which he outlined in his writings and later put into practice. An "Atlantic Confederacy," a world with "more centers of decision," and a set of "basic principles" to restrain international competition: these were the pillars of his alternative to containment. "The decade of the 1960's," Kissinger wrote, "will require heroic effort and we will not always have the solace of popular acclaim. . . . We must be willing to face the paradox that we must be dedicated both to military strength and to arms control, to security as well as to negotiation, to assisting the new nations towards freedom and self-respect without accepting their interpretation of all issues. If we cannot do *all* these things, we will not be able to do *any* of them."[74]

"Atlantic Confederacy"

As one would expect, Kissinger's transatlantic identity overlapped with a transatlantic view of security. His federalist strategy began with the assertion that the United States must strengthen its core alliance in western Europe. Close relations within the North Atlantic Treaty Organization (NATO) would protect fundamental values and interests. This was the key area of contestation in the Cold War and the central location for possible accommodation with adversaries. In western Europe Washington would display its determination to prohibit communist aggression, articulate its commitment to international peace, and showcase the possibilities of liberal-capitalist society. Security in this region was essential for broadening American efforts to build cooperation elsewhere. A strong NATO would facilitate federalist overtures by coordinating the efforts of the United States and its allies. It would also provide the force to convince adversaries that their best option was negotiation rather than conflict. The transatlantic community was for a federalist global vision in the twentieth century what the eastern seaboard had been for a federalist continental vision in the nineteenth century. It was the Holy Land.

"For more than a decade now," Kissinger wrote in 1961, "the nations bordering the North Atlantic have been living off the capital provided by the great initiative of the Marshall Plan." American aid had financed reconstruction and alliance after the Second World War. It had solidified a set of common purposes that, in the face of growing communist challenges, needed renewed attention: "The leap forward required in the next decade is the creation of a political framework that will go beyond the nationalism which has dominated the past century and a half." Kissinger called for an "Atlantic Confederacy," a deeper integration of diplomatic aims and force capabilities. The "North Atlantic Community" would "increase its political cohesion so that it begins to approach a federal system."[75]

Kissinger was not advocating more bureaucracy or anything like a superstate. These things would violate the federal idea, as he defined it. Instead, he called for an alliance of "sovereign states" in which "the delegation of authority will clearly have to be limited." Borrowing from the proposals for a "Directorate" of transatlantic leaders put forward by French president Charles de Gaulle, Kissinger argued that a federal arrangement for diplomatic and military policy should work through an "Executive Committee" of the leaders from the largest transatlantic states. They would forge a common position for negotiations with the Soviet Union, they would formulate overtures for peace and stability in Europe, and they would pool their resources to increase the military pressures on Moscow to avoid conflict. Diplomacy, not international bureaucracy, provided the structure for Kissinger's federalist hopes.[76]

More organized, consensual, and effective coordination among leaders would instill confidence in citizens. It would counteract democratic tendencies toward neutrality and defeatism. It would also give NATO a positive goal beyond the reactive posture of containing communism. "A great leader," Kissinger wrote in this context, "is not so much clever as lucid and clear-sighted. Grandeur is not simply physical power but strength reinforced by moral purpose." A functioning Executive Committee from the largest states, in Kissinger's eyes, would provide the transatlantic community with needed direction and inspiration.[77]

Unlike most other American observers, Kissinger praised de Gaulle's understanding of this point: "His diplomacy is in the style of Bismarck, who strove ruthlessly to achieve what he considered Prussia's rightful place, but who then tried to preserve the new equilibrium through prudence, restraint, and moderation." Kissinger reminded readers that de Gaulle had "repeatedly urged the coordination of Western policies on a world-wide basis," with equal and acknowledged American, British, and French dominance. The United States rejected this scheme because it excluded other key allies. Kissinger agreed with this decision, but he lamented the rigidity of American opposition to the French leader: "No attempt was made to explore de Gaulle's reaction to the possibility of a wider forum." Washington had, in Kissinger's eyes, missed an important opportunity for enhancing the sovereignty of major European states like France, and forging new mechanisms for policy coordination at the same time.[78]

Kissinger wanted to take de Gaulle's Directorate proposal and expand it slightly in size and scope. He argued that an Executive Committee of the largest states—including West Germany (and perhaps Italy), as well as France, Great Britain, and the United States—was a necessary federal structure for assuring the future dynamism of the transatlantic community. These were the natural leaders on the European continent. They were also the states, because of their economic and military resources, with the most leverage over Soviet policy. As de Gaulle had argued, the Executive Committee would provide a forum for consistent consultation among the most important international actors, replacing the ad hoc approach of the early Cold War years. Real coordination needed a federalist mechanism of this kind. "European history demonstrates," Kissinger explained, "that stability in Europe is unattainable except through the cooperation of Britain, France, and Germany." In a Cold War world, the United States was now a central part of this process, and it had to facilitate strategic unity in place of "old national rivalries."[79]

Despite their enormous destructive power, nuclear weapons had the potential to replace traditional markers of conflict in western Europe with new anchors of alliance. Returning to his earlier advocacy of more diverse fighting capabilities, Kissinger argued that the most effective mechanism for assuring transatlantic strategic coordination came through the sharing of nuclear weapons. In response to widespread criticisms of his alleged recklessness, he deemphasized (though never rescinded) his earlier calls for planned use of small nuclear weapons in conflict. Instead, Kissinger argued for a controlled proliferation of nuclear capabilities to the states on the proposed Executive Committee. A "European nuclear force," Kissinger wrote, was preferable to the alternatives proposed for static American dominance; "it is likely," he predicted, "that nuclear autonomy is the least divisive form of European unity."[80]

According to this scheme, west European leaders would no longer depend on American consent to use the weapons stationed on their territory. They would now operate them independently. Great Britain and France (already developing their own forces) and West Germany and Italy would gain greater assurance in their ability to determine their own futures. Most significant, Kissinger argued, these allies would now feel a stronger stake in coordinating European defense with American activities, rather than carping about a set of policies and weapon systems they could not control:

> In military matters—and particularly in the nuclear field—the closest association between Europe and the United States is in the self-interest of both sides. Whatever their formal autonomy, it is highly improbable that our allies would *prefer* to go to war with the relatively small nuclear forces available or in prospect for them and *without* the support of our necessarily preponderant arsenal. Close coordination between Europe and the United States in the nuclear field is dictated by self-interest; and Europe has more to gain from it than the United States.[81]

Nuclear independence would breed responsibility, maturity, and mutual benefits, Kissinger argued. It would build a closer alliance as states chose to follow Washington's lead because they freely determined that doing so was in their best interests. France, West Germany, and Great Britain would also gain self-confidence from a more credible deterrent posture within NATO, assured of their access (without American veto) to nuclear weapons if their countries came under limited attack. They would no longer have to rely on Washington's willingness to imperil New York for the defense of Paris or West Berlin. Similarly, Moscow would entertain fewer doubts about retaliation for incursions across the Iron Curtain.

Kissinger's strategic vision rested upon building a stronger, more confident Atlantic community of states. The federalization of NATO would occur primarily through the federalization of nuclear weapons. Soviet thermonuclear forces posed the greatest threat to the transatlantic community, and only new methods for sharing retaliatory capabilities would preserve flexibility, cohesion, and strength. Kissinger's thinking on this point was highly revisionist; it ran against the emerging norms of nuclear nonproliferation in the 1960s and 1970s, advocated most consistently by the proponents of containment. He continued to see nuclear weapons as useful symbols and tools for leverage short of full-scale thermonuclear conflict. The spread of small nuclear capabilities would create opportunities for local defense—including limited wars—in Europe against communist adversaries, when necessary.

Upon entering the White House in 1961, John F. Kennedy and his closest advisors were initially attracted to Kissinger's ideas on nuclear strategy and relations with western Europe. Like Eisenhower, the new president did not agree with all his proposals, but the promise of a creative approach to an increasingly stalemated foreign-policy doctrine was exciting. In this sense, both Rockefeller and Kennedy saw a similar value in Kissinger's iconoclasm. McGeorge Bundy, who had been Kissinger's dean at Harvard and was now the president's special assistant for national security affairs, rebuffed Secretary of State Dean Rusk's attempts to hire the professor. Kissinger was too valuable; Kennedy wanted him in the White House, where he would use the National Security Council to make foreign policy in the most crucial areas. The "president has asked me to talk with you at your early convenience about the possibility of joining up down here," Bundy wrote Kissinger. "The only complication in the situation, from his point of view, is that more than one part of the government may want to get you. He does not want to seem to interfere with any particular department's needs, but he does want you to know that if you should be interested, he himself would like to explore the notion of your joining the small group which Walt Rostow and I will be putting together for his direct use." Bundy later added: "We count on having your help, particularly in the general area of weapons and policy and in the special field of thinking about all aspects of the problem of Germany."[82]

In March 1961 Kissinger began part-time work as a White House advisor. He immediately applied his ideas about federalizing nuclear weapons and building an "Atlantic Confederacy" to his evaluations of government policy. In his first memorandum for the president on "major defense options" he called for broader access to weapons short of thermonuclear war in Europe. Referring to the United States and its allies, he advised Kennedy: "We must be prepared to use both nuclear and conventional weapons, though we will make every effort to shift the responsibility for initiating the use of nuclear weapons to the other side." He coupled this call for an expansion of force with suggestions for increased consultation with west European allies, negotiation with the Soviet Union, and commitment to German unification through peaceful means. The last issue, Kissinger argued, was crucial for demonstrating American resolve to serve the interests of citizens in western Europe, particularly Germany, giving them a voice and therefore a larger stake in the transatlantic alliance. Kissinger was careful not to advocate immediate and violent German unification, but he emphasized that the nation's division could not be accepted as legitimate. The burden for the separation must rest with the Soviet Union. Kissinger admitted that although "nobody really wants German unification—with the significant exception of the Germans—a great deal for us depends on demonstrating why German unity is not achievable. The West may have to acquiesce in the division of Germany, but it can condone it only at the risk of undermining the pro-Western orientation of the Federal Republic."[83]

Kissinger shared precisely the same assessment with his other boss, Nelson Rockefeller. In the summer of 1961 he encouraged the New York governor to support improvements in "our military strength, particularly the forces suitable for limited war." He also indicated that we "must be prepared to negotiate. But we should take our stand in the principle of self-determination." Soviet threats to West Germany and other American allies had reached a crisis, but better transatlantic coordination could turn uncertainty to positive purposes. "The opportunity," Kissinger counseled both Rockefeller and Kennedy, "should be grasped to push forward constructive programs moving in the direction of a Confederation of the North Atlantic states."[84]

Once again, Kissinger's expertise on Germany and his imaginative approach to international problems made him a valuable presence for established figures from both political parties. He was one of the few strategy experts to serve both Republican and Democratic leaders. Before Rockefeller and Kennedy, he had worked for Truman and Eisenhower in lower-level positions. As one would expect, Kissinger's bipartisan activities raised questions about his loyalty. This would become a recurring point of controversy, especially in 1968, when he aided President Lyndon Johnson's Vietnam negotiating team while continuing to work for the Republican party through Rockefeller. Kissinger's dual loyalty reflected his personal choices, but it was also part of the circumstances he confronted because of his background. From Harvard to Washington, powerful people sought Kissinger's expertise and his creative mind; they needed a transatlantic bridge figure with his intellectual and organizational capabilities. At the same time, they did not see him as one of them. Bundy was a Boston Brahmin who, despite his own Republican loyalties, fitted the part of Kennedy's New Frontiersman. Kissinger was a German Jew who contributed important ideas but did not belong among the optimistic, privileged men of America's best clubs. He was still an outsider. His clear recognition of this fact made him acutely sensitive about his position.

In October 1961 Kissinger resigned from his role as a part-time advisor to the White House, angered by what he perceived as Bundy's efforts to exclude him from key policy meetings. Despite Kennedy's invitation for him to serve as a personal advisor on matters involving nuclear strategy and Germany, Kissinger's contacts with the president were severely restricted. Referring to his Jewish outsider status from the circle of Kennedy insiders, Kissinger complained that the administration was using him as a "kibitzer"—"shouting random comments from the side-lines" with little say over their implementation. In a rare moment of reflection on anti-Semitic attitudes, Kissinger recounted how both at Harvard and in the White House, Bundy "tended to treat me with the combination of politeness and subconscious condescension that upper-class Bostonians reserve for people of, by New England standards, exotic backgrounds and excessively intense personal style."[85]

Kissinger's objections were not only personal. He argued that the Kennedy White House had, following the East German construction of a wall separating the two halves of Berlin, accepted the permanent division of the nation. Washington failed to articulate continued support for German unification, it offered no plan for a positive change in the status quo, and it assumed that West Germany would remain deferential to American interests. Kennedy refused to give West Germany access to an independent nuclear capability, and at the same time he demanded increased "off-set" payments to cover the costs of U.S. forces in Europe. Kissinger predicted a West German "crisis" of confidence and a profound loss of faith in American leadership. "If present trends continue," he wrote, "the outcome will be a decaying, demoralized city [of West Berlin] with some access guarantees, a Germany in which neutralism will develop, and a substantially weakened NATO." Seeing his calls for a federalization of nuclear weapons and a broader Atlantic Confederacy ignored, Kissinger faulted the White House for choosing short-term tactical maneuvers over a required strategic overhaul: "I am in the position of a man riding next to a driver heading for a precipice who is being asked to make sure that the gas tank is full and the oil pressure adequate."[86]

Like many other American leaders, President Kennedy was intrigued by Kissinger's calls for reforming the transatlantic alliance, but unwilling to abandon the static division of Europe and the established American predominance within NATO. These were the anchors of containment and the familiar sources of stability in U.S. strategic thought. Nuclear nonproliferation policy and negotiations with the Soviet Union during the 1960s emphasized more centralized and overweening management of European affairs by Washington and Moscow. The Limited Nuclear Test Ban Treaty of 1963, for example, banned atmospheric tests, making it more difficult for states like Italy and West Germany to experiment with nuclear capabilities. France had already developed its own small nuclear arsenal, but it too would have to rely on the United States for its defense. Instead of an Atlantic Confederacy, in which power became more flexible and diffuse, Kennedy and his successor, Lyndon Johnson, reinforced an Atlantic sphere of American predominance.[87]

"More Centers of Decision"

Kissinger's federalist approach to foreign policy focused on Europe, his primary area of expertise, but it extended over a wider landscape. The dominance of the United States and the Soviet Union after the Second World War created what most observers identified as a "bipolar" world, largely divided among allies of these two states. Nations generally turned to Washington or Moscow for aid and defense. These two great powers possessed available resources and sought to distribute them as a mechanism for building political influence. The price of assistance was alliance with the United States or the Soviet Union, and conflict with its counterpart. In a bipolar world the friend of one superpower was the adversary of the other. Every small gain for one superpower became a loss for the other. This was a predictable, but also rigid and conflict-prone environment.

Numerous countries—including Yugoslavia, India, Indonesia, Ghana, and eventually the People's Republic of China—sought to navigate a "neutral" position between the superpowers. They attempted to assert their independence and to draw on the resources of both blocs. Although states the size of India could pursue this approach with some success, their efforts often produced intensified conflict with their neighbors and their patrons in Washington and Moscow. India, for example, fought wars in 1962, 1965, and 1971 with states that benefited from either American or Soviet support. In each case, leaders in New Delhi felt compelled, despite their espousal of neutralism, to enlist assistance from one of the superpowers in responding to a rival supplied from outside the region. In 1962 this meant an emergency Indian request for U.S. aid against Soviet-supported China. In 1965 and 1971 New Delhi moved closer to Moscow, in response to conflict with American-allied Pakistan. Like other states, India could not transcend the pressures and constraints of a bipolar Cold War. Kissinger joined many other observers when he condemned neutralism as a false hope for escape from the exercise of power in the international system. Nations emerging from colonialism were especially susceptible to the "new cult of neutralism," but they opened themselves to more deprivation and conflict, not less, through this attempt to avoid hard choices.[88]

For many commentators bipolarity was not only a fact of life, but a source of strategic stability. It made calculations of power easy, and the need for superpower restraint during moments of direct conflict obvious. It eliminated the uncertainty that could lead to a thermonuclear war no one wanted through miscalculation or blundering. Most significant, it created a set of common interests among adversaries in preserving the status quo against potentially catastrophic alternatives. This was most evident during the Cuban Missile Crisis, when both Kennedy and Khrushchev backed down from their respective aims in the Caribbean and accepted a stable basis for superpower peace, rather than nuclear war, in the region. Across Europe and Northeast Asia similar thinking underlay the movement toward U.S.-Soviet cooperation after 1962, often against the wishes of local actors. Bipolarity, in the words of one writer, transformed the Cold War into a "long peace," at least for the dominant nuclear states.[89]

Kissinger did not accept this argument. In the aftermath of the Cuban Missile Crisis he wrote that bipolarity had, in fact, encouraged Soviet aggression. Convinced that the United States would not risk war to prevent Moscow's incursions in Cuba or other small states, Khrushchev felt he could safely provide Fidel Castro with nuclear missiles, close to American territory. This move would show support for an ally, increase Soviet striking capabilities against the United States, and humiliate Washington. In a bipolar world, Kissinger explained, Khrushchev believed that the balance of power and resolve had shifted in his direction; he perceived that American fears of growing Soviet power would deter Washington from acting forcefully in response. Bipolarity encouraged risk-taking by a leader who was convinced of his counterpart's aversion to such behavior.[90]

The solution to this situation involved a demonstration of American resolve and a widening of the range of actors who could deter Soviet aggression. Kissinger praised Kennedy for displaying a firm commitment to force Moscow's retreat from Cuba, even at the risk of war. American military superiority and its willingness to use it were crucial: "The crisis could not have ended so quickly and decisively but for the fact that the United States can win a general war if it strikes first and can inflict intolerable damage on the Soviet Union even if it is the victim of a surprise attack." The brandishing of ready military capabilities moderated the policies of an aggressive adversary.[91]

At the same time, Kissinger joined former Secretary of State Dean Acheson and others who worried that Washington would not show the same firmness in future confrontations. American leaders needed to avoid the swings between "tough" and "soft" policies that characterized domestic debate—swings the Kennedy administration had perpetrated as much as any of its predecessors. Instead of returning to the "weary treadmill" of business as usual, Kissinger called for concrete actions to resolve disputes, particularly in Europe, through an American posture of strength combined with serious negotiation proposals. Anything less would make the firmness of Washington's position in the Cuban Missile Crisis a fleeting asset as citizens and allies became distracted from pressing strategic needs. This was the moment for the American president to take the initiative. "We now have the opportunity," Kissinger wrote, "to define what we stand for rather than go through a shopping list of Soviet demands in an effort to determine which of them may be tolerable. In particular, the best time to articulate our notion of a settlement in Central Europe is before another Berlin crisis is upon us and while the impetus of our action in Cuba still invigorates the alliance."[92]

Kissinger did not expect events to follow this course in the 1960s. The U.S. government, under Presidents Kennedy and Johnson, was too hesitant and unimaginative. Bipolarity numbed the ability of Americans to think in creative strategic terms. Kissinger lamented that Soviet-American rigidity had become the unquestioned framework for all foreign-policy decisions, making members of the White House "prisoners of events." They prepared to react, not to lead. Anxieties about antagonizing Moscow or about altering its relationship with Washington stifled initiative. Despite the rhetoric about a "New Frontier," Kissinger observed that international experts produced "too many warmed-over versions of the policies of the previous administration." He was not optimistic that an enlightened, charismatic leader would emerge to cut through the inertia of bipolar strategic presumptions. In some ways, Kennedy had been "our best, perhaps our last, hope"—but he too had failed to redefine the American relationship with the Soviet Union.[93]

The only practical solution to Cold War stalemate and Soviet risk-taking was to transform the structure of the international system, encouraging a diffusion of power on terms favorable to the United States. A world with "more centers of decision," Kissinger explained, would provide flexibility for innovative diplomacy and consensus-building, rather than the enforced dominance of two bullies. In a "multipolar" framework, the superpowers would feel less directly threatened by their counterpart's every move. They would have less at stake because the shifting roles of other powerful states could compensate for setbacks in "peripheral" parts of Africa, Asia, and Latin America. Instead of a duel between two heavily armed gunslingers, the Cold War would become a contest among fluid coalitions of countries, working to ensure basic peace as they jockeyed for advantage.[94]

The diffusion of power "was fully compatible with our interests as well as our ideals" because it encouraged governments to work with the United States out of free choice rather than in response to perceived American arm-twisting. In western Europe, this strategic architecture would allow Washington to draw more effectively on the potential strengths of its allies, and it would ensure their firmer and more self-confident engagement with the White House. Outside western Europe—especially within the communist bloc and among nations emerging from colonialism—a greater American recognition of regional power centers would allow the U.S. government to formulate more appealing policies. Instead of imposing an external model for political relations, or simply ignoring particular areas, Kissinger argued, a multipolar vision of the international system would enable Washington to escape simple slogans and find common interests with diverse states. Americans would now have a clear incentive to seek international compromise rather than impose their way of life on others. They would look to work with legitimate, empowered local figures rather than create politicians in their own image.

This was the central logic of both classical nineteenth-century diplomacy and pluralism as formulated by James Madison in the *Federalist Papers.* A larger and more varied range of actors elicited adaptation, innovation, and cooperation. It prevented the tyranny of any one or two superpowers. Most significant, it benefited those who defended local autonomy, broadly defined. With more power centers, there were more options for transformation, more possibilities for the individual to make a difference. In a pluralistic world, skilled diplomacy could have its greatest effect—far beyond the confines of a stalemated Cold War system.[95]

During the 1960s Kissinger laid out a strategy for the United States to nurture a multipolar world that would serve its interests. It would replace the nuclear stalemate with a politics of movement that emphasized close working relationships with new partners. It would provide for increased American leverage, despite overstretched U.S. resources, by relying on regional actors rather than direct U.S. dominance. Particularly in Asia, the recognition of more power centers would solve the twin dilemmas of America's long-standing conflict with Communist China and its self-defeating war in Vietnam. Kissinger's multipolar plans promised to reverse the tragic, almost paralyzing, Cold War inertia in each of these areas. The "age of the superpowers is now drawing to an end," Kissinger explained. "A new concept of international order is essential."[96]

China stood at the center of Kissinger's new strategic framework. He shared with many other observers, including French president Charles de Gaulle, a belief in the inner greatness of Chinese civilization. One of Kissinger's frequent interlocutors from Europe remembers: "He was fascinated by China." Despite two decades of disastrous communist rule, this was a society with self-confidence, accumulated learning, and a sense of its historical role as a world leader. The "Middle Kingdom," like Germany, dominated its neighbors not through brute force alone, but also from cultural accomplishment, from *Bildung*. Although Kissinger knew little about the substance of Chinese society, he came to believe that it could play an effective role in providing order to the emerging nations in its region. Geopolitical and ideological antagonisms with the Soviet Union, combined with vivid memories of the brutal Japanese occupation of the mainland during the Second World War, held out the possibility that Beijing would look to the United States as a less offensive regional partner than the available alternatives. Despite his image as a cold-blooded analyst of *Realpolitik,* Kissinger believed that the Chinese were a natural cultural anchor for stable relations, and even cooperation, in Asia. He later commented that their society did not possess an "expansionist" disposition, but was instead "inward looking"—with "slow, patient resolve," "deliberative thought, not impulsive action."[97]

These are remarkable judgments, especially in light of Chinese aggression during the Korean War and the radical violence that swept the mainland during the late 1960s as Mao Zedong encouraged a "Great Proletarian Cultural Revolution" against all vestiges of traditional society. Kissinger was not blind to the viciousness of the regime in Beijing, but he contended that "Communist China is a major fact of international life, especially in Asia." He called for "contacts without illusion":

> We cannot take over the responsibility for bringing Mainland China into a more normal and communicative relationship with the community of nations; she must bring herself out of the isolation which is principally self-imposed. But we can do more to advance the day when China will be able to recognize that it is in her interest to join in rational and constructive relationships with the outside world.[98]

Kissinger believed that China would respond positively to American overtures that returned this civilization to its rightful place as a great power, living in a stable world community. If anything, the violence and deprivation of communist rule created a powerful urge for this reversion to geopolitical normalcy. "We must encourage Communist China," Kissinger explained, "to play a role in a peaceful and progressive order in Asia, in which her own security would not be threatened and her legitimate interests would be represented." Kissinger included this recommendation in one of presidential candidate Nelson Rockefeller's major foreign-policy addresses, delivered on 1 May 1968. The speech called for nurturing international openness, limiting American military commitments, and expanding consensual relations with foreign societies. It also affirmed the importance of particular regional powers, especially China. "We gain nothing, and we prove nothing," Rockefeller announced, "by aiding or encouraging the self-isolation of so great a people. Instead, we should encourage contact and communication—for the good of us both." Chinese-American partnership in Asia, as cultural and political centers of power, would assure broad benefits for the entire region, with less conflict.[99]

Many other prominent Americans, including President Lyndon Johnson and presidential candidate Richard Nixon, joined these calls for diplomatic engagement with Communist China after nearly two decades of hostility. In July 1966 Johnson pledged to pursue "reconciliation" between Washington and Beijing. "Lasting peace can never come to Asia," he explained, "as long as the 700 million people of mainland China are isolated by their rulers from the outside world." In late 1967 Nixon, despite his long history of condemning communist brutality, admitted: "We simply cannot afford to leave China outside the family of nations, there to nurture its fantasies, cherish its hates and threaten its neighbors." "Asia after Vietnam" would require cautious but consistent Sino-American "dialogue." Kissinger's advocacy of improved relations between the two adversaries in 1968 was neither unique nor imaginative. It had become quite obvious to even the most hardened anticommunists that Mao Zedong's regime was a fact of international life, a necessary participant in any discussion of global security.[100]

American overtures to China were almost inevitable in the 1970s. As Nixon's comments indicated, the escalation of the Vietnam War increased the importance of China as a regional power. Mao Zedong's government offered extensive support to the North Vietnamese forces fighting American soldiers in Southeast Asia; a settlement to the conflict would benefit from an accommodation between Beijing and Washington. China had growing incentive to match American peace feelers as the Vietnam War threatened to expand throughout the region, and tensions exploded around its long, disputed border with the Soviet Union. The two communist giants entered a period of low-level warfare during the late 1960s, with direct military clashes that threatened to include nuclear weapons. The prospect of Sino-Soviet armageddon motivated both regimes to improve relations with the United States. Like Washington, Beijing and Moscow had strong interests in limiting their military commitments and enlisting adversaries against common enemies. Nixon and Kissinger recognized these circumstances, as did most careful observers at the time.[101]

Kissinger's thinking was distinctive for its effort to integrate China in a systematic global strategy. Improved relations with Beijing were part of a fundamental structural shift from bipolar containment to multipolar federalism. Kissinger wrote in 1968 of building "triangular relationships between Moscow, Beijing, and Washington." This vision was about more than Vietnam and the future of Southeast Asia. It was part of Kissinger's consistent attempt to create avenues for American global influence and flexibility by integrating calibrated force with diverse negotiations. A triangular relationship would increase Washington's regional leverage in Asia, Europe, and other continents. It would acknowledge the limits on direct American intervention, but it would also create opportunities for diplomacy. The United States would retreat from its Cold War assertion of global military dominance, and it would push forward as a preponderant political influence among both communist and noncommunist states. "The chances of peace are increased," Kissinger explained, "as we are able to develop policy options toward both Communist powers." Instead of containment's emphasis on isolating adversaries, continual dialogue would emphasize "accommodation" for mutual benefits.[102]

In Kissinger's federalist framework, the United States would stand above its new partners as *the* central diplomatic player, *the* worldwide mediator. Leaders in Washington would become the only figures with effective networks of influence throughout the major regions and among the major powers. They would be the transcendent statesmen for the indispensable nation. Amidst what Kissinger identified as the weakening of large authority structures, and the emergence of new local allegiances, the international system needed leaders who could supply an overarching vision to organize and coordinate diverse interests. International organizations and expert bureaucracies could not substitute. This was the role for the United States, and the president in particular, ensuring that state-to-state competition remained civilized—peaceful, stable, and respectful of cultural achievements. Only the White House had the resources and the reach to act effectively on this scale. Only Washington could manage a multipolar world without falling prey to tyranny or bankruptcy.

Nurturing an "Atlantic Confederacy," opening relations with China, and seeking accommodation with other regional powers—these were the building blocks for a new U.S. global preeminence. They also made American political leadership more essential than ever before. Echoing his writings from more than a decade earlier, Kissinger returned to his judgment that "pragmatism is not enough; it becomes meaningful only in terms of values and purpose." American leadership was not about dominance and imposition. In a world with multiplying centers of decision, the president had to create consensus: "He must bridge the gap between our people's experience and future; between our realities and our aspirations. Every great achievement was once an ideal. The world we shall live in a decade from now will reflect the vision and dedication we can muster today."[103]

"Basic Principles"

Kissinger sought to position the United States as a global manager and consensus-builder in a hierarchical world. He rejected both the imperialist impulse for a single state's dominance over a distant landscape and, at the other extreme, the assumed equality of all nations in an institution like the United Nations General Assembly. Empire, as he knew from the history of modern Germany, overextended the resources of society and inspired resistance. Democracy, as he had witnessed in Europe after the First World War, was prone to chaos, conflict, and weakness when challenged by determined evildoers. Kissinger sought to use military posturing, negotiations, and persuasion to support a hierarchy in which the most powerful and most "advanced" countries had greatest international influence, followed by proportional gradations for less powerful and less advanced nations. By definition, this vision placed the transatlantic community—with its industrialized economies, nuclear weapons, and civilized traditions—at the top of the global hierarchy, and the United States at the apex. China, Japan, and the Soviet Union were also near the top. The countries of Africa and Latin America, with few exceptions, ranked close to the bottom.[104]

Racial and cultural prejudices contributed to this vision, as did a legacy of colonial attitudes from Europe. The great powers of the nineteenth century were at the "center" of Kissinger's international system; their former colonial subjects remained "peripheral" to decisionmaking. This judgment reflected the rough allocation of military and economic power. It also illustrated the importance of *Bildung* to Kissinger's strategy. He could admit China to his pantheon of great powers because he—like many others—recognized its deep, sophisticated cultural achievements, even if his familiarity with them was superficial. Chinese society had the wisdom and maturity to act as a responsible anchor for peace in a multipolar world. To Kissinger's eyes, most third-world societies lacked these qualities. They were impulsive, unpredictable, and still "awakening." Kissinger's hierarchical ordering of international power began with this common categorization, and his strategy made it more permanent.[105]

For all his calls to increase the flexibility of American foreign policy, Kissinger's federalist framework was static in its cultural elitism. It drew heavily on the worldview that Kissinger and other German Jews brought to the United States at midcentury. Intellectual preparedness and political experience would guide governance among states, rather than notions of national sovereignty and plans for international institutions. The allocation of authority would follow a meritocratic model that assumed certain countries deserved priority because of their superior achievements. Kissinger advised policymakers to recognize the limits on American power in distant territories, and he argued for the encouragement of local initiative; but he continued to view newly independent societies as recipients of the history made in the capitals of the great states. This was a federalist vision structured by cultural hierarchy. Peace would not come from the free expression of national will or the blueprints of idealists. The great powers would make the peace, and the smaller states would adapt it to local practice.[106]

Kissinger advocated the recognition of "basic principles" in this context. He did not use the term to promote individual or human rights; nor did he think along the lines of international legal procedures. His basic principles constituted a set of international rules to assure the functioning of hierarchy. They set standards for acceptable behavior, the protection of particular interests, and the management of disputes. Once established, they would civilize global affairs by building consensus around practice, and thus lend the functioning of Kissinger's system widespread legitimacy. Federalism and hierarchy would "generate willing cooperation" as the presumed method for structuring the world; alternatives, including Cold War containment, would become unthinkable.[107]

Morality and justice mattered deeply to Kissinger, but not as a universal code for right and wrong. The world was too complex for that. The choices confronting leaders did not conform to abstract ethical standards. Kissinger had witnessed the paralysis of the self-righteous in Weimar Germany, and he had participated in the prosecution of a world war that relied on inhumane actions, including frequent attacks on civilian populations, to defeat a threat to humanity as a whole. International justice required principles that allowed tough decisions about greater and lesser evils. "A country that demands moral perfection of itself as a test of its foreign policy," he warned, "will achieve neither perfection nor security."[108]

International ethics, for Kissinger, turned on the application of basic principles that minimized but did not eliminate injustice. This was the true art of statesmanship, as distinguished from the work of the philosopher. It was also the place where Kissinger believed that moderation born of learning and experience, rather than the impulses of youth, should define the terms of acceptable conduct. Human rights were alluring to the naïve ear, but they were too divorced from geopolitical context. Basic principles of cultural hierarchy held out far more promise for preventing some of the worst threats to morality, especially nuclear war. They allowed space for diversity and differential power, and yet they created order out of international chaos.[109]

Kissinger's consistent emphasis on "principles of international conduct" reflected this basic judgment about ethics in an unethical world. His perspective emerged from his experiences as a German Jewish refugee and a Cold War intellectual. It reinforced the federalist vision for the international system that he formulated as a strategist. Most significant, it opened new avenues for American foreign policy that recognized the limits of the nation's power and ideals. Consensus on the allocation of authority among unequal states would ensure greater stability and open space for a "burst of creativity" that did not risk global annihilation. Basic principles were necessary for liberation from Cold War stalemate and nuclear fear.[110]

To the surprise of those who did not take his scholarly writings seriously, Kissinger applied this vision to the negotiation of a treaty on basic principles with the Soviet Union in 1972. It pledged the signatories "to behave with restraint and with a maximum of creativity in bringing about a greater degree of stability and peace." The agreement laid out a "roadmap" to govern an "age in which a cataclysm depends on the decisions of men." Kissinger possessed a coherent and imaginative grand strategy that guided his negotiation of this landmark treaty with America's main Cold War adversary. Kissinger's grand strategy defined the general conduct of his policies.[111]

Vietnam

By the 1960s Henry Kissinger had become one of the most recognized, respected, and influential strategic experts in the world. His writings were ubiquitous, appearing in bestselling books, scholarly journals, and popular magazines throughout the United States and Europe. He was also a tireless traveler, meeting frequently with leading politicians, diplomats, and intellectuals across the globe. As in the Army and at Harvard, Kissinger distinguished himself by his energy, his powerful mind, and his iconoclasm. He offered establishment figures compelling and contrarian proposals for addressing contemporary challenges. He brought a fresh and useful outsider perspective to foreign-policy debates among insiders. Hamilton Fish Armstrong, the editor of the preeminent insider international affairs journal, *Foreign Affairs,* commented that "Kissinger has one of the most intelligent and original minds operating in the field." Ernst Van der Beugel, one of the leading officials in western Europe, who worked with Kissinger for more than three decades, recounts: "from the time we first met, I have always been listening to his analyses with the greatest admiration. They reach a level that you hardly ever come across. Never, in fact. . . . He is one of the most brilliant 'minds' of our generation. It sparkles with astonishing brilliance."[112]

For all his insights, Kissinger had little to say about the escalating war in Vietnam that consumed more American blood and treasure than any other conflict at the time. His prolific writings from the 1950s and 1960s largely avoided the topic. Like other strategic experts, he paid close attention to the fighting in Southeast Asia, including a number of trips to the region. He also followed the emerging domestic debate about the war with anguish and trepidation. As public controversy about Vietnam grew in the United States and among allies, it became a shadow presence in Kissinger's writings. "In 1965 when I first visited Vietnam," he explained to Hans Morgenthau, "I became convinced that what we were doing was hopeless. I then decided to work *within* the government to attempt to get the war ended. Whether this was the right decision we will never know."[113]

Kissinger's calls for a more federal, multipolar, and hierarchical world sought to escape the Cold War logic that embroiled the United States in a conflict it could afford neither to win nor to lose. He struggled in vain to find a mechanism for ending America's disastrous intervention without damaging U.S. power irreparably. This was the predicament that confronted all the best strategic minds. When asked to write an article for *Foreign Affairs* that might point to a potential solution, Kissinger initially lamented: "I do not know what I could write about Vietnam that would not in the final analysis be highly critical and give aid and comfort to a point of view with which I do not agree."[114]

The essay that Kissinger eventually published in early 1969 offered few options other than a recognition that the United States must disengage. Kissinger advocated a strengthening of South Vietnamese forces (later called "Vietnamization") in place of American soldiers. He also supported negotiations with the North Vietnamese government and with its allies in the National Liberation Front for South Vietnam (often called the Vietcong) in order to smooth the U.S. withdrawal and preserve the credibility of American power in other areas: "However we got into Viet Nam, whatever the judgment of our actions, ending the war honorably is essential for the peace of the world. Any other solution may unloose forces that would complicate prospects for international order." If statesmen allowed events in Southeast Asia to diminish U.S. prestige and resolve, the emerging multipolar world would lose its global manager; it would turn chaotic. Kissinger was determined to prevent this from happening.[115]

As early as 1966, Kissinger used his broad Cold War network to open secret "channels" for discussion between Washington and Hanoi. Working with W. Averell Harriman, the seasoned diplomat who became President Johnson's chief negotiator for the Vietnam War, Kissinger sought to establish indirect and informal communications with North Vietnamese representatives. He drew on a mix of French and east European figures, often academics, to probe Hanoi. These men had personal and professional ties to America's adversary, and they could operate without intense public scrutiny. Although Secretary of State Dean Rusk was skeptical about these endeavors, Kissinger impressed Secretary of Defense Robert McNamara, General Maxwell Taylor, and President Johnson with his ability to nurture promising foreign contacts. As at Harvard, Kissinger became a bridge figure for established leaders in need of new diplomatic options. International knowledge, cosmopolitan connections, and patronage by elite politicians—not the standard foreign-policy bureaucracy—made Kissinger a valued contributor to the White House. Kissinger continued to work for Republican Nelson Rockefeller, but Lyndon Johnson needed him too.[116]

Following his own advice about strategy, Kissinger sought to mix force and diplomacy, increasing the military pressure on the ground and in the air, while also offering accommodation and compromise. He attempted to link an American bombing halt to assurances from Hanoi that it would limit its infiltration of the south and enter "productive discussions" about a settlement to the war. This exercise failed because the leaders in North Vietnam continued to believe that they could gain more on the battlefield than at the negotiating table. The poor performance of the American and South Vietnamese militaries, Kissinger admitted, encouraged this conclusion.[117]

In May 1968, months after the Tet Offensive dramatically escalated the level of conflict, the United States and North Vietnam finally opened face-to-face negotiations. The Paris peace talks stalemated around Washington's demand that Hanoi limit its military activities as a condition for an American bombing halt. Despite its alliance with the United States, the South Vietnamese government contributed to the deadlock. Leaders in Saigon recognized that an American withdrawal would bring about the collapse of their regime. South Vietnam as a separate country could not survive without a U.S. military presence. Although American negotiators, particularly Averell Harriman, argued otherwise, their friends in Saigon knew a settlement that preserved North Vietnamese strength was suicide.[118]

As the 1968 U.S. presidential election approached, Lyndon Johnson grew increasingly desperate to make some headway in the negotiations. Military pressure did not appear to help; neither did public calls for peace. In late September Washington dropped its demand for North Vietnamese military restraint in exchange for an American bombing halt. Harriman's personal correspondence makes it clear that he and other U.S. policymakers believed that evidence of some progress in the Paris peace talks was "essential to give Hubert [Humphrey, the Democratic presidential candidate] a fighting chance." North Vietnam's representatives showed some interest in the new American overtures, but South Vietnam, predictably, objected. When President Johnson on 31 October announced a unilateral U.S. bombing pause, along with a promise of expanded negotiations in Paris, he did so without South Vietnamese consent.[119]

Kissinger remained peripheral to the negotiations in 1968, but he monitored events closely through his network of foreign and domestic contacts. He also worked as an informal foreign-policy consultant to both the Humphrey and Nixon campaigns after his primary patron, Nelson Rockefeller, failed to win the Republican nomination. Journalist Seymour Hersh has alleged that Kissinger exploited his position to pass information to Nixon that his campaign used to encourage South Vietnamese obstructionism in Paris. The Republicans feared that an apparent breakthrough in negotiations would hand the election to the Democrats. According to this allegation, Kissinger undermined the chances for peace and boosted his placement in a prospective Nixon White House.[120]

Kissinger does not deny that he talked to both Democrats and Republicans in 1968 about the Vietnam negotiations. He calls assertions that he and others in the Nixon campaign unraveled a possible peace agreement "vicious misrepresentation." Although the evidence on what information he passed to the two campaigns remains unclear, there is no reason to believe that his actions harmed the negotiations in Paris. North Vietnam was not going to conclude a major agreement with a weakened, lame-duck president. Nor was South Vietnam going to accept a suicidal agreement from a weakened, lame-duck president. Both sides were waiting for the outcome of the election.[121]

Despite these stalemated circumstances, Kissinger's role as a bridge figure between countries, cultures, and parties was once again both a source of power, and a target of suspicion. By the late 1960s he was a valued provider of strategic analysis for nearly every major American political figure. Men like Lyndon Johnson and Richard Nixon encouraged him to play this role. He was particularly effective at nurturing new networks and formulating new ideas for politicians in need of new policies. He was the floating advisor who helped leaders work around the bureaucratic, military, and political impediments to change. He first established this niche within the Cold War University, under William Elliott's tutelage. He made it a central element of his contributions to global strategy, working for both Rockefeller and Kennedy and, later, Johnson. Kissinger's behind-the-scenes acumen, and its encouragement by powerful patrons, brought him to the center of presidential politics in 1968.

Condemnations of Kissinger for talking to all sides neglect this context. In passing information to Nixon and Humphrey about the Paris peace talks he acted out of self-interest, but he also worked to encourage more effective foreign policy. As throughout his career, Kissinger used his knowledge to push for wiser American strategic thinking. In 1968 this entailed a broad reconceptualization of the nation's power in a world with multiplying states and challenges to traditional authority. Kissinger called for recognition of the limits on American capabilities, integration of diplomacy with force, and acceptance of a more federal international structure, with the United States acting as a restrained global manager. Kissinger pursued these large aims through informal information sharing and network-building. He consistently supported negotiations with the North Vietnamese, including the Paris peace talks. These meetings, however, were unlikely to yield any serious settlement without the broader alteration in strategic view that Kissinger advocated. Such a sharp change of direction was not possible for a broken and disgraced president during his last months in office. Kissinger turned to Nixon, among many others, as a possible anchor for necessary policy reform.

Silences

Kissinger's position on the Vietnam War in the late 1960s deserves deepest criticism for its silences. He was one of the most perceptive, imaginative, and energetic members of the strategic community that came of age in the early decades of the Cold War. He was a product of this community, sharing many of its conceptual limitations. If anything, Kissinger's exceptional dynamism as a thinker made him exceptionally susceptible to common blind spots. He worked so hard to analyze the "big issues" of the day, particularly nuclear weapons policy, that he neglected to interrogate some of the conventional assumptions underpinning strategic discussions. For all his attempts to transcend his times, Kissinger remained a man of the Cold War. In Vietnam and other regions he neglected three crucial transformations that challenged the common framework for grand strategy.

The proliferation of nonstate actors. Kissinger and most other observers after 1945 assumed that world affairs would continue to be dominated by states. States had fought the last war, and they dominated the postwar landscape. From his earliest studies of nineteenth-century diplomacy through his later writings on American policy toward China, Kissinger emphasized the challenge of negotiation among a widening circle of presidents, prime ministers, dictators, and despots. He recognized that the international system of the twentieth century was not centered on Europe, but he believed that the exercise of power on a wider geographic canvas would continue to look European. He also assumed that states, not ideological movements, would continue to command loyalty and offer the best protections for citizens. This was, after all, the recent historical experience of German Jews.

The Vietnam War did not fit this experience. It was a civil war in which the main belligerents were not traditional states. They were nationalist, communist, and religious activists—often allied, but not subsumed within states—who had formed strong bonds in opposition to the existing international system. They did not react in predictable ways to the combinations of force and diplomacy that, in other contexts, assured stability. Vietnamese citizens and their counterparts invested their loyalty in a movement for independence and an idea of nationhood that did not conform to Kissinger's hierarchy of states, and did not affirm a European-style system of authority. Most significant, they would not accept a settlement—at the Geneva Conference of 1954 or the Paris peace talks—that preserved the interests of states above the claims of their people. This was not an entirely new phenomenon, but nonstate activism of this scale, determination, and resilience had little place in Kissinger's grand strategy.[122]

Popular attacks on state power, inspired in part by the Vietnam War, created a crisis for Kissinger's worldview. During the late 1960s citizens in every major state, especially the United States, challenged not only the content of policy, but also the legitimacy of the statesmen who made policy. The image of the enlightened, courageous leader that Kissinger exalted, many protesters condemned. They denied that the state and its traditional authorities could constitute an international system of peace and stability. In this context, visions of an "Atlantic Confederacy" and a multipolar world were at best irrelevant, and at worst reactionary. "Liberation" movements, both in newly emergent nations and within the dominant states, were a central feature of global politics by the late 1960s, but they had little place in Kissinger's grand strategy.

Complexity. Although he recognized that the proliferation of actors, weapons, and other technologies complicated the task of managing global change, Kissinger still believed that such management was possible. He continued

A fairly typical image from a student demonstration in 1968. Protests of this sort, around the world, frightened Kissinger. He feared domestic upheaval and popular revolt against established leadership. He feared the violence and irrationality of mass politics. He feared a return to conditions that approximated Weimar Germany during his childhood. (© Bettmann / CORBIS)

to place great store in the ability of the charismatic statesman—a Bismarck or a Churchill—to see beyond the barrage of technical details and the cacophony of conflicting claims. Figures of this kind were essential to keep his system functioning and to prevent a descent into chaos and war. Kissinger lamented the fact that transcendent leaders were not only rare, but when they appeared they rarely groomed adequate successors. Kissinger's strategy depended on an almost mythic grand master.[123]

Waiting for such a figure was tantamount to waiting for a Messiah. He would eventually come, but you could not predict when. During the 1970s Kissinger aspired to this stature. Despite the fact that his career had emerged from the particular circumstances of the twentieth century, he believed he was a transcendent thinker and politician. He would dominate both the global concepts and their local applications. As national security adviser, and later as secretary of state, he placed himself simultaneously at the center of intricate, laborious negotiations with the Soviet Union, China, Japan, Israel, Egypt, and North Vietnam, among many other states. Following Kissinger's daily schedule in the early 1970s leaves the historian breathless. Shuttling frantically from one set of deliberations to another, Kissinger attempted to calibrate all these endeavors within a carefully balanced architecture for American gain. He drew the blueprints and assembled the timber with ever-pressing deadlines. An artist of vision and a genius of detail, he cultivated an image of himself as "Super K"—the savior for the Cold War world. *Time* magazine called him "the world's indispensable man." He accepted and encouraged this all-encompassing aura.[124]

In biblical terms, Kissinger approached too close to God. He set ambitions for himself and made claims about his personal capabilities that were superhuman. This was a result not only of personal ego but also of the basic structure of his grand strategy. For all his admonitions about the limits on power, he allocated to the statesman omniscient knowledge and initiative. In Vietnam and elsewhere the proliferation of influential actors—local and global, domestic and international—exceeded the intellectual capacity of any single individual, even Kissinger. He could not devote his days to tedious negotiations in Paris and at the same time understand the aims of the Vietnamese villagers who would have to accept his settlement. He could not engage in extended meetings with his Soviet and Chinese counterparts and at the same time follow the course of military affairs in Southeast Asia with any seriousness. Like a swimmer struggling against a swirl of ocean currents, the harder Kissinger swam, the closer he came to drowning.

These challenges of international politics were not unique to the Cold War. As Kissinger recognized, his historical heroes had fallen victim to international and domestic crises that exceeded their intellectual scope. After 1945, however, the multiplication of perspectives, ideas, and weapons made the world extraordinarily complex—with perhaps more diverse sources of power than ever before. The rapid proliferation of global actors with access to influence made the aspiration to omniscience self-defeating. How could anyone really grasp the full range of challenges? How could anyone identify all the "key issues" and accurately assess them? Kissinger tried and failed. Throughout his career, he remained profoundly ignorant of the effects of his policies, especially in places far from Europe. He was naïve in his assumption that a single statesman, and a single country, could manage international affairs.[125]

Emotion and faith. Kissinger conceived a world of states and statesmen. This was a rational system of calculated interests and negotiations. It was a club of intelligent, energetic, and courageous men, served by gifted figures—like Kissinger. It globalized the Harvard International Seminar, where a network of the best and the brightest reconciled the interests of their societies for mutual gain. Kissinger's and de Gaulle's ideas about a "Directorate" within the "Atlantic Confederacy" set a model for international management as a whole.

Despite the rhetoric of *Realpolitik* surrounding it, this vision embodied inherited assumptions about cultural hierarchy and emotional reactions to the prospect of chaos. For Kissinger, the statesman was both a philosopher and a politician, a scholar of *Bildung* and a practitioner of policy. Although this was the intellectual foundation for his worldview, the language of his advice, like that of other strategic experts, emphasized "objective" judgments about international behavior. Leaders who followed his counsel made dispassionate choices. Sacrifices and suffering were the unavoidable consequences of circumstances that decisionmakers could not change; they could only choose carefully among lesser evils. In contrast to the sentimentality of many citizens, Kissinger's statesman made tough, rational decisions.

Politics, however, is the stuff of emotion, faith, and sentimentality. Kissinger fell victim to a double standard common to intellectuals—particularly those authoring grand strategy. He defined his subjective judgments about values in terms that did not allow for analysis and debate. Cultural hierarchy was not open to discussion. The moral content of state interests was taken for granted. American benevolence went unquestioned. By turning these interpretations into "facts," and by formulating policy based upon them, Kissinger closed off alternative possibilities. Did the large powers really have to play a guiding role in regions like Southeast Asia? Did states, on the European model, necessarily dominate international affairs? Was the United States always a force for good across the globe?

These were open issues, and they remain so to this day. Differing judgments create differing assessments of "reality." In denying this fact, Kissinger and other grand strategists of his generation artificially narrowed the range of policy options for their patrons. The slow, steady American embroilment in Vietnam over the course of more than two decades occurred because leaders failed to question basic assumptions. They failed to take account of the emotions, faiths, and sentiments that would prevent people—in Vietnam and elsewhere—from accepting what looked like the most rational solutions. They failed to think with the objectivity and dispassion, the creativity and imagination, that they so strongly advocated.[126]

I. F. Stone recognized this problem at the time. "Sensible and sane men" made decisions about nuclear weapons, limited warfare, and international management that looked wise in their Cold War context. If one questioned basic assumptions, however, strategic wisdom appeared arbitrary and shortsighted. Few people could interrogate their own limitations so effectively. This is, as Stone indicated, the advantage of the historian, removed from the period under study. Kissinger had a broad historical sensibility, but he was, like all strategists, a captive of his particular history. He was a victim of his own limits.[127]

FIVE | *A Statesman's Revolution*

The late 1960s mark a historical divide. In nearly every society, the tenor of life changed. Social and cultural traditions endured concerted attack. Authority figures faced direct challenges from "ordinary" citizens. Fears of worldwide chaos replaced assumptions about international order. Like balls of yarn, the stable lines of geopolitics after the Second World War came undone as people pulled at them from multiple directions. This was an era of global revolution from within and without.[1]

State leaders, particularly in the United States and western Europe, were traumatized by this upheaval. They struggled to run their governments as the world collapsed around them. They grasped for political legitimacy when their inherited values lost public suasion. British foreign secretary Michael Stewart captured this sense of pervasive crisis in his private diary. "The 10: P.M. television news presents a depressing picture," he wrote. "The great difficulty of the world is the moral deficiencies of what should be the free world . . . Germany distracted, France selfish, ourselves aimless, U.S.A. in torment."[2]

Hamilton Fish Armstrong, the editor of *Foreign Affairs* and the figure who helped to articulate an American global vision at midcentury, echoed Stewart's foreboding. Armstrong explained to one of his younger associates—Henry Kissinger—that never since the days of President Warren Harding had "the prestige of the United States stood so low. We have the military power and we have the economic power . . . to command the world. But we do not have the moral prestige, because abroad governments and people know what we know in our hearts ourselves, that our life forces, the forces that we felt made us great, are dispersed and sullied."[3]

Kissinger shared Armstrong's sentiment. In 1968, working for both Lyndon Johnson and Nelson Rockefeller, he positioned himself as a high-level advisor to Democrats and Republicans. He did not, however, expect great policy successes in the near future. He worried that the upheavals of the period would undermine rational decisionmaking. He feared a return to the violence, chaos, and collapse of Weimar Germany in "the turmoil surely ahead of us." "The next Presidency is likely to be tragic," Kissinger predicted. "Nothing suggests that any of the prospective candidates can unify the country or restore America's position in the world. The next four years are likely to witness mounting crises—disorder at home, increasing tension abroad."[4]

"In the best of circumstances," Kissinger warned, "the next administration will be beset by crises. In almost every area of the world, we have been living off capital—warding off the immediate, rarely dealing with underlying problems. These difficulties are likely to multiply when it becomes apparent that one of the legacies of the war in Vietnam will be a strong American reluctance to risk overseas involvements." Like the democracies on the eve of the Second World War, the citizens of the transatlantic community had become weak, divided, and cowardly. The Cold War had encouraged a dangerous mix of strident rhetoric and stale policy.[5]

Democratic optimists, including President Lyndon Johnson, had hoped to address the sources of contention through government programs, compromise policies, and personal persuasion. They would rebuild public consensus from the bottom up. They would follow the inspiration of the New Deal, which restored the faith of Depression-era Americans in the continued viability of a capitalist society and an activist foreign policy. For Johnson, more democracy, not less, was the solution. Citizens had to feel a deeper connection to their nation's foreign and domestic activities.[6]

Kissinger's experiences as a German Jew in the 1930s had led him to draw a very different lesson. He had witnessed the collapse of civilization at the hands of frightened and frustrated citizens. He had suffered the pain of heightened violence and prejudice amidst upheaval. Like many other people from a similar background, Kissinger was profoundly skeptical about the prospects for democratic deliberation during a moment of crisis. Efforts at political compromise and public persuasion were not enough. The global revolution of the late 1960s demanded a fundamental redirection of policy. The heroic statesman had to channel the energies and emotions of citizens into a new framework for political thought, with a revised set of expectations.[7]

Metternich, Bismarck, and Churchill—leaders who thrived in moments of crisis—again provided Kissinger with his model. Confronting a combination of domestic and international challenges, they courageously moved their societies in a new direction. They acknowledged the limits of prior policy assumptions, centralized decisionmaking authority, and implemented a coherent grand strategy. Metternich built the Concert of Europe on the ashes of the Napoleonic Wars; Bismarck forged German unity from splintered states; Churchill constructed a vibrant transatlantic alliance from the edges of fascist defeat. Each of these men avoided the temptation to get entangled excessively in redressing specific political grievances. They enhanced their power and diminished their enemies' by creating a new system of relations, a new architecture for the exercise of authority. They did not manage crises; they transcended them.[8]

Watching the United States sink ever deeper into the military quicksand of Vietnam as citizens set American cities aflame, Kissinger believed that the nation needed imaginative leadership more than ever before. He agreed with public protesters who argued that the old assumptions about containment and liberal politics no longer offered hope. The problem was not the content of American power; the United States had the military capability to destroy its adversaries in Vietnam, and it had the resources to satisfy domestic grievances. The problem was the way in which power was organized, exercised, and judged. The United States needed to revise the basic concepts underpinning its policies. "The shape of the future," Kissinger wrote, "will depend ultimately on convictions which far transcend the physical balance of power."[9]

When asked in 1971 "where the administration wants to end up after four years," Kissinger invoked both his sense of contemporary crisis and the strategic ideas he had articulated for more than a decade. "This administration came into office when the intellectual capital of U.S. postwar policy had been used up and when the conditions determining postwar U.S. policy had been altered," he explained. "We had to adjust our foreign policy to the new facts of life. It is beyond the physical and psychological capacity of the U.S. to make itself responsible for every part of the world. We hope in the first term to clear away the underbush [*sic*] of the old period. In the second term, we could try to construct a new international settlement—which will be more stable, less crisis-conscious, and less dependent on decisions in one capital."[10]

All Kissinger's experiences—as a refugee, a counterintelligence officer, a scholar, and a strategist—had prepared him to remake foreign policy, "to clear away the underbush of the old period." He rejected "ready made solutions" and encouraged the formation of a small, elite "directorate" of leaders—on the model of the International Seminar at Harvard—that would craft new initiatives. Echoing his earlier writings, Kissinger asserted that this directorate could replace assumptions about a bipolar Cold War with an international system keyed to a federal distribution of authority, multiple centers of decision, and ordered hierarchy. More than almost any other historical figure, Kissinger attempted to put a coherent and transformative grand strategy into action. During a time of crisis, this effort would be his source of transcendence. Confronted by revolution overseas and in the streets, he would make his own "statesman's revolution."[11]

Kissinger thought of himself as a statesman, protecting the security of the American state as a bulwark of freedom against its enemies at home and abroad. He was also a revolutionary, eager to shake up standard policies and implement alternatives. The combined posture of the statesman and the revolutionary involved an uneasy balance between order and change, pragmatism and idealism, leadership and accountability. Implementing his strategy as President Nixon's special assistant for national security affairs and later as secretary of state, Kissinger ultimately failed to balance these contradictions. He was too much of an elite statesman for advocates of popular revolution, too revolutionary for traditional diplomats.

Kissinger's policies, and his relationship with Nixon, reflect this unresolved tension. During his years in office and the decades since, the controversies surrounding him continue to center on the same questions of how the statesman should relate to revolution. Kissinger came of age in a mid-twentieth-century world where leaders struggled to manage overwhelming social and political changes. He focused much of his professional thinking on this topic. He ended his career, however, in the same boat as the figures he had observed as a young man—beset by multiplying crises that he could not satisfactorily resolve. For all his preparation and effort, Kissinger did not transcend the upheavals surrounding him. As he predicted in the late

1960s, Kissinger and other statesmen remained subjects of larger revolutionary forces they could not control.

From Rockefeller to Nixon

Kissinger was a tireless correspondent with prominent Cold War figures, but his letters were generally formal in tone. In late December 1968, however, he wrote a rare emotional note to his longtime patron Nelson Rockefeller. As he prepared to enter the Nixon White House, Kissinger expanded on how much Rockefeller's "friendship and our association has meant to me":

> You cannot imagine what a wrench it was for me to interrupt our collaboration. But even though we will not be working together directly, your values and inspiration will continue to be crucial to me. I hope we can stay in close touch. And I count on the fact that in the years to come our paths will join again. . . . Whatever you may do I hope you know that you can count on my friendship and devotion.[12]

Kissinger expressed deep affection for Rockefeller, and sincere appreciation for his personal support. His words also highlighted that this was an unequal relationship based on the beneficent patronage of a wealthy and established figure for a poor outsider. Kissinger apologized for interrupting his service to Rockefeller. He pledged continued loyalty. Most significant, he acknowledged permanent guidance from his patron through his "values and inspiration." Kissinger wrote to Rockefeller as an adopted son who had achieved success. Even after his appointment to the Nixon White House, he remained deferential to Rockefeller.

Kissinger's gratitude appears heartfelt, but it is the gratitude of a subordinate. The two men developed a productive, trusting, and hierarchical friendship. Kissinger was a servant, Rockefeller a patron. Rockefeller's response to Kissinger's letter reinforced this point. He thanked his advisor for his "counsel" and "service." As a symbol of his "friendship" and "appreciation"—as well as a reminder of Rockefeller's greater wealth and status—he sent Kissinger a gift of $50,000. This was quite a large sum for the time, and it solidified their unequal relationship. With this act of generosity, Kissinger owed his patron an even greater debt of service.[13]

Richard Nixon never elicited the same personal connection from his advisors. Kissinger's contact with Nixon began in May 1955, when he sent the vice president a letter of invitation to speak at Harvard's International Seminar that summer. Nixon did not attend, although he did read Kissinger's book *Nuclear Weapons and Foreign Policy.* The two men had at least one brief social encounter, at a cocktail party in Washington, D.C., during the 1960s, but they hardly talked to one another. They were, in fact, social outsiders who did not have much opportunity for interaction. Kissinger focused on building professional contacts with respected Cold War figures such as Rockefeller. Nixon operated on the fringes of the Republican party. As late as August 1968, Kissinger wrote of Nixon in distant and condescending terms. He doubted the former vice president's "suitability" for the highest national office. Kissinger's personal regard for Nixon was even lower. He told one of his regular correspondents: "I detest Nixon."[14]

These two estranged outsiders did not come together in later months out of common beliefs, affections, or a patron-client arrangement, as in Kissinger's other professional relationships. Despite their claims concerning the importance of grand strategy, there is no evidence that they ever had a heart-to-heart conversation about their shared hopes for the future. They ranted about their perceived enemies—political insiders, liberal intellectuals, and the media—but they never outlined a future vision. How did they want to change the world? What was their desired legacy? Kissinger thought extensively about these matters alone, but he and the president never broached the subject together with any documented seriousness.

Theirs was not a collaboration for higher purposes. It was a marriage of convenience, filled with all the suspicion, hostility, and jealousy that accompanies these dysfunctional alliances. Nixon and Kissinger respected and resented each other at the same time. They worked closely together but remained strangers to one another. Looking back on his time in the White House, Kissinger is amazed at how personally distant he remained from the president who gave him so much power.[15]

Nixon and Kissinger joined forces in the face of public crisis. One of Nixon's foreign-policy advisors, Richard Allen, suggested Kissinger as a possible national security official because of his reputation for brilliance, creativity, and administrative acumen. William F. Buckley Jr., the prominent journalist who had opposed Nixon in earlier years because he lacked consistent conservative convictions, also endeavored to bring the candidate and Kissinger together. Despite some philosophical differences with

Kissinger, Buckley recognized that he possessed the energy and brilliance to protect political authority against a "stampede into chaos." Buckley and other observers of diverse political backgrounds looked to Nixon and Kissinger as strong leaders who would restore order and reason at a time when both were in short supply. Asked about Kissinger's prospective appointment in the Nixon White House, his former Harvard colleague and Kennedy aide, Arthur Schlesinger Jr., replied: "I urged him to accept. He's the best they'll get."[16]

Fears of democratic chaos and anxieties about pervasive threats were the anchors for Nixon and Kissinger's working relationship. They always had adversaries, particularly within the United States, to bring them together. They always had schemes, both domestic and foreign, to outmaneuver their enemies. Nixon and Kissinger were emotionally bound by a strong

Kissinger with President Richard Nixon at the White House, 1973. Although the two men worked closely together and contributed to each other's power, their relationship was filled with animosity and distrust. Nixon resented Kissinger's fame, questioned his loyalty, and derided his Jewish background. Kissinger considered Nixon unstable, anti-Semitic, and frequently self-defeating. (Courtesy of National Archives / Getty Images News / Getty Images)

desire to protect the imperiled institutions of the United States that had made their careers possible. They would "stick it" to those citizens and leaders who condescended to them. In a time of crisis, their relationship inverted political tradition, placing the outsiders who had operated on the fringes of power in the driver's seat.

Nixon and Kissinger had a dark view of human nature and democratic society, born of their own experiences with social prejudice. Nixon never confronted the anti-Semitic virulence of Nazi Germany, but he faced the disdain of East Coast elites—like the Kennedys and Rockefellers—for a hard-working man from rural America, without polish or prestigious connections. He and Kissinger had to scrape and struggle for their advancement, and they viewed life in these terms. They did not believe that an expansion of freedoms would naturally make for a better society. Free citizens were often hateful and destructive, as the urban riots of the late 1960s seemed to prove once again. For Nixon and Kissinger, social progress required firm national leadership to limit human excesses and restrict human hatreds. The same applied to the international system, where competitive states would pummel one another to death without the force of imposed order from a superior power. On the basis of their own personal experiences, Nixon and Kissinger saw themselves as benevolent strongmen rather than Jeffersonian democrats.

Nixon took the image of toughness seriously. As president, he operated as a boss politician, organizing policy around his close personal advisors, dispensing favors to his friends, and lashing out—often illegally—against a long list of enemies. He created an atmosphere of constant recrimination in the White House. He needled everyone who worked for him, including Kissinger, to identify critics and discredit them. Watching and isolating adversaries—including other elected American officials—was legitimate, according to Nixon. Observing constitutional restrictions on executive power and formulating disinterested policies was "touchy," and frankly laughable for a politician who thought in terms of unending struggle. Nixon's notion of national security included a presidential prerogative to stand above the law. He would mobilize the power of his office to maximize the benefits for his supporters. He would act as a personal broker for the needs of his constituents. He would destroy his adversaries, especially those from the "damned establishment."[17]

In his daily behavior and rhetoric, Nixon acted more like a gangster than a statesman. He told Kissinger that in confronting critics, including the mainstream American press, "You can't fight this with gentlemanly gloves." Nixon ordered his aides to reject standard strictures about decency and civility. When confronting an adversary, they should "kick him" and "keep whacking, whacking, and whacking." "Scare the shit out of them."[18]

Nixon believed that he would live and die by the sword. His enemies would exploit his weaknesses, as he perceived they had in the past. Domestic and international observers would respect only strength. Nixon had intricate knowledge of policy, particularly of foreign affairs, but he was, in Kissinger's words, a simple "gut fighter" by instinct and habit:

> he turned without hesitation to uses of Presidential power that he never ceased believing—with much evidence—had been those of his predecessors as well. Such tactics were inappropriate for our national anguish. Bridges needed building and the Chief Executive of the country, the only nationally elected official, should have taken the first step. Yet this is something Nixon just did not know how to do. He was too insecure and, in a strange way, too vulnerable.[19]

Insecurity and vulnerability pervaded the government. Nixon's distrust of the diplomatic elite in various offices led him to centralize foreign-policy power in the White House. He intended to direct the details of strategy more than any of his predecessors. Presidents Eisenhower and Kennedy had begun the process of converting the National Security Council (NSC), created in 1947 as an administrative organ, into a policymaking body. Nixon expanded this function, using the NSC as his personal creature, often excluding the Departments of State and Defense from key deliberations. He feared that other members of his own administration would undercut him.[20]

This personalization of policy led Nixon to empower his NSC advisor as the dominant day-to-day overseer of foreign activities. The president had too many responsibilities; he could not follow the details of even the most important issues. By necessity more than design, Nixon turned to Kissinger as the preeminent foreign-policy figure in the administration. As Richard Allen, William F. Buckley, and others had attested, Kissinger possessed the brains and ambition to play this role. He was a renowned scholar with extraordinary political access, but he was also an outsider to the clubby establishment elite. Nixon recognized, as Rockefeller had before, that he could use Kissinger's talents and control him at the same time. The NSC advisor would take on numerous responsibilities, but he would remain dependent on the president for his continued power. He would not have the prestige conferred by the State Department (at least not until 1973), nor would he benefit from a broad constituency within the administration. "Kissinger's power derived from Nixon," the president's longtime speechwriter, William Safire, observed. In the first year of the administration, Safire recalled, "Kissinger was more organizer and codifier than stimulant to Nixon, because a sense of bringing order out of chaos was what the President needed most."[21]

The NSC advisor served the president as a skilled business manager would serve his gangster boss. Nixon barked orders, and Kissinger dutifully listened. He then had to interpret the chief's intemperate remarks in ways that would serve intended purposes and address neglected issues. This was a tricky undertaking that could incur the wrath of the president if his unwise remarks were followed too closely or his deeply considered statements ignored. In his memoirs, Kissinger refers to the "several warring personalities" struggling within the president: "There was a reflective, philosophical, stoical Nixon; and there was an impetuous, impulsive, and erratic one. Sometimes one set of traits prevailed; sometimes another; occasionally they were in uneasy balance. One could never be certain which Nixon was dominant from meeting to meeting." Kissinger recounted that the president's closest advisors "learned to discount much of what he said and filter out many assertions made under stress. We were expected, we believed, to delay implementing more exuberant directives, giving our President the opportunity to live out his fantasies and yet to act, through us, with the calculation that his other image of himself prescribed."[22]

Like all gangsters, Nixon refused to respect the boundaries of his servants' personal space. Kissinger worked for a man who demanded that he remain "on call" at all hours, ever ready to bear the brunt of his boss's angry outbursts and to bolster his fragile self-esteem. One such telephone conversation occurred a few minutes before midnight on 17 April 1973, when Nixon called Kissinger to lament the mounting pressures surrounding the Watergate scandal:

Nixon: Some of these people will even piss on the President if they think it will help them. It's pretty hard. . . . Maybe we'll even consider the possibility of, frankly, just throwing myself on the sword . . .

Kissinger: That is out of the question, with all due respect, Mr. President. That cannot be considered. The personality, what it would do to the presidency, and the historical injustice of it. Why should you do it, and what good would it do? Whom would it help? It wouldn't help the country. It wouldn't help any individual involved. . . . You have saved this country, Mr. President. The history books will show that, when no one will know what Watergate means.[23]

This conversation captures the dysfunctional nature of the president's relationship with his advisor. Nixon's words are filled with anger and self-pity, and he demands sycophantic validation from his subordinate. Late at night, Kissinger finds himself forced to assess his volatile boss, prove his loyalty, and also contain any further eruption. Kissinger has to allay and affirm Nixon at the same time. He has to separate the posturing from the purposeful, and quickly discern how the president's words affect pressing policy decisions. Nixon was an imposing boss whom Kissinger had to manage from a position of weakness. If he misjudged, he could find himself cut off from power on the president's whim. Like the gangster's assistant, Kissinger felt pressure to display supreme competence in policy and psychology. This was a far cry from the more refined, though no less unequal, world of the Cold War University and the Rockefeller campaign.

Kissinger had confronted anti-Semitic attitudes in all his professional activities, but around Nixon these prejudices were particularly grating. In contrast to Rockefeller, who avoided explicit anti-Semitism, Nixon was more open in his prejudices. He frequently lashed out against Jewish conspiracies. He identified Jewish enemies in the media, business, academia, and the state of Israel. They were untrustworthy, secretly organized, and un-American in their attacks on the president. When Nixon learned that Mark Felt, the second-highest-ranking FBI official and the man later identified as "deep throat," was leaking damaging information, he immediately focused on Felt's background: "It could be the Jewish thing. I don't know. It's always a possibility." Nixon generalized about the treachery of Jews and the need to isolate them from political power: "we've been trying to run this town by avoiding the Jews in the government, because there were very serious questions. . . . Because there were leaks in the government itself." Nixon surrounded himself with men who he believed would not be "soft on the Jews." He subjected Jewish critics to the same rough, gangsterlike tactics reserved for other enemies.[24]

Nixon, of course, recognized that he was investing enormous foreign-policy power in a German Jew. His belief in the supreme capabilities of Jews, especially for intrigue, surely encouraged this decision. It also confirmed his profound suspicion of Kissinger. The NSC advisor was at once an ally and an adversary. Fearing that Kissinger was collaborating with Nixon's Jewish critics in the media, the president ordered close surveillance of his telephone conversations. Referring to Max Frankel, an editor at the *New York Times,* Nixon explained: "Henry is compulsive on Frankel. He's Jewish . . . Henry—the *New York Times,* see if he talked to Frankel." Kissinger did share information with the press, but the attribution of this activity to a Jewish conspiracy highlighted the depth of the president's prejudices.[25]

Kissinger confronted Nixon's anti-Semitism on a variety of issues, particularly policy toward Israel. When Kissinger received the Nobel Peace Prize in 1973 for his role in the Vietnam negotiations, a jealous Nixon called with advice about how he should donate the award money. Without warning, the president thundered: "I would not put any in for Israel." Taken aback, Kissinger responded: "Absolutely not. That would be out of the question. I never give to Israel." "You should not," Nixon repeated. "No. That is out of the question," Kissinger confirmed. The sting of this dialogue remained with Kissinger more than three decades later, when he published the transcript of the conversation but excluded the material illustrating the president's suspicion about his aide's excessive loyalty to Israel.[26]

Kissinger worried that anti-Semitic attitudes were growing more common among citizens and politicians horrified by the chaos of the late 1960s. "I speak as a Jew," he explained to journalist C. L. Sulzberger: "I very much wonder what the President's own repercussions and reactions will be." Sulzberger recounts that Kissinger "was astonished at how many people in the Establishment told him of their own feelings, which were evidently although unconsciously anti-Semitic. Because of his high White House position they seem to forget that he is Jewish. One very important man had most recently said to him in confidence that he was convinced there was a Jewish-communist plot. Henry was appalled."[27]

No one really forgot that Kissinger was Jewish, and he knew that. Leonard Garment, another Jew who served Nixon as a domestic policy advisor and later as legal counsel, recalls that Kissinger privately complained about the "goddamn anti-Semites" in the administration. Garment explains that "Kissinger was treated at the White House as an exotic wunderkind—a character, an outsider. His colleagues' regard for him was genuine, but so were the endless gibes at his accent and style, and so were the railings against Jewish power that were part of the casual conversation among Nixon's inner circle. . . . just as a black man can never change his skin," Garment observed, "Kissinger could never—in fact, would never—shed his Jewishness."[28]

In his relationship with a prejudiced president and public, Kissinger worked hard to anticipate and diffuse potential accusations about a world-wide Jewish conspiracy. On this issue he was in a permanently defensive position, ever fearful of the suspicion emanating from the Oval Office and other parts of society. Ironically, his attempts to preempt anti-Semitism compelled him to address the issue directly, rather than avoid it as he had in the past. In October 1973, when Kissinger (now secretary of state as well as NSC advisor) prepared to present a list of appointees to the U.S. Senate for confirmation, he noticed an overwhelming preponderance of Jewish names:

> *Kissinger:* I've got to reserve one position for a WASP on this. I know it takes 10 in the Jewish religion for a prayer service, but I can't have them all on the seventh floor [of the State Department]. One WASP. Am I entitled to that for congressional reasons?
>
> *Assistant Secretary of State David Abshire:* I'm trying. I've just come up with the wrong names.
>
> *Kissinger:* Well, you got me [Joseph] Sisco; can you imagine the line-up on the seventh floor—Kissinger, Sisco, [Helmut] Sonnenfeldt, [Henry] Wallich?
>
> *Abshire:* You want people to keep a sense of humor.
>
> *Kissinger:* It's a talented country, but there is a limit. And maybe a Negro . . .
>
> *Abshire:* I'm going to the Baptist church to look around.[29]

Serving a president who expressed anti-Semitic sentiments, Kissinger had to emphasize his Jewishness in some settings, to prevent its exploitation in others. The reference to African Americans in this context also shows that Kissinger felt pressure not just from those who distrusted Jews, but also from activists who sought to diversify foreign policy by limiting the number of people in office who looked like Kissinger, at least in terms of perceived skin color. Confronted with calls for more black appointees, he responded: "I feel embarrassed being Jewish; I know how it feels to be discriminated against. I feel embarrassed to say we have hired more black ambassadors—more deputy assistant secretaries; I think it sounds patronizing."[30]

Kissinger found himself in a very precarious position. He had to deflect popular presumptions of Jewish treachery. He also had to address growing criticisms of insufficient minority representation in the U.S. Foreign Service. Nixon's appeals to the anti-Semitic and racist attitudes within the "silent majority" encouraged attention to these issues. In this context, Kissinger could not sidestep the emerging ethnic-group politics of the 1970s. For an outsider who had climbed to power by avoiding direct discussion of his background, an explicit defense of Jewish loyalty was painful, despite its obvious correctness. For an immigrant who had benefited from the privileging of German Jews following the Second World War, building bridges with other minority groups sounded good in theory, but it proved unworkable in practice. Kissinger's experiences emphasized vertical mobility, ascending American society by appealing to mainstream white figures—the William Elliotts and Nelson Rockefellers. He avoided horizontal links to less successful outsider groups, especially African Americans. Kissinger had neither the experience nor the disposition to bring foreign policy into line with the transformed landscape of American politics after the Civil Rights Movement. Nixon's personal prejudices and political manipulations only deepened Kissinger's difficulties.[31]

The president and his chief foreign-policy aide defined their relationship in response to the crisis they perceived around them. They struggled to govern a society torn apart by a failed foreign intervention and what Nixon called a "war at home." They both sought to rebuild national authority, but they did not act in unison. Quite the contrary: Nixon and Kissinger were more rivals than partners, more antagonists than friends. The sense of crisis that brought them together also made them suspicious, resentful, and insecure. They were outsiders who, despite the invective they hurled at the establishment, distrusted other outsiders.[32]

Nixon empowered a Jew with remarkable skills to guide his foreign policy, but he did not like doing that. Kissinger played the role of sycophantic advisor to a mercurial president, and he did not like that either. Together they transformed the White House into more of a gangster den than a place for considered policy deliberation. They expended inordinate time and energy conspiring against enemies, including themselves. This was the imperial presidency in action.[33]

Nixon and Kissinger became mutual dependents. They needed each other, despite their contrary inclinations. Nixon relied on his brilliant and energetic aide to manage his foreign policies. Kissinger required a strong president to give him the power to pursue controversial initiatives. Their relationship was built on fear and frustration. Their policies were built on obsessions with toughness and secrecy. For Kissinger, the bright optimism of Rockefeller's presidential campaign mutated into the dark intrigue of Nixon's White House. This environment left little room for the statesmanship promised by Kissinger's grand strategy.

Credible Force

Nixon and Kissinger inherited a mess in Vietnam. Writing less than a decade after he assumed his duties in the White House, Kissinger remembered:

> When we came into office over a half-million Americans were fighting a war ten thousand miles away. Their numbers were still increasing on a schedule established by our predecessors. We found no plans for withdrawals. Thirty-one thousand had already died. Whatever our original war aims, by 1969 our credibility abroad, the reliability of our commitments, and our domestic cohesion were alike jeopardized by a struggle in a country as far away from the North American continent as our globe permits.

Despite evidence that the military situation was improving for the United States, the new administration was "determined to end our involvement in Vietnam."[34]

Throughout the 1960s Kissinger had defended America's commitment to South Vietnam, but at the end of the decade he had also joined a chorus of opinion advocating a negotiated settlement to the war. In line with his broad strategic vision, Kissinger called for a combination of more effective military force, multilateral diplomacy involving the big regional powers, and serious proposals for compromise among the belligerents. As early as 1965 he explained that negotiations would "begin a new phase of the struggle rather than mark its end. The stakes remain high and the conduct of affairs grows more complicated because it depends on so many intangibles. Negotiations require as careful and thoughtful preparation as do our military campaigns." Negotiations were not an alternative to the use of force, but an opportunity to coordinate military and political capabilities—more firepower and more diplomatic maneuver.[35]

Although he believed that the United States could improve its military performance, Kissinger argued that the nation could not "win" in Vietnam by destroying the region with unremitting force. Brutality on this scale would further inflame domestic opinion. It would also antagonize neighboring China, as well as the Soviet Union. Kissinger vividly remembered the experience of the Korean War two decades earlier, when reckless expansion of the conflict had sparked nearly three years of bloody fighting between American and Chinese soldiers, with the looming danger of nuclear escalation. Washington had to pursue a negotiated solution in Vietnam that avoided this dangerous course, while also preserving American strength. Force alone would not do the job.[36]

The United States could not shoot its way to victory, but it could not pick up tail and run either. For more than a decade, Washington had been the primary sponsor of South Vietnam. American leaders of both political parties had argued that success in the Cold War required an effective stand against communist expansion in Southeast Asia. Vietnam was a strategic fulcrum for the future of Asia, and it was a testing ground for American claims about containment. Efforts to transform South Vietnam into a vibrant capitalist economy during the 1960s further enhanced the U.S. stake in the region. If Washington admitted failure in South Vietnam, it would become harder for leaders to justify the pursuit of communist containment and capitalist transformation elsewhere. Perceiving weakness in U.S. determination, adversaries would become more likely to challenge America's assertions across the globe.

Even critics of the war recognized that an ignominious departure from Vietnam would undermine the nation's Cold War standing. Adlai Stevenson, the standard-bearer of the liberal wing in the Democratic party, captured this ambivalence when he told Lyndon Johnson: "I shudder at getting too deeply involved there [in Vietnam], and everybody thinks that's the only alternative. . . . I've been shuddering on this thing for three years, and I am afraid we're in a position now where you don't have any alternative, and it's a hell of an alternative. It really gives me the shakes."[37]

Kissinger and Stevenson were not far apart in their basic approach to Vietnam. Kissinger was appalled by the disaster the war had become for the United States, and he sought to end it. This was easier said than done. "We could not," Kissinger explained, "simply walk away from an enterprise involving two administrations, five allied countries, and thirty-one thousand dead as if we were switching a television channel." Millions of Americans "opposed" the Vietnam War after 1968, but only a fraction of the public supported immediate and unconditional withdrawal. The strategic and ideological stakes were too high, even for those who wanted instant relief.[38]

American leaders struggled to preserve the nation's "credibility" as they accepted a major setback—perhaps the most damaging U.S. military experience in the twentieth century. They emphasized the importance of displaying continued resolve to defeat threatening enemies, and continued commitment to support loyal friends. The experiences of appeasement before the Second World War loomed large, when the fascist dictators came to believe their adversaries were weak and irresolute. Men like Hitler acted on this assumption and initiated a global conflagration. Policymakers from all backgrounds in the Cold War feared that evidence of American weakness in Vietnam would have a similar effect.[39]

The United States had to appear willing and able to deploy overwhelming force if it wished to forestall the need to use it. Threats of U.S. retaliation underpinned deterrence of communist aggression, especially in Europe and Asia. In order to avoid fighting everywhere, Washington had to frighten its adversaries, convincing them that they faced a crushing response if they challenged local American vulnerabilities in places like West Berlin and South Korea. Although the United States was the most powerful nation in the world, it relied on intimidation (the prospect of force) as much as on the actual use of force to protect its extensive interests. The perceived willingness to fight ferociously was necessary for war avoidance. Any apparent slackening in Washington's ability to fight, as in Vietnam, made it more difficult for the nation (and the Western alliance as a whole) to maintain an intrepid posture against challengers. Credibility was about appearing tough, and even brutal when necessary. It was about showing that American leaders would fulfill their commitments and put their force to use.

Thomas Schelling, Kissinger's former colleague at Harvard, explained the importance of credibility—what he called "face"—most effectively in the late 1960s: "If one side yields on a series of issues, when the matters at stake are not critical, it may be difficult to communicate to the other just when a vital issue has been reached. . . . It is undoubtedly true," Schelling admitted, "that false pride often tempts a government's officials to take irrational risks or to do undignified things—to bully some small country that insults them, for example. But there is also the more serious kind of 'face,' the kind that in modern jargon is known as a country's 'image,' consisting of other countries' beliefs (their leaders' beliefs, that is) about how the country can be expected to behave." Anticipating Kissinger's position on the Vietnam War, Schelling argued:

> If the question is raised whether this kind of "face" is worth fighting over, the answer is that this kind of face is one of the few things worth fighting over. Few parts of the world are intrinsically worth the risk of serious war by themselves, especially when taken slice by slice, but defending them or running risks to protect them may preserve one's commitments to action in other parts of the world and at later times. "Face" is merely the interdependence of a country's commitments; it is a country's reputation for action, the expectations other countries have about its behavior.[40]

As much as Americans might have wished otherwise, the nation's credibility (its "face") was deeply entangled with developments in Vietnam after more than a decade of intervention. For the United States to withdraw from the region and at the same time maintain its credibility as a superpower, it needed a settlement that recognized American strength, not weakness. Achieving this objective required combining serious negotiation efforts with increased military pressure on North Vietnam. "Our military effort leaves a great deal to be desired," Kissinger wrote the president, "but it remains one of our few bargaining weapons." The administration's emerging "game plan" called for escalated attacks on enemy positions. Nixon wanted to "crack them pretty hard" with massive air strikes: "My inclination is to crack this one, and crack another one—plenty of places to hit." Nixon would send a signal of toughness to the world. Everyone, especially the North Vietnamese and their supporters in Moscow and Beijing, should "know that there's still a lot of snap left in the old boys."[41]

Air power offered the perfect mechanism for reducing American casualties and maintaining the credibility of U.S. force. Nixon blew hard about his desire to "*punish* the enemy in ways that he will really hurt. . . . I want you to get this spirit inculcated in all hands and particularly I want the military to get off its back side," he ordered Kissinger.

> I think we have had too much of a tendency to talk big and act little. This was certainly the weakness of the Johnson Administration. . . . We have the power to destroy [the North Vietnamese] war making capacity. The only question is whether we have the *will* to use that power. What distinguishes me from Johnson is that I have the *will* in spades. . . . For once, I want the military and I want the NSC staff to come up with some ideas on their own which will recommend *action* which is very *strong, threatening,* and *effective.*[42]

The president lashed out about his qualities as a tough guy. Kissinger had the difficult task of translating that sentiment into daily policy. He had to manage his boss, and he took the blame when toughness did not produce the desired outcomes. He also had to manage the Paris negotiations among the main belligerents—the North Vietnamese and South Vietnamese governments, the National Liberation Front for South Vietnam (the "Vietcong"), and the United States—as well as ongoing discussions with the Soviet Union. Kissinger calibrated Nixon's gangsterlike pronouncements for various international audiences. Here again, his cosmopolitanism and his network of foreign contacts were invaluable assets.

Mixing Nixon's invocations of toughness with diplomacy and force, Kissinger devised a three-point strategy. First, the White House would make it clear through public statements, private negotiations, and unilateral actions that it wanted to withdraw from Vietnam. The Nixon administration began reducing the American troop presence in the region soon after taking office, announcing the first removal of 25,000 soldiers ("Vietnamization" of the war) in June 1969. Second, Washington would enlist support from the Soviet Union and other nations to help the United States achieve favorable settlement terms. Kissinger would condition better relations with Moscow on the Kremlin's assistance in ending the war. Third, and most important, Nixon and Kissinger would display a disposition to act creatively—often in violation of the normal limits on American action. They would transcend the rules of the Cold War and fight on their own terms if their enemies did not respect their wishes. This was a strategy of movement, uncertainty, and hope—in contrast to the policy stalemate of the late 1960s.[43]

Nixon had spoken of a "madman" approach to intimidating his adversaries, but the administration's Vietnam strategy was a more intricate and explicit application of Kissinger's long-standing thinking about foreign policy. Since the end of the Second World War American leaders had alternated between the use of overwhelming force and the pursuit of negotiations. In the Korean War, for example, President Truman had initially orchestrated a strong response to communist aggression, then accepted a more passive approach after fighting bogged down and cease-fire discussions began. President Johnson had applied the same methods to Vietnam, initially escalating American operations in response to enemy attacks, then curtailing bombing operations for the sake of negotiations. Kissinger broke out of these rules for limited war. More than Nixon, he pursued creative and flexible uses of American capabilities for the purpose of encouraging a mutually beneficial settlement.[44]

Applying his own writings as well as those of Thomas Schelling and others, Kissinger attempted to assert new leverage over events surrounding Vietnam. His approach presumed that war fighting and diplomatic negotiation were integrated activities, part of the larger bargaining process that constituted military conflict. Kissinger emphasized the importance of seizing the initiative rather than merely containing the enemy. Like Bismarck, he sought to bring transformative leadership and action to a moment of crisis. Nixon called this the "big play," but Kissinger saw it as a deeper reflection of the statesman's role in imagining a new future—a "conceptual" shift. Nixon was concerned primarily with ending the Vietnam War on favorable terms for political purposes; Kissinger sought to remake the international system and the global positioning of the United States. Nixon focused on military and political tactics; Kissinger sought to address "the generally deteriorating strategic position of the United States" on a worldwide scale. Nixon was the pragmatist, Kissinger the revolutionary.[45]

Kissinger's effort to shape an international revolution reflected his accumulated thinking about politics and foreign policy since he fled Nazi Germany. He focused considerable energy on formulating new military options for the United States. Traditional modes of behavior in a moment of crisis were self-defeating. A strong leader, according to Kissinger, was one who created new instruments of power for new challenges. In the context of the Vietnam War, this meant a rejection of the generally accepted confines for American activities.

In addition to the conventional bombing of North Vietnamese targets, the napalm attacks on Vietcong-controlled villages in the South, and the efforts to "pacify" the countryside, Kissinger advocated expanding American operations into neighboring states—particularly Cambodia. The Johnson administration had already begun some limited raids against enemy "sanctuaries" across the border, but "Operation Breakfast" made it clear that the White House would now bring overwhelming force against communist forces operating in neutral countries. Washington would no longer allow its adversaries to hide behind claims of sovereignty, and it would no longer deploy its air power with careful restraint. In the year after the Cambodia bombings began in March 1969, the United States launched 3,650 B-52 strikes, dropping 110,000 tons of TNT on this nonbelligerent nation. On 30 April 1970, Nixon announced that in addition to the air strikes, 31,000 American soldiers had entered Cambodia to pursue North Vietnamese forces. Kissinger expressed some reservations about this escalation of ground operations—and two of his assistants, Roger Morris and Anthony Lake, resigned in protest—but he had strongly encouraged the president to seize control of the war by widening the terrain for American force. This was a calculated set of measures designed to send a "signal that things might get out of hand." Kissinger expected that the North Vietnamese and their supporters in Moscow and Beijing would now find themselves on the defensive.[46]

Conventional military raids into neutral territory were not enough. The attacks on Cambodia had a minimal effect on North Vietnamese fighting strength. Kissinger also sought to expand the range of weapons in play. He returned to his calls for the United States to make its nuclear arsenal useful for diplomatic purposes. Kissinger did not advocate launching a nuclear attack, but he pushed for creative maneuvers with these weapons to frighten and cajole adversaries. This was a strategy of aggressive nuclear posturing and calculated risk-taking. It was an attempt to convert the prospect of total destruction into daily leverage over faraway events.

In October 1969 Kissinger applied his ideas about nuclear posturing to the pursuit of a settlement in Vietnam. President Nixon demanded a negotiated cessation to the war by the end of the year; otherwise he would unleash a new set of massive and unprecedented attacks on North Vietnam. On Nixon's instructions, Kissinger warned Soviet ambassador Anatoly Dobrynin: "the train had just left the station and was now headed down the track." Dobrynin and other observers assumed that "the train" referred to a prospective escalation of conventional forces, particularly aerial bombardments. Kissinger, however, encouraged the president to add a series of nuclear maneuvers to his conventional threats. He did not intend to initiate nuclear war over Vietnam, but to shock the Soviet leadership into pursuing a peace settlement for fear of dire and unpredictable consequences. Kissinger attempted to create the prospect of "irrational" American behavior, in line with Nixon's vague remarks about adopting a "madman" posture. Kissinger devised a method for calibrating feigned madness to U.S. nuclear capabilities and the demands of the Vietnam War. As in the widening of the conflict into Cambodia, Kissinger sought to send a "signal that things might get out of hand."[47]

On the morning of 6 October 1969, Kissinger triggered planning for American nuclear maneuvers when he asked Secretary of Defense Melvin Laird to increase the nation's preparations for war so that "the other side" will "pick this up." Later that evening Nixon ordered Laird to "initiate a series of increased alert measures designed to convey to the Soviets an increasing readiness by U.S. strategic forces." Nixon's charges were vague. Kissinger had to transform these cryptic comments into a specific set of actions. The president wanted to appear tough, but his NSC advisor had to figure out how to do this effectively with nuclear weapons. Kissinger and his assistant, General Alexander Haig, pressed the military bureaucracy to assemble a proposal that would

1. "be discernible to the Soviets and be both unusual and significant"
2. "not be threatening to the Soviets"
3. "not require substantial additional funding or resources"
4. "not require agreement with the allies"
5. "not degrade essential missions"
6. "have minimum chance of public exposure"[48]

Senior military planners resisted this scheme because it violated standard assumptions about nuclear deterrence and diverted American resources from other planned exercises and activities. It also appeared unlikely to frighten U.S. adversaries. Lieutenant General Robert Pursley, Secretary of Defense Laird's military aide, explained that without a real mobilization for nuclear war, this isolated act would look like a bluff—a "sham." Pursley attempted to convince Kissinger and Haig that they should find other ways of meeting the president's demand for symbolic acts of toughness.[49]

These objections gave Kissinger a compelling reason to call off the nuclear maneuvers, but he pushed forward. More than the president, the NSC advisor believed that nuclear weapons could compel favorable behavior around Vietnam. In particular, he anticipated that a strong signal of mounting frustration and potential belligerence in the White House would convince the Kremlin to help end the war on acceptable American terms. It would also set a precedent for constructive nuclear diplomacy in the future, rather than passive nuclear deterrence. Kissinger's thinking drew on ideas he had articulated as early as the mid-1950s and had continued to advocate through three different presidential administrations. In 1969 he now had the opportunity, for the first time, to put these ideas into action.

On 9 October Kissinger recommended that Nixon approve a series of specific nuclear maneuvers, including:

1. Communications silence in selected Strategic Air Command and Polaris nuclear submarine commands
2. Cessation of regular combat aircraft exercises in select areas
3. Increased surveillance of Soviet ships en route to North Vietnam
4. Increased ground alert actions for Strategic Air Command bombers and tankers
5. Dispersal of Strategic Air Command aircraft with nuclear weapons to forward positions[50]

Nixon approved these recommended actions. Together they constituted a nuclear alert—preparations for a possible use of nuclear weapons against the Soviet Union. The alert did not make a nuclear attack likely, but it did reduce the time and preparation Washington would need to launch its weapons, if the president gave the order. Most significant, actions of this kind surely elicited the attention of the Soviet military, and they must have raised questions about American intentions. That was Nixon and Kissinger's objective: to sow uncertainty in the minds of Moscow's leaders, and thus encourage them to accommodate the United States in Vietnam for the sake of international stability.[51]

Before its termination on 30 October, the nuclear alert included the loading of thermonuclear weapons on B-52 aircraft stationed at March Air

Force Base in southern California and Fairchild Air Force Base in Washington State. Nuclear-armed B-52s flew eighteen-hour missions over the northern polar cap, toward the Soviet border, in a pattern they would use if they were indeed launching a nuclear strike. These were dangerous missions that could have initiated a direct clash between Washington and Moscow, especially if a nuclear-armed aircraft strayed into Soviet airspace or crashed near Soviet territory. Observers in the Kremlin also might have misconstrued this alert as the real thing. Fortunately that did not happen. Kissinger's calculated nuclear risk-taking did not have immediate policy costs.[52]

It did not produce positive results either. Kissinger expected that Soviet ambassador Dobrynin would refer to the nuclear alert and become more accommodating. These responses never materialized. Nonetheless, Kissinger continued to advocate the repositioning of nuclear weapons, as well as occasional nuclear threats, to throw adversaries off balance. He remained convinced that nuclear weapons could serve diplomatic purposes, intimidating enemies and encouraging favorable negotiations.[53]

Confronting the frustrating limits on American leverage in Vietnam, Kissinger reaffirmed his long-standing belief that the nation's overwhelming military power, including its nuclear arsenal, "is no better than the willingness to use it." Seeking to extricate the United States from a self-defeating war and to preserve the nation's credibility, Kissinger attempted to bolster the American negotiating position by growling and flexing the nation's muscles even while offering adversaries an outreached hand. He followed the same script in October 1973, when, threatened by the prospect of Soviet intervention in the Middle East, he raised the U.S. nuclear-alert status to "DefCon III"—the highest state of readiness in peacetime—while also encouraging political cooperation between Washington and Moscow. This was precisely the strategy Kissinger had long advocated; it was precisely the opposite of the "peace policies" endorsed by good democrats in the 1930s and the 1960s.[54]

Domestic protest over the Vietnam War and other deployments of American force convinced Kissinger that he had to pursue his maneuvers in secrecy, without public accountability. This conviction explains the curious organization of the October 1969 nuclear alert as an action that would be obvious to Soviet officials, but hidden from American citizens. Drawing on his experiences in Germany during the 1930s and in the United States during the late 1960s, Kissinger believed that democratic citizens were not prepared to manage the necessary uses of military power, especially during a period of extreme political turbulence. His policies of escalation in Vietnam attempted to end the war, as many protesters demanded, without diminishing America's global position, as many protesters hoped. This was more than just a matter of strategy for Kissinger; it was a reflection of his own personal history as a German Jewish immigrant to the United States:

> The principles of America's honor and America's responsibility were not empty phrases to me. I felt them powerfully. I had been born in Germany in the Bavarian town of Fürth, six months before Hitler's attempted beerhall putsch in Bavaria's capital, Munich. Hitler came to power when I was nine years old. . . . Until I emigrated to America, my family and I endured progressive ostracism and discrimination. My father lost the teaching job for which he had worked all his life; the friends of my parents' youth shunned them. I was forced to attend a segregated school. . . . Even when I learned later that America, too, had massive problems, I could never forget what an inspiration it had been to the victims of persecution, to my family, and to me during cruel and degrading years. I always remembered the thrill when I first walked the streets of New York City. Seeing a group of boys, I began to cross to the other side to avoid being beaten up. And then I remembered where I was.

Connecting his personal history to his policymaking in Vietnam, Kissinger criticized the "self-hatred" of many protesters in the late 1960s. Despite American misdeeds in Vietnam, he still believed he had to defend the nation's global position for "its idealism, its humanity, and its embodiment of mankind's hopes." Kissinger had a responsibility, as he saw it, "to help end the war in a way compatible with American self-respect and the stake that all men and women of goodwill had in America's strength and purpose. It seemed to me important," Kissinger explained, "for America not to be humiliated, not to be shattered, but to leave Vietnam in a manner that even the protesters might later see as reflecting an American choice made with dignity and self-respect."[55]

Kissinger was defending his American dream in Vietnam—his salvation as a Jewish immigrant from Nazism, his coming of age in the U.S. Army, his rise as a postwar intellectual, and his power as a Cold War policymaker. His American dream was threatened by international communists *and* by domestic critics who sought to undermine the very institutions that made his career possible—the Army, the universities, and the government. To defend the moral vision he attached to the power of the American state, Kissinger implemented foreign policies that excluded public interference and accountability. He often acted against what he saw as dangerous domestic opinion. To do otherwise, in his eyes, would repeat the mistakes of the democratic purists in the 1930s and bow to the weaknesses and extremes of mass politics. For Kissinger, the American dream was too important to be left to the people protesting in the streets.[56]

The Soviet Back Channel

Diplomacy, as Kissinger saw it, was also too delicate a matter for public oversight. He had little experience with the pomp and circumstance of formal ambassadorial work, but he was a seasoned practitioner of behind-the-scenes discussions. From his years directing the International Seminar at Harvard and his work as an advisor to Kennedy, Rockefeller, and Johnson, Kissinger excelled at organizing diverse elites for common purposes. He brought unparalleled energy, drive, and resourcefulness to these endeavors. He was a natural bridge figure with an instinctive sense of how to build discrete connections between people.

Throughout his career Kissinger displayed a combination of perseverance and charm that wore down his interlocutors and made them feel attached to him. Mixing deference and wit with intellectual firepower, Kissinger knew how to "handle" people. Despite his short stature and dour appearance, he was a "larger-than-life personality" in direct meetings. He could impress the most jaded observer and manipulate the most guarded discussant.[57]

This behind-the-scenes role was hardly unique to Kissinger. Jews had long served in this position for monarchs, elected officials, and other leaders. Paradoxically, their valuable skills as bridge figures between societies made them unacceptable as holders of the most distinguished public offices in any nation; they did not appear sufficiently "American," "French," or "German." Instead, Jews operated as unseen advisors, shadow figures, secret agents. Kissinger defined his diplomacy in these terms—working in the shadows, away from public oversight and among a small group of individuals empowered in different societies. He approached international negotiations as he approached his career—with a commitment to strong and decisive leadership and a distrust of democratic institutions.

Upon entering office, Kissinger immediately moved to take diplomatic power away from the State Department and the Foreign Service—its traditional centers in the U.S. government—and transfer it to the NSC advisor, acting on behalf of the president. He emphasized a very tight concentration of decisionmaking in the White House, and he advocated the creation of secret links to elite figures abroad. Nixon and Kissinger would circumvent the public, Congress, and the basic government bureaucracy—all of which they distrusted. Instead, they would work nimbly with their foreign counterparts through a web of "back channels" that Kissinger managed.

The most important of these back channels led to the Soviet Union. This was America's main Cold War rival, and a government that exerted powerful influence over communist belligerents around the globe. Despite their ideological differences, Kissinger believed, Moscow and Washington shared interests in avoiding conflict and assuring international stability. In Vietnam, the "vital interests of the United States and the Soviet Union" were "not in conflict." Both superpowers had "a responsibility to keep it that way. Which is another way of saying we both have an interest in getting the war ended." Ending the war required frequent and productive Soviet-American negotiations. Instead of relying on containment and toughness alone, President Nixon pledged to "keep the lines of communication open . . . to recognize that great powers will differ and to insure that differences be resolved by peaceful means." The White House gave coordination and consultation with the Soviet Union high priority.[58]

Kissinger had long advocated diplomacy along these lines. He consistently criticized earlier leaders for having neglected the hard work of compromise with adversaries. As the United States displayed its willingness to use force, it also had to pursue negotiations to settle dangerous disputes. The two went hand in hand. This approach required nurturing personal relations between representatives from Moscow and Washington—individuals who could integrate the key issues confronting their societies, build mutual trust, and insulate their frank exchanges from political exploitation in the public sphere. The last concern was paramount in Kissinger's mind. Both he and the president feared that democratic pressures for moral clarity would undermine the necessary ambiguities, compromises, and half-measures involved with negotiation. Successful back channels had to be secret channels—secret, above all, from the American people. Previous presidents, especially Kennedy, had come to the same conclusion during moments of heightened crisis. Nixon and Kissinger elevated this practice to the central operating feature of their relations with the Soviet Union.[59]

Kissinger maneuvered to make himself the key American figure in the back channel with Moscow. After meeting briefly with Soviet ambassador Anatoly Dobrynin on 14 February 1969, he reported to Nixon that the Kremlin's representative appeared "eager to move forward on a broad front . . . to conduct his conversations in Washington with some person you designate who has your confidence, but who was not part of the diplomatic establishment." The implication was clear. Relations between Moscow and Washington could improve if they escaped traditional posturing, and nurtured close collaboration between designated figures who commanded influence but were not tied to entrenched policy interests. Henry Kissinger, not Secretary of State William Rogers, was the obvious American to fill this role.[60]

Dobrynin's memoirs indicate that he did not, in fact, suggest this special role for Kissinger or anyone else. The national security advisor took the initiative in proposing a back channel that subverted established diplomatic procedures. He positioned the Soviet and U.S. governments to accept it as a desirable method for circumventing public pressures. Dobrynin recounts that at Kissinger's urging, Nixon explained to him that handling relations through the State Department would "open to an excessively broad range of officials. This might occasionally cause unpredictable leaks of information. But there were questions that needed to be restricted to a very narrow circle, and for some questions that circle should be limited to the president alone, who would receive information via the channel of Kissinger and Dobrynin." The Soviet ambassador affirmed, according to Kissinger, that the Kremlin welcomed a "strictly confidential exchange on delicate and important matters" through the NSC advisor. Only a few weeks in office, Kissinger had changed the form of Soviet-American interactions.[61]

Substance followed form. In their frequent—often daily—conversations, Kissinger and Dobrynin exchanged information, tested ideas, and built trust between their respective leaders. Many conflicts remained unresolved, but an assumption of Soviet-American cooperation on basic international stability took shape. Kissinger spoke frankly with Dobrynin about American desires for an honorable withdrawal from Vietnam, a settlement to tensions in Europe, and a control on the spiraling arms race. Dobrynin also appeared to expand sincerely on Soviet desires for "peaceful coexistence" with the United States under Leonid Brezhnev's leadership. In an unprecedented manner, Moscow and Washington cooperated to implement agreements on the permanent division of Berlin (the Four Power Agreement), nuclear nonproliferation (the Nuclear Non-Proliferation Treaty), arms limitations (the Strategic Arms Limitation Treaty and the Anti-Ballistic Missile Treaty), security and cooperation in Europe (the Helsinki Accords), and even basic principles of international conduct.

Kissinger played a direct role in the negotiation of all these agreements, working as the bridge between the White House and the Kremlin. He used his position to smooth over differences, suggest compromises, and manipulate his Soviet and American interlocutors. He made negotiations an accepted part of relations between Moscow and Washington, as they

Kissinger orchestrated a sea-change in relations between the United States and the Soviet Union. He used "back channel" discussions with Moscow's representatives to set the stage for President Nixon's trip to the Soviet Union in May 1972. This summit produced the first Strategic Arms Limitation Treaty (SALT I) and an agreement on "basic principles" to encourage peace and cooperation in superpower relations. In this photograph, Nixon and Kissinger toast their accomplishments, with Soviet leader Leonid Brezhnev between them. (© Bettmann / CORBIS)

had not been before. As he had counseled in his writings during the previous decade, Kissinger replaced the icy superpower estrangement of containment with "irreversible" engagement between the two societies.[62]

This was the essence of Kissinger's détente strategy—an attempt to use superpower cooperation, rather than conflict, to manage the multiplying centers of power around the world. It involved continued deployments of force, but also extended negotiations. It emphasized international stability, but also encouraged new forms of collaboration among leaders. Most significant, détente reinforced hierarchy, expanding American and Soviet efforts to shape developments in different societies, to define appropriate behavior, and to designate chosen surrogates. None of this activity was entirely new, but back-channel deliberations on the future of the world facilitated these efforts. Although Kissinger pursued negotiations with the Soviet Union because of the limits on American power, détente greatly extended the claims of White House authority. It also excluded most citizens, including elected leaders, from the policymaking process. Congressmen, senators, and even expert-trained Foreign Service officers were not invited to participate in the Soviet back channel.[63]

Negotiating with North Vietnam

The North Vietnamese were also absent from the Soviet back channel. Kissinger assumed that the Kremlin exerted influence over Hanoi, but he recognized that this influence was limited. If he wished to combine force with diplomacy for an honorable end to the war, Kissinger had to negotiate directly with the leaders of North Vietnam. He made this point repeatedly before going to work for Nixon. In December 1968 Kissinger drew upon his French contacts with Hanoi to send the following message: "The Nixon administration is prepared to undertake serious talks. . . . If Hanoi wishes to communicate some of their general ideas prior to January 20, they will be examined with a constructive attitude and in strictest confidence." This was an invitation for secret negotiations in "good faith," with Kissinger acting as the president's personal representative. The NSC advisor did not inform Secretary of State William Rogers of these communications until the end of January 1969—more than a month after the fact.[64]

Peace talks among four groups—the United States, North Vietnam, South Vietnam, and the National Liberation Front for South Vietnam—

had already begun in Paris, but Kissinger wanted to avoid the complicated structure of these discussions and to engage his opposites from Hanoi one on one. He hoped that through secret talks he could mix promises, threats, and charm to obtain an honorable settlement to the war. He was also prepared to force an agreement on America's South Vietnamese allies, who opposed any reduction in support for what Kissinger clearly recognized as an unsustainable regime. Though he would later deny it, the NSC advisor received consistent information that Saigon could not sustain an American troop withdrawal. Kissinger hoped to use his secret talks with North Vietnam to forestall the collapse of the U.S.-supported regime as American troops withdrew. By 1971 he and Nixon would accept a "decent interval" between U.S. disengagement and a North Vietnamese takeover in the south. Secret talks with Hanoi would allow Kissinger to manage this process, preserving the image of American strength and credibility.[65]

On 22 May 1969 he initiated a secret channel for negotiations with North Vietnam, sending a message through his French contacts: "The President would like to exploit channels outside the current framework of the negotiations. Conceivably, delegates from the United States and Vietnam could meet outside the Paris framework to discuss the general principles of a solution." This was vintage Kissinger. He emphasized private discussions removed from normal diplomatic venues, in which he and a North Vietnamese representative would confer with minimal public interference. He also focused on "general principles," not on specific claims, hoping to articulate a common set of American and North Vietnamese interests that would provide a basis for the warring parties to reach agreement. The main question for Kissinger was not who had wronged whom, but how the two sides could devise a mutually beneficial settlement. This was the purpose of his proposed back channel with North Vietnam.[66]

Le Duc Tho, a member of the North Vietnamese leadership, took up Kissinger's offer for secret negotiations. The two men first met on 21 February 1970, and for the next three years they jousted over a mutually acceptable settlement to the war. They agreed on the virtues of a rapid American departure from Vietnam, but they differed significantly on the conditions for it. Kissinger pushed for a mutual withdrawal of U.S. and North Vietnamese forces from the south, accompanied by some provisions for national unification behind a popularly chosen government. Le Duc Tho rejected this proposal. In his first meeting with Kissinger he stated unequivocally: "We have won the war. You have failed." He would not accept any agreement that did not give the North Vietnamese and their allies the dominant position on the ground that they demanded.[67]

Kissinger proved unflappable in his response to Le Duc Tho's categorical statements. He did not dispute the North Vietnamese assessment of the war. Instead he appealed to Le Duc Tho's desire to end the conflict, and reminded him of Nixon's evident willingness to escalate the fighting. Kissinger also made a personal appeal, emphasizing his sincerity and his goodwill. He showed respect for North Vietnam's courage in battle, and he acknowledged the justice in Hanoi's criticisms of the "puppet" regime in Saigon. "I was very impressed by what you said," Kissinger told Le Duc Tho. "I would point out only that our assessment of the situation might be wrong, but it is sincere." This private deference, mixed with implied threats, was characteristic of Kissinger's negotiating style. It differed significantly from the White House's more belligerent public statements about the war.[68]

Kissinger avoided condescending to his counterpart. He approached Le Duc Tho as an equal—a political leader who had struggled against great odds, pursued what he perceived as the best interests of his people, and understood the difficulties of policymaking. Kissinger positioned himself as not only a representative of the United States, but also a bridge figure who could bring the warring parties together, often in spite of contrary inclinations within circles of the U.S. government. Kissinger was the insider with the president's ear, but he was an outsider to the missionary impulses and simple geopolitical judgments that had long characterized American approaches to Vietnam. When Le Duc Tho called Kissinger a "philosopher," he acknowledged that the NSC advisor had managed through his statements to transcend, in some small way, the hardened divisions between Washington and Hanoi. Le Duc Tho never spoke in the same way about the less cosmopolitan American figures who had attended earlier discussions.[69]

Kissinger did not dominate the negotiations with Le Duc Tho, but he "handled" him as he had done with powerful interlocutors since the 1950s. Although the two did not become trusted friends, they grew into negotiators who respected each other. They also developed a mutual interest in securing an agreement that would justify their long and tedious work, while promising their respective countries some relief from the fighting. Intensive discussions produced an unmistakable personal bond. During one of their sessions in late 1972, amidst laughter and fatigue, Le Duc Tho admitted: "you and I have made very great effort."[70]

The Nixon administration's escalation of the war did not make the North Vietnamese more accommodating at the negotiating table, but it did increase their desire for a temporary reduction in hostilities. One historian writes that by 1972 North Vietnamese leaders feared for the basic sustenance of their regime as intensified American bombings destroyed agriculture and industrial facilities. Through an uneasy combination of threat and deference, as well as sheer perseverance, Kissinger convinced Le Duc

Le Duc Tho (on the right) was the North Vietnamese leader with whom Kissinger negotiated most intensively. The two men met frequently from 1970 into 1973 for detailed, confidential, and often contentious discussions. Despite their differences, Kissinger and Le Duc Tho developed mutual respect. They also shared a commitment to negotiating a withdrawal of American forces from South Vietnam. They concluded a final agreement on 23 January 1973 and received the Nobel Peace Prize for their efforts. (© Bettmann / CORBIS)

Tho that it was imperative to help the United States save face in Vietnam. He made a diplomatic settlement something the North Vietnamese cared about.[71]

By the second half of 1972 both Kissinger and Le Duc Tho were anxious to conclude an agreement. Running for reelection, Nixon sought to position himself as the president who had extracted the nation from Vietnam. As the United States continued to bomb enemy positions, the White House drew down American forces stationed in South Vietnam; 23,516 U.S. soldiers remained at the end of 1972, in contrast to the half-million deployed when Nixon entered office. Kissinger pushed the North Vietnamese to make a deal at this moment, before the election. He also recognized that the troop reductions would soon diminish his military leverage.

North Vietnam felt similar pressure to negotiate a settlement. Le Duan, the general secretary of the ruling party in Hanoi, later admitted that the American bombing and mining of the port of Haiphong in May 1972 had "completely obliterated our economic foundation." The regime faced setbacks on the battlefield and confronted major shortages in basic resources. It also feared that Nixon, following his likely reelection, would have a stronger domestic mandate to prosecute the war. In this context, the Soviet Union and China might curtail their support for Hanoi. Kissinger was correct when he advised the president that "the North Vietnamese want a settlement if at all possible before our elections." After reaching a series of interim agreements with Le Duc Tho, on 26 October 1972 Kissinger dramatically announced to reporters: "peace is at hand."[72]

Despite concerted efforts, the negotiators did not hammer out a final settlement until early 1973. Resistance from their respective allies—the South Vietnamese government and the National Liberation Front for South Vietnam—scuttled an early agreement. The American-supported government in Saigon, under Nguyen Van Thieu, objected to provisions that allowed North Vietnamese forces to remain in the south after the United States departed. Hanoi's allies in the south objected to the maintenance of Thieu's government. Nixon and Kissinger escalated American bombing again in late December to place additional pressure on North Vietnam and to prove their commitment to Saigon. In the end, however, they jettisoned South Vietnam's objections. The North Vietnamese similarly sidelined the concerns of the National Liberation Front.[73]

On 23 January 1973 the Vietnam back channel reached fruition as Kissinger and Le Duc Tho initialed the "Paris Agreements." They included provisions for a cease-fire, the final departure of American soldiers, and an exchange of prisoners of war. The agreements left the Saigon government in place, but they also allowed North Vietnamese and National Liberation Front forces to maintain their positions in the south. The fighting between these groups intensified after the U.S. withdrawal. In a little more than two years the communists overran the South Vietnamese government, uniting the country under Hanoi's dominance. On 29 April 1975 the last American diplomatic personnel in Saigon, along with about 4,000 local allies, fled South Vietnam. The images of frightened Vietnamese surrounding the American embassy, grasping helplessly for the last departing U.S. helicopters, marked the conclusion of a nearly seven-year White House effort to end the war.[74]

This searing image of the last Americans fleeing Saigon by helicopter on 29 April 1975 led many Americans to question whether Kissinger's efforts really preserved U.S. power and credibility in the world. Some observers viewed this image as evidence of American weakness in the 1970s. (© CORBIS SYGMA)

President Gerald Ford, who had replaced Nixon in August 1974 after his resignation over the Watergate scandal, declared to a relieved public: "the war in Vietnam is over as far as America is concerned." Observers, however, had only begun to debate the efficacy of Kissinger's activities. In 1973 the Norwegian Nobel Committee jointly awarded Kissinger and Le Duc Tho the Nobel Peace Prize, citing their perseverance in negotiations. Henry Cabot Lodge Jr. congratulated Kissinger on "the miracles which you have wrought." Lodge went so far as to call for the Republican party to draft Kissinger as its next presidential candidate, despite constitutional prohibitions against foreign-born immigrants. Lodge extolled Kissinger's "superhuman" energy and his "brilliant intellect"—two characteristics that he had displayed during the tortuous negotiations with Le Duc Tho. Kissinger's old mentor Nelson Rockefeller also praised his former advisor's "miraculous" "handling of the Vietnam situation." In 1974 *Time* magazine used the Kissinger-as-magician imagery for its cover. Under the headline "How Henry Does It," the jowly German Jew pulled a dove from his hat as the leaders of the world watched passively. He was "the great Kissinger"—a virtuoso and an enigma at the same time.[75]

Not everyone agreed on the nature of Kissinger's greatness. Frank Snepp, a senior intelligence analyst for the CIA in Saigon who helped manage the American evacuation in 1975, condemned Kissinger's "penchant for the virtuoso performance." By centralizing all decisionmaking through his back channel, he lost touch with events on the ground. During his extended negotiations, more than 20,000 American soldiers died in action, and many more thousands of Vietnamese perished. Kissinger's conversations with Le Duc Tho responded to political pressures, especially from the antiwar movement in the United States, but they were strangely isolated from the realities on the ground in South Vietnam. The two men negotiated about the war, but they rarely grappled with the gruesome nature of the fighting. Kissinger, in particular, never seemed to question whether the national credibility he sought to preserve was worth the mounting human costs.[76]

The chaos and humiliation of the final U.S. departure from Saigon also raises questions about whether the prolonged disengagement, rather than a unilateral withdrawal, really contributed to American credibility. This judgment is very difficult to assess. The negotiations between Kissinger and Le Duc Tho coincided with increased Soviet and Cuban interventions throughout Africa. Leaders in Moscow, in particular, perceived a weakening in U.S. power and resolve, despite Kissinger's efforts. The image of the last Americans fleeing from Saigon in 1975 probably confirmed this analysis.[77]

The years after the end of the Vietnam War were a very difficult time for U.S. foreign policy. Kissinger's "miraculous" maneuvers were unable to halt an international slide in American influence. At home, protests became less common, but recriminations and controversies proliferated, especially after Nixon's forced resignation. Kissinger extracted the United

Henry Kissinger frequently appeared on the cover of popular magazines in the 1970s. He became one of the most recognized figures in the world. This *Time* magazine cover from 1 April 1974 captures his image as a magician, capable of superhuman feats that amazed international leaders and citizens alike. He also appears as an exotic, ethnic figure—awkward in his role as global celebrity. (Courtesy of Time & Life Pictures / Getty Images)

States from a nightmare conflict in Vietnam, but he did so in a way that reinforced the moral crisis Hamilton Fish Armstrong and others had identified at the start of the decade. Technical acumen in negotiations did not produce the promised conceptual breakthrough. Although Kissinger's back-channel diplomacy increased his tactical flexibility, fears of democratic weakness amidst pervasive domestic upheaval limited his strategic imagination. Hard though he tried, Kissinger never transcended the Vietnam War.

Personal Politics in China and the Third World

Kissinger's strategic vision had its most immediate revolutionary effects outside Vietnam—in China and parts of Latin America and Africa. Most observers separate these areas of policy because of their obvious geographic diversity. At first glance the famous "opening" to China appears to stand alone for political reasons as well. In his memoirs, Kissinger singles out his secret maneuvers with Beijing as "one giant step" that "transformed our diplomacy": "We had brought new flexibility to our foreign policy. We had captured the initiative and also the imagination of our own people." He does not say similar things about his policies in Latin America and Africa.[78]

China held a special place in Kissinger's strategic vision because of its size and its history. Despite his relative ignorance of the society, Kissinger understood its traditional role as a cultural magnet for much of Asia. China was a great civilization, with the will and wisdom to anchor regional stability. The excesses of the communist regime—particularly the devastating "Great Proletarian Cultural Revolution" of the late 1960s—were aberrations from what Kissinger perceived as China's natural position as a leader of Asia. "The Chinese," he explained, "are very impressive. They have a certain moral quality, which maybe makes them a peril."[79]

Like many other observers, Kissinger perceived China as a regional power, interested in "cooperation on the basis of congruent interests." The American withdrawal from Vietnam increased Beijing's relative stature. The communist regime had aided the North Vietnamese in their struggle against France and the United States. It gained security and respect from the forced departure of American forces near its southeastern border. In addition, Chinese tensions with the Soviet Union encouraged Beijing to assert its leadership over progressive world forces while seeking new partners—potentially even the United States—as allies in a possible war against Moscow. China was a sleeping giant beginning to awaken, fitfully, from a nightmarish slumber and regain its rightful place in the world.[80]

Kissinger sought to turn China's reemergence to American advantage by negotiating a limited partnership with the regime. He aimed to forge a personal bond between leaders that would provide a basis for trust and cooperation, insulated from the extremes of public rhetoric and political contention. A back channel to Beijing would allow for more effective management of conflicts in Asia, with less danger to American lives. It would also give Washington a new source of leverage over events. Instead of relying on anticommunist containment alone, the United States could work with the assistance of a leading communist state to shape the region.

This was precisely the diplomatic flexibility that Kissinger had advocated before he entered office, when he extolled the virtues of an international system with more centers of decision, and more points of entry for American influence. Returning to his extensive writings on the limits of U.S. military power, Kissinger explained: "This Administration is reducing its commitments and is reducing its anti-communist ideology, for example, with China." From his first months in office, Kissinger made a series of secret overtures to Beijing—many without Nixon's knowledge—in hopes of creating a useful back channel.[81]

These secret maneuvers were not limited to China. Kissinger pursued a consistent policy of building back channels with leaders of non-Western states whom he identified as potential American regional partners. This was his federalist grand strategy in action. The United States would curtail its direct military presence outside the transatlantic community, working closely with local authorities in the third world. Washington would shift its emphasis from the deployment of armed force, as in Vietnam, to the negotiation of diplomatic arrangements, often with unsavory but friendly figures. The White House nurtured dual power, using its resources to bolster and manipulate independent local authorities, rather than building its own governments from scratch. This was a policy of regime collaboration rather than regime change or nation-building. It followed Kissinger's earliest thoughts about defense of what he called the "grey areas," and it implemented his counsel for transforming American strategy in the wake of Vietnam:

> The United States is no longer in a position to operate programs globally; it has to encourage them. It can no longer impose its preferred solution; it must seek to evoke it. In the forties and fifties, we offered remedies; in the late sixties and in the seventies our role will have to be to contribute to a structure that will foster the initiative of others. We are a superpower physically but our designs can be meaningful only if they generate willing cooperation. We can continue to contribute to defense and positive programs, but we must seek to encourage and not stifle a sense of local responsibility. Our contribution should not be the sole or principal effort, but it should make the difference between success and failure. . . . Regional groupings supported by the United States will have to take over major responsibility for their immediate areas, with the United States being concerned more with the overall framework of order than with the management of every regional enterprise.[82]

Nixon announced this policy shift during his first year in office. Speaking to reporters in July 1969, he explained that the United States must avoid "that kind of policy that will make countries in Asia so dependent upon us that we are dragged into conflicts such as the one that we have in Vietnam." Describing what he later dubbed the "Nixon Doctrine," the president pledged to "reduce American involvement" in future regional conflicts. The White House encouraged independence, power, and initiative in friendly regimes. Regional partnerships now took priority over programs for development and democratization. Washington offered increased support to authoritarians—even communists—who guaranteed continued American influence. Overall, a division of responsibilities between the United States and its local allies replaced direct American intervention. A pragmatic focus on pliable agents assumed priority over ideological rigidity.[83]

Nixon's words focused on Asia, but for Kissinger this was a well-considered global strategy. He had come of age with grave doubts about the effectiveness of democracy as a guide for making policy. He was a believer in the central importance of Europe, and the inherited values of "Western civilization," to American society. The third world, including China, did not figure as a space for the extension of democracy or the defense of vital interests. It was a "grey area" where the United States had to project a powerful image and weaken potential enemies before they grew strong enough to challenge Washington where it really mattered. Militant regimes, including those in North Vietnam and North Korea, for example, were not dangers by themselves. If they were left unhindered, however, their growth and expansion—like those of the fascist governments before the Second World War—would imperil American security. They were emerging threats that had to be addressed through a combination of international diplomacy and local force.

The United States did not have a compelling reason to rule the third world, but it had a strong incentive to target aid against regional challengers. In Africa this strategy entailed an effort to work informally with the white South African government, despite its atrocious apartheid policies. Pretoria shared Washington's interest in controlling what Kissinger called a "revolutionary situation" among newly independent black states on the continent. When the Portuguese finally retreated from Angola and other parts of southern Africa in 1975, Kissinger encouraged President Ford to use covert aid as a mechanism for encouraging a "peaceful transition" to in-

Before 1975 Kissinger paid little attention to political developments in Africa. For all his contacts with international diplomats, throughout his career he had few interactions with African leaders. This photo shows a rare Kissinger meeting with ambassadors from the Organization of African Unity in August 1974. (Courtesy of National Archives, Washington, D.C.)

dependent governments that were "stable" and followed a "policy of cooperation and friendship with the United States."[84]

Kissinger made it clear that, in the case of Angola, this approach involved supporting a thuggish nationalist fighter, Jonas Savimbi, who was willing to work with the United States, South Africa, and even China. Savimbi strongly opposed the growing Cuban and Soviet influences in the region. Africa had become a cockpit of international conflict, with as many as 30,000 Cuban soldiers fighting on the continent and growing arms shipments from abroad. Amidst this postcolonial chaos, Kissinger felt compelled to identify a friendly influence. Hinging policy on abstract notions of democracy or good government made little sense. Kissinger acted to ensure that the United States did not lose leverage in the region as violence spread. "Look," he warned his staff; "a great country that cannot give military aid in these revolutionary situations is going to become irrelevant." South African soldiers helped protect American relevance in the region.[85]

In Latin America, Kissinger sought to assure American leverage against what he perceived as the growing influence of Fidel Castro's regime. Under his direction, Washington expanded its long-standing policy of supporting "moderate" regional figures who rejected Marxist influences, protected American-owned property, and cooperated with Washington. As political leaders emerged during the early 1970s to challenge these assumptions, especially Salvador Allende in Chile, Kissinger looked for strong and reliable alternatives. He found them in the Latin American armed forces, filled with ambitious men who were willing to use cold-blooded violence against their own people to repress reforms and empower themselves. Fully aware of these circumstances, Kissinger authorized U.S. officials to nurture back channels with military leaders as anchors for American influence. President Nixon confirmed this approach when he explained: "I will never agree with the policy of downgrading the military in Latin America. They are power centers subject to our influence."[86]

These military back channels repressed political openness in the name of regional stability. The United States provided covert support—including weapons, cash, and propaganda—for a coup against what Kissinger described as an elected "socialist State" in Chile. Without strong action, he warned, Allende would "consolidate his position and then move ahead against us." Nixon elaborated:

> If Chile moves as we expect and is able to get away with it—our public posture is important here—it gives courage to others who are sitting on the fence in Latin America. . . . No impression should be permitted in Latin America that they can get away with this, that it's safe to go this way. All over the world it's too much the fashion to kick us around. We are not sensitive but our reactions must be coldly proper. We cannot fail to show our displeasure. We can't put up with "Give Americans hell but pray they don't go away." There must be times when we should and must react, not because we want to hurt them but to show we can't be kicked around.[87]

Nixon and Kissinger did not orchestrate the assault that overthrew Allende's government in September 1973 and initiated a repressive military regime under Augusto Pinochet. They did, however, encourage and facilitate this action. Kissinger approved a series of CIA operations that included efforts to "sow dissension within the coalition of parties and individuals supporting Allende," "take advantage of Allende's weaknesses and sensitivity to direct criticism," and expand contacts "within the Chilean military forces." After the coup, CIA director William Colby confirmed: "U.S. policy has been to maintain maximum covert pressure to prevent the Allende regime's consolidation." CIA activities included "financial support totaling $6,476,166 for Chilean political parties, media, and private sector organizations opposed to the Allende regime." Colby contended that "the CIA played no direct role in the events which led to the establishment of the new military government," but the U.S. government was "instrumental in enabling opposition political parties and media to survive." Colby intentionally avoided a discussion of American cooperation with the Chilean military, which was also "instrumental" in the coup.[88]

Kissinger did not extol the domestic brutality and frequent cold-blooded viciousness of the regimes he supported in Chile, South Africa, and other parts of the third world. He did, however, nurture personal relations with their leaders as strongmen who could mobilize force effectively against threats to themselves and the United States. These were not "freedom fighters," but shady partners who could do America's dirty work. In 1976 Kissinger acknowledged the mass killings conducted by the military juntas in Chile, Argentina, and other Latin American countries that received Washington's aid, but he confidentially explained to Argentine foreign minister Cesar Guzzetti: "We have followed events in Argentina closely. We wish the new government well. We wish it will succeed. We will do what we can to help it succeed. We are aware you are in a difficult period. It is a curious time, when political, criminal, and terrorist activities tend to merge without any clear separation. We understand you must establish authority."[89]

Kissinger then went on to explain his commitment to assuring regional stability despite "crazy" public pressures for American disengagement: "A stable Argentina is of interest to the hemisphere. That has always been true. It is basic. . . . We do not want to harass you. I will do what I can. Of course, you understand, that means I will be harassed. But I have discovered that after the personal abuse reaches a certain level you become invulnerable."[90]

Political "harassment" of White House policies in the 1970s increased the incentives for Kissinger to work with regional dictators. They were reliable alternatives to direct U.S. intervention. Their departures from democratic governance in fact made it easier for them to accomplish what more consensual regimes could not in the light of intense public scrutiny. Secret arrangements with figures like Zhou Enlai in China, Augusto Pinochet in Chile, and John Vorster in South Africa helped skirt what Kissinger perceived as the limits on American power, especially during a period of domestic turmoil. These leaders would act as regional "policemen," enforcing common rules negotiated between their governments and the White House. "We face," Kissinger explained to South Africa's foreign minister in 1973, "a tragic situation in a world that reverberates with shibboleths of political and social doctrines. . . . I will curb any missionary zeal on the part of my officers in the State Department to harass you." Kissinger later confided that, in his eyes, South Africa and the United States faced similar problems at home and abroad, "although employing different tactics."[91]

"Different tactics" reflected a division of international responsibility between indirect American support for regional stability and local applications of force to ensure that end. This arrangement distanced Kissinger and other American officials from the violence and human degradation that they bankrolled. In his memoirs, Kissinger vehemently denies any personal responsibility for the 1973 coup in Chile, the "dirty wars" against dissidents in Latin America, the prolonged life of apartheid in South Africa, and the continued brutality of communist rule in China during the Nixon and Ford administrations. In all of these cases, Kissinger did not control local events, and he did not determine outcomes. He did, however, attach American policy in the third world to a set of brutal dictators who could wield regional force in ways that served U.S. international interests, often with grave human costs for their societies. This was a trade-off that Kissinger knowingly made, believing that he had to protect America's global standing while simultaneously addressing domestic opposition to U.S. force. Faced with what he viewed as a popular revolution against a strong and effective foreign policy, Kissinger created his own revolution in directing power toward selected dictators.

The citizens of Chile, Argentina, South Africa, China, and other countries suffered the extremes of this revolution as the United States benefited

Fearful of Cuban and Soviet influence in Chile, Kissinger provided support for coup plotters who brought Augusto Pinochet to power in September 1973. Pinochet oversaw one of the most brutal dictatorships in Latin America during the 1970s. Despite calls from many activists and politicians to place intensive pressure on Pinochet for human rights reforms, Kissinger maintained friendly U.S. relations with this violent regime. (© Bettmann / CORBIS)

from greater regional leverage on the cheap. Instead of deploying half a million soldiers to Southeast Asia, Washington now sent bags of cash and caches of weapons to Augusto Pinochet and his third-world counterparts. Pinochet used these American-provided resources to conduct a domestic reign of terror. One historian of Chile explains: "The repression in Chile was large in scale and layered in its implementation. In a country of only 10 million people in 1973, individually proved cases of death or disappearance by state agents (or persons in their hire) amount to about 3,000; torture victims run in the dozens of thousands; documented political arrests exceed 82,000; the exile flow amounts to about 200,000. These are lower-end figures, suitable for a rock-bottom baseline." They are also figures with depressing parallels in Argentina and other third-world allies of the United States.[92]

Resisting congressional limitations on aid to regimes practicing domestic terror, Kissinger told Pinochet: "we are sympathetic with what you are trying to do here. I think that the previous government was headed toward Communism. We wish your government well. At the same time, we face massive domestic problems, in all branches of government, especially Congress, but also in the Executive, over the issue of human rights. As you know, Congress is now debating further restraints on aid to Chile. We are opposed . . . we don't want to intervene in your domestic affairs."[93]

Kissinger did not invent this policy. During the Cold War the United States frequently worked with anticommunist dictators. Kissinger reduced the importance of anticommunism, emphasizing international stability and American influence at least as much. He also made support for third-world strongmen more central to U.S. foreign policy. Programs for economic development and democratization now received minimal support from the White House. After Kissinger became secretary of state in 1973, the State Department also turned against these initiatives. Personalized politics and a regional division of responsibilities transformed the United States from an inconsistent advocate of third-world political reform into a consistent supporter of local muscle. "Statesmanship," in this context, amounted to leadership through the barrels of hired guns.

Human Rights

Resistance within the third world, the United States, and western Europe to Kissinger's "statesmanship" inspired a flowering of human rights activism—at the very same time that he disparaged these claims in conversations with Pinochet and others. The atrocities committed by American allies, combined with the images of suffering from the Vietnam War, raised broad international concern about the human effects of foreign policy in the 1970s. The brutalities in Chile had particular resonance because of the cosmopolitan community that had resided there before the coup. Residents of Chile had strong familial and professional connections to other countries, including the United States and Spain. They used their personal networks to circulate information about Pinochet's oppression and to condemn Kissinger's support for the regime. The flight of 200,000 political exiles from Chile gave the news of the death squads an immediacy that could not be ignored.

As refugees from Nazi hatred in the 1930s had entered the U.S. Army and other state institutions to combat fascism, refugees from third-world brutality in the 1970s found a home in nongovernmental organizations. From 1974 through 1976, for example, membership in Amnesty International, one of the leading nongovernmental human rights groups, grew from 3,000 to 50,000. Pepe Zalaquette is representative of many of these new activists. He escaped from Chile in 1976, joined the board of directors of Amnesty International USA, and eventually served on its international executive committee. Joe Eldridge, a Methodist minister working in Chile at the time of the coup, is another representative from the new network of activists. "Human rights entered my vocabulary on September 11, 1973," he recalled, "when it was suddenly denied to one-third of the Chilean population. That was a watershed. That defining moment has sustained my vision of what abuses of human rights are about. It has driven me." Eldridge moved to Washington, D.C., where he served as director of the Washington Office on Latin America—one of the many human rights organizations that sprouted into existence during Kissinger's years in power.[94]

These new advocates made their presence felt in the media, on college campuses, and especially before congressional committees. They provided, in the words of two supporters, "a bridge between the massive activism of the Vietnam War years" and subsequent opposition to White House policies. By 1975 they succeeded in procuring two major congressional restrictions on U.S. aid to Chile: the Kennedy Amendment of December 1974, which limited military and later economic assistance to the Pinochet government; and the Harkin Amendment of November 1975, which prohibited aid to regimes violating basic human rights. The Friends Committee on National Legislation, a long-standing lobby group with a strong interest in Latin America, wrote the initial language for the Harkin Amendment and coordinated its passage through Congress. By the mid-1970s nongovernmental organizations had found a powerful legislative mechanism for restricting White House policy.[95]

Human rights activists also gained a strong advocate in Senator Henry "Scoop" Jackson from Washington State. Though more focused on the Soviet Union, anticommunism, and his own presidential ambitions than most of the nongovernmental actors around Latin America, Jackson gave voice to criticisms of U.S. cooperation with oppressive leaders. He linked trade and assistance to evidence that foreign regimes were improving the treatment of their citizens. In the case of the Soviet Union, the senator demanded that the Kremlin allow more of its Jewish population to emigrate, in return for "most-favored-nation" trade arrangements with the United States. Kissinger had promised favored trade to Soviet leaders, but he had to backtrack with the passage of the Jackson-Vanik Amendment to the Trade Act of 1974. Jackson was a product and a producer of the popular human rights critique inspired by Kissinger's policies.[96]

Jackson and other members of Congress forced Kissinger to create a new position in the State Department for a "coordinator of human rights and humanitarian affairs," soon upgraded to assistant secretary of state for human rights. Public advocates in the 1970s helped the Senate Select Committee to Study Government Operations (the "Church Committee") publish two unprecedented reports detailing CIA covert activities in Chile. Kissinger had shaped public discussions about foreign policy during his first years in office, but now he found himself on the rhetorical defensive against human rights activists. They revised the public agenda.[97]

These attacks on American policy were, in Kissinger's judgment, a form of "isolationism"—"the proposition that we were too depraved to participate in international politics." Kissinger responded with a public-relations campaign centered on a series of "heartland speeches" that explained the moral purposes behind his activities. From the summer of 1975 through the summer of 1976, despite a grueling foreign travel schedule, Kissinger spoke to audiences in Milwaukee, Minneapolis, Cincinnati, Pittsburgh, Detroit, San Francisco, Dallas, Chicago, and Seattle. In Detroit he called on citizens

> to end the self-flagellation that has done so much harm to this nation's capacity to conduct foreign policy. It is time that we outgrew some of the illusions that characterized the long-past period of our isolationism: the idea that we are always being taken in by foreigners; the fear that military assistance to allies leads to involvement rather than substitutes for it; the pretense that defense spending is wasteful and generates conflict; the delusion that American intelligence activities are immoral; the suspicion that the confidentiality of diplomacy is a plot to deceive the public; or the illusion that tranquility can be achieved by an abstract purity of motive for which history offers no example.

Kissinger avoided the term "human rights." Referring to the controversy over American aid to third-world dictators, he argued: "We must maintain our defenses and a prudent program of economic and military assistance to other countries with whom we have productive political relations. . . . It is the responsibility of this nation to exercise creative leadership in a moment of uncertainty, in a world that cries out for inspiration."[98]

The invocation of moral purpose through force and diplomacy, and faith in strong leaders, were long-standing elements of Kissinger's thought. In defending his policies, he returned to these core beliefs—his basic worldview. Kissinger's words received favorable treatment in the press, but they failed to persuade his audience at home or his critics abroad. He admitted, in a somewhat self-serving manner, that after Vietnam and Watergate he could not satisfy the public's demand for an immediate moral cleansing: "we affirmed gradualism, the critics urged fulfillment."[99]

Mounting human rights criticisms of American foreign policy were symptomatic of a deeper shift in society. For Kissinger, an emerging transatlantic community at midcentury provided an engine for mobility and influence. His career reflected the growth of a powerful network of Cold War policy experts—men who thought in terms of a common "Western civilization" and the need to use force in its defense. For escaped third-world dissidents and sympathetic observers, a growing transnational community of discontented citizens offered an alternative avenue for recognition and publicity. Their activism in the 1970s and subsequent decades tracked the growth of a vibrant network that set itself against not just Kissinger's policies, but the social and political framework that made his career possible.

In August 1975 the successful multinational push for the codification of human rights in the Final Act of the Conference on Security and Cooperation in Europe ("the Helsinki Accords"), despite initial opposition from Washington and Moscow, symbolized the emerging power of new advocates. A rising political generation perceived the Cold War, and the assumptions that underpinned it, as sources of repression both inside and outside Europe. They identified Kissinger as the foremost representative of an inherited but now discredited worldview. The Jewish refugee from Nazi Germany was the old politics; the human rights activists who protested the Vietnam War, fled the violence of Latin America and Africa, and supported the Helsinki Accords were the new politics—or so it seemed at the time.[100]

Kissinger's policies reflected the accumulated wisdom and experience of his formative years. They were keyed to his early and lasting skepticism of democracy, his sense of cultural hierarchy, his faith in state power, and his fear of political chaos. These assumptions captured the personal concerns of a middle-class Jewish boy who witnessed virulent anti-Semitism and public passivity. They neglected, and frequently silenced, the very different concerns of peoples struggling against the legacies of colonialism, poverty, and exploitation—especially outside Europe. Kissinger's policies simultaneously hardened and drew attention to these struggles. He made human rights a prominent issue by so obviously excluding them from the language of his strategy. To the end of his career, he remained a German Jewish thinker focused on limits and "statesmanship," uncomfortable with the somewhat simplistic "rights talk" of the late twentieth century.[101]

The Kissinger Revolution in Retrospect

What can we say about Kissinger's policies in retrospect? Was he a war criminal, as some claim?[102]

Kissinger was, above all, a revolutionary. "History," he told reporter James Reston, "has, I think, placed me in a key position at a time when we are moving from the relics of the postwar period toward a new international structure." Kissinger used his intimate knowledge of the early Cold War to shape the future. As NSC advisor and secretary of state he transformed the conduct of foreign policy in enduring ways.[103]

First, he extricated the United States from the Vietnam War, at great cost, but with a renewed sense of purpose. Mixing escalation with negotiation, he transformed the nature of anticommunist containment. He placed a premium on engaging adversaries—the North Vietnamese, the Chinese, and the Soviets—in face-to-face discussion, rather than relying on forced isolation. He pushed for compromise, rather than victory or defeat, in areas of dispute. Kissinger articulated a new, if controversial, emphasis on diplomacy. Summitry, not separation, would dominate the final decades of the Cold War. In the 1970s and 1980s Washington defined itself as *the* global diplomatic leader, *the* indispensable negotiating partner. It maintained better relations with the most powerful states—the Soviet Union, China, Japan, West Germany, and Great Britain—than any of them had with the others. This leadership was not possible before Kissinger entered office.

Second, Kissinger redefined the use of force in international affairs. Under his direction, the United States rejected its earlier commitment to "pay any price and bear any burden." Drawing on his own writings, he replaced assumptions about the destruction of enemies with a more thoughtful, if still inexact, calibration of military power for political purposes. In his dealings with Vietnam, the Soviet Union, China, and the third world Kissinger devised limited military maneuvers that he could link to threats and overtures at the negotiating table. Force was an essential bargaining tool, but not a solution to disputes. Through détente the United States would accept the permanence of its adversaries, and it would use its power for competitive leverage instead of life-and-death struggle.

Third, and most significant, Kissinger insulated the day-to-day management of foreign policy from public interference. In a time of domestic upheaval across societies this was no small feat. It required an intensive centralization of authority in the White House and an almost superhuman ability to juggle the details of countless undertakings. Foreign-policy insulation allowed for consistency and flexibility despite social disorder. It facilitated rapid breaks with established modes of behavior despite constant distraction. In the darkest days of Watergate—when the president, according to Kissinger, exhibited "suicidal states of mind"—he managed to hold things together and continue moving forward with a coherent grand strategy. Regardless of how one judges the substance of Kissinger's policies, he exhibited extraordinary leadership in his ability to manufacture opportunities out of chaos.[104]

Kissinger created a foreign-policy revolution that set the course for the rest of the century. His successors, including Ronald Reagan, condemned

Kissinger's emphasis on limits, but they continued to draw on the diplomatic networks and the maneuvers of force that he pioneered. Despite all the controversy surrounding him, he remained one of the most influential foreign-policy figures in the world long after he left office.

Thousands of people died because of Kissinger's activities. His preoccupations with credibility and leverage closed off opportunities for peace, especially in Vietnam and Chile. Kissinger also neglected legitimate concerns about human rights and broader criticisms of his hierarchical world order. These were all failings of imagination on his part, failures of his foreign-policy revolution to address the social revolution in the streets and in third-world states. Kissinger was unprepared for these challenges from groups he did not understand, and from ideas that ran against his basic assumptions and experiences. He was a revolutionary strategist, but also a conservative thinker. He was a mix of the creative policymaker and the German Jewish believer in *Bildung.* He was a man who made many mistakes in trying circumstances, but he was not a war criminal.

SIX | *From Germany to Jerusalem*

On 22 September 1973 Henry Kissinger became U.S. secretary of state. Since 1969 he had played a dominant role in the making of American foreign policy, but he had done so as Richard Nixon's special assistant for national security affairs—an appointee, Kissinger explained, "on the president's own staff, unconfirmed by the Senate, totally dependent on the president's goodwill and confidence." His elevation to secretary of state now gave Kissinger constitutional standing, with a large constituency in the nation's bureaucracy of diplomats and other Foreign Service personnel. More important, Kissinger emerged from a shadow White House position into a public role filled with great prestige. He now occupied the same government office once held by Thomas Jefferson, John Quincy Adams, and Dean Acheson, among many other heroic figures.[1]

Kissinger was deeply moved by his accession to such a prominent public role. He had never held a comparable position. He was, in fact, the first foreign-born citizen to preside over U.S. foreign policy. Introducing Kissinger at his swearing-in ceremony, Nixon explained that it was "very significant in these days when we must think of America as part of the whole world community that for the first time in history a naturalized citizen is the Secretary of State of the United States." Surrounded by his parents, children, and brother, Kissinger could not hide his emotions. The *New York Times* reported that his voice "cracked with feeling":

> Mr. President, you referred to my background, and it is true, there is no country in the world where it is conceivable that a man of my origin

> could be standing here next to the president of the United States. And if my origin can contribute anything to the formulation of our policy, it is that at an early age I have seen what can happen to a society that is based on hatred and strength and distrust, and that I experienced then what America means to other people, its hope and its idealism. And therefore, in achieving a structure of peace under your leadership, Mr. President, we will strive not just for a pragmatic solution to this or that difficulty, but to recognize that America has never been true to itself unless it meant something beyond itself.[2]

Kissinger recounts in his memoirs that his parents watched the ceremony "as in a dream": "they had been driven out of their native country; thirteen members of our family had become victims of man's prejudices. They could hardly believe that thirty-five years later their son should have reached our nation's highest appointive executive office." How far Kissinger had climbed.[3]

At this moment of extraordinary achievement, Kissinger chose to emphasize his immigrant background, his experience with public intolerance, and his commitment to protecting the promise of American society. He also chose to avoid any mention of his Jewish background. Talking on the telephone with Nixon the next day, Kissinger went so far as to thank the president for not mentioning his Jewishness:

> *Nixon:* when you made your comment about this only in America could a man with my background be standing here beside the President of the United States which was done with great understatement but nevertheless, that must have appealed to an enormous number of people. . . . You just didn't reach people who happen to have a Jewish background.
>
> *Kissinger:* No, and of course you never mentioned that, which I was very grateful for.
>
> *Nixon:* Of course not. That's the point: you reached people with all sorts of backgrounds. It could reach Italians and others. They sort of feel a little pride for that sort of thing . . . the idea that we had, of this idealism in policy is good. You and I both know Henry that a lot of that's malarkey, but it's very important malarkey.[4]

This moment encapsulated Kissinger's entire career. He achieved power and influence by working with men who shared his skepticism about the virtues of public opinion. Nixon was only one of many international figures who agreed with Kissinger's emphasis on strong leadership rather than the "malarkey" of simple slogans about justice and human rights. "What I meant," the president elaborated, "is you and I both know that as far as our Soviet friends are concerned, to them it's pure pragmatism and power. It's true of China, and Japan, and others."[5]

The reporters who hounded Nixon about the alleged moral and legal misdeeds of his administration did not understand this point. They threatened to undermine the necessary exercise of national power. Kissinger encouraged Nixon's hostility to the press: "I would treat the bastards with contempt, Mr. President. They asked me about Watergate. I said you cannot play with the central authority of the country without paying a price."[6]

Kissinger's experiences as a German Jew informed his anxieties about public attacks on political authority. He feared a "suicidal" breakdown in

This was one of the proudest moments in Kissinger's career. On 22 September 1973 his parents and children watched as he took the oath of office as the first foreign-born U.S. secretary of state. Referring at this event to his German Jewish background, Kissinger explained: "there is no country in the world where it is conceivable that a man of my origin could be standing here next to the president of the United States." (Courtesy of AP / Wide World Photos)

domestic order and a turn toward social intolerance and policy paralysis. In July 1973 he spoke in grave terms about the recriminations of the White House during the height of the Watergate scandal: "At no crisis in the last fifteen years did I think the country was in danger. But I genuinely now believe that we could suffer irreparable damage." He warned of imminent American decline; the country had approached the "edge of a precipice."[7]

Kissinger sought to rescue the United States by reasserting national leadership and diverting attention from domestic differences. This was how he had made his own career. Kissinger climbed from Washington Heights to the White House by associating himself with powerful authority figures and by avoiding frequent hostilities targeted at immigrants, Jews, and other groups. He was deeply committed to what he called the "hope" and "idealism" of American society, but he emphasized toughness and pragmatism in pursuing these ends. Self-righteousness and sentimentality had not saved his community in Fürth; they threatened, in Kissinger's eyes, to produce the same weakness in America. As secretary of state, Kissinger sought to project internal strength and national unity, not self-doubt and ethnic particularism.

Among citizens who remained suspicious about Jewish loyalties, Kissinger had to walk a tightrope, accentuating the general "lessons" of his personal experience without mentioning the specific attributes that had helped to shape it. He had to articulate the wisdom derived from his life as a German Jew, without explicit reference to German and Jewish characteristics. Nixon contributed to the difficulty of this endeavor. Although he made frequent (usually negative) references to Kissinger's Jewish background, he encouraged Kissinger to remain silent about his Jewishness. In the White House, as throughout his career, Kissinger avoided public acknowledgment of his Jewishness for fear of the reactions among the public and among his patrons. The domestic controversies of the early 1970s only reinforced this tendency.

Kissinger therefore limited his involvement in Middle East politics during the first years of the Nixon administration. The Arab-Israeli dispute raised uncomfortable questions about his loyalties. Never before had a person with a spiritual connection to one side in this conflict played such a prominent, and potentially controversial, role in the U.S. government. Kissinger initially ceded leadership in Middle East policy to his predecessor at the State Department, William Rogers. And indeed, throughout his career before the 1970s, in all his prolific writings Kissinger had rarely expressed a public position on Israel and its neighbors. He maintained an intentional distance from the region and its ethnic politics. "When I entered office," Kissinger admits, "I knew little of the Middle East. I had never visited any Arab country; I was not familiar with the liturgy of Middle East negotiations." Kissinger did have some familiarity with the Jewish community: "My personal acquaintance with the area before 1969 was limited to three brief visits to Israel during the 1960s."[8]

Nixon viewed Kissinger's background as a liability in the Middle East, and he suspected his advisor's biases. The president, Kissinger recounts, "suspected that my Jewish origin might cause me to lean too much toward Israel." In contrast to other regions, Nixon limited Kissinger to a "planning" role in the Middle East, with little direct policy implementation. The president distrusted the Jewish political lobby in the United States, the Israeli government, and their potential sympathizers in his own government. He associated Kissinger with these groups, calling on him to use his "enormous influence on them." "He is harassing the hell out of me," Kissinger complained to his former military assistant and the president's chief of staff, Alexander Haig. "He wants me to call the Jewish leaders. . . . Well, the Jewish heads of organizations. You know that this is going to backfire."[9]

Only two weeks after he became secretary of state, the outbreak of war between Israel and its Arab neighbors forced Kissinger to confront his Jewishness and its relationship to his activities as an American statesman in the Cold War. With a president preoccupied by the Watergate scandal at home and with ominous signs of widening conflict in the Middle East, Kissinger became the most influential mediator between Jews and Arabs in their struggle for control of the Holy Land. He was torn between a personal attachment to the plight of the Jewish people and political pressure to prove his impartiality. "I could never forget," Kissinger explains, "that thirteen members of my family had died in the Nazi concentration camps. I had no stomach for encouraging another holocaust by well-intentioned policies that might get out of control. Most Israeli leaders were personal friends." In one of the most introspective passages in his memoirs, Kissinger recounts: "I had to subordinate my emotional preferences to my perception of the national interest. Indeed, given the historical suspicions toward my religion, I had a special obligation to do so. It was not always easy;

occasionally it proved painful. But Israel's security could be preserved in the long run only by anchoring it to a strategic interest of the United States, not to the sentiments of individuals."[10]

Israeli and Arab leaders did not always see it that way. Yitzhak Rabin, who served as Israel's ambassador to Washington and prime minister during the 1970s, remembered that Kissinger's connections to Israel contributed to frustration and disappointment: "He was not always understood in Israel. Frequently, many forgot that he was a representative of the U.S., not the Jewish diaspora. He faced exaggerated demands. Often we treated him improperly, state officials and citizens alike."[11]

Arab leaders also expected too much from Kissinger. They believed that his Jewish background meant that he had control over Israel as well as American policy. Meeting with Egyptian foreign minister Ismail Fahmy on 30 October 1973, Kissinger pledged to "move Israel" toward a settlement with Cairo. Despite his suspicions about Kissinger's alleged anti-Arab bias, Fahmy explained: "we have faith in you, Dr. Kissinger. We have confidence in you." Fahmy was referring not to American goodwill, which he doubted, but to his recognition that Kissinger sought to enforce a stable peace in the Middle East by creating a rough balance between Israeli and Arab power. "I do not believe it is in your interest to put us into an inferior position," Fahmy explained. He assumed that the American secretary of state could push the Israelis and deliver where earlier American statesmen had failed.[12]

Kissinger understood the curious way in which conspiracy theories about Jewish power boosted Arab expectations, and even respect for him. In mid-October 1973, amidst continued warfare and preparations for his first trip to Arab countries in the Middle East, Kissinger noted Cairo's anxious anticipation of his visit. Speaking with Brent Scowcroft, the deputy special assistant for national security affairs, he asked: "Have you heard about the Egyptians? They have already prepared for my arrival there."

Scowcroft: That's beautiful! They are something else.
Kissinger: In the nutty Arab world I am sort of a mythical figure. The Arabs think I am a magician.
Scowcroft: That's right. Might not be possible right now.[13]

Despite Scowcroft's caution, Kissinger achieved what had appeared impossible in the Middle East. He established a personal connection with the leaders of Israel, Egypt, Saudi Arabia, Jordan, and Syria that gave each of them a strong stake in diplomatic progress. As in his relations with European elites during the 1950s and 1960s, and North Vietnamese and Chinese leaders during the early 1970s, Kissinger made himself the indispensable bridge figure between societies, translating and revising their respective demands for the purposes of mutual compromise. He created personal networks of mutual dependence, with himself at the center. He built respect, awe, and even personal trust with his counterparts—including those who suspected his Jewish loyalties. Although he faced frequent criticisms, Kissinger convinced the Israelis that he was the most sympathetic secretary of state they could get. He persuaded Arab leaders that he alone had the power to deliver on changes in the map of the region.

Kissinger was simultaneously a political outsider and an emotional insider to the Middle East. This was a complicated but effective hinge for bringing religious enemies to the negotiating table. Through his famous "shuttle diplomacy," Kissinger literally carried proposals from one capital to another—pleading, cajoling, and, when necessary, threatening his counterparts to accept strategic compromises.

Perseverance paid large dividends. Kissinger helped to formulate and enforce the cease-fire that curtailed Arab-Israeli fighting in late October 1973. In the process, he marginalized the Soviet Union and increased American influence throughout the region. Under Kissinger's leadership, the United States became the dominant foreign power in the Middle East. American pressures contributed to a series of agreements that established stable relations between long-standing belligerents. Egypt and Israel withdrew their forces from a war footing and began a process of reconciliation. The United States provided both countries with security assurances and massive amounts of foreign aid. Relations between Syria and Israel remained hostile, but the two countries refrained from direct military confrontation. Saudi Arabia, despite its participation in the oil embargo that accompanied the fighting in 1973, lent its support to improved relations between Egypt and Israel. The Saudi regime also became a reliable supplier of oil to the United States and its allies. In the aftermath of the Arab-Israeli war, Kissinger's diplomacy brought peace and stability to the Middle East, on terms favorable to Washington. As a result of his efforts, the most powerful states in the region would not fight another major war—as they had in 1956, 1967, and 1973.[14]

These were great achievements, unmatched by any other American policymaker. They failed, however, to settle the Arab-Israeli conflict. Arab leaders continued to seek recovery of the Holy Land and destruction of the state of Israel. They blamed the United States for preventing this outcome. Israel continued to seek more landholdings and security against hostile neighbors. Israeli leaders and citizens blamed the United States for preventing this outcome. Many American citizens, including numerous non-Jews, came to believe that Washington must provide Israel with absolute assurance against a replay of events in 1973. They blamed Kissinger, in particular, for preventing this outcome. Most significant, the people living in Israeli-occupied territories and in despotic Arab societies looked for opportunities to challenge and reform the repressive politics of the region. Palestinians and other residents of the region blamed the United States for supporting unjust regimes and undermining progressive political movements. As in other parts of the third world, Kissinger's achievements in relations between states inspired powerful resistance from citizens within those states, including his own.

Kissinger's successes and failures stemmed from the same qualities. His ability to operate between societies and to win over powerful people made him the most effective Middle East diplomat of the twentieth century. He turned his Jewish background into an asset for Israeli and Arab advocates alike. Kissinger's ingenious maneuvers between societies, however, created a distance between him and the people who had to live with his policies. He spent so much time and energy shuttling between capitals as secretary of state that he could not penetrate beyond palace walls. He became a streaking figure across the television screens and newspaper headlines of Arab, Jewish, and American societies. He inspired fascination and awe, but not trust from "ordinary" citizens. In this sense, his Jewish background became a liability for those who perceived either unfair bias to Israel on his part, or an attempt to overcompensate by showing excessive deference to non-Jewish claims. As a bridge figure (an "inside-outsider"), Kissinger elicited suspicion from nationalists of all stripes.

This was not unique to the Middle East or Kissinger's tenure as secretary of state. He faced similar contradictions between his empowerment and his exclusion throughout his life. From Fürth to Jerusalem, Kissinger's German Jewish background reinforced valued skills and it raised grave suspicions. Kissinger learned to turn this duality to his advantage, especially when negotiating with foreign adversaries. In so doing, he greatly expanded America's global influence. He also, however, inspired widespread resistance to the United States.

This is the story of politics in the contemporary Middle East—Kissinger's most enduring and complex legacy. His policies set the contours for future stability and conflict in the region. His activities raised hopes for American mediation and anger about American meddling. Like the combined encouragement and suspicion of Jewish accomplishments that Kissinger confronted throughout his career, the United States faces attraction and revulsion among foreign populations today. America became a necessary and a resented global presence during Kissinger's years. In the twenty-first century, America's contested international standing reflects the contradictions surrounding Kissinger's Middle East legacy.

The Yom Kippur War

Kissinger was only one of many observers to anticipate another Arab-Israeli war, but he was surprised to learn on the morning of 6 October 1973 that Egypt, Syria, and their allies were poised for attack. He did not believe that they could defeat Israeli forces on the battlefield. The 1967 Six-Day War had made Arab weaknesses abundantly clear. Egypt and Syria were "insane," Kissinger believed, to start another war they could not win. Although Israeli citizens were unprepared to fend off an attack on Yom Kippur, the holiest day of the Jewish year, the secretary of state was confident that, as in 1967, the Israeli army would prevail in just a few days.[15]

Before the outbreak of hostilities, Israeli leaders shared this underestimation of Arab military capabilities. They discounted the ability of their adversaries to challenge Israel's proven battlefield superiority. They also doubted the possibility of coordinated and effective action among the various Arab states. Even in the early hours of 6 October 1973, when Egyptian and Syrian forces made their final preparations for attack, Israeli prime minister Golda Meir ruled out the kind of preemptive military strike employed by her predecessors in the 1967 war. She believed that Israel could repel an Arab attack, and she also recognized the importance of maintaining a defensive position. "If we strike first," Meir explained to her advisors, "we won't get help from anybody." She sought to repulse Arab aggression and gain foreign support form the United States and other countries.[16]

The Arab armies fought better than either the Americans or the Israelis expected. During the first day they drove deep into Israeli-held territory on the Sinai peninsula (across the Suez Canal) and in the Golan Heights. They had momentum, and they appeared ready to extend their gains. The Israeli army quickly lost its attitude of invincibility. It was on its heels, disorganized, and uncertain. Surveying his country's early battlefield losses, Israel's defense minister, Moshe Dayan, warned that the initial Arab successes would mobilize more support within those societies. Soon his nation of 3 million Jews would confront 80 million confident and zealous Arabs. "This is the war of Israel against the Arabs," he proclaimed. Dayan worried that Israel would now get smothered in a sea of enemies.[17]

Though aware of the Arab battlefield gains, Nixon and Kissinger were less alarmed by the military situation than their counterparts in Jerusalem. They believed that the Israelis would halt the Egyptian and Syrian advances and eventually launch an effective counterattack. Instead of the details on the ground, they focused on how the United States could turn this crisis into a source of stability and influence in the region. Speaking with the president in the first hours of the war, Kissinger explained that "the primary problem is to get the fighting stopped and then use the opportunity to see whether a settlement could be enforced."

Nixon: You mean a diplomatic settlement of the bigger problem?
Kissinger: That is right. . . . I think it is impossible now to keep maintaining the status quo ante.[18]

Nixon and Kissinger agreed that they should adopt a "neutral approach" as they sought an end to hostilities. They also worked through diplomatic channels to bring an American-led peace to the region. Washington consulted with Moscow, but the United States moved to "take the initiative." In a flurry of phone calls and meetings, Kissinger opened a series of intense discussions with Egyptian and Israeli representatives, as well as with the Soviet ambassador to the United States, Anatoly Dobrynin. "Your Arab friends were terribly deceitful," Kissinger scolded Dobrynin. "We are taking this matter extremely seriously. If you will let your colleagues know we would appreciate it as quickly as possible."[19]

American neutrality, as this last comment indicated, did not mean indifference to the outcome of the war. Nixon and Kissinger agreed that neither side should be allowed a clear and decisive victory. The United States initially stalled on aid requested by Israel. Kissinger spoke of letting the belligerents beat upon one another "for a day or two, and that will quiet them down." After more desperate requests from Jerusalem, particularly a personal appeal to the president from Golda Meir, Nixon approved an emergency airlift of military supplies on 13 October 1973. This was also a reaction to the evidence of increased Soviet aid to the Arab countries, particularly Syria. Over the next month the United States transported 11,000 tons of ammunition, electronic equipment, and other matériel to Israel. Kissinger wanted to maintain a low profile for the relationship between Israel and the United States, but the pressures of the war forced a more decisive and obvious expression of Washington's support.[20]

With the assistance of American supplies, Israel finally gained the upper hand over the attacking Arab armies. Forces under the command of General Ariel Sharon broke through Egyptian lines on 15 October. During the night of 16 October Israeli units began to cross the Suez Canal into Egypt.

During and after the Yom Kippur War, Kissinger and Israeli prime minister Golda Meir had a contentious relationship. Meir expected Washington to provide more support to the Jewish state; Kissinger found Meir's demands excessive. Drawing on his personal connection to Israel, Kissinger encouraged compromise with Arab claims and pursued a diplomatic settlement among regional leaders. (© Henri Bureau / Sygma / Corbis)

Israeli soldiers also pushed through the Arab-held sections of the Golan Heights, entering Syrian territory. After this turn of events, Kissinger reported to the president that "things may be breaking."[21]

On the retreat, Arab leaders now looked to the United States for a diplomatic solution to the war. During the conflict, Washington had acquired unique leverage. Israel felt beholden for American military assistance. The Soviet Union, in contrast, had discredited itself in many capitals through its support for a failed Arab war. Moscow also lacked serious relations with Israel. "Everyone," Kissinger explained, "knows in the Middle East that if they want a peace they have to go through us." He set out to exploit this position in the last days of the Yom Kippur War.[22]

As he had long advocated, Kissinger mixed diplomacy with force—negotiations with nuclear weapons. On 24 October, when the Soviet Union threatened to send soldiers to the region, Kissinger ordered American nuclear and conventional forces to a heightened state of readiness. Like the nuclear alert he had initiated four years earlier, this maneuver signaled U.S. resolve and the possibility of "irrational" American actions if the Soviets challenged Washington. Kissinger followed the advice he had given former Israeli ambassador Yitzhak Rabin earlier that year: "I have learned that when you use force it is better to use 30 percent more than is necessary than five percent less than necessary . . . whenever we use force we have to do it slightly hysterically."[23]

This logic matched the "madman" image of the president that Nixon and Kissinger had espoused in 1969. It also fitted with Kissinger's consistent attempts, since the 1950s, to make nuclear weapons useful in moments of crisis. Nixon's increasing entanglement in the Watergate scandal strengthened an impression that the president might do something risky and dramatic at this troubling moment. Nixon, in fact, was largely distracted from the deliberations about the nuclear alert, and from Middle East diplomacy in general. He was, as Kissinger admitted at the time, no longer a "functioning president."[24]

Unlike the events of October 1969, in October 1973 the American nuclear alert reached public attention, despite Kissinger's claims that he wished otherwise. The U.S. government brought its forces to "Defcon III," the state of readiness just short of actual nuclear war. When questioned, Kissinger spoke explicitly of the threat to regional stability: "The United States does not favor and will not approve the sending of a joint Soviet–

United States force into the Middle East. . . . The United States is even more opposed to the unilateral introduction by any great power, especially by any nuclear power, of military forces into the Middle East in whatever guise those forces should be introduced."[25]

Most significant, Kissinger asserted that the United States would use its full power to pursue a settlement in the region—even at the risk of nuclear war. This was a major shift from the cautious American diplomacy before October 1973. It was also an international "coming out" for Kissinger as the most prominent statesman in the Middle East. When Arab and Israeli forces halted their hostilities, all the belligerents, as well as foreign observers, looked to him for a negotiated settlement. All the belligerents accepted that he was uniquely situated—because of his influence in the U.S. government, his international standing, and his background—to shape a future course for the region. An embattled president in the Oval Office and a discredited leadership in the Kremlin left a vacuum that Kissinger energetically filled.

Less than a year after the end of the Yom Kippur War, Anwar Sadat, Egypt's president and the main strategist behind the Arab attack on Israel, looked to Kissinger as "a magician," capable of building "a new image of America" in the Middle East. "I don't want to be imaginative," Sadat told Kissinger in confidence. "I want to be practical. I have confidence in you, you know."[26]

Sadat and the Arab "Moderates"

Sadat was the figure on whom Kissinger hinged his efforts to bring American-led stability to the Middle East. In his memoirs, the former secretary of state recounts the admiration he developed for the Egyptian leader, dating to their first meeting on 7 November 1973, just two weeks after the cessation of Arab-Israeli hostilities:

> Sadat had emerged, dressed in a khaki military tunic, an overcoat slung carelessly over his shoulders. . . . He was taller, swarthier, and more imposing than I had expected. He exuded vitality and confidence. That son of peasants radiated a natural dignity and aristocratic bearing as out of keeping with his revolutionary history as it was commanding and strangely calming. He affected nonchalance.[27]

Sadat explained to Kissinger that he had planned the 6 October 1973 attack on Israel as an effort to restore Arab dignity and convince the Israelis that they could not dominate the region through force. The Egyptian leader was also frustrated by American passivity. He had expelled Soviet military personnel from his country in July 1972, hoping that the United States would play a mediating role between Israeli and Arab interests. Sadat understood that Arab belligerence and alliance with Moscow only reinforced U.S. support for Israel. Instead of antagonizing Washington, he wanted to turn America's influence to his advantage. Sadat pursued a strategy that encouraged U.S. leaders to press concessions on Israel, in return for promises that his state would promote peace and pro-American sentiment in the region. "Egypt leads the Arab world," Sadat told Nixon and Kissinger. "We started promoting better relations with the United States.

Egyptian president Anwar Sadat became one of Kissinger's most important diplomatic partners in the Middle East. Kissinger perceived Sadat as the kind of strong and visionary leader who could bring peace to the region through negotiations. Kissinger and Sadat met frequently and developed a close, trusting, and affectionate personal relationship. Sadat viewed Kissinger's Jewish background as an asset; the Egyptian leader believed that Kissinger could deliver compromises from Israel that non-Jewish American figures could not. Kissinger did not disabuse Sadat of this judgment. (Courtesy of Getty Images)

The United States has all the cards in its hands and Israel should heed the United States."[28]

In the aftermath of the Yom Kippur War, the Egyptian leader correctly surmised that his efforts to enhance his power through cooperation with the United States matched Kissinger's pursuit of a multicentered world order. Washington did not seek to dominate the Middle East directly, nor did it want to build up Israel as a regional giant, isolated from its Arab neighbors. The 1973 war made it clear to Kissinger that the Middle East needed a cluster of strong states—Jewish and Arab, oil rich and desert poor—roughly balanced in military capabilities. The leaders of these states would recognize that victory in war was not conceivable, and they would seek cooperative relations instead. Following from his long-standing thoughts on how the United States should manage the "grey areas," Kissinger sought to use American power to insure military balance and to stabilize Arab-Jewish relations. This is what the president meant when he explained to members of Congress: "If your goal is peace in the Middle East and the survival of Israel, we have to have some stake with Israeli neighbors." The United States pushed for what Kissinger called "a diplomatic revolution" in the region predicated upon "a triumph for the moderates."[29]

Sadat was exactly the kind of Arab "moderate" Kissinger needed. He ruled a powerful and influential state in the region. He rejected extremist calls for socialist or religious proselytism. Instead, he desired a working partnership with the United States. Most significant, Sadat sought to build an enduring structure of relations in the Middle East that supported Egyptian interests but also accommodated the needs of Israel and the United States. He wanted to move beyond conflict.

Sadat fitted Kissinger's definition of a transcendent leader. Referring to him in his memoirs, Kissinger proclaimed: "The great man has a vision of the future that enables him to put obstacles in perspective." Echoing his assessment of Metternich, Bismarck, and Churchill, Kissinger explained: "Sadat bore with fortitude the loneliness inseparable from moving the world from familiar categories toward where it has never been." In place of religious intolerance and sectarian strife, Sadat and Kissinger sought to enforce diplomatic "normality"—including collegial state-to-state relations and political cooperation among diverse groups. Kissinger believed this was "the best chance to transcend frozen attitudes that the Middle East had known since the creation of the State of Israel."[30]

Sadat described Kissinger as "the real face of the United States, the one I had always wanted to see." He and the American secretary of state became, in Sadat's words, "friends." "There was no difficulty in understanding one another." Both men sought to assure Egyptian strength as a bulwark against Arab extremism and Soviet meddling. Both men envisioned a stable Middle East dominated by roughly balanced regional powers in Egypt and Israel that cooperated to restrain belligerent forces and to work with the United States. "I want us to make progress; to make a complete peace," Sadat told Kissinger and Nixon's successor in the White House, Gerald Ford. "And I want the United States to achieve it, not the Soviet Union."[31]

Kissinger was the "real face of the United States," according to Sadat, because he appreciated power and he was Jewish. The Egyptian leader assumed that Kissinger's position as the most prominent international Jewish figure gave him unique leverage with Israel. Sadat pledged that he would manage the other Arab leaders, and he expected the United States to "put pressure" on Israel. Egyptian foreign minister Fahmy brushed aside Kissinger's protestations about Israeli intransigence, exclaiming that Prime Minister "Rabin is your boy."[32]

Sadat expected Kissinger to make Israel accept territorial transfers to Egypt "pill by pill." He did not merely anticipate that Washington would use its military and economic might to shape Israeli policy; he believed that the secretary of state could exert unique personal leverage. Kissinger was an outsider to the region who could mediate between warring parties for Sadat, and he was also a Jewish insider who could move Israel from within. These "inside-outsider" qualities, once again, made Kissinger particularly valuable for a powerful leader—in this case, Sadat.[33]

Kissinger did not deny his personal leverage over Israel. When Fahmy said "Rabin is your boy," Kissinger responded: "I need a few months to work on him." The secretary of state affirmed the asserted link between him and the Israeli prime minister. Earlier in the same conversation, Kissinger compared Rabin to his predecessor during the Yom Kippur War, Golda Meir: "he doesn't have her guts. He's more intellectual. But we can get him to move in the right direction. . . . We need a few months to work on him."[34]

Kissinger's "shuttle diplomacy" between Cairo, Jerusalem, and other capitals followed the model of his transatlantic networking in earlier years.

He established himself as the closest and most effective link between different leaders. He turned their prejudices to his advantage. Most significant, he made himself indispensable to political negotiations. Kissinger needed Sadat for a "moderate" and American-influenced Middle East; Sadat needed Kissinger as his effective go-between with Israel. Kissinger combined personal politics, skillful diplomacy, and a coherent grand strategy for regional stability. He made himself not just a "mystical figure," but also a bridge between warring societies.

He retains this unique position in the twenty-first century. No other person outside government wields comparable influence in *both* the Arab states and Israel. No other person outside government is so connected to the sources of power in multiple societies, yet so suspected for his multiple loyalties.

Israel and the American Jewish Community

Kissinger could not control Israeli leaders or the opinions of the American Jewish community. Sadat and his counterparts overrated him. In fact, Kissinger frequently complained about the opposition he confronted from these groups. "They are," he told Brent Scowcroft, "as obnoxious as the Vietnamese." In another conversation, Kissinger joked: "I'm going to be the first Jew accused of anti-Semitism."[35]

Israelis and American Jews feared that Kissinger was overcompensating for his background by making excessive concessions to the Arabs, that he was trading Israel's security for his own international influence. Menachem Begin, the leader of Israel's Likud party and a future prime minister, reminded Kissinger: "You are a Jew. You are not the first [Jew] who has reached a high position in one's country of residence. Remember the past. There were such Jews, who out of a complex feared non-Jews would charge them with acting for their people, and therefore did the opposite." "Dr. Kissinger," Begin warned, "should be careful about such a distortion in his seemingly objective thinking."[36]

American Jews had similar concerns. Rabbi Daniel J. Silver of Cleveland accused Kissinger of trying too hard to show the Arabs that "being a Jew doesn't count." Gershon Jacobson, a Jewish literary figure in New York, explained that "Kissinger was determined to gain the confidence of the Arabs as a Jew, and to do so at the expense of Israel." Norman Podhoretz, the editor of *Commentary* magazine, told Kissinger that Israeli and American Jews feared he was an appeaser—a "Chamberlain"—seeking to conciliate enemies bent on destroying the Jewish people.[37]

Fame and celebrity made Kissinger an international giant, but he remained all too human for those who felt closest to him in background. He disappointed those who expected the most of him. He seemed disloyal to those who demanded a champion for their group. Most of all, he refused to focus his energies on moral claims rather than on diplomatic compromises. As Yitzhak Rabin remembered, Kissinger enraged those who wanted a Jewish representative in office, rather than an American secretary of state.[38]

This was a major handicap for Kissinger, particularly when he negotiated in the Middle East, but it also had its advantages. Kissinger was a Jew, who had experienced the worst forms of anti-Semitism. None of his Israeli

Many Israelis and their American supporters opposed the agreement that Kissinger negotiated for Israel's withdrawal from Egyptian territory on the Sinai peninsula. Kissinger's peace efforts drew criticism from powerful Arab, Israeli, and American Jewish constituencies. He emphasized territorial compromise in a region where many groups pursued broad and exclusive territorial ambitions. This 1975 cartoon gave voice to Israeli concerns that Kissinger forced a settlement on a supplicant Jewish state, enriching Arab leaders in the process. (© David Rubinger / CORBIS)

and American Jewish detractors ever forgot that fact. Much as they might criticize him for not doing enough on behalf of Jews, he was still one of them. He was still part of their family. This personal history did not produce agreement on policy, but it did create a foundation for basic trust and empathy. Non-Jewish secretaries of state did not benefit from the same Israeli bond.

Henry Rosovsky, who participated in some of Kissinger's meetings with American Jewish leaders after the Yom Kippur War, recalls the "comfort" and "mutual respect" that pervaded these discussions. Despite the anxieties that Rosovsky voiced about insufficient U.S. support for Israel in December 1973, "this was an all-Jewish meeting, with a shared concern and commitment to Israel." Rosovsky remembers that he and others who talked with the first Jewish secretary of state knew "Kissinger would not be a person to betray Israel." Rabbi Alexander Schindler, speaking on behalf of many American Jewish organizations, made the same point. He and other Jewish leaders paid tribute to Kissinger "because we sense in his depths, a commitment to Israel and the Jewish people. He may have been objective, but he was never detached."[39]

Kissinger appealed to this sentiment. He asked for his fellow Jews "to understand what we're trying to do" and to "avoid slogans." Warning that Israel was "in great danger" if it remained isolated and surrounded by belligerent enemies, he called for help in pursuing compromises on territory, particularly in the Sinai peninsula, that would reduce conflict throughout the region. "With some wisdom in the Jewish community, and among friends of Israel, maybe we can manage it. . . . Certainly this government will never participate in anything that we believe involves any risk of its destruction."[40]

When negotiating directly with Israeli leaders, Kissinger similarly drew on a presumed bond. Meeting with Prime Minister Yitzhak Rabin one month after Nixon's resignation of the presidency and during a particularly difficult moment in Middle East peace efforts, Kissinger explained: "We read often of disagreements. One, there are no disagreements. Two, if there are, they're family disagreements. We are working for a common strategy, one element of which is a strong Israel." Kissinger reminded the Israeli leader of their close personal relationship before 1973, when Rabin was ambassador to the United States. "We worked together for five years in an atmosphere of trust and confidence."[41]

Rabin reciprocated these sentiments, despite his evident anxiety about

Kissinger's calls for Israeli concessions to the Arab states: "We believe very much in Israel that there is friendship between our two countries. I have had the experience of this friendship, especially with you, and all our intentions are to continue this—to have the basis to speak frankly, but the basis is a common interest and a common understanding." Following Kissinger's prodding, Rabin agreed to push forward with further negotiations for territorial withdrawals from Egyptian-claimed lands, as well as discussions with Jordan and Syria. Kissinger, in turn, pledged to increase American support for Israel through an expanding list of military supplies and billions of dollars in foreign aid. Kissinger and Rabin trusted each other "to find a constructive solution" for mutual concerns.[42]

Public controversy in Israel and the United States proliferated, but relations between the leaders of the two countries grew closest during the tenure of the first Jewish secretary of state. Yigal Allon, Israel's deputy prime minister and a former participant in Kissinger's International Seminar at Harvard, confirmed this point: "I trusted him to the extent that I could trust the foreign minister of any other country. I trusted his friendship, but not always his judgment. I never doubted I was talking to a friend of Israel. He was loyal to Israel in his way."[43]

By the time Kissinger left office, in January 1977, he had succeeded in redrawing the map of the Middle East. Following a war that threatened to unleash years of armed conflict between the Arab states and Israel, with possible superpower participation, he created a framework for peace among some of the most powerful governments in the region—particularly those in Cairo and Jerusalem. He negotiated intensively for armed disengagement near their border, the exchange of territory occupied by Israel on the Sinai peninsula, and a commitment to basic cooperation between the states. He used the full range of American pressure, pleading, and bribery to achieve this end. Most significant, Kissinger made the United States a trusted mediator for Egypt and Israel—the one government both Arabs and Jews could look to for assurance.

Kissinger's Middle East policy was a natural extension of the strategy he applied to other parts of the world. The regimes in Egypt and Israel provided local authority, supported and managed indirectly by the United States from afar. Peace in the region was not about justice or democracy, but instead about stability through negotiation. Basic freedoms derived from enlightened and strong leadership rather than popular consensus. This was a vision for the region that self-consciously approximated Metternich's or Bismarck's Europe, much more than the religious prophecies of the Bible or the Koran. It was the well-considered worldview of a German Jew seeking to protect cherished values—and his heritage—from political extremes.

Speaking "from the heart" to a conference of presidents from American Jewish organizations in January 1977, Kissinger explained:

> I thought it was important for the future of Israel and for the future of the Jewish people, that the actions that the U.S. Government took were not seen to be the result of a special, personal relationship; that the support we gave Israel reflected not my personal preferences alone but the basic national interests of the United States, transcending the accident of who might be in office at any particular period. I have never forgotten that thirteen members of my family died in concentration camps, nor could I ever fail to remember what it was like to live in Nazi Germany as a member of a persecuted minority. I believe, however, that the relationship of Israel to the United States transcends these personal considerations. I do not believe that it is compatible with the moral conscience of mankind to permit Israel to suffer in the Middle East a ghetto existence that has been suffered by Jews in many individual countries throughout their history. The support for a free and democratic Israel in the Middle East is a moral necessity of our period to be pursued by every Administration, and with a claim to the support of all freedom-loving people all over the world.[44]

Kissinger closed by invoking his own continued Jewish faith and his attachment to Israel: "Throughout their history, Jews have been saying to themselves: 'Next year in Jerusalem.' I would like to think that sometime soon *we* can say this in its deepest sense—in an Israel that is secure, that is accepted, that is at peace."[45]

Troubled Legacy

In many ways, Kissinger's vision became a reality. On the eve of 11 September 2001 Israel and Egypt remained at peace. Kissinger's map of the Middle East endured twenty-five years of continued low-scale Arab-Israeli fighting, in addition to other conflicts in the region. The United States served as a mediator between the sides and as a sponsor of "moderate" regimes. It was the dominant external power in the region—a fact it had proven by leading an international coalition of forces, including Arab states, to turn back Saddam Hussein's invasion of Iraq's oil-rich neighbor Kuwait. An Islamic revolution in Iran had expelled U.S. influence from that country and humiliated Americans through a prolonged seizure of hostages, but it had not changed the borders of the region or sparked a renewed Arab-Israeli war. American access to inexpensive oil seemed assured until the supply of hydrocarbons ran out.[46]

Geopolitical stability in the Middle East masked deeper domestic disturbances. Kissinger's strategy had the effect of reinforcing dictatorship and discontent. His policies made the United States a visible sponsor of oppressors, including Sadat, his successor Hosni Mubarak, the Shah of Iran, King Faisal in Saudi Arabia, and Saddam Hussein before 1990. These men cooperated with Washington while they brutalized their populations. Kissinger's policies did not address the anger, resentment, and desires for political change voiced by citizens living in Arab societies and the territories occupied by Israel after 1967. In the latter case, Washington became an indirect financier of new Israeli settlements on land claimed by Palestinians. The United States built peace in the Middle East on the backs of iron-fisted Arab and Israeli leaders.

Kissinger understood both the nature of this policy and its shortcomings. It was not unique to his endeavors in the Middle East. He constructed his career around the presumption that in a cruel and violent world powerful leaders, not democratic politics, offered the best protection for life and liberty. Statesmanship, for Kissinger, required the tolerance of brutality as a bulwark against worse suffering. Transcendent leaders needed the courage to make tough choices among lesser evils. This is how he interpreted recent history. During the 1940s the United States and Great Britain had to fight one of history's most destructive wars to rescue Europe from Nazi genocide. After Germany's surrender, the Western nations had to deploy the most deadly weapons to assure the survival of civilization in the face of communist expansion. Kissinger believed that the United States had to follow similar logic in the Middle East. Washington would work closely with unsavory regimes to prevent the region from immolating itself in a fire of mass hatred.

Kissinger believed that more democracy in countries like Egypt and Saudi Arabia would only increase the urge to war. Anti-Semitism and other hatreds had popular appeal; violence was a simple and attractive option for angry citizens. Wasn't it better to work with figures like Sadat, who ruled as dictators but who also used their power to repress popular calls for war? Wasn't it better to acquiesce in Israeli occupation of Palestinian territories than to allow those lands to become a base for renewed attacks on the Jewish state? The United States had to build a sustainable process for political stability in the region before it could pursue far-reaching reform. The Middle East, like other areas of the world, needed reliable and rational local authorities. Only after these authorities asserted themselves, with American support, could Washington "let history take its course."[47]

History did take its course in the Middle East, but not as Kissinger hoped. Arab and Israeli leaders after 1973 used American aid to continue brutalizing the people of the region. The governments of Egypt and Saudi Arabia deployed force to crush internal critics, and they simultaneously sponsored anti-Semitic appeals to local popular prejudices. They manipulated hatred of Israel to divert attention from their failings. The government of Israel sustained its democracy for Jewish citizens, but it made itself a permanent occupier of territories with dense Palestinian populations. Israeli rule in Gaza and on the West Bank involved military force against civilians and a hardening of racist attitudes about Arab society.

Kissinger searched for transcendent leaders in the Middle East and found effective strongmen. Like their counterparts in Latin America and Africa, they were, generally, reliable partners. They did not, however, transcend the pathologies of hatred and violence in the region. If anything, they deepened the tendency toward extremism.

Terrorism, in this context, became part of the region's daily politics in the 1970s and successive decades. Disfranchised citizens in Arab-ruled and Israeli-occupied territories turned to paramilitary violence as a mechanism for political change. They had few alternatives. Islamic fundamentalism and the cult of personal martyrdom were attractive to young men and women because the most powerful state leaders choked off internal mechanisms for reform. They offered citizens little hope. Ruling by force, they also encouraged resistance by force. The anchors of regional stability, particularly American influence, became targets for those who wanted a different life.

The diffusion of Middle East terrorism to territories outside the region—particularly in western Europe and the United States—is an extension of this dynamic. As the dominant foreign power in the area after 1973, America is also a primary focus of anger among critics with access to destructive capabilities. Terrorist strikes on U.S. interests are launched by a small and reprehensible minority that enjoys the sympathy of many groups discontented with the domestic costs of the policies pursued after the Yom Kippur War. As in other parts of the world, Kissinger's strategic accomplishments—working with state leaders like Sadat and Rabin—inspired new political challenges from stateless figures like Yasir Arafat and Osama bin Laden.

In the aftermath of the 11 September 2001 attacks on the United States, President George W. Bush sought to address the internal sources of violence in the Middle East by pursuing a program for muscular democratization of the region. "We are led," he proclaimed in his Second Inaugural Address, "to one conclusion: The survival of liberty in our land increasingly depends on the success of liberty in other lands. The best hope for peace in our world is the expansion of freedom in all the world." Bush announced that "it is the policy of the United States to seek and support the growth of democratic movements and institutions in every nation and culture, with the ultimate goal of ending tyranny in our world."[48]

In accordance with this boundless vision, Bush had gone to war in Iraq. The American military, with limited aid from Great Britain and other countries, overthrew a violent and tyrannical regime that had long undermined regional peace. Washington set out to build a functioning democracy in Iraq under American tutelage. This was a radical departure from the diplomatic policies the United States had pursued in the region since 1973. It was also a rejection of Kissinger's more cautious and less democratic approach to power.

Bush identified the problem of absent democracy in the Middle East, but a poorly planned military occupation did not offer a viable solution. His rhetoric about "the expansion of freedom" proved hollow as armed gangs terrorized ordinary people in Iraq. Popular rule produced more violence, not less. Iraq needed order and strong leadership, beyond the limited and isolated U.S. presence.[49]

The evidence that the United States could not bring peace to the Middle East through rapid democratization inspired a return to Kissinger's emphasis on stability and negotiation with local leaders. Although proponents of the "war on terror" initially looked to reform America's relationship with dictatorial governments in Saudi Arabia, Pakistan, and other countries, the United States quickly grew more dependent on these very regimes. They offered invaluable resources and support for the war effort. They helped to defend stability amidst regional unrest and insurgency.

Kissinger supported this undemocratic arrangement. Consistent with his entire career, Kissinger argued against treating "democratization as an end in itself." He pointed to the success of "non-democratic regimes in places like Korea, Taiwan, and Turkey" that used firm authority to establish stability, wealth, and eventually "representative institutions and checks and balances." Returning to his long-standing reflections on the limits of American power, Kissinger explained: "The advocates of the important role of a commitment to democracy in American foreign policy have won their intellectual battle. But institution-building requires not only doctrine but a vision recognizing cultural and historical circumstance. Such humil-

After he left office, Kissinger worked hard to remain an influential figure in policy circles. Leaders from both American political parties and many foreign countries looked to him for guidance. In the aftermath of the 11 September 2001 terrorist attacks on the United States, Kissinger's influence grew in President George W. Bush's White House. Kissinger provided advice on Middle East politics, international diplomacy, and conducting a distant war. (© Brooks Craft / CORBIS)

ity is not an abdication of American values; it is the only way to implement these values effectively."[50]

This well-rehearsed argument won attention from a frustrated and increasingly desperate White House. Kissinger once again became an influential figure for an administration embroiled in a difficult war, seeking new avenues for political leverage and new arrangements with regional elites. The reversion to a model of peace through local strongmen proved the durability of Kissinger's worldview. The repression and violence that accompanied this model, particularly in Iraq, fueled the controversies surrounding Kissinger's activities. He left a troubling but enduring legacy.[51]

Kissinger's critics, including this author, have analyzed the many failings in his thought—particularly the tendency for his antidemocratic fears to empower repressive regimes and violent rebellions. Kissinger's policies contributed to the anti-Americanism that breeds terrorism. Nonetheless, no alternative strategic vision for managing the Middle East and other regions of the world has emerged in its place. Rhetoric about democracy does not provide a path forward in dealing with violence and hatred. International peace requires a careful calibration of means and ends, as well as a coherent integration of various challenges. It requires trade-offs that defy simple slogans.

From Germany to Jerusalem, Kissinger offered policymakers in multiple societies imperfect but practical options for dealing with a troubled world. He provided a path for policy beyond slogans. This was the foundation for his remarkable career. This remains his source of influence, until someone else offers a more effective foreign-policy strategy. Kissinger's critics have failed in this task. The twenty-first century awaits Kissinger's successor.

NOTES

ACKNOWLEDGMENTS

INDEX

Notes

The following abbreviations are used in the notes.

Adenauer Papers	Adenauer Nachlass, Stiftung Bundeskanzler-Adenauer-Haus, Rhöndorf, Germany
Armstrong Papers	Hamilton Fish Armstrong Papers, Seeley Mudd Manuscript Library, Princeton University
Brodie Papers	Bernard Brodie Papers, Special Collections, Charles Young Research Library, University of California at Los Angeles
Buckley Papers	William F. Buckley Papers, Manuscripts and Archives, Yale University Library
DDE	Dwight D. Eisenhower Presidential Library, Abilene, Kans.
Elliott Papers	William Y. Elliott Papers, Hoover Institution, Stanford, Calif.
FRUS	*Foreign Relations of the United States*
Galbraith Papers	Papers of John Kenneth Galbraith, JFKL
JFKL	John F. Kennedy Presidential Library, Boston, Mass.
Lodge Papers	Papers of Henry Cabot Lodge II, Massachusetts Historical Society, Boston
NAR	Nelson A. Rockefeller Papers, RAC
Nixon Papers	Nixon Presidential Materials Project, National Archives, College Park, Md.
NSA	Digital National Security Archive Document Database, http://nsarchive.chadwyck.com

NSF	National Security Files, JFKL
RAC	Rockefeller Archive Center, Pocantico Hills, N.Y.
Schlesinger Papers	Arthur Schlesinger Jr. Papers, JFKL
State FOIA	U.S. Department of State Freedom of Information Act website: http://foia.state.gov/SearchColls/CollsSearch.asp

Introduction

1. Henry Luce, "The American Century," *Life,* 17 February 1941. See also James L. Baughman, *Henry R. Luce and the Rise of the American News Media* (Boston: Twayne Publishers, 1987), esp. 130–133; Olivier Zunz, *Why the American Century?* (Chicago: University of Chicago Press, 1998); James T. Patterson, *Grand Expectations: The United States, 1945–1974* (Oxford: Oxford University Press, 1996); David Reynolds, *One World Divisible: A Global History Since 1945* (New York: W. W. Norton, 2000); John Lewis Gaddis, *The Cold War: A New History* (New York: Penguin, 2005), esp. 259–266.

2. Henry Kissinger, *White House Years* (Boston: Little, Brown, 1979), 229.

3. Luce, "The American Century"; Henry A. Kissinger, "The Meaning of History (Reflections on Spengler, Toynbee and Kant)" (Undergraduate thesis, Department of Government, Harvard University, 1950), 348. See also Eric Hobsbawm's brilliant discussion of these paradoxes in *The Age of Extremes: A History of the World, 1914–1991* (New York: Pantheon, 1995).

4. Henry Kissinger, *Does America Need a Foreign Policy? Toward a Diplomacy for the 21st Century* (New York: Simon and Schuster, 2001), 285.

5. The historical literature on Kissinger is enormous. Some of the most important books include Jussi Hanhimäki, *The Flawed Architect: Henry Kissinger and American Foreign Policy* (New York: Oxford University Press, 2004); Walter Isaacson, *Kissinger: A Biography* (New York: Simon and Schuster, 1992); Robert D. Schulzinger, *Henry Kissinger: Doctor of Diplomacy* (New York: Columbia University Press, 1989); Raymond Garthoff, *Détente and Confrontation: American-Soviet Relations from Nixon to Reagan,* rev. ed. (Washington, D.C.: Brookings Institution, 1994); Seymour M. Hersh, *The Price of Power: Kissinger in the White House* (New York: Summit Books, 1983); John Lewis Gaddis, *Strategies of Containment: A Critical Appraisal of American National Security Policy during the Cold War,* rev. ed. (New York: Oxford University Press, 2005); Bruce Mazlish, *Kissinger: The European Mind in American Diplomacy* (New York: Basic Books, 1976); Ralph Blumenfeld and the staff and editors of the *New York Post, Henry Kissinger: The Private and Public Story* (New York: Signet, 1974); Stephen R. Graubard, *Kissinger: Portrait of a*

Mind (New York: W. W. Norton, 1973); David Landau, *Kissinger: The Uses of Power* (Boston: Houghton Mifflin, 1972).

6. David Halberstam, *The Best and the Brightest* (New York: Random House, 1972). For some excellent examples of books that probe the social and political contexts for policymaking in different ways, see Kai Bird, *The Color of Truth: McGeorge Bundy and William Bundy, Brothers in Arms* (New York: Simon and Schuster, 1998); Robert D. Dean, *Imperial Brotherhood: Gender and the Making of Cold War Foreign Policy* (Amherst: University of Massachusetts Press, 2001); Geoffrey M. Kabaservice, *The Guardians: Kingman Brewster, His Circle, and the Rise of the Liberal Establishment* (New York: Henry Holt, 2004); Andrew Preston, *The War Council: McGeorge Bundy, the NSC, and Vietnam* (Cambridge, Mass.: Harvard University Press, 2006).

7. Henry Kissinger, *Years of Renewal* (New York: Simon and Schuster, 1999), 1071.

8. See Geir Lundestad, "Empire by Invitation? The United States and Western Europe, 1945–1952," *Journal of Peace Research* 23 (September 1986), 263–277; Tony Judt, *Postwar: A History of Europe since 1945* (New York: Penguin, 2005), esp. 63–164; John Lewis Gaddis, *We Now Know: Rethinking Cold War History* (Oxford: Oxford University Press, 1997), 26–53.

9. By many counts the number of governments with democratic institutions grew considerably during the Cold War. I do not dispute this claim. My argument is that the *practice* of democracy, particularly in the realm of foreign policy, was constrained by fears of weakness in the face of internal and external threats—especially communist subversion. For a contrary perspective, see Gaddis, *The Cold War,* 264–266.

10. Kissinger, *Years of Renewal,* 1074–75.

11. Despite decades of quotas and other forms of exclusion before the Second World War, after 1945 Jews became, in the words of one historian, "the most educated of all Americans"—"almost all college-age Jews are in college, and the concentration of Jews in professional occupations is double that of non-Jews." As Yuri Slezkine points out, the numbers are astonishing, and they merit reflection: "50 percent of the most influential American intellectuals (published and reviewed most widely in the top twenty intellectual journals) were Jews. Among the academic elite (identified in the same fashion), Jews made up 56 percent in the social sciences and 61 percent in the humanities." Jews also made up "between one-quarter and one-third of the 'media elite' (the news divisions of the three television networks and PBS, the three leading news magazines, and the four top newspapers). More than one-third of the most 'influential' critics of film, literature, radio, and television were of Jewish background, as were almost half of the Hollywood producers of prime-time television shows and about two-thirds of the directors,

writers, and producers of the fifty top-grossing movies between 1965 and 1982." Jews suffered from deep-seated anti-Semitism in the United States and other countries, but they also achieved remarkable success. Looking at their aggregate accomplishments, one could easily forget that Jews accounted for less than 3 percent of the American population. Yuri Slezkine, *The Jewish Century* (Princeton: Princeton University Press, 2004), 368. See also David A. Hollinger, *Cosmopolitanism and Solidarity: Studies in Ethnoracial, Religious, and Professional Affiliation in the United States* (Madison: University of Wisconsin Press, 2006), 135–165. I understand why many Jews, including Kissinger, fear that a discussion of their achievements as a group will inflame racist tropes about a world Jewish "conspiracy." As a Jew myself, I firmly believe that intentional silence about Jewish accomplishments only gives ammunition to those who condemn alleged secret and illegitimate powers. We need to address the social and political circumstances that encouraged and distorted Jewish achievements. We need to demystify Jewish accomplishments, not pretend to ignore them. Another historian, David Hollinger, makes the same point: "Some people think it unwise to speak at all of the demographic overrepresentation of Jews among the wealthiest, most politically powerful, and most intellectually accomplished of Americans. . . . Although I understand the reasons for this reticence—e.g., do we want to feed anti-Semitic fantasies of a Jewish conspiracy to run the world?—I believe the time has come for historians and social scientists to apply their skills to the question. . . . failure to address the question at this point in time may actually facilitate the perpetuation of racist and other biocentric ideas. The truth is the best defense against bigotry." Hollinger, *Cosmopolitanism and Solidarity,* 154. Kissinger and I have discussed these issues at length, but he has asked that I refrain from quoting our conversations on this specific subject.

12. On Kissinger's attempts to manipulate his image through appearances with female celebrities, see Walter Isaacson's excellent account, *Kissinger,* 355–370.

13. Hollinger, *Cosmopolitanism and Solidarity,* 154. Hollinger writes that the historical experiences of Jews "over many centuries do much to explain Jewish preeminence in the many practices of modernity, just as the conditions of slavery and Jim Crow racism do much to explain the overrepresentation of black men in American prisons. History, not essentialist ideas about communities of dissent, tells us what we most need to know." Ibid., 154–155. Among other things, this book examines the influence of Jewish history, particularly German Jewish history, on Kissinger's career. This book argues that Kissinger's *interpretation* of his experiences as a German Jew—not Jewish ritual or doctrine—deeply influenced his politics.

14. Kissinger, *White House Years,* 54. See also John Lewis Gaddis, "Rescuing Choice from Circumstance: The Statecraft of Henry Kissinger," in Gordon A.

Craig and Francis L. Loewenheim, eds., *The Diplomats, 1939–1979* (Princeton: Princeton University Press, 1994), 564–592.

15. For an excellent discussion of this point, see Melvyn P. Leffler, *A Preponderance of Power: National Security, the Truman Administration, and the Cold War* (Stanford: Stanford University Press, 1992), esp. 1–24. See also Frank Ninkovich, *Modernity and Power: A History of the Domino Theory in the Twentieth Century* (Chicago: University of Chicago Press, 1994); Anders Stephanson, *Kennan and the Art of Foreign Policy* (Cambridge, Mass.: Harvard University Press, 1989).

16. My thinking draws extensively on Alexander L. George's seminal article "The 'Operational Code': A Neglected Approach to the Study of Political Leaders and Decision-Making," *International Studies Quarterly* 13 (June 1969), 190–222.

17. Kissinger, *White House Years,* 55. Kissinger emphasized the importance of a "moral framework" in the author's interview with Henry Kissinger, 27 July 2004. He made similar references in interviews with the author on 7 June 2004 and 26 October 2005.

18. Kissinger, *White House Years,* 230.

19. Quotation from Henry Kissinger's videotaped oral history interview with Louise Bobrow, 11 January 2001, Museum of Jewish Heritage, New York. Kissinger made a very similar statement in the author's interview with him, 27 July 2004.

20. Author's interview with Kissinger, 27 July 2004.

1. Democracy and Its Discontents

1. Sigmund Freud, *Civilization and Its Discontents,* trans. James Strachey (1930; reprint, New York: W. W. Norton, 1961), 111–112.

2. See Stanley G. Payne, *A History of Fascism, 1914–1945* (Madison: University of Wisconsin Press, 1995); George L. Mosse, *The Fascist Revolution: Toward a General Theory of Fascism* (New York: Howard Fertig, 2000); Eugen Weber, *Varieties of Fascism: Doctrines of Revolution in the Twentieth Century* (Princeton: Van Nostrand, 1964).

3. Hannah Arendt, *The Origins of Totalitarianism* (1948; reprint, New York: Harcourt Brace, 1979), 312. See also idem, *On Revolution* (New York: Viking, 1963), esp., 13–52; idem, "Personal Responsibility under Dictatorship" (1964), reprinted in idem, *Responsibility and Judgment* (New York: Schocken Books, 2003), 17–48. Theodor Adorno et al., *The Authoritarian Personality* (New York: Harper, 1950). For a perspective with parallels to Adorno's argument, rooted more explicitly in social psychological analysis, see Erich Fromm, *Escape from Freedom* (New York: Farrar and Rinehart, 1941).

4. Winston Churchill, *The Gathering Storm* (Boston: Houghton Mifflin,

1948), 17–18. For two insightful historical assessments of appeasement, and its complex motivations in the early twentieth century, see Paul Kennedy, *Strategy and Diplomacy, 1870–1945: Eight Studies* (London: Allen and Unwin, 1983), 13–39; Zara Steiner, *The Lights That Failed: European International History, 1919–1933* (Oxford: Oxford University Press, 2005), esp. 635–816.

5. See Melvyn P. Leffler, *A Preponderance of Power: National Security, the Truman Administration, and the Cold War* (Stanford: Stanford University Press, 1992), esp. 15–24; Robert L. Beisner, *Dean Acheson: A Life in the Cold War* (New York: Oxford University Press, 2006), esp. 151–157; Ernest R. May, *"Lessons" of the Past: The Use and Misuse of History in American Foreign Policy* (New York: Oxford University Press, 1973), esp. 19–86.

6. George Kennan, "The Sources of Soviet Conduct," *Foreign Affairs* 25 (July 1947), reprinted in *Foreign Affairs* 65 (Spring 1987), 852–868; quotations on 861, 867–868. For more on Kennan's formulation of containment doctrine, and its connections to domestic society, see John Lewis Gaddis, *Strategies of Containment: A Critical Appraisal of American National Security Policy during the Cold War*, rev. ed. (New York: Oxford University Press, 2005), 24–52; Leffler, *A Preponderance of Power*, esp., 108–109, 179–181; Wilson D. Miscamble, *George F. Kennan and the Making of American Foreign Policy* (Princeton: Princeton University Press, 1992); Anders Stephanson, *Kennan and the Art of Foreign Policy* (Cambridge, Mass.: Harvard University Press, 1989).

7. Lawrence S. Kaplan, *NATO and the United States: The Enduring Alliance*, rev. ed. (New York: Twayne Publishers, 1994), 1–11. See also Michael J. Hogan, *A Cross of Iron: Harry S. Truman and the Origins of the National Security State, 1945–1954* (Cambridge: Cambridge University Press, 1998); Aaron L. Friedberg, *In the Shadow of the Garrison State: America's Anti-Statism and Its Cold War Strategy* (Princeton: Princeton University Press, 2000).

8. For a similar argument, see Mark Mazower, *Dark Continent: Europe's Twentieth Century* (New York: Random House, 1998), esp. 3–40. The biographies that criticize Kissinger for being out of touch with a common American democratic sensibility include Walter Isaacson, *Kissinger: A Biography* (New York: Simon and Schuster, 1992); Robert D. Schulzinger, *Henry Kissinger: Doctor of Diplomacy* (New York: Columbia University Press, 1989); Peter W. Dickson, *Kissinger and the Meaning of History* (Cambridge: Cambridge University Press, 1978); Bruce Mazlish, *Kissinger: The European Mind in American Policy* (New York: Basic Books, 1976); John G. Stoessinger, *Henry Kissinger: The Anguish of Power* (New York: W. W. Norton, 1976); Stephen R. Graubard, *Kissinger: Portrait of a Mind* (New York: W. W. Norton, 1973).

9. Nazi Judenkartei for Louis Kissinger, Stadtarchiv Fürth. This large index

card, compiled and updated by Nazi officials, includes detailed data on the Kissinger family, its various places of residence, professions, etc.

10. For an excellent account of Napoleonic influences on the German states, particularly Bavaria, during the early nineteenth century, see James J. Sheehan, *German History, 1770–1866* (Oxford: Oxford University Press, 1989), 253–274.

11. See James F. Harris, *The People Speak! Anti-Semitism and Emancipation in Nineteenth-Century Bavaria* (Ann Arbor: University of Michigan Press, 1994), 19–30.

12. Ibid., 51–80.

13. Ibid., 5.

14. Petition from Hirschau, 18 December 1848, translated and reprinted in ibid., 253–255; quotation on 254. See also ibid., 87–187.

15. Ibid., 209–231. This assessment agrees with the general argument in Ian Kershaw, *Popular Opinion and Political Dissent in the Third Reich: Bavaria, 1933–1945*, rev. ed. (Oxford: Clarendon Press, 2002), xx–xxviii, 377–385.

16. Walter Isaacson writes that Louis Kissinger "liked the kaiser and yearned for him after his abdication"; Isaacson, *Kissinger*, 19. I have found no evidence for this, or for Louis Kissinger's attachment to any monarchist groups.

17. Author's interview with Henry Kissinger, 26 October 2005. In Bavaria the Center party competed with another conservative nationalist party, the Bavarian People's party (Bavarian Volkspartei), which broke with the Center on Jewish issues in particular. The Bavarian People's party appealed more strongly than the Center to Catholic anti-Semitism. It came to dominate Bavaria during the Weimar years. For an excellent examination of all these issues, see Peter Pulzer, *Jews and the German State: The Political History of a Minority, 1848–1933* (Detroit: Wayne State University Press, 2003), esp. 121–147, 239–247, 322–323. On Christian Democracy and Konrad Adenauer's leadership in post-1945 West Germany, see Chapter 2. Henry Kissinger's strong attraction to Adenauer followed, in part, from his family's attachment to the vision of the Center party in the early twentieth century.

18. Hans Mauersberg, *Wirtschaft und Gesellschaft Fürths in neuer und neuester Zeit* (Göttingen: Vandenhoeck and Ruprecht, 1974), 111–117; Baruch Ophir and Falk Wiesemann, "Fürth," in *Die jüdischen Gemeinden in Bayern 1918–1945: Geschichte und Zerstörung* (Munich: R. Oldenbourg, 1979), 179–187. Middle Franconia is a largely Protestant region in Catholic-dominated Bavaria.

19. Heinrich Strauss, "Fürth in der Weltwirtschaftskrise und nationalsozialistischen Machtergreifung" (Ph.D. diss., University of Erlangen-Nuremberg, 1979), 457–463.

20. Quotation from Henry Kissinger's videotaped oral history interview with

Louise Bobrow, 11 January 2001, Museum of Jewish Heritage, New York. Louis Kissinger's quotation comes from a speech he gave in December 1975, upon returning to Fürth for the first time with his wife and his now famous son. See *Amtsblatt Fürth,* December 1975, 342. I thank Holger Klitzing for helping me to track down this text.

21. Quotation from Henry Kissinger's videotaped oral history interview, Museum of Jewish Heritage. In this interview Kissinger recounts that he "studied Talmud" and "had regular religious instruction." The Nazis suspended Louis Kissinger from his teaching position at the Fürth Mädchenlyzeum in the fall of 1933. In 1935 they forced him to leave his teaching position permanently. See the discussion later in this chapter and Manfred Mümmler, *Fürth, 1933–1945* (Emskirchen: Verlag Maria Mümmler, 1995), 122, 144.

22. Henry Kissinger's boyhood friend Menachem Lion emphasized that social life for Kissinger and other Orthodox Jews in Fürth centered on Jewish groups. Although they considered themselves Germans, they were not assimilated in German society. Menachem Lion's interview with my student Vanessa Walker, conducted in Rehovot, Israel, 7 December 2004. On the unique social space—a "subculture"—occupied by German Jews, see David Sorkin, *The Transformation of German Jewry, 1780–1840* (New York: Oxford University Press, 1987), 107–178. On German Jewish cultural creativity, see George Mosse, *German Jews beyond Judaism* (Bloomington: Indiana University Press, 1985), esp. 21–41.

23. Louis Kissinger was born in 1887. He was twenty-seven years old when the First World War began in 1914. Many other Jews of similar age served in the German military. Louis Kissinger did not. I have not found any documented explanation for his lack of military service. When I asked Henry Kissinger why his father did not fight in the First World War, he answered: "I don't know. We never discussed it." Author's interview with Kissinger, 26 October 2005.

24. Mosse, *German Jews beyond Judaism,* 1–20; quotation on 8. My understanding of *Bildung* draws heavily on David Sorkin, "Wilhelm von Humboldt: The Theory and Practice of Self-Formation *(Bildung),* 1791–1810," *Journal of the History of Ideas* 44 (January–March 1983), 55–73; idem, *The Transformation of German Jewry,* 15–21, 86–104; George Mosse, "Jewish Emancipation: Between *Bildung* and Respectability," in Jehuda Reinharz and Walter Schatzberg, eds., *The Jewish Response to German Culture* (Hanover, N.H.: University Press of New England, 1985), 1–16; W. H. Bruford, *The German Tradition of Self-Cultivation: "Bildung" from Humboldt to Thomas Mann* (Cambridge: Cambridge University Press, 1975); idem, *Culture and Society in Classical Weimar, 1775–1806* (Cambridge: Cambridge University Press, 1962), esp. 418–425.

25. Rudolf Reiser, *Alter Häuser-Große Namen: Nürnberg mit Fürth und Er-*

langen (München: Bruckmann, 1990), 203–206. See also Mosse, *German Jews beyond Judaism,* 60.

26. Henry Kissinger, *Years of Renewal* (New York: Simon and Schuster, 1999), 1078.

27. Henry A. Kissinger, "The Meaning of History (Reflections on Spengler, Toynbee and Kant)" (Undergraduate thesis, Department of Government, Harvard University, 1950), 330, 341–342, 345. For an extended analysis of Kissinger's undergraduate thesis that is consistent with my interpretation, though more focused on broader philosophical issues, see Dickson, *Kissinger and the Meaning of History,* 28–50.

28. Kissinger, "The Meaning of History," 340, 127–128. Kissinger frequently refers to mysticism in general and to a "mystic relationship to the Infinite." See ibid., esp. 340–349.

29. Ibid., 347, n. 1.

30. See Modris Eksteins, *Rites of Spring: The Great War and the Birth of the Modern Age* (Boston: Houghton Mifflin, 1989); Peter Gay, *Weimar Culture: The Outsider as Insider* (New York: Harper and Row, 1968); Fritz Stern, *The Politics of Cultural Despair: A Study in the Rise of the Germanic Ideology* (Berkeley: University of California Press, 1961).

31. Henry Kissinger, *Diplomacy* (New York: Simon and Schuster, 1994), 289.

32. See Michael Burleigh, *The Third Reich: A New History* (New York: Hill and Wang, 2000), 83–121; Richard J. Evans, *The Coming of the Third Reich* (New York: Penguin, 2003), 217–230; Jeffrey Herf, *Reactionary Modernism: Technology, Culture, and Politics in Weimar and the Third Reich* (New York: Cambridge University Press, 1984); George Mosse, *The Crisis of German Ideology: Intellectual Origins of the Third Reich* (New York: Grosset and Dunlap, 1964). Russian, and even some Soviet, leaders had long claimed that they represented the "Third Rome."

33. Kissinger tellingly contrasts the statesmanship of German foreign minister Gustav Stresemann in the 1920s with Hitler's demagoguery in the 1930s. See *Diplomacy,* 266–287.

34. Kershaw, *Popular Opinion and Political Dissent,* 228–229.

35. Ibid., 229–231. Kershaw is careful to argue that although virulent anti-Semitism was common, especially in Franconia, it was not the primary source of Nazi support throughout Bavaria. See also Burleigh, *The Third Reich,* 121.

36. Raffael Mibberlin, "Kesseltreiben gegen 'Judenärzte,'" in *Sie durften nicht mehr Deutsche sein: Jüdischer Alltag in Selbstzeugnissen, 1933–1938* (Frankfurt: Campus Verlag, 1990), 54–60; quotation on 57.

37. Ibid., 54–60.

38. Fred Hahn, *Lieber Stürmer: Leserbriefe an das NS-Kampfblatt 1924 bis 1945*

(Stuttgart: Seewald Verlag, 1978), 115. For circulation figures see Dennis E. Showalter, *Little Man, What Now? Der Stürmer in the Weimar Republic* (Hamden, Conn.: Archon Books, 1982), 78; Richard J. Evans, *The Third Reich in Power* (New York: Penguin, 2005), 145–146, 537–538. The quoted phrase came from historian Heinrich von Treitschke's infamous 1879 essay, "Unsere Aussichten" (Our Future Prospects). The essay is reprinted in Walter Boehlich, *Der Berliner Antisemitismusstreit* (Frankfurt: Insel-Verlag, 1965), 5–12; quotation on 11.

39. Randall L. Bytwerk, *Julius Streicher* (New York: Stein and Day, 1983), 63. See also William P. Varga, *The Number One Nazi Jew-Baiter: A Political Biography of Julius Streicher, Hitler's Chief Anti-Semitic Propagandist* (New York: Carlton, 1981); Showalter, *Little Man, What Now?*, 4–19, 200–232.

40. Strauss, "Fürth in der Weltwirtschaftskrise und nationalsozialistischen Machtergreifung," 381–383; Varga, *The Number One Nazi Jew-Baiter*, 73–179; Showalter, *Little Man, What Now?*, 20–48.

41. Interview with Menachem Lion, 7 December 2004.

42. *Nürnberg-Fürther Israelitischer Gemeindeblatt*, 1 December 1929. This important German Jewish newspaper was published in Nuremberg from 1921 through 1938. Copies of the newspaper are available at the Bibliothek der Jüdisches Museum Franken, Fürth, Germany. See also *Nürnberg-Fürther Israelitischer Gemeindeblatt*, 1 July and 1 October 1930, 1 March 1931, 1 January 1933; *Centralverein Zeitung*, 30 January 1931.

43. Interview with Menachem Lion, 7 December 2004.

44. On the absent civil courage *(Zivilcourage)* and abundant fatalism that characterized many German, and especially German Jewish, responses to Nazism, see Fritz Stern's powerful memoir, *Five Germanys I Have Known* (New York: Farrar, Straus and Giroux, 2006), 71–72, 96–97. Stern was raised in a German Jewish family that converted to Christianity, but he explains that Nazi targeting of Jews made him identify with other German Jews.

45. Rabbi Dr. Heilbronn, "Assimilation," *Nürnberg-Fürther Israelitischer Gemeindeblatt*, 1 December 1933; *Das Jüdische Echo: Bayerische Blätter für die jüdischen Angelegenheiten*, May 1929, August 1930, 26 September 1930, 3 October 1930. Selected copies of the latter newspaper are available at the Nürnberger Institut für NS-Forschung und Jüdische Geschichte des 20. Jahrhunderts, Nuremberg, Germany. I want to thank Peter Zinke for his generous assistance during my visit to this institute. See also *Nürnberg-Fürther Israelitischer Gemeindeblatt*, 1 June 1933, 1 March 1934.

46. This analysis does not deny the courage of various figures who resisted Nazi authority. Many Jews did resist the Nazis, particularly through the Berlin-based Central Association of German Citizens of the Jewish Faith *(Centralverein)*. At least 250,000 German Jews—more than half the German Jewish population—

emigrated to escape Nazism. Jews from Fürth emigrated, including eventually the Kissingers. Heroic resistance among those who stayed, however, was almost nonexistent in Fürth. All the available evidence points to passivity and fatalism rather than resistance in Kissinger's hometown. In this particular context, the central lesson for Kissinger and many other survivors was that democratic resistance proved ineffectual in curtailing the regime's brutality. For a very suggestive set of essays on resistance to Nazi authority, see Michael Geyer and John W. Boyer, eds., *Resistance against the Third Reich, 1933–1990* (Chicago: University of Chicago Press, 1994). On Jewish resistance and the *Centralverein,* see Avraham Barkai, *"Wehr Dich!": Der Centralverein deutscher Staatsbürger jüdischen Glaubens (C.V.), 1893–1938* (Munich: C. H. Beck, 2002); Arnold Paucker, *Der jüdische Abwehrkampf gegen Antisemitismus und Nationalsozialismus in den letzten Jahren der Weimarer Republik* (Hamburg: Leibniz-Verlag, 1968). See also Marion A. Kaplan's analysis of the ambiguities surrounding Jewish responses to Nazism, *Between Dignity and Despair: Jewish Life in Nazi Germany* (New York: Oxford University Press, 1998), esp. 212–216, 229–232.

47. Henry Kissinger, *A World Restored: Metternich, Castlereagh, and the Problems of Peace, 1812–1822* (1957; reprint, London: Phoenix, 2000), 329. Kissinger employs identical language in his Ph.D. dissertation, upon which *A World Restored* is based. Henry Alfred Kissinger, "Peace, Legitimacy, and the Equilibrium (A Study of the Statesmanship of Castlereagh and Metternich)" (Department of Government, Harvard University, April 1954), 541–542.

48. Henry A. Kissinger, "The White Revolutionary: Reflections on Bismarck," *Daedalus* 97 (Summer 1968), 910.

49. Kissinger, *Years of Renewal,* 1065.

50. Henry Kissinger, *Does America Need a Foreign Policy? Toward a Diplomacy for the Twenty-first Century* (New York: Simon and Schuster, 2001), 286. The reference to "normal electoral processes" comes from *Years of Renewal,* 1065.

51. Mümmler, *Fürth, 1936–1945,* 122, 144; Louis Kissinger's speech in *Amtsblatt Fürth,* December 1975, 342.

52. Mümmler, *Fürth, 1936–1945,* 137–144; Kershaw, *Popular Opinion and Political Dissent,* 238. For accounts of Jewish adjustment to Nazism in daily life, see Kaplan, *Between Dignity and Despair,* esp. 17–73; Evans, *The Third Reich in Power,* esp. 555–579.

53. Mümmler, *Fürth, 1936–1945,* 109–131; Stefan Niedermeier, "Antisemitismus, Abwehr und Selbstbehauptung in Nürnberg und Fürth in der Weimarer Republik und in der NS-Zeit" (Master's thesis, Friedrich-Alexander-Universität Erlangen-Nürnberg, 1990), 48–51; Peter Zinke, *Flucht nach Palästina: Lebenswege Nürnberger Juden* (Nuremberg: Antogo Verlag, 2003), 17–19; interview with Paula Kissinger, quoted in Isaacson, *Kissinger,* 26; interview with Menachem Lion, 7 December 2004.

54. Paula Kissinger comments on her husband's shock and confusion in Isaacson, *Kissinger,* 27.

55. Kershaw, *Popular Opinion and Political Dissent,* 236–238; "Jüdisches Leben in Gunzenhausen," Stephani-Volksschule Gunzenhausen, http://www.gunnet.de/stephani/step_pix.htm (accessed 26 July 2005).

56. Kershaw, *Popular Opinion and Political Dissent,* 236.

57. Quotations from Kissinger's videotaped oral history interview, Museum of Jewish Heritage.

58. On Falk and Fanny Stern see the Nazi Judenkartei for Falk Stern, Stadtarchiv Fürth. See also Isaacson, *Kissinger,* 20, 24. On 31 July 1932, 911 of 1,016 voters in Leutershausen cast their ballots for the Nazi party. On 6 November 1932, 791 of 933 voters in Leutershausen cast their ballots for the Nazi party. Nürnberger Staatsarchiv LRA 499 and 500. I thank Peter Zinke of the Nürnberger Institut für NS-Forschung und Jüdische Geschichte des 20. Jahrhunderts for his assistance with sources on Leutershausen and the surrounding region. Zinke also led me on an informative tour of the region.

59. Ernst Engelhardt oral history, 9 September 1989, included in Karl Ernst Stimpfig, "Jüdische Familien in Leutershausen in der 1930er Jahren," 1999, Nürnberger Institut für NS-Forschung und Jüdische Geschichte des 20. Jahrhunderts, Nuremberg; Nazi Judenkartei for Falk Stern, Stadtarchiv Fürth; Kershaw, *Popular Opinion and Political Dissent,* 258–259; Yad Vashem, Central Database of Shoah Victims' Names, www.yadvashem.org (accessed 26 July 2005).

60. This assessment of Nazi followers draws especially on Ian Kershaw, *Hitler: 1889–1936, Hubris* (New York: W. W. Norton, 1999), esp. 527–591; Burleigh, *The Third Reich,* 281–322.

61. Quotations from Kissinger's videotaped oral history interview, Museum of Jewish Heritage. Louis and Paula Kissinger lived in this same apartment until they died.

62. Ibid. On the Jewish community in Washington Heights during the late 1930s and early 1940s, see Steven M. Lowenstein, *Frankfurt on the Hudson: The German-Jewish Community of Washington Heights, 1933–1983* (Detroit: Wayne State University Press, 1989), esp. 22–152; idem, *The Mechanics of Change: Essays in the Social History of German Jewry* (Atlanta: Scholars Press, 1992), 215–226.

63. Quotation from Kissinger's videotaped oral history interview, Museum of Jewish Heritage. Kissinger reprints a long extract from his father's 1946 letter in Kissinger, *Years of Renewal,* 1079. See also Louis Kissinger's speech in Fürth, December 1975, reprinted in *Amtsblatt Fürth,* December 1975, 342. On the crisis of paternal authority among German Jews created by immigration, see Lowenstein, *Frankfurt on the Hudson,* 93.

64. See Carl J. Friedrich, "Anti-Semitism: Challenge to Christian Culture," in Isacque Graeber and Steuart Henderson Britt, eds., *Jews in a Gentile World: The Problem of Anti-Semitism* (New York: Macmillan, 1942), 1–18; Leonard Dinnerstein, *Antisemitism in America* (New York: Oxford University Press, 1994), 128–149; Jonathan D. Sarna, *American Judaism: A History* (New Haven: Yale University Press, 2004), 208–271; Hasia R. Diner, *The Jews of the United States, 1654 to 2000* (Berkeley: University of California Press, 2004), 205–258.

65. "Awake, America," *Aufbau*, 24 May 1940; Thomas Mann, "Die Juden warden bestehen," ibid. Archived copies of *Aufbau* are available at the New York Historical Society Library, New York. On the circulation of *Aufbau* and the German press in the United States in general, see Lowenstein, *Frankfurt on the Hudson*, 50.

66. *Aufbau*, 8 January 1999.

67. George Washington High School had a large cohort of Jewish students, many of whom participated in various extracurricular activities, including sports, literary clubs, and performance arts. Historian Paula Fass explains that at George Washington and other high schools in the 1930s these extracurricular activities played a crucial role in "Americanization," bringing different ethnic groups together while also encouraging continued ethnic identification. Fass uses a close reading of high school yearbooks to document the range and participation in extracurricular activities. See Paula S. Fass, *Outside In: Minorities and the Transformation of American Education* (New York: Oxford University Press, 1989), 73–111. The George Washington High School yearbooks for the years 1939–1941, when Kissinger attended, show this proliferation of extracurricular activities, but they also point to Kissinger's nonparticipation. He is absent from every discussion and photo of "high school life." See *The Hatchet*, yearbook of George Washington High School, 1939–1941, available at the George Washington Educational Campus, New York. I thank my colleague William Reese for his assistance in understanding the social environment of American high schools in the early twentieth century.

68. See Martin Jay, *Permanent Exiles: Essays on the Intellectual Migration from Germany to America* (New York: Columbia University Press, 1985); Donald Fleming and Bernard Bailyn, eds., *The Intellectual Migration: Europe and America, 1930–1960* (Cambridge, Mass.: Harvard University Press, 1969); David Sorkin's review of Reinhard Bendix's memoir, *From Berlin to Berkeley: German-Jewish Identities*, in *Theory and Society* 17 (March 1988), 285–291.

69. Quotation in Barnard Law Collier, "The Road to Peking, or How Does This Kissinger Do It?" *New York Times Magazine*, 14 November 1971. In our discussions, Kissinger has not been quite so categorical.

70. Author's interview with Henry and Walter Kissinger in Fürth, Germany, 7 June 2004; press conference by Henry and Walter Kissinger at the Kartofel restau-

rant in Fürth, 7 June 2004. Ian Buruma describes the international anti-Semitism that often links Kissinger to various alleged Jewish conspiracies. See Buruma, "How to Talk about Israel," *New York Times Magazine*, 31 August 2003.

71. Kissinger, *Years of Renewal*, 1078.

72. Freud, *Civilization and Its Discontents*, 111–112. See also Eksteins, *Rites of Spring;* Michael Geyer, "The Place of the Second World War in German Memory and History," *New German Critique* 71 (Spring–Summer 1997), 5–40. For insightful explorations of the role of emotion in policymaking, see Frank Costigliola, "'Unceasing Pressure for Penetration': Gender, Pathology, and Emotion in George Kennan's Formation of the Cold War," *Journal of American History* 83 (March 1997), 1309–39; idem, "'Like Animals or Worse': Narratives of Culture and Emotion by U.S. and British POWs and Airmen behind Soviet Lines, 1944–1945," *Diplomatic History* 28 (November 2004), 749–780. For a classic political science model that emphasizes the lasting influence of emotions, memories, and remembered lessons in a policymaker's early experiences, see Alexander L. George, "The 'Operational Code': A Neglected Approach to the Study of Political Leaders and Decision-Making," *International Studies Quarterly* 13 (June 1969), 190–222.

73. Quotation from Kissinger's videotaped oral history interview, Museum of Jewish Heritage; Stern, *Five Germanys I Have Known*, 4. Stern also refers to the "fragility of freedom" on the same page.

74. Quotation from Kissinger's videotaped oral history interview, Museum of Jewish Heritage.

75. Churchill, *The Gathering Storm*, 17–18. George Kennan's quotation comes from his famous "long telegram." See Chargé in the Soviet Union (George Kennan) to the Secretary of State, 22 February 1946, available at http://www.gwu.edu/~nsarchiv/coldwar/documents/episode-1/kennan.htm (accessed 11 August 2005).

2. Transatlantic Ties

1. The scholarship on the transatlantic nature of American history is enormous, particularly for the colonial period and the Revolution. For some representative works, see Felix Gilbert, *To the Farewell Address: Ideas of Early American Foreign Policy* (Princeton: Princeton University Press, 1961); Alan Taylor, *American Colonies* (New York: Penguin, 2001); Bernard Bailyn, *Atlantic History: Concept and Contours* (Cambridge, Mass.: Harvard University Press, 2005); J. H. Elliott, *Empires of the Atlantic World: Britain and Spain in America, 1492–1830* (New Haven: Yale University Press, 2006). The scholarship on immigration, citizenship, and the construction of "whiteness" in America is also vast. For some representative works, see David R. Roediger, *The Wages of Whiteness: Race and the Making of the American Working Class* (New York: Verso, 1991); Matthew Frye Jacobson, *Whiteness of a Dif-*

ferent Color: European Immigrants and the Alchemy of Race (Cambridge, Mass.: Harvard University Press, 1998); George Lipsitz, *The Possessive Investment in Whiteness: How White People Profit from Identity Politics* (Philadelphia: Temple University Press, 1998).

2. President Franklin Roosevelt, "Arsenal of Democracy" radio address ("Fireside chat" number 16), 29 December 1940, text and audio recording available at http://millercenter.virginia.edu/scripps/diglibrary/prezspeeches/roosevelt/fdr_1940_1229.html (accessed 15 August 2005). See also Warren F. Kimball, *The Juggler: Franklin Roosevelt as Wartime Statesman* (Princeton: Princeton University Press, 1991), 21–41, 83–105; David Kennedy, *Freedom from Fear: The American People in Depression and War, 1929–1945* (New York: Oxford University Press, 1999), 426–464.

3. President Woodrow Wilson's Address to a Joint Session of Congress, 2 April 1917. In this speech Wilson asked Congress to recognize that a state of war existed between the United States and the German Empire. Arthur Link, ed., *The Papers of Woodrow Wilson*, vol. 41 (Princeton: Princeton University Press, 1983), 519–527; quotation on 525. President Franklin Roosevelt, "On the Fall of Mussolini" radio address ("Fireside chat" number 25), 28 July 1943, text and audio recording available at http://millercenter.virginia.edu/scripps/diglibrary/prezspeeches/roosevelt/fdr_1943_0728.html (accessed 15 August 2005). See also Robert A. Divine, *Second Chance: The Triumph of Internationalism in America during World War II* (New York: Atheneum, 1967); Melvyn P. Leffler, *A Preponderance of Power: National Security, the Truman Administration, and the Cold War* (Stanford: Stanford University Press, 1992), esp. 1–24.

4. See Warren F. Kimball, *Forged in War: Roosevelt, Churchill, and the Second World War* (New York: W. Morrow, 1997); David Reynolds, *Rich Relations: The American Occupation of Britain, 1942–1945* (New York: Random House, 1995); Petra Goedde, *GIs and Germans: Culture, Gender, and Foreign Relations, 1945–1949* (New Haven: Yale University Press, 2003). For a thoughtful discussion of how warfare and its memories create new connections between societies—including both allies and belligerents—see Ute Frevert, "Europeanizing German History," *Bulletin of the German Historical Institute* 36 (Spring 2005), 12–15. Wendell Wilkie most famously used the phrase "one world" in his bestselling 1943 book, *One World* (New York: Simon and Schuster).

5. Secretary of State George C. Marshall Address at Harvard University, 5 June 1947, available at http://www.bnt.com/marshall/speech.html (accessed 19 August 2005). See also Leffler, *A Preponderance of Power*, 151–164; Michael J. Hogan, *The Marshall Plan: America, Britain, and the Reconstruction of Western Europe, 1947–1952* (New York: Cambridge University Press, 1987).

6. George F. Kennan, lecture to the National War College, 18 June 1947, quoted in idem, *Memoirs, 1925–1950* (London: Hutchinson, 1967), 351. Thomas

Schelling calculates that in the first year of the Marshall Plan American outlays for this single program totaled approximately 1.5 percent of the U.S. gross national product. No other single American foreign aid program has transferred a comparable percentage of U.S. wealth. See Thomas C. Schelling, "Greenhouse Effect," in *The Concise Encyclopedia of Economics,* available at http://www.econlib.org/LIBRARY/Enc/GreenhouseEffect.html (accessed 11 November 2006).

7. See Geir Lundestad, "Empire by Invitation? The United States and Western Europe, 1945–1952," *Journal of Peace Research* 23 (September 1986), 263–277; John Lewis Gaddis, *We Now Know: Rethinking Cold War History* (New York: Oxford University Press, 1997), 26–53.

8. Quoted by Kissinger in *Does America Need a Foreign Policy? Toward a Diplomacy for the Twenty-first Century* (New York: Simon and Schuster, 2001), 285. Kissinger cites the following source for Bismarck's words in German: Paul Liman, *Fürst Bismarck nach seiner Entlassung: Neue vermehrte Volksausgabe* (Leipzig: Historisch-politischer Verlag, 1901), 3. My research assistant Gil Ribak helped me to acquire a 1904 edition of the same book, published in Berlin by C. A. Schwetschke and Son. A more literal translation of Bismarck's words would be "The statesman can never create anything himself; he can only wait and listen until he hears the footsteps of God through the course of events, then lunge forward and seize the hem of His coat—that is all" ("Der Staatsmann kann nie selber etwas schaffen, er kann nur abwarten und lauschen, bis er den Schritt Gottes durch die Ereignisse hallen hört; dann vorzuspringen und den Zipfel seines Mantels zu sassen, das ist alles"). Kissinger's translation of Bismarck gives agency to the statesman—"walk with Him a few steps of the way"—that is not in Bismarck's words. I thank Sonja Mekel for her help with this translation.

9. Quotation from Henry Kissinger's videotaped oral history interview with Louise Bobrow, 11 January 2001, Museum of Jewish Heritage, New York. Kissinger made similar comments in a discussion with the author, 11 June 2005. Henry A. Kissinger, "The White Revolutionary: Reflections on Bismarck," *Daedalus* 97 (Summer 1968), 910.

10. For a provocative reflection on the experience of Jews as familiar strangers and "service nomads" in the twentieth century, see Yuri Slezkine, *The Jewish Century* (Princeton: Princeton University Press, 2004), 4–104.

11. For some of the seminal works on nationalism and identity, see Benedict Anderson, *Imagined Communities: Reflections on the Origin and Spread of Nationalism,* rev. ed. (London: Verso, 1991); Eric Hobsbawm and Terence Ranger, eds., *The Invention of Tradition* (Cambridge: Cambridge University Press, 1983); Ernest Gellner, *Nations and Nationalism* (Oxford: Blackwell, 1983); Partha Chatterjee, *The Nation and Its Fragments: Colonial and Postcolonial Histories* (Princeton: Princeton University Press, 1993).

12. For one of the earliest and clearest examples of Kissinger's self-defined role as a transatlantic translator for American policymakers, see Kissinger, "Reflections on American Diplomacy," *Foreign Affairs* 35 (January–February 1956), 37–56.

13. Kissinger quoted in Joseph Kraft, "In Search of Kissinger," *Harper's Magazine*, January 1971, 57.

14. Quotations from Kissinger's videotaped oral history interview, Museum of Jewish Heritage.

15. Deborah Dash Moore, *GI Jews: How World War II Changed a Generation* (Cambridge, Mass.: Harvard University Press, 2004), 49–85. On the social distance between New York and Spartanburg, South Carolina, see Stephen R. Graubard, *Kissinger: Portrait of a Mind* (New York: W. W. Norton, 1973), 2.

16. These quotations come from Walter Isaacson's 1988 interviews with Henry and Walter Kissinger. See Isaacson, *Kissinger: A Biography* (New York: Simon and Schuster, 1992), 40, 56–57.

17. Quotations from Kissinger's oral history interview, Museum of Jewish Heritage. On the anti-Semitism in the American military during the Second World War, see Moore, *GI Jews*, 59–60, 79; Jonathan D. Sarna, *American Judaism: A History* (New Haven: Yale University Press, 2004), 266; Joseph Bendersky, *The "Jewish Threat": Anti-Semitic Politics of the U.S. Army* (New York: Basic Books, 2000), 287–347.

18. Moore, *GI Jews*, 21. See also Sarna, *American Judaism*, 264–265; Jay M. Eidelman, ed., *Ours to Fight For: American Jewish Voices from the Second World War* (New York: Museum of Jewish Heritage, 2003).

19. Carl J. Friedrich, "Anti-Semitism: Challenge to Christian Culture," in Isacque Graeber and Steuart Henderson Britt, eds., *Jews in a Gentile World: The Problem of Anti-Semitism* (New York: Macmillan, 1942), 1–18; quotations on 7, 12, 15.

20. Mark Silk, "Notes on the Judeo-Christian Tradition in America," *American Quarterly* 36 (Spring 1984), 67–68.

21. Friedrich, "Anti-Semitism," 15.

22. See David A. Hollinger, *Science, Jews, and Secular Culture: Studies in Mid-Twentieth-Century American Intellectual History* (Princeton: Princeton University Press, 1996), 17–41; Sarna, *American Judaism*, 267.

23. Deborah Dash Moore, "Jewish GIs and the Creation of the Judeo-Christian Tradition," *Religion and Culture* 8 (Winter 1998), 47; Friedrich, "Anti-Semitism," 14–15.

24. Moore, "Jewish GIs," 37.

25. Moore, *GI Jews*, 118–155; Sarna, *American Judaism*, 267.

26. Quotations from Henry Kissinger, *Diplomacy* (New York: Simon and Schuster, 1994), 833.

27. For a more extensive analysis of the role of religion in American identity during the twentieth century, and particularly the dominance of Judeo-Christian faith, see Hollinger, *Science, Jews, and Secular Culture,* 17–41; Silk, "Notes on the Judeo-Christian Tradition in America," 65–85.

28. On "Orientalism" see the classic work of Edward Said, *Orientalism* (New York: Vintage, 1979). For thoughtful applications of this concept to international history, see Andrew J. Rotter, "Saidism without Said: *Orientalism* and U.S. Diplomatic History," *American Historical Review* 105 (October 2000), 1205–17; Douglas Little, *American Orientalism: The United States and the Middle East since 1945* (Chapel Hill: University of North Carolina Press, 2002); Salim Yaqub, *Containing Arab Nationalism: The Eisenhower Doctrine and the Middle East* (Chapel Hill: University of North Carolina Press, 2004), esp. 11–15, 269–276.

29. On this point, and the "tilt" of Nixon and Kissinger toward white supremacist voices at home and abroad, see Thomas Borstelmann, *The Cold War and the Color Line: American Race Relations in the Global Arena* (Cambridge, Mass.: Harvard University Press, 2001), 223–242.

30. Friedrich, "Anti-Semitism," 17–18.

31. Quotation from Kissinger's oral history interview, Museum of Jewish Heritage; Ralph Blumenfeld and the staff and editors of the *New York Post, Henry Kissinger: The Private and Public Story* (New York: Signet, 1974), 48–53; quotation on 52.

32. In the popular movie about his career, *The Fog of War* (2004), Robert McNamara effectively depicts himself as a hard-working, patriotic, and virtuous American everyman. Kissinger could never play this part because of his appearance and background, as well as his personality.

33. Author's interview with Henry Kissinger, 7 June 2004.

34. Peter Gay, *My German Question* (New Haven: Yale University Press, 1998), 155; George L. Mosse, *Confronting History: A Memoir* (Madison: University of Wisconsin Press, 2000), 219.

35. For two of the most influential books by Gay and Mosse, displaying their deep connection to twentieth-century Germany and their ability to translate German history into a compelling narrative for American readers, see Peter Gay, *Weimar Culture: The Outsider as Insider* (New York: Harper and Row, 1968); George L. Mosse, *The Crisis of German Ideology: Intellectual Origins of the Third Reich* (New York: Grosset and Dunlap, 1964).

36. Henry Kissinger's speech at the German Historical Institute, Washington D.C., 18 March 2003, reprinted in *Remembering Willy Brandt,* Schriftenreihe der Bundeskanzler-Willy-Brandt-Stiftung, no. 10 (Berlin, 2003), 43.

37. Quotation in Guy Stern, "The Jewish Exiles in the Service of U.S. Intelligence: The Post-War Years," *Leo Baeck Institute Year Book* 40 (1995), 52; quotations

from Kissinger's oral history interview, Museum of Jewish Heritage. Recounting his own response to the defeat of the Nazi regime as a nineteen-year-old German Jewish refugee in New York, Fritz Stern echoes Kissinger's comments: "We assumed that many Germans still clung to the Nazi faith, and we soon came to realize that many of them, certain of their own innocence, were consumed with self-pity. . . . The punitive decisions taken at the Potsdam Conference, and the ensuing expulsion of some ten million Germans from the east, aroused little or no compassion. It was the Germans themselves who had begun a program of 'ethnic cleansing' in Eastern Europe." See Fritz Stern, *Five Germanys I Have Known* (New York: Farrar, Straus and Giroux, 2006), 170.

38. Guy Stern, "In the Service of American Intelligence: German-Jewish Exiles in the War against Hitler," *Leo Baeck Institute Year Book* 37 (1992), 463; quotation from Kissinger's oral history interview, Museum of Jewish Heritage. See also Blumenfeld, *Henry Kissinger,* 65; Isaacson, *Kissinger,* 48–49. On the proportion of refugees in intelligence work, see Hans Habe, *All My Sins: An Autobiography,* trans. E. Osers (London: George Harrap, 1957), 324. See also Barry M. Katz, *Foreign Intelligence: Research and Analysis in the Office of Strategic Services, 1942–1945* (Cambridge, Mass: Harvard University Press, 1989), 10–13; Thomas F. Troy, *Donovan and the CIA: A History of the Establishment of the Central Intelligence Agency* (Langley, Va.: CIA Center for the Study of Intelligence, 1981), 494, n. 38.

39. Quoted from interviews with Henry Kissinger in Blumenfeld, *Henry Kissinger,* 75–76.

40. Quotation from McGeorge Bundy, "The Battlefields of Power and the Searchlights of the Academy," in E. A. J. Johnson, ed., *The Dimensions of Diplomacy* (Baltimore: Johns Hopkins Press, 1964), 3. See also Katz, *Foreign Intelligence,* esp. 1–28; Robin W. Winks, *Cloak and Gown: Scholars in the Secret War, 1939–1961* (New Haven: Yale University Press, 1987).

41. One can contrast Kissinger's outsider position in the intelligence community with the insider activities of a figure like Allen Dulles. See Peter Grose, *Gentleman Spy: The Life of Allen Dulles* (New York: Houghton Mifflin, 1994).

42. Quotation from Kissinger's oral history interview, Museum of Jewish Heritage. See also Henry Kissinger's report on West German society to the Psychological Strategy Board, July 1952, folder 91, box 6, Records of the Psychological Strategy Board, White House Central Files, Harry S Truman Presidential Library, Independence, Mo. I thank Thomas Alan Schwartz for initially bringing this document to my attention. See also Henry Kissinger's speech at the German Historical Institute, Washington D.C., 18 March 2003, 43; author's interview with Henry Kissinger, 26 October 2005.

43. Quotations from Kissinger's oral history interview, Museum of Jewish Heritage. Ralph Farris quotation from Blumenfeld, *Henry Kissinger,* 60.

44. Quotation from Kissinger's oral history interview, Museum of Jewish Heritage.

45. Henry Kissinger's speech at the German Historical Institute, Washington D.C., 18 March 2003, 46.

46. See Saul K. Padover, *Experiment in Germany: The Story of an American Intelligence Officer* (New York: Duell, Sloan, and Pearce, 1946), 286; Blumenfeld, *Henry Kissinger,* 66. Padover was an intelligence officer in the Psychological Warfare Division of the U.S. Army. He arrived in Krefeld, briefly, in early March 1945, just before Kissinger took over as military administrator.

47. See Brigitte Elsässer, "Kissinger in Krefeld und Bensheim," *Deutsch-amerikanischer Almanach* 1 (1994), 15–17; Blumenfeld, *Henry Kissinger,* 63–64. I thank Stephan Fuchs and Gil Ribak for their assistance in acquiring the first source—a periodical that proved difficult to find.

48. Padover, *Experiment in Germany,* 284–326. See also Earl F. Ziemke, *The U.S. Army in the Occupation of Germany, 1944–1946* (Washington D.C.: Center of Military History, United States Army, 1990), 186.

49. Padover, *Experiment in Germany,* 297–298.

50. Fritz Kraemer quoted in Marvin Kalb and Bernard Kalb, *Kissinger* (Boston: Little, Brown, 1974), 40.

51. Fritz Kraemer quoted in Blumenfeld, *Henry Kissinger,* 67; Elisabeth Heid quoted in *Newsweek,* 8 October 1973, 48; Jerry Bechhofer quoted in Blumenfeld, *Henry Kissinger,* 73.

52. See Elsässer, "Kissinger in Krefeld und Bensheim," 18–30.

53. Author's interview with Kissinger, 26 October 2005.

54. Quotation from Henry A. Kissinger, "The New Cult of Neutralism," *The Reporter* (24 November 1960), 29.

55. See Thomas Alan Schwartz, *America's Germany: John J. McCloy and the Federal Republic of Germany* (Cambridge, Mass.: Harvard University Press, 1991), 29–155; Carolyn Woods Eisenberg, *Drawing the Line: The American Decision to Divide Germany, 1944–1949* (New York: Cambridge University Press, 1996), 363–410; Leffler, *A Preponderance of Power,* 182–219, 277–286; Gaddis, *We Now Know,* 113–129. On Soviet postwar expansionism in central Europe, see Vladislav Zubok and Constantine Pleshakov, *Inside the Kremlin's Cold War: From Stalin to Khrushchev* (Cambridge, Mass.: Harvard University Press, 1996), 36–173; Norman Naimark, *The Russians in Germany: A History of the Soviet Zone of Occupation, 1945–1949* (Cambridge, Mass.: Harvard University Press, 1995); Vojtech Mastny, *The Cold War and Soviet Insecurity: The Stalin Years* (New York: Oxford University Press, 1996).

56. Henry Kissinger's eulogy of Fritz Kraemer, 8 October 2003, provided by Kissinger to the author.

57. Ibid. Kissinger's math is mistaken here. He was born in 1923, and therefore turned twenty-one in 1944. Angered by Kissinger's policies, Kraemer cut off all contact with Kissinger in 1975. They never spoke directly again. Kraemer died on 8 September 2003. Despite Kraemer's explicit orders to prohibit Kissinger's attendance at his funeral, Kraemer's children granted Kissinger his request to eulogize his old friend and mentor. Author's interviews with Sven Kraemer, 16 June and 23 June 2005.

58. Kissinger's eulogy of Fritz Kraemer, 8 October 2003. See the discussion of *Bildung* in Chapter 1.

59. Fritz Kraemer to Henry Kissinger, 1 November 1956, folder 38, box 4, Series 4A, Record Group 5, Rockefeller Brothers Fund, Special Studies Project Collection, Rockefeller Archive Center, Pocantico Hills, N.Y.

60. Ibid. For a revealing personal account of Kraemer's demeanor, outlook, and belief in "great men," see Peter F. Drucker, *Adventures of a Bystander* (New York: Harper and Row, 1979), 141–157. For accounts of Kraemer's broad influence on policymakers in the second half of the twentieth century, see Nick Thimmesch, "The Iron Mentor of the Pentagon: Why Even Henry Kissinger Needs Dr. Fritz Kraemer," *Washington Post Magazine,* 2 March 1975; Michael T. Kaufman, "Fritz Kraemer, 95, Tutor to U.S. Generals and Kissinger, Dies," *New York Times,* 19 November 2003, A24.

61. See Maximiliane Saalfrank, "Kissinger in Oberammergau," *Deutsch-amerikanischer Almanach* 1 (1994), 36–40; "Unterwegs in geheimer Mission: Henry Kissinger und Oberammergau," *Garmisch-Partenkirchen Journal* 4 (August/September 1993), 34–37.

62. Dick Van Osten, quoted in Blumenfeld, *Henry Kissinger,* 79; author's interview with Henry Rosovsky, 3 December 2005.

63. On the presence of Nazi rocket scientists in the area, their surrender to U.S. Army Counterintelligence, and the role of Wernher von Braun, see Dennis Piszkiewicz, *The Nazi Rocketeers: Dreams of Space and Crimes of War* (Westport, Conn.: Praeger, 1995), 195–238. For a discussion of the strong Nazi presence in Oberammergau, see Willard A. Heaps, "Oberammergau Today," *Christian Century* 63 (4 December 1946), 1468–69.

64. On the attraction of the Center party for many German Jews, see Peter Pulzer, *Jews and the German State: The Political History of a Minority, 1848–1933* (Detroit: Wayne State University Press, 2003), 142–144, 239–247.

65. A number of scholars have written detailed biographies of Adenauer that elaborate on these points. See Hans-Peter Schwarz, *Adenauer: Der Aufstieg, 1876–1952* (Stuttgart: Deutsche Verlags-Anstalt, 1986); Henning Köhler, *Adenauer: Eine politische Biographie* (Frankfurt am Main: Propyläen, 1994); Charles Williams, *Adenauer: The Father of the New Germany* (New York: John Wiley, 2000).

66. Daniel E. Rogers, "Transforming the German Party System: The United States and the Origins of Political Moderation, 1945–1949," *Journal of Modern History* 65 (September 1993), 515.

67. See Adenauer Rede in der Freien Universität, West Berlin, 5. Dezember 1958, 16.25, 1958/Band 2, Reden, Interviews, Aufsätze; Konrad Adenauer an dem Herrn Staatssekretär, 9. Dezember 1960, III/50; Ansprache des Bundeskanzlers auf dem Festakt anläßlich der 10. Sommertagung des Politischen Clubs an der Evangelischen Akademie, Tutzing, 19. Juli 1963 (Unkorrigiertes Manuskript), 02.31, 1963/Band 1, Adenauer Papers. On the crucial role of religious values and influences in the formation of the CDU, see Maria Mitchell, "Materialism and Secularism: CDU Politicians and National Socialism, 1945–1949," *Journal of Modern History* 67 (June 1995), 278–308. See also Ronald Granieri, "Political Parties and German-American Relations: Politics beyond the Water's Edge," in Detlef Junker, ed., *The United States and Germany in the Era of the Cold War, 1945–1990: A Handbook,* vol. 1 (Cambridge: Cambridge University Press, 2004), 141–148.

68. Kissinger, *Diplomacy,* 502–503; idem, "The White Revolutionary," 898.

69. Kissinger, *Diplomacy,* 502.

70. Ibid., 503.

71. See Kissinger's speech at the German Historical Institute, Washington, D.C., 18 March 2003, 43.

72. On 16 October 1963 the CDU forced Adenauer, then eighty-seven years old, to leave the chancellorship after more than fourteen years in office. Adenauer remained the chairman of the CDU until 1966. He died at age ninety-one on 19 April 1967. The dates of Kissinger's meetings with Adenauer are listed in the card file on Adenauer's appointments, available at the Stiftung Bundeskanzler-Adenauer-Haus, Rhöndorf. The notes on Adenauer's discussions with Kissinger on 18 May 1961, 16 February 1962, and 17 May 1963 are available in the Adenauer Papers, III/59, III/60, and III/79 respectively. Attached to the card file notations on Kissinger's discussions with Adenauer is a letter Kissinger wrote on 8 February 1967, after their last meeting. Kissinger wrote: "It always means a great deal to me to be able to share the wisdom of one of the great men of our period."

73. For some representative works from the enormous literature on the expansion of U.S. cultural influence, see Reinhold Wagnleitner, *Coca-Colonization and the Cold War: The Cultural Mission of the United States in Austria after the Second World War,* trans. Diana M. Wolf (Chapel Hill: University of North Carolina Press, 1994); Uta G. Poiger, *Jazz Rock and Rebels: Cold War Politics and American Culture in a Divided Germany* (Berkeley: University of California Press, 2000); Victoria de Grazia, *Irresistible Empire: America's Advance through 20th Century Europe* (Cambridge, Mass.: Harvard University Press, 2005); Christopher Endy, *Cold War Holi-*

days: American Tourism in France (Chapel Hill: University of North Carolina Press, 2004); Penny M. Von Eschen, *Satchmo Blows Up the World: Jazz Ambassadors Play the Cold War* (Cambridge, Mass.: Harvard University Press, 2004).

74. See Arthur M. Schlesinger Jr., *The Vital Center: The Politics of Freedom* (Boston: Houghton Mifflin, 1949).

75. For insightful examinations of the intersection between gender, emotion, and masculinity in Cold War policymaking, see Frank Costigliola, "'Unceasing Pressure for Penetration': Gender, Pathology, and Emotion in George Kennan's Formation of the Cold War," *Journal of American History* 83 (March 1997), 1309–39; idem, "The Nuclear Family: Tropes of Gender and Pathology in the Western Alliance," *Diplomatic History* 21 (April 1997), 163–183; Robert D. Dean, *Imperial Brotherhood: Gender and the Making of Cold War Foreign Policy* (Amherst: University of Massachusetts Press, 2003); Andrew Rotter, *Comrades at Odds: The United States and India, 1947–1964* (Ithaca: Cornell University Press, 2000), 188–219.

76. See Mark Atwood Lawrence, *Assuming the Burden: Europe and the American Commitment to War in Vietnam* (Berkeley: University of California Press, 2005); Gary R. Hess, *The United States' Emergence as a Southeast Asian Power, 1940–1950* (New York: Columbia University Press, 1987).

77. Quotation from author's interview with Kissinger, 26 October 2005.

3. The Cold War University

1. Author's interview with Henry Kissinger, 26 October 2005.

2. On MIT and Stanford see Stuart W. Leslie, *The Cold War and American Science: The Military-Industrial-Academic Complex at M.I.T. and Stanford* (New York: Columbia University Press, 1993). See also Rebecca S. Lowen, *Creating the Cold War University: The Transformation of Stanford* (Berkeley: University of California Press, 1997); Margaret Pugh O'Mara, *Cities of Knowledge: Cold War Science and the Search for the Next Silicon Valley* (Princeton: Princeton University Press, 2005), 17–141.

3. My use of the term "Cold War University" draws on the work of others, including Ellen W. Schrecker, *No Ivory Tower: McCarthyism and the Universities* (New York: Oxford University Press, 1986), 63–160, 338–341; R. C. Lewontin, "The Cold War and the Transformation of the Academy," in Noam Chomsky et al., eds., *The Cold War and the University: Toward an Intellectual History of the Postwar Years* (New York: New Press, 1998), 1–34; Christopher Simpson, "Universities, Empire, and the Production of Knowledge," in Simpson, ed., *Universities and Empire: Money and Politics in the Social Sciences during the Cold War* (New York: New Press, 1998); Michael A. Bernstein and Allen Hunter, eds., "The Cold War and Expert

Knowledge," special issue of *Radical History Review* 63 (Fall 1995), 1–139; David Engerman, "Rethinking Cold War Universities: Some Recent Histories," *Journal of Cold War Studies* 5 (July 2003), 80–95.

4. See James Conant's influential address, "Our Unique Heritage," 30 June 1942, reprinted in idem, *Our Fighting Faith: Six Addresses to College Students* (Cambridge, Mass.: Harvard University Press, 1944), 25–39. See also Peter Novick, *That Noble Dream: The "Objectivity Question" and the American Historical Profession* (Cambridge: Cambridge University Press, 1988), 281–413; David W. Noble, *Death of a Nation: American Culture and the End of Exceptionalism* (Minneapolis: University of Minnesota Press, 2002).

5. McGeorge Bundy, "The Battlefields of Power and the Searchlights of the Academy," in E. A. J. Johnson, ed., *The Dimensions of Diplomacy* (Baltimore: Johns Hopkins Press, 1964), 3. See also Morton Keller and Phyllis Keller, *Making Harvard Modern: The Rise of America's University* (New York: Oxford University Press, 2001), 93–95; James Hershberg, *James B. Conant: Harvard to Hiroshima and the Making of the Nuclear Age* (New York: Alfred A. Knopf, 1993), 412; Robin W. Winks, *Cloak and Gown: Scholars in the Secret War, 1939–1961,* 2d ed. (New Haven: Yale University Press, 1987), 60–115, 439–469. For a much more negative appraisal of the relationship between the U.S. government and the Russian Research Center, see Sigmund Diamond, *Compromised Campus: The Collaboration of Universities with the Intelligence Community, 1945–1955* (New York: Oxford University Press, 1992), 50–110.

6. Author's interview with Kissinger, 26 October 2005.

7. My analysis of the integration of knowledge and power in the Cold War University draws, most obviously, on Michel Foucault, *Discipline and Punish: The Birth of the Prison,* trans. Alan Sheridan (New York: Vintage Books, 1995), esp. 3–31; idem, *The Birth of the Clinic: An Archaeology of Medical Perception,* trans. A. M. Sheridan Smith (New York: Vintage Books, 1994); idem, *Power/Knowledge: Selected Interviews and Other Writings, 1972–1977,* ed. Colin Gordon (New York: Pantheon Books, 1980).

8. Selma Stern, *The Court Jew,* trans. Ralph Weiman (Philadelphia: Jewish Publication Society, 1950), 266–267. See also Michael Graetz, "Court Jews in Economics and Politics," in Vivian B. Mann and Richard I. Cohen, eds., *From Court Jews to the Rothschilds* (New York: Prestel, 1996), 27–43; Steven Lowenstein, "Court Jews, Tradition and Modernity," in Rotraud Ries and J. Friedrich Battenberg, eds., *Hofjuden: Ökonomie und Interkulturalität die Jüdische Wirtschaftselite in 18 Jahrhundert* (Hamburg: Christians, 2002), 369–381; Jonathan Israel, *European Jewry in the Age of Mercantilism, 1550–1750* (Oxford: Clarendon Press, 1985); *Encyclopedia Judaica,* vol. 5 (Jerusalem: Macmillan, 1971), 1006–11.

9. Pierre Birnbaum, *The Jews of the Republic: A Political History of State Jews in France from Gambetta to Vichy,* trans. Jane Marie Todd (Stanford: Stanford University Press, 1996), 2. See also Ernst Hamburger, *Juden im öffentlichen Leben Deutschlands: Regierungsmitglieder, Beamte und Parlamentarier in der monarchischen Zeit, 1848–1918* (Tübingen: Mohr Siebeck, 1968), 170–540.

10. I thank my colleague David Sorkin for suggesting this term and elucidating its historic relationship to the experiences of Jews in earlier political-social systems.

11. For a personal reflection on this point by one of Kissinger's distinguished contemporaries of German Jewish background, see Fritz Stern, *Five Germanys I Have Known* (New York: Farrar, Straus and Giroux, 2006), esp. 280–281.

12. Interview with Dr. Albert Cohen, Harvard class of 1938, in Nitza Rosovsky, *The Jewish Experience at Harvard and Radcliffe* (Cambridge, Mass.: Harvard University Press, 1986), 92. Theodore White, a poor Jewish boy from Boston who later became a famous journalist, confirms Cohen's assessment. White describes the somewhat isolated experience of "meatballs" at Harvard—"day students or scholarship students": "We were at Harvard not to enjoy the games, the girls, the burlesque shows of the Old Howard, the companionship, the elms, the turning leaves of fall, the grassy banks of the Charles. We had come to get the Harvard badge, which says 'Veritas,' but really means a job somewhere in the future, in some bureaucracy, in some institution, in some school, laboratory, university, or law firm." Theodore H. White, *In Search of History: A Personal Adventure* (New York: Harper and Row, 1978), 43.

13. Recollections of Arthur Schlesinger Jr., Harvard class of 1938, in Jeffrey L. Lant, ed., *Our Harvard: Reflections on College Life by Twenty-two Distinguished Graduates* (New York: Taplinger 1982), 109–121; quotation on 115–116. See also Arthur M. Schlesinger Jr., *A Life in the Twentieth Century: Innocent Beginnings, 1917–1950* (Boston: Houghton Mifflin, 2000), 108–186.

14. Dr. Albert Cohen, in Rosovsky, *The Jewish Experience at Harvard and Radcliffe,* 91. See also Samuel Eliot Morison, *Three Centuries of Harvard, 1636–1936* (Cambridge, Mass.: Harvard University Press, 1936), 323–481; Donald Fleming, "Harvard's Golden Age?" in Bernard Bailyn, Donald Fleming, Oscar Handlin, and Stephan Thernstrom, eds., *Glimpses of the Harvard Past* (Cambridge, Mass.: Harvard University Press, 1986), 77–95; Keller and Keller, *Making Harvard Modern,* 3–10.

15. Schlesinger in Lant, *Our Harvard,* 116–117.

16. Morison, *Three Centuries of Harvard,* 481.

17. Keller and Keller, *Making Harvard Modern,* 7–8; Schlesinger in Lant, *Our Harvard,* 117.

18. James Bryant Conant, Baccalaureate Sermon, 7 June 1942, reprinted in idem, *Our Fighting Faith*, 69–83; quotation on 69–70. See also idem, *My Several Lives: Memoirs of a Social Inventor* (New York: Harper and Row, 1970), 207–233.

19. Keller and Keller, *Making Harvard Modern*, 165.

20. Ibid., 163–165; Conant, *My Several Lives*, 339–350; William L. Langer, *In and out of the Ivory Tower: The Autobiography of William L. Langer* (New York: Neale Watson Academic Publications, 1977), 180–193.

21. *Alumni Bulletin* quotation in Keller and Keller, *Making Harvard Modern*, 168; Langer, *In and out of the Ivory Tower*, 194–208.

22. Charles J. V. Murphy, "GIs at Harvard," *Life*, 17 June 1946, 16–22; John T. Bethell, *Harvard Observed: An Illustrated History of the University in the Twentieth Century* (Cambridge, Mass.: Harvard University Press, 1998), 178–179.

23. Quotations from Conant, *My Several Lives*, 368. These words come from Conant's instructions to the committee he created during the Second World War to suggest educational reforms at Harvard and throughout the nation. In October 1945 the "Harvard Report" became the basis for postwar curricular reforms at Harvard. It also inspired similar curricular reforms at many other schools and universities. On the popularity of social science courses, particularly in government, after 1945, see Murphy, "GIs at Harvard."

24. Interview with Sherman H. Starr, Harvard class of 1946 (graduated in 1947), in Rosovsky, *The Jewish Experience at Harvard and Radcliffe*, 100. Conant used the term "Hebraic-Christian tradition" in his public advocacy of ethnic, religious, and ideological diversity. See Keller and Keller, *Making Harvard Modern*, 167.

25. Jerome Karabel, *The Chosen: The Hidden History of Admission and Exclusion at Harvard, Yale, and Princeton* (Boston: Houghton Mifflin, 2005), 181–199; quotation on 183; author's interview with Henry Rosovsky, 3 December 2005. See also Seymour Martin Lipset and David Riesman, *Education and Politics at Harvard* (New York: McGraw-Hill, 1975), 179–180; Marcia Graham Synnott, *The Half-Opened Door: Discrimination and Admissions at Harvard, Yale, and Princeton, 1900–1970* (Westport, Conn.: Greenwood, 1979), 199–231.

26. See Synnott, *The Half-Opened Door*, 199–231.

27. Quotation in Keith W. Olson, *The G.I. Bill, the Veterans, and the Colleges* (Lexington: University Press of Kentucky, 1974), 33. See also Suzanne Mettler, *Soldiers to Citizens: The G.I. Bill and the Making of the Greatest Generation* (New York: Oxford University Press, 2005), 41–105.

28. Quotation in Murphy, "GIs at Harvard," 18. See also Olson, *G.I. Bill, Veterans, and Colleges*, 3–78.

29. See Mettler, *Soldiers to Citizens*, esp. 106–135; quotation on 134.

30. Author's interview with Henry Kissinger, 27 July 2004.

31. On female exclusion from G.I. Bill benefits and the Cold War University, see Lizabeth Cohen, *A Consumers' Republic: The Politics of Mass Consumption in Postwar America* (New York: Alfred A. Knopf, 2003), 137–143; Mettler, *Soldiers to Citizens,* 144–162. On African American exclusion from G.I. bill benefits and the Cold War University, see Ira Katznelson, *When Affirmative Action Was White: An Untold History of Racial Inequality in Twentieth-Century America* (New York: W. W. Norton, 2005), 113–141; David H. Onkst, "'First a Negro . . . Incidentally a Veteran': Black World War Two Veterans and the G.I. Bill of Rights in the Deep South, 1944–1948," *Journal of Social History* 31 (Spring 1998), 517–543. For a more positive appraisal of African American benefits from the G.I. Bill, see Mettler, *Soldiers to Citizens,* esp. 136–143.

32. On the growing perception of Jews as "white" in the 1940s, see Eric L. Goldstein, *The Price of Whiteness: Jews, Race, and American Identity* (Princeton: Princeton University Press, 2006), 189–208. For a contrary argument about Jewish and African American solidarity after the Second World War, see Cheryl Lynn Greenberg, *Troubling the Waters: Black-Jewish Relations in the American Century* (Princeton: Princeton University Press, 2006), 169–204.

33. On African American criticisms of U.S. Cold War policy and Henry Kissinger, among others, see Brenda Gayle Plummer, *Rising Wind: Black Americans and U.S. Foreign Affairs, 1935–1960* (Chapel Hill: University of North Carolina Press, 1996); Thomas Borstelmann, *The Cold War and the Color Line: American Race Relations in the Global Arena* (Cambridge, Mass.: Harvard University Press, 2001); Penny Von Eschen, *Satchmo Blows Up the World: Jazz Ambassadors Play the Cold War* (Cambridge, Mass: Harvard University Press, 2004); Carol Anderson, *Eyes off the Prize: The United Nations and the African-American Struggle for Human Rights, 1944–1955* (New York: Cambridge University Press, 2003).

34. Author's interview with Rosovsky, 3 December 2005; reminiscences by Anthony Lewis, Harvard class of 1948, in Rosovsky, *The Jewish Experience at Harvard and Radcliffe,* 100; Kissinger quotation in Ralph Blumenfeld and the staff and editors of the *New York Post, Henry Kissinger: The Private and Public Story* (New York: Signet, 1974), 80.

35. Quotations in Walter Isaacson, *Kissinger: A Biography* (New York: Simon and Schuster, 1992), 61.

36. Quotation from Stephen R. Graubard, *Kissinger: Portrait of a Mind* (New York: W. W. Norton, 1973), 4. See also Blumenfeld, *Henry Kissinger,* 80–86; Isaacson, *Kissinger,* 59–62.

37. Summary of remarks by Professor W. Y. Elliott at the Constitutional Reform session of the American Political Science Association Convention, Buffalo, 27 August 1952, folder: Buffalo Speech—Spare Copies, 8/27/52, box 30, Elliott Papers.

38. William Yandell Elliott to Paul Nitze, Policy Planning Staff, U.S. State Department, 11 December 1950, folder N, box 55, Elliott Papers. Elliott's major work of scholarship was an extensive criticism of pragmatism as a political philosophy. He linked pragmatism, with its rejection of moral universals, to the rise of fascism. See William Yandell Elliott, *The Pragmatic Revolt in Politics: Syndicalism, Fascism, and the Constitutional State* (New York: Macmillan, 1928).

39. Quoted in Blumenfeld, *Henry Kissinger,* 88.

40. Transcript of William Elliott and Henry Kissinger in Elliott's Contemporary Political Theory Seminar 204 at Harvard University, 21 March 1955, folder: Henry Kissinger, 21 March 1955, box 55, Elliott Papers. An audio recording of this seminar is available, on plastic disk, in the Elliott Papers. I converted the disk for this seminar, and two others with Elliott and Kissinger (9 March 1953, 8 March 1954), to audiocassette. The audio quality is often poor, but one can clearly hear Kissinger's German accent and Elliott's southern drawl. Their dialogue in all three recorded seminars focuses on the failures of pragmatism as a political philosophy and on the contemporary need for transcendent moral will. Their dialogue is frequently pedantic. Elliott, in particular, comes across as a condescending windbag. Kissinger sounds super-serious but also deferential to Elliott.

41. William Elliott, Summary of Paper: "An Extension of National Security Council Machinery: The Creation of a High-Level Continuing Advisory Board to Review National Security Programs for Policy Priority Treatment," 1950, folder: National Security, 1950, box 5, Elliott Papers.

42. William Elliott to Undersecretary of State Christian Herter, 6 November 1958, folder: WYE–State Department Memos, box 23, Elliott Papers.

43. Henry A. Kissinger, "The Meaning of History (Reflections on Spengler, Toynbee and Kant)" (Undergraduate thesis, Department of Government, Harvard University, 1950), quotations on 11 and 27. See also idem, "The Relation between Metaphysics, Epistemology, and Empirical Knowledge," paper presented at William Elliott's Harvard Government Seminar 204, 8 March 1954, folder: Henry Kissinger, March 8, 1954, box 68, Elliott Papers.

44. Henry Kissinger to William Elliott, 12 December 1950, folder: Memos—U.S. Strategy—Kissinger, Henry, 1951, box 27, Elliott Papers.

45. Ibid.

46. See Bruce Kuklick, *Blind Oracles: Intellectuals and War from Kennan to Kissinger* (Princeton: Princeton University Press, 2006), 182–203.

47. Josiah Lee Auspitz, "Cabbages and Kings," *Harvard Crimson,* 16 January 1962, in Greg Lawless, ed., *The Harvard Crimson Anthology: 100 Years at Harvard* (Boston: Houghton Mifflin, 1980), 187–191.

48. On the tendency of Jewish thinkers to seek universal political principles as

an antidote to social prejudice, see Isaac Deutscher, *The Non-Jewish Jew and Other Essays* (New York: Oxford University Press, 1968), 25–41.

49. Kissinger to Elliott, fall 1950, folder: International Seminar, Harvard, 1951–1959, box 2, Elliott Papers.

50. Report of the Sub-committee on Academic Programs, early 1951, folder: International Seminar, Harvard, 1951–1959, box 2, Elliott Papers.

51. Summer School Foreign Student Project, Report of the First Regular Meeting of the Steering Committee, 14 November 1950, ibid.

52. See Bruce Mazlish, *Kissinger: The European Mind in American Policy* (New York: Basic Books, 1976), 66–71; Holger Klitzing, "The Nemesis of Stability: Henry A. Kissinger's Ambivalent Relationship with Germany" (Ph.D. diss., Historisches Seminar, Ruprecht-Karls-Universität Heidelberg, 2005), 73–77.

53. Dean McGeorge Bundy to Dr. Paul McGhee, New York Foundation, 5 March 1954, folder: International Seminar, Harvard, 1951–1959, box 2, Elliott Papers.

54. Elliott to Don K. Price, Ford Foundation, 30 August 1956; Joseph McDaniel, Ford Foundation to Nathan Pusey, President of Harvard University, 10 October 1956, both in ibid. See also Volker R. Berghahn, *America and the Intellectual Cold Wars in Europe: Shepard Stone between Philanthropy, Academy, and Diplomacy* (Princeton: Princeton University Press, 2001), esp. 143–213; Oliver Schmidt, "Small Atlantic World: U.S. Philanthropy and the Expanding International Exchange of Scholars after 1945," in Jessica C. E. Gienow-Hecht and Frank Schumacher, eds., *Culture and International History* (New York: Berghahn Books, 2003), 115–134.

55. Kissinger quoted in the government report he wrote: "Psychological and Pressure Aspects of Negotiations with the USSR," November 1955, Psychological Aspects of United States Strategy: Source Book of Individual Papers, box 10, White House Office, Office of the Special Assistant for National Security Affairs, NSC Series, Subject Subseries, Dwight D. Eisenhower Presidential Library, Abilene, Kans. I thank Kenneth Osgood for bringing this document to my attention and elucidating its context. See Kenneth Osgood, *Total Cold War: Eisenhower's Secret Propaganda Battle at Home and Abroad* (Lawrence: University Press of Kansas, 2006). See also Klitzing, "The Nemesis of Stability," 80–86. In 1952 Kissinger worked as a consultant to the Truman administration's Psychological Strategy Board. See Kissinger's report on West German society to the board, July 1952, folder 91, box 6, Records of the Psychological Strategy Board, White House Central Files, Harry S Truman Presidential Library, Independence, Mo.

56. Gene M. Lyons and Louis Morton, *Schools for Strategy: Education and Research in National Security Affairs* (New York: Praeger, 1965), 3–11; quotation on 9.

57. This connection between philanthropies, government policies, and American assumptions about political culture predated the Cold War. See Emily S. Rosenberg, *Spreading the American Dream: American Economic and Cultural Expansion, 1890–1945* (New York: Hill and Wang, 1982), esp. 108–121. For the Cold War and the emerging "culture of national security" that included more philanthropic activism and an emphasis on limits to direct government interference, see Michael J. Hogan, *A Cross of Iron: Harry S. Truman and the Origins of the National Security State, 1945–1954* (New York: Cambridge University Press, 1998), 1–22; Aaron L. Friedberg, *In the Shadow of the Garrison State: America's Anti-Statism and Its Cold War Grand Strategy* (Princeton: Princeton University Press, 2000), 9–80.

58. See Berghahn, *America and Intellectual Cold Wars,* 214–249; Simpson, "Universities, Empire, and Production of Knowledge."

59. See Scott Lucas, "A Document from the Harvard International Summer School," in Gienow-Hecht and Schumacher, eds., *Culture and International History,* 258–263; idem, "USA OK? Beyond the Practice of (Anti)-American Studies," *49th Parallel* 8 (Summer 2001); Isaacson, *Kissinger,* 70.

60. Siegfried Unseld quoted in Blumenfeld, *Henry Kissinger,* 102.

61. Blumenfeld, *Henry Kissinger,* 95.

62. Isaacson, *Kissinger,* 73.

63. See John Kenneth Galbraith to Walter Mallory, 23 September 1958, folder: Council on Foreign Relations, 11/1/56–10/24/58, box 19, Galbraith Papers; Galbraith to John J. McCloy, 3 November 1966, folder: McCloy Correspondence about Council on Foreign Relations, November–December 1966, box 72, Galbraith Papers; Bernard Brodie to Henry Kissinger, 26 August 1966, folder K, box 6, Brodie Papers; Kissinger to Brodie, 31 August 1966, folder: European Trip, September–October 1966, box 9, Brodie Papers.

64. For two examples from numerous cases in which Kissinger reported to high-ranking U.S. government officials on his foreign meetings, see the following documents from the Kennedy and Johnson administrations: Henry Kissinger to McGeorge Bundy, 1 June 1961 (with notation from Bundy indicating he forwarded Kissinger's memorandum to President Kennedy), and attached summary of Kissinger's 10 May 1961 meeting with West German Minister of Defense Franz-Josef Strauss, folder: Kissinger, Henry A., 6/1/61–8/28/62, box 31, President's Office File, John F. Kennedy Presidential Library, Boston; Henry Kissinger, Memorandum of Conversation with West German Chancellor Ludwig Erhard, 28 January 1966, folder: CO 81 France (1966), box 8, White House Central File, Confidential File, Lyndon Baines Johnson Presidential Library, Austin, Texas. See also Klitzing, "The Nemesis of Stability," 119–208.

65. Henry Kissinger, *A World Restored: Metternich, Castlereagh, and the Problems of Peace, 1812–1822* (1957; reprint, London: Phoenix, 2000), 326.

66. Metternich quoted in ibid., 320.

67. Richard Rovere to Peter Viereck, 31 October 1952, folder 4, box 1, Richard Rovere Papers, Wisconsin Historical Society, Madison. I thank Julie Lane and Justin King for bringing this document to my attention.

68. For accounts of Kissinger's personal networking and its criticism by people like Thomas Schelling, see Isaacson, *Kissinger,* 69–74; Mazlish, *Kissinger,* 66–71; Jussi Hanhimäki, *The Flawed Architect: Henry Kissinger and American Foreign Policy* (New York: Oxford University Press, 2004), 6–7.

69. Quotation in Henry Kissinger, *Years of Renewal* (New York: Simon and Schuster, 1999), 1071.

70. Sigmund Diamond, "Kissinger and the F.B.I.," *The Nation,* 10 November 1979, 467.

71. For an alternative interpretation, highly critical of Kissinger personally, see Diamond, *Compromised Campus,* 138–150. For an excellent analysis of the damage caused by academic collaboration with McCarthyism, see Schrecker, *No Ivory Tower,* esp. 338–341.

72. These quotations come from an FBI report on Kissinger's communications with the agency in July 1953; Diamond, "Kissinger and the F.B.I.," 468. For an account of Kissinger's sharing of information with the FBI after early July 1953, as well as Elliott's relations with the FBI, see Diamond, *Compromised Campus,* 142–150.

73. Yosef Hayim Yerushalmi, *The Lisbon Massacre of 1506 and the Royal Image in the Shebet Yehuda,* Hebrew Union College Annual Supplement, No. 1 (Cincinnati: Hebrew Union College, 1976), xi. Hannah Arendt, writing during the years when Kissinger created the International Seminar, made the same point. See *The Origins of Totalitarianism* (1951; reprint, New York: Harcourt, Brace, 1976), 11–28. See also Benjamin Ginsberg, *The Fatal Embrace: Jews and the State* (Chicago: University of Chicago Press, 1993), esp. 1–58; Ismar Schorsch, *From Text to Context: The Turn to History in Modern Judaism* (Hanover, N.H.: Brandeis University Press, 1994), 118–129.

74. The first quotation appears in the preface to Kissinger's dissertation, but not in the published version; Henry Alfred Kissinger, "Peace, Legitimacy, and the Equilibrium (A Study of the Statesmanship of Castlereagh and Metternich)" (Ph.D. diss., Department of Government, Harvard University, 1954), i.

The second quotation is in both the original dissertation and the published version: Kissinger, "Peace, Legitimacy, and the Equilibrium," 544–545; idem, *World Restored,* 331.

75. Kissinger, *World Restored,* 331–332. Kissinger's dissertation includes an ambiguous gesture to "historical tact" before the closing phrase: "the most difficult task of statesmanship." Kissinger, "Peace, Legitimacy, and the Equilibrium," 545.

76. Draft prospectus for the Harvard Center for International Affairs, 11 October 1957, folder: Harvard University—International Affairs Center, box 2, p. 4, Elliott Papers.

77. Ibid., 10, 7.

78. Ibid., 15–16. In practice, the CFIA often did not nurture scholarly consensus. Faculty tended to pursue their own research rather than work in close collaboration. I thank Robert Jervis for his insights, based on his experiences at the CFIA in the 1960s. Author's conversation with Robert Jervis, 15 September 2006.

79. Draft prospectus for the Harvard Center for International Affairs, 11 October 1957, 21.

80. Henry Kissinger to Bernard Brodie, 4 September 1959; Brodie to Kissinger, 28 September 1959, both in folder: K Correspondence, box 1, Brodie Papers; Lyons and Morton, *Schools for Strategy,* 146–154. Kissinger became the director of the Defense Studies Program in 1958. He also edited a journal, *Confluence,* published through the Harvard Summer School, in association with the International Seminar. Appearing quarterly from March 1952 to the summer of 1958, *Confluence* printed articles from leading international figures. Kissinger procured and edited these articles, but he published only two letters of his own in the journal. See *Confluence,* vols. 1–7 (March 1952–Summer 1958); Isaacson, *Kissinger,* 72–74; Mazlish, *Kissinger,* 69–71; Graubard, *Kissinger,* 58–59.

81. Author's interview with Sven Kraemer, 23 June 2005; David Landau, "The Salad Days of Henry Kissinger," *Harvard Crimson,* 21 May 1971; idem, *Kissinger: The Uses of Power* (Boston: Houghton Mifflin, 1972), 73–102; Graubard, *Kissinger,* 117–119; Blumenfeld, *Henry Kissinger,* 121–136. Kissinger became an associate professor with tenure in 1959 and a full professor in 1962.

82. For an eloquent articulation of the importance of "scholarly dispassion" to the mission of the university, see John W. Boyer, "Judson's War and Hutchins's Peace: The University of Chicago and War in the Twentieth Century," in *Occasional Papers of Higher Education,* no. 12 (Chicago: University of Chicago, 2003), esp. 92–95. I thank Jonathan Reischl for bringing this publication to my attention.

83. Author's interview with Kissinger, 26 October 2005; Henry Kissinger's videotaped oral history interview with Louise Bobrow, 11 January 2001, Museum of Jewish Heritage, New York. See also David Halberstam, *The Best and the Brightest* (New York: Random House, 1972); Kai Bird, *The Color of Truth: McGeorge Bundy and William Bundy, Brothers in Arms* (New York: Simon and Schuster, 1998). For an excellent study of the social origins of anticommunism within the education of policy elites, see Robert D. Dean, *Imperial Brotherhood: Gender and the Making of Cold War Foreign Policy* (Amherst: University of Massachusetts Press, 2001).

84. Kissinger, *World Restored,* 320–321.

85. On Bundy and Schelling's simultaneous promotion and criticism of Kissinger, see Isaacson, *Kissinger,* 69–81, 94–101, 104–105.

4. A Strategy of Limits

1. I. F. Stone, "National Suicide as a Form of Defense," *I. F. Stone's Weekly,* 28 November 1955; idem, "Words to Be Engraved on a New Rosetta Stone," ibid., 21 June 1961, both reprinted in Stone, *The Haunted Fifties* (New York: Merlin, 1963), 119–123, 378–380.

2. See Spencer R. Weart, *Nuclear Fear: A History of Images* (Cambridge, Mass.: Harvard University Press, 1988); Paul Boyer, *By the Bomb's Early Light: American Thought and Culture at the Dawn of the Atomic Age* (New York: Pantheon, 1985); Lawrence S. Wittner, *The Struggle against the Bomb,* 2 vols. (Stanford: Stanford University Press, 1993, 1997).

3. The literature on the nuclear strategists is enormous. For some of the best works see Bruce Kuklick, *Blind Oracles: Intellectuals and War from Kennan to Kissinger* (Princeton: Princeton University Press, 2006); Sharon Ghamari-Tabrizi, *The Worlds of Herman Kahn: The Intuitive Science of Thermonuclear War* (Cambridge, Mass.: Harvard University Press, 2005); Fred Kaplan, *The Wizards of Armageddon* (New York: Simon and Schuster, 1983); Gregg Herken, *Counsels of War,* rev. ed. (New York: Oxford University Press, 1987); Marc Trachtenberg, *History and Strategy* (Princeton: Princeton University Press, 1991), 3–46; Lawrence Freedman, *The Evolution of Nuclear Strategy,* 3d ed. (New York: Palgrave Macmillan, 2003).

4. Henry Kissinger, *White House Years* (Boston: Little, Brown, 1979), 54, 70. See also John Lewis Gaddis, "Rescuing Choice from Circumstance: The Statecraft of Henry Kissinger," in Gordon A. Craig and Francis L. Loewenheim, eds., *The Diplomats, 1939–1979* (Princeton: Princeton University Press, 1994), 564–592.

5. Henry Kissinger, Memorandum to Arthur Schlesinger Jr., 8 December 1954, folder: Kissinger, Henry A., 1954–57, box 39, Armstrong Papers; Bernard Brodie, "War in the Atomic Age," in idem, ed., *The Absolute Weapon: Atomic Power and World Order* (New York: Harcourt, Brace, 1946), 21–69.

6. Thomas Schelling, *Arms and Influence* (New Haven: Yale University Press, 1966), 33–34.

7. Kissinger, *White House Years,* 66–67. For Kissinger's early views on nuclear weapons and American weakness in Korea and Vietnam, see Henry Kissinger to William Elliott, 12 December 1950; Kissinger to Elliott, 2 March 1951, both in folder: Memos—US Strategy—Kissinger, Henry, 1951, box 27, Elliott Papers; Kissinger, Memorandum to Schlesinger, 8 December 1954; Henry A. Kissinger, *Nuclear Weapons and Foreign Policy* (New York: Harper and Brothers, 1957), 134.

8. Bernard Brodie to Henry Kissinger, 11 July 1955, and Brodie to Mac Hoag, 5 September 1963, in folder K Correspondence, box 1, Brodie Papers; Brodie to Kissinger, 26 August 1966, folder K, box 6, ibid. See also Brodie to Kissinger, 11 May 1966, folder K Correspondence, box 1, ibid.

9. Stanley Kubrick's movie *Dr. Strangelove, or How I Learned to Stop Worrying and Love the Bomb* was released in 1964. On Kissinger, see I. F. Stone, "Military Minuet," *I. F. Stone's Weekly,* 9 September 1957; idem, "Partnership with Krupp," ibid., 26 October 1959, both reprinted in Stone, *The Haunted Fifties,* 189–191, 279–280. On *Dr. Strangelove* and its reception, see Margot A. Henriksen, *Dr. Strangelove's America: Society and Culture in the Atomic Age* (Berkeley: University of California Press, 1997), esp. 303–344. Historians and political scientists writing after the early 1970s have generally dismissed Kissinger's work as a nuclear strategist. They have emphasized his unoriginal synthesis of other people's writings and his distortion of serious intellectual thought to ingratiate policymakers. There is some truth in these criticisms, but they are overstated. This chapter will show that Kissinger was an original and important contributor to the development of strategy as an intellectual field. Fellow thinkers, especially Brodie, acknowledged this fact frequently at the time. Kissinger adapted intellectual thought for policy purposes, but so did other strategists. That, after all, was the point of strategy—to formulate and implement policy. Kissinger was more successful at this than his ambitious, and later resentful, counterparts. With regard to the charge that Kissinger simply synthesized the work of others, the correspondence between Brodie and Kissinger is very revealing. On 25 April 1958 Kissinger wrote Brodie about rumors that "you were extremely unhappy with me because I did not give you full credit in my book [*Nuclear Weapons and Foreign Policy*] either for the help you had given me personally or for the influence of your thought on me." On 2 May 1958 Brodie responded with a description of his "surprise at your refraining from mentioning *anyone* as a source or inspiration of any of your ideas, or even as someone who happened to think along the same lines." After outlining some of the writings, particularly his own, that Kissinger should have referenced, Brodie concluded: "None of the above comments have the slightest bearing on the intrinsic quality or value of your book, which has received enough praise and renown by now to make any words of mine on the matter superfluous." When questioned by reporters in 1974, Brodie reaffirmed the intrinsic quality of Kissinger's book. See Kissinger to Brodie, 25 April 1958; Brodie to Kissinger, 2 May 1958; Kissinger to Brodie, 12 May 1958, all in folder K Correspondence, box 1, Brodie Papers; Kissinger to Brodie, 22 July 1974, folder K, box 8, ibid. Also see Brodie's published review of *Nuclear Weapons and Foreign Policy,* in which he attests: "it is clearly the best that has thus far appeared in the field of United States national security policy." Brodie praises the "novelty" of Kissinger's "several outstanding articles" that preceded the book; review in *Scientific*

Monthly 85 (October 1957), 206–207. Hans Morgenthau, one of the most prominent international-relations scholars of the postwar years, agreed with Brodie. He wrote that Kissinger's intellect and his 1957 book "put him in the forefront of the new breed of political-military thinkers"; "Henry Kissinger: Secretary of State," *Encounter* 43 (November 1974), 57–61. The evidence indicates that Kissinger was seen as a serious strategist by his contemporaries. Scholars writing in the aftermath of his White House service have, it appears, allowed their personal and political disagreements with Kissinger to distort their view of his record. For thoughtful, but perhaps too dismissive, accounts of Kissinger's strategic thought, see Campbell Craig, "The Illogic of Henry Kissinger's Nuclear Strategy," *Armed Forces and Society* 29 (Summer 2003), 547–568; Lawrence Freedman, "Henry Kissinger," in John Baylis and John Garnett, eds., *Makers of Nuclear Strategy* (New York: St. Martin's, 1991), 98–119.

10. Kissinger, *Nuclear Weapons and Foreign Policy,* 431–436; quotation on 431. See also Schuyler Schouten's very suggestive thesis, "Kissinger's Realist Ethics: Morality and Pragmatism in American Foreign Policy" (Senior thesis, Yale University, 2003).

11. President Dwight Eisenhower to Acting Secretary of State Christian Herter, 31 July 1957, folder: July 1957—DDE Dictation, box 25, DDE Diary Series, Ann Whitman File, DDE.

12. The quotations on strategy come from Bernard Brodie's seminal article "Strategy as a Science," *World Politics* 1 (July 1949), 467–488; quotations on 477, 484. For other helpful discussions about the meaning of grand strategy, see Stephen M. Walt, "The Search for a Science of Strategy: A Review Essay," *International Security* 12 (Summer 1987), 140–165; Richard K. Betts, "Is Strategy an Illusion?" ibid., 25 (Fall 2000), 5–50; John Lewis Gaddis, *Surprise, Security, and the American Experience* (Cambridge, Mass.: Harvard University Press, 2004), esp. 107–113.

13. See Henry A. Kissinger, "American Policy and Preventive War," *Yale Review* 44 (March 1955), 321–339; idem, "Military Policy and Defense of the 'Grey Areas,'" *Foreign Affairs* 33 (April 1955), 416–428; idem, "The Limitations of Diplomacy," *New Republic* (9 May 1955), 7–8. Kissinger's first *Foreign Affairs* article is a revised version of his 8 December 1954 memo to Arthur Schlesinger Jr. See also Robert L. Beisner, *Dean Acheson: A Life in the Cold War* (New York: Oxford University Press, 2006), esp. 151–157, 642–654. For an excellent discussion of the ways in which a "peace through strength" doctrine encourages military conflict, see Coral Bell, *Negotiation from Strength: A Study in the Politics of Power* (London: Chatto and Windus, 1962); Robert Jervis, "Was the Cold War a Security Dilemma?" *Journal of Cold War Studies* 3 (Winter 2001), 54.

14. Kissinger, *Nuclear Weapons and Foreign Policy,* 8, 21; idem, "American Policy and Preventive War," 323. For the best analysis of the "American Way of War" and

its relevance for the Cold War, see Russell F. Weigley, *The American Way of War: A History of United States Military Strategy and Policy* (New York: Macmillan, 1973), esp. 363–477.

15. Kissinger, *Nuclear Weapons and Foreign Policy,* 9, 20.

16. Idem, "American Policy and Preventive War," 329–330.

17. See idem, "Reflections on American Diplomacy," *Foreign Affairs* 35 (October 1956), 37–56. For a similar analysis forty years later, see idem, *Diplomacy* (New York: Simon and Schuster, 1994), 29–55, 218–245. For alternative interpretations of Woodrow Wilson, see John Milton Cooper Jr., *The Warrior and the Priest: Woodrow Wilson and Theodore Roosevelt* (Cambridge, Mass.: Harvard University Press, 1983); Thomas J. Knock, *To End all Wars: Woodrow Wilson and the Quest for a New World Order* (New York: Oxford University Press, 1992); Frank Ninkovich, *The Wilsonian Century: U.S. Foreign Policy since 1900* (Chicago: University of Chicago Press, 1999).

18. Henry A. Kissinger, "The Meaning of History (Reflections on Spengler, Toynbee and Kant)" (Undergraduate thesis, Department of Government, Harvard University, 1950), 326.

19. Idem, "The Conservative Dilemma: Reflections on the Political Thought of Metternich," *American Political Science Review* 48 (December 1954), 1029–30. This is the first piece of writing that Kissinger published.

20. Idem, "The Meaning of History," 26, 347; idem, "The White Revolutionary: Reflections on Bismarck," *Daedalus* 97 (Summer 1968), 898; idem, "The Conservative Dilemma," 1017–30.

21. Idem, "The Meaning of History," 348.

22. Ibid., 26, 340, 346; Hans J. Morgenthau, "Ethics and Politics," in Lyman Bryson, Louis Finkelstein, and R. M. Maciver, eds., *Approaches to Group Understanding: Sixth Symposium* (New York: Cooper Square, 1964), 341.

23. Kissinger, "Reflections on American Diplomacy," 41.

24. C. Vann Woodward, *The Burden of Southern History* (Baton Rouge: Louisiana University Press, 1960), 188; idem, "The Age of Reinterpretation," *American Historical Review* 66 (October 1960), 2, 7–8.

25. Reinhold Niebuhr, *The Irony of American History* (New York: Charles Scribner's, 1952), 74.

26. Ibid., 44.

27. Kissinger, "The Meaning of History," 1; idem, *White House Years,* 55–56.

28. For a similar assessment of Kissinger's thinking, particularly on the limits of power, see Peter W. Dickson, *Kissinger and the Meaning of History* (New York: Cambridge University Press, 1978), 83–116; Bruce Mazlish, *Kissinger: The European Mind in American Policy* (New York: Basic Books, 1976), 171–186; Kuklick, *Blind Oracles,* 184–190. In his thinking about religion, history, and limits, Kissinger drew on

another German émigré, Karl Löwith. See Löwith, *Meaning in History: The Theological Implications of the Philosophy of History* (Chicago: University of Chicago Press, 1949); idem, *My Life in Germany before and after 1933: A Report,* trans. Elizabeth King (1940; reprint, Urbana: University of Illinois Press, 1994). Kissinger also drew on the writings of Fyodor Dostoyevsky, particularly *The Brothers Karamazov,* originally published in 1880. I thank my colleague Lawrence Dickey for helping me to understand Kissinger's philosophy of history, and the influence of Löwith and Dostoyevsky in particular.

29. Kissinger, "Military Policy and Defense of 'Grey Areas,'" 425; idem, *Nuclear Weapons and Foreign Policy,* 20, 61.

30. Idem, *Nuclear Weapons and Foreign Policy,* 7; idem, "Military Policy and Defense of 'Grey Areas,'" 420. On "overkill," see David Alan Rosenberg, "The Origins of Overkill: Nuclear Weapons and American Strategy," reprinted in Norman A. Graebner, ed., *The National Security: Its Theory and Practice, 1945–60* (New York: Oxford University Press, 1986), 123–195. For a powerful defense of the U.S. strategic posture in the 1950s, contrary to the criticisms voiced by Kissinger and others, see Campbell Craig, *Destroying the Village: Eisenhower and Thermonuclear War* (New York: Columbia University Press, 1998).

31. Kissinger to Elliott, 12 December 1950.

32. Ibid.; Kissinger, "Military Policy and Defense of 'Grey Areas.'"

33. Idem, "Military Policy and Defense of 'Grey Areas.'"

34. Idem, *Nuclear Weapons and Foreign Policy,* 41; Kissinger to Elliott, 2 March 1951. Kissinger offered the same criticisms of containment policy and of Acheson's rhetoric about "situations of strength" in his memoirs published in 1979. See *White House Years,* 61–63. For a detailed and thoughtful evaluation of Acheson's policymaking and its problems, see Beisner, *Dean Acheson,* esp. 151–157, 333–337, 375–389, 642–654.

35. Kissinger, Memorandum to Schlesinger, 8 December 1954; idem, "Military Policy and Defense of 'Grey Areas,'" 424.

36. Idem, "Military Policy and Defense of 'Grey Areas,'" 419, 427. Kissinger used the terms "psychological condition" and "will-to-fight" as synonyms. Kissinger to Elliott, 2 March 1951. See also Kissinger, "American Policy and Preventive War," 326–327; idem, "Force and Diplomacy in the Nuclear Age," *Foreign Affairs* 34 (April 1956), 349–366. For a historical account of containment policy that criticizes the U.S. government for failing to coordinate military threats with effective diplomacy, see Fredrik Logevall, "A Critique of Containment," *Diplomatic History* 28 (September 2004), 473–499.

37. Kissinger to Elliott, 2 March 1951; Kissinger, "Military Policy and Defense of 'Grey Areas.'"

38. Idem, *Nuclear Weapons and Foreign Policy,* 144–145.

39. Ibid., 147, 189.

40. Ibid., 201–202; Thomas Schelling, *The Strategy of Conflict* (Cambridge, Mass.: Harvard University Press, 1960), 53–80, 257–266; idem, *Arms and Influence,* 92–125, 215–220.

41. Kissinger, *Nuclear Weapons and Foreign Policy,* 136, 140. On war as "the pursuit of policy by other means," see Carl von Clausewitz, *On War,* ed. and trans. Michael Howard and Peter Paret (Princeton: Princeton University Press, 1984), esp. 86–87, 99, 585, 592–593.

42. Bernard Brodie review in *Scientific Monthly* 85 (October 1957), 206–207; Reinhold Niebuhr, "Limited Warfare," *Christianity and Crisis* 17 (11 November 1957), 146–147.

43. Schelling, *The Strategy of Conflict,* 257–266. See also William Kaufmann, "The Crisis in Military Affairs," *World Politics* 10 (July 1958), 579–603; Alain Enthoven, "American Deterrent Policy," *Survival* 5 (May–June 1963), 96; Craig, "Illogic of Kissinger's Nuclear Strategy," 557–558.

44. Kissinger, *Nuclear Weapons and Foreign Policy,* 20. For Kissinger's more tempered advocacy of limited nuclear capabilities in the 1960s, see idem, *The Necessity for Choice: Prospects of American Foreign Policy* (New York: Harper and Row, 1961), 75–98; idem, *The Troubled Partnership: A Re-appraisal of the Atlantic Alliance* (New York: McGraw-Hill, 1965), 161–186. On the increase in the American tactical nuclear arsenal in western Europe during the 1960s, see *The Troubled Partnership,* 178–179; "Table of U.S. Nuclear Warheads," Natural Resources Defense Council, http://www.nrdc.org/nuclear/nudb/datab9.asp (accessed 21 July 2006). On the British military's interest in tactical nuclear capabilities, see June–July 1968, DEFE 4/228, Public Records Office, Kew, London.

45. Kissinger, "Force and Diplomacy in the Nuclear Age," 360; idem, *Nuclear Weapons and Foreign Policy,* 18–19.

46. Kissinger's formulation of this strategic vision, in response to U.S. containment doctrine and reliance on massive thermonuclear retaliation, is most evident in his Memorandum to Arthur Schlesinger Jr., 8 December 1954. This paper by Kissinger became the basis for his first *Foreign Affairs* article, "Military Policy and Defense of 'Grey Areas,'" praised by Bernard Brodie and other major nuclear strategists. Kissinger's thinking drew on the ideas of Brodie and many others, but his consistency and iconoclasm going back to 1950 show his independence and originality.

47. Eisenhower to Christian Herter, 31 July 1957. General Andrew Goodpaster prepared a 24-page synopsis of Kissinger's *Nuclear Weapons and Foreign Policy* for Eisenhower. The president circulated this synopsis within his administration. See Synopsis of "Nuclear Weapons and Foreign Policy," folder: Kissinger Book, box 23, Administration Series, Ann Whitman File, DDE.

48. Kissinger, *White House Years,* 61–62.

49. Idem, "Force and Diplomacy in the Nuclear Age," 361; idem, "Reflections on American Diplomacy," 46–47; idem, "The Limitations of Diplomacy," 7–8.

50. Idem, "Psychological and Pressure Aspects of Negotiations with the USSR," November 1955, Psychological Aspects of United States Strategy: Source Book of Individual Papers, box 10, White House Office, Office of the Special Assistant for National Security Affairs, NSC Series, Subject Subseries, DDE. I thank Kenneth Osgood for bringing this document to my attention and elucidating its context. See Osgood, *Total Cold War: Eisenhower's Secret Propaganda Battle at Home and Abroad* (Lawrence: University Press of Kansas, 2006), 181–183. On the Geneva summit of 1955, see ibid., 189–195; Gunter Bischof and Saki Dockrill, eds., *Cold War Respite: The Geneva Summit of 1955* (Baton Rouge: Louisiana State University Press, 2000).

51. Kissinger, "Psychological and Pressure Aspects of Negotiations"; idem, "Reflections on American Diplomacy," 53–56.

52. Idem, *Diplomacy,* 78–136, 350–422.

53. Idem, "American Policy and Preventive War," 328.

54. Kissinger quotes the same lines from Winston Churchill's 9 October 1948 speech at Llandudno, Wales, in *White House Years,* 63; idem, *Diplomacy,* 466; idem, "Reflections on Containment," *Foreign Affairs* 73 (May–June 1994). The 1994 *Foreign Affairs* article is largely a reprint of the equivalent section in *Diplomacy.* For the original text of Churchill's speech, see Winston Churchill, *Europe Unite: Speeches 1947 and 1948* (London: Cassell, 1950), 409–424; quotation on 414. See also Logevall, "A Critique of Containment," 473–499.

55. Kissinger, "American Policy and Preventive War," 325. Kissinger echoed Walter Lippmann's criticism of American assumptions that "all we can do is to 'contain' Russia until Russia changes, ceases to be our rival, and becomes our partner. . . . For a diplomat to think that rival and unfriendly powers cannot be brought to a settlement is to forget what diplomacy is about"; Lippmann, *The Cold War: A Study in U.S. Foreign Policy* (New York: Harper and Row, 1972), 50. Lippmann initially published these articles in 1947. For Kissinger's positive assessment of Lippmann's argument, see *Diplomacy,* 463–466.

56. Kissinger, *White House Years,* 62. Kissinger argued that Stalin might have accepted a less repressive status for the eastern European states after the Second World War. Kissinger blamed the authors of containment policy for failing to pursue this possibility. "Unexpectedly, we deferred serious negotiations until we had mobilized more of our potential strength. Thus we gave the Soviet Union time—the most precious commodity it needed to consolidate its conquests and to recover from the war"; *White House Years,* 62–63.

57. Kissinger to Elliott, 12 December 1950 and 2 March 1951; Kissinger, *White*

House Years, 63–64; idem, *Diplomacy,* 473–492. On 27 July 1953 the belligerents signed an armistice that created a cease-fire, but not a peace settlement, on the Korean peninsula. Through the end of the twentieth century, the Korean peninsula remained divided, with North and South Korea in a state of suspended war.

58. Kissinger, "American Policy and Preventive War," 327.

59. Idem, *White House Years,* 62, 55. George Kennan shared Kissinger's belief in the utility of negotiations during the 1950s, but Kennan did not agree with Kissinger's emphasis on the development of more extensive war-fighting capabilities. Kennan was far less confident than Kissinger in the effective uses of limited force. On Kennan and his differences with U.S. policy during the 1950s in particular, see John Lewis Gaddis, *Strategies of Containment: A Critical Appraisal of American National Security Policy during the Cold War,* rev. ed. (New York: Oxford University Press, 2005), 24–104.

60. Kissinger, *White House Years,* 55.

61. Idem, "Reflections on Cuba," *The Reporter,* 22 November 1962, 24.

62. See Kissinger, Memorandum to Schlesinger, 8 December 1954. Schlesinger recommended this memorandum to the editor of *Foreign Affairs,* Hamilton Fish Armstrong. It became the basis for Kissinger's first article in the journal, "Military Policy and Defense of 'Grey Areas.'" Through the next decade, Armstrong would look to Kissinger for a series of articles articulating foreign-policy alternatives. Between 1955 and 1969 Kissinger published more articles in *Foreign Affairs* than any other author. On Henry Cabot Lodge Jr.'s advocacy of Kissinger's ideas to President Eisenhower see Lodge to Eisenhower, 25 July 1957, folder: Kissinger Book, box 23, Administration Series, Ann Whitman File, DDE; Henry Cabot Lodge, *As It Was: An Inside View of Politics and Power in the '50s and '60s* (New York: W. W. Norton, 1976), 202. On the West German government's efforts to cultivate Kissinger, see Dienstreise Ministerialdirigent Dr. Reute nach Boston/USA, 1 February 1965, IIA6, Band 225, Seite 110–115; Protokoll der Konsularkonferenz 1966 in Washington, 28–30 March 1966, IIA6, Band 240, Seite 208–216, 291–295, all in Politisches Archiv des Auswärtigen Amts, Berlin, Germany; Holger Klitzing, "The Nemesis of Stability: Henry A. Kissinger's Ambivalent Relationship with Germany" (Ph.D. diss., Historisches Seminar, Ruprecht-Karls-Universität Heidelberg, 2005), chap. 5.

63. On Eisenhower's psychological warfare strategy and Rockefeller's role, see Osgood, *Total Cold War,* esp. 46–75, 80–85; Scott Lucas, *Freedom's War: The American Crusade against the Soviet Union* (New York: New York University Press, 1999), esp. 235–248; Gregory Mitrovich, *Undermining the Kremlin: America's Strategy to Subvert the Soviet Bloc, 1947–1956* (Ithaca: Cornell University Press, 2000), esp. 122–176; James Marchio, "The Planning Coordination Group: Bureaucratic Casualty in

the Cold War Campaign to Exploit Soviet-Bloc Vulnerabilities," *Journal of Cold War Studies* 4 (Fall 2002), 3–28.

64. Rockefeller quotations from an 11 March 1974 interview, in Ralph Blumenfeld and the staff and editors of the *New York Post, Henry Kissinger: The Private and Public Story* (New York: Signet, 1974), 108, 115. On the August 1955 meeting and the work of the "Quantico II panel" that grew out of it, see *FRUS*, 1955–1957, vol. 19, 153–154; Lucas, *Freedom's War*, 242–244.

65. Rockefeller quoted from his 11 March 1974 interview in Blumenfeld, *Henry Kissinger*, 116.

66. Henry Kissinger to Nelson Rockefeller, 18 November 1960, folder 184, box 31, Series J.2, Record Group 4, NAR, Personal, RAC. Above Kissinger's typewritten "dynamic conservatism," Rockefeller wrote "creative."

67. Kissinger to Rockefeller, 24 February 1961, folder 184, box 31, Series J.2, Record Group 4, NAR, Personal, RAC.

68. Nelson A. Rockefeller, *The Future of Federalism* (Cambridge, Mass.: Harvard University Press, 1962), 3–4. Rockefeller delivered his three Godkin Lectures at Harvard on 7–9 February 1962. For a reference to Kissinger's work on the Godkin Lectures, see Kissinger to Rockefeller, 24 February 1961. Other prominent advocates of policy reform had delivered the Godkin Lectures in prior years, including Adlai Stevenson and Chester Bowles.

69. Rockefeller, *The Future of Federalism*, 57. Kissinger emphasized the limits on American capabilities most emphatically in one of the first reports he wrote for a Rockefeller-sponsored study on "America at Mid-Century": "International Security—The Military Aspect," Panel Report II of the Special Studies Project, published as a stand-alone report in 1958. See folder 204, box 18, Series 4B, Record Group 5, Rockefeller Brothers Special Studies, RAC.

70. Rockefeller, *The Future of Federalism*, 4, 6–7.

71. Henry A. Kissinger, "Coalition Diplomacy in a Nuclear Age," *Foreign Affairs* 42 (July 1964), 542; idem, "The White Revolutionary," 909–918; idem, *Diplomacy*, 120–136. Kissinger's understanding of federalism drew on the pioneering work of one of his mentors at Harvard, Carl J. Friedrich. Kissinger adopted Friedrich's belief in the wisdom of federalism as "the process by which a number of separate political communities enter into arrangements for working out solutions, adopting joint policies, and making joint decisions on joint problems." Kissinger did not share Friedrich's belief that international federalism would contribute to the development of world government. Kissinger contended that international federalism would function best without the creation of an official central authority. See Carl J. Friedrich's seminal book *Constitutional Government and Democracy: Theory and Practice in Europe and America*, rev. ed. (Boston: Ginn, 1950), esp. 73–88,

173–221. Kissinger became familiar with this book as a student at Harvard. See also Friedrich, *Trends of Federalism in Theory and Practice* (New York: Praeger, 1968), esp. 3–10, 82–88; quotation on 7. I thank Alison Alter for sharing her expertise on comparative federalism.

72. Kissinger to Rockefeller, 18 November 1960. This is the same language Kissinger used to describe leadership throughout his career. See "Peace, Legitimacy, and the Equilibrium (A Study of the Statesmanship of Castlereagh and Metternich)" (Ph.D. diss., Department of Government, Harvard University, 1954), 541–542; idem, *Nuclear Weapons and Foreign Policy,* 247; idem, "The Congress of Vienna," in John G. Stoessinger and Alan F. Westin, eds., *Power and Order: Six Cases in World Politics* (New York: Harcourt, Brace, 1964), 32; idem, *Does America Need a Foreign Policy? Toward a Diplomacy for the 21st Century* (New York: Simon and Schuster, 2001), 283–288.

73. Kissinger, *The Troubled Partnership,* 251.

74. Idem, *The Necessity for Choice,* 7–9.

75. Idem, "For an Atlantic Confederacy," *The Reporter,* 2 February 1961, 20; idem, *The Necessity for Choice,* 121.

76. Idem, *The Troubled Partnership,* 246.

77. Ibid., 47.

78. Ibid., 47, 54–55.

79. Ibid., 244. See also idem, "Coalition Diplomacy in a Nuclear Age," 544–545. Kissinger did not always include Italy in his Executive Committee proposal. He excluded Italy in his discussion of the scheme in 1961, and then added it in 1965. See idem, *The Necessity of Choice,* 167; idem, *The Troubled Partnership,* 245–246.

80. Idem, "For a New Atlantic Alliance," *The Reporter,* 14 July 1966, 27.

81. Ibid.

82. McGeorge Bundy to Henry Kissinger, 28 January 1961 and 18 February 1961, folder: Staff Memoranda, Henry Kissinger, 5/61, NSF. See also McGeorge Bundy to President Kennedy, 8 February 1961, folder: Staff Memoranda, Henry Kissinger, 1/61–4/61, box 320, NSF.

83. Kissinger to the President, 22 March 1961, folder: Staff Memoranda, Henry Kissinger, 5/61, NSF. In June 1961 Kissinger explained: "The need for a flexible nuclear response remains"; Kissinger to Bundy, 15 and 21 July 1961, folder: Staff Memoranda, Henry Kissinger, 6/61–7/61, box 320, NSF. When Kissinger wrote that "nobody really wants German unification," he meant that none of the non-German states in Europe wanted it. The key point, with regard to U.S. policy, was that the Germans strongly desired unification. Kissinger pressed the Kennedy administration to formulate a policy that would convince the Germans of an American commitment to reunification even while assuring neighboring states that unification would not occur anytime soon.

84. Kissinger to Rockefeller, ca. 20 July 1961, folder 69, box 12, Series 1, Record Group 15, NAR, Gubernatorial, RAC. For Kissinger's use of similar language in memoranda for the White House, see Kissinger to Bundy, 21 July 1961; Kissinger to Bundy, 18 August 1961, folder: Staff Memoranda, Henry Kissinger, 8/61, box 320, NSF.

85. Kissinger to Arthur Schlesinger Jr., 8 September 1961, folder: Kissinger, Henry, 4/19/61–12/2/61, box WH-13, Schlesinger Papers; Kissinger, *White House Years,* 13–14; Kissinger to Bundy, 19 October 1961, folder: Staff Memoranda, Henry Kissinger, 9/61–10/61, box 320, NSF; Kissinger to Bundy, 3 November 1961, folder: Staff Memoranda, Henry Kissinger, 11/61–12/61, ibid.

86. Kissinger to Schlesinger, 8 September 1961.

87. See Marc Trachtenberg, *A Constructed Peace: The Making of the European Settlement, 1945–1963* (Princeton: Princeton University Press, 1999), 379–402; John Lewis Gaddis, *We Now Know: Rethinking Cold War History* (Oxford: Clarendon Press, 1997), 278–280; Anders Stephanson, "The United States," in David Reynolds, ed., *The Origins of the Cold War in Europe: International Perspectives* (New Haven: Yale University Press, 1994), 23–51; Jeremi Suri, *Power and Protest: Global Revolution and the Rise of Détente* (Cambridge, Mass.: Harvard University Press, 2003), 41–43. Thomas Schwartz has shown that Lyndon Johnson did take some measures, particularly with French president Charles de Gaulle, to ensure more consultation and consensus within NATO; *Lyndon Johnson and Europe: In the Shadow of Vietnam* (Cambridge, Mass.: Harvard University Press, 2003).

88. Henry A. Kissinger, "The New Cult of Neutralism," *The Reporter,* 24 November 1960, 26–29. Kissinger's thinking matched a general American anxiety about neutrals in the Cold War. See H. W. Brands, *The Specter of Neutralism* (New York: Columbia University Press, 1990).

89. John Lewis Gaddis, *The Long Peace: Inquiries into the History of the Cold War* (New York: Oxford University Press, 1987), 215–245. For the most influential theoretical articulation of this perspective, see Kenneth Waltz, *Theory of International Politics* (New York: McGraw-Hill, 1979).

90. Kissinger, "Reflections on Cuba," 21–24. Evidence from Russian archives indicates that Khrushchev did not act according to the logic that Kissinger assumed. See Aleksandr Fursenko and Timothy Naftali, *Khrushchev's Cold War: The Inside Story of an American Adversary* (New York: W. W. Norton, 2006); William Taubman, *Khrushchev: The Man and His Era* (New York: W. W. Norton, 2003), esp. 529–577.

91. Kissinger, "Reflections on Cuba," 23.

92. Ibid., 23–24. See also Dean Acheson, "Dean Acheson's Version of Robert Kennedy's Version of the Cuban Missile Affair: Homage to Plain Dumb Luck," *Esquire,* February 1969, 76–78, 94, 96.

93. Kissinger to Schlesinger, 8 September 1961.

94. Kissinger, *White House Years,* 69. Kissinger's comments in his memoirs are consistent with his earlier writings. See idem, "American Policy and Preventive War," 330; idem, "Coalition Diplomacy in a Nuclear Age," 529–530; idem, "Central Issues of American Foreign Policy," in Kermit Gordon, ed., *Agenda for the Nation* (Washington: Brookings Institution, 1968), 585–614.

95. See Kissinger's link between nineteenth-century diplomacy, Madison's writings on pluralism, and multipolar balance of power politics in *Diplomacy,* 21–22. For Madison's seminal essays on pluralism and federalism, see *Federalist* 10, 37, and 51, available at http://www.constitution.org/fed/ (accessed 20 July 2006). For a particularly insightful account of Madison's thought, see Jack N. Rakove, *Original Meanings: Politics and Ideas in the Making of the Constitution* (New York: Alfred A. Knopf, 1996), esp. 161–202.

96. Kissinger, "Central Issues of American Foreign Policy," 588.

97. Ernst Hans Van der Beugel oral history, chap. 7, Archive Location 2.21.183.08, Inventory 60-65, National Archive, The Hague; author's interview with Henry Kissinger, 11 June 2005. See also Stephen Graubard, *Kissinger: Portrait of a Mind* (New York: W. W. Norton, 1974), 250–253. On the prevalent fascination with China's cultural greatness and its influence on foreign-policy considerations (especially in France), see Suri, *Power and Protest,* 71–87. I thank Floris Kunert for helping me to use the Van der Beugel materials, and Danielle Kleijwegt for her translation of the Van der Beugel oral history. All quotations from this oral history are her translations.

98. "Recommended Position: Communist China," prepared by Kissinger for Nelson Rockefeller's briefing book, 15 May 1968, folder 89, box 5, Series 35, Record Group 15, NAR, Gubernatorial, RAC. The same text is included in another section of the same briefing book: folder 88, ibid.

99. Kissinger, "Recommended Position: Communist China"; Excerpts of Remarks by Governor Nelson A. Rockefeller, World Affairs Council of Philadelphia, 1 May 1968, folder: 5/1/68—World Affairs Council, box 59, Series 33, Record Group 15, NAR, Gubernatorial, RAC. See also Walter Isaacson, *Kissinger: A Biography* (New York: Simon and Schuster, 1992), 334; Graubard, *Kissinger,* 250–253.

100. Lyndon Johnson, "Remarks to the American Alumni Council: Asian Policy," 12 July 1966, in *Public Papers of the Presidents: Lyndon Baines Johnson, 1966,* 720–722; Richard M. Nixon, "Asia after Viet Nam," *Foreign Affairs* 46 (October 1967), 121, 123. See also Suri, *Power and Protest,* 226–235.

101. On Kissinger's recognition of the importance of Sino-Soviet tensions in 1968 see "Recommended Position: U.S.-U.S.S.R.," prepared by Kissinger for Nelson Rockefeller's briefing book, 15 May 1968, folder 8, box 5, Series 35, Record Group 15, NAR, Gubernatorial, RAC; Excerpts of Remarks by Governor Nelson

A. Rockefeller, World Affairs Council of Philadelphia, 1 May 1968, Folder: 5/1/68—World Affairs Council, box 59, Series 33, Record Group 15, NAR, Gubernatorial, RAC. See also Jussi Hanhimäki, *The Flawed Architect: Henry Kissinger and American Foreign Policy* (New York: Oxford University Press, 2004), 40–42; Yang Kuisong, "The Sino-Soviet Border Clash of 1969: From Zhenbao Island to Sino-American *Rapprochement,*" *Cold War History* 1 (August 2000), 21–37; William Burr, "Sino-American Relations, 1969: The Sino-Soviet Border War and Steps towards *Rapprochement,*" *Cold War History* 1 (April 2001), 73–112.

102. "Recommended Positions: United States' Relations with the USSR," prepared by Kissinger for Nelson Rockefeller's briefing book, 15 May 1968, folder 89, box 5, Series 35, Record Group 15, NAR, Gubernatorial, RAC; Kissinger, "Recommended Position: Communist China."

103. On 3 May 1968 Professor James MacGregor Burns from Williams College wrote Rockefeller inquiring about his views on the presidency. These quotations come from a letter that Kissinger drafted to Burns on Rockefeller's behalf, 23 May 1968, folder 111, box 7, Series 35, Record Group 15, NAR, Gubernatorial, RAC.

104. For Kissinger's reflections on "advanced" and "new" countries, see "Central Issues of American Foreign Policy," 603–606.

105. Ibid., 603.

106. Kissinger criticized Americans for thinking of peace in terms similar to the "hidden hand" of Adam Smith's economic market. According to this flawed image, peace would arise as the organic outcome of fair and equal relations among states. "No idea," Kissinger wrote, "could be more dangerous." He argued that peace was not a "normal" condition of international relations. It emerged from the decisions of the biggest powers. Kissinger, "Reflections on American Diplomacy," 42–43.

107. Idem, "Central Issues of American Foreign Policy," 612.

108. Idem, *Diplomacy,* 471.

109. Idem, *A World Restored,* 316–317; idem, "The Policymaker and the Intellectual," *The Reporter,* 5 March 1959, 30–35; idem, *White House Years,* 55.

110. Kissinger, "Recommended Position: U.S.-U.S.S.R."; idem, "Central Issues of American Foreign Policy," 585–589, 610–614.

111. "Basic Principles of Relations between the United States of America and the Union of Soviet Socialist Republics," 29 May 1972, *U.S. Department of State of Bulletin* 66 (26 June 1972), 898–899; Kissinger's news conference, Kiev, 29 May 1972, ibid., 890–897. See also Suri, *Power and Protest,* 256–258. In his memoirs, Kissinger claims that Soviet leaders pushed for a "Declaration of Principles" in 1972, while he and Nixon were initially somewhat reluctant. The Soviets certainly saw value in a document that legitimized their authority, but the evidence above indicates that Kissinger had long sought a consensus on basic principles to manage international conflict. The 1972 Soviet-American "Basic Principles" agreement reflected Kissin-

ger's long-standing thought, in addition to Soviet interests. See Kissinger, *White House Years,* 1131–32.

112. Hamilton Fish Armstrong to the John Simon Guggenheim Memorial Foundation, 2 December 1964, folder: Kissinger, Henry A., 1963–1972, box 39, Armstrong Papers; Van der Beugel oral history. Van der Beugel oversaw Dutch administration of American Marshall Plan aid. He became deputy foreign minister in the Dutch Ministry of Foreign Affairs, with special oversight for NATO matters. He also served as the president of KLM Royal Dutch Airlines and the secretary-general of the Bilderberg Group, organizing annual meetings of influential transatlantic elites. More biographical information is available at http://www.parlement.com/9291000/biof/01847 (accessed 10 July 2006).

113. Kissinger to Hans Morgenthau, 13 November 1968, folder 1, box 4, Hans Morgenthau Collection, Leo Baeck Institute, New York. A copy of the letter is available in folder: Kissinger, Henry, box 33, Papers of Hans J. Morgenthau, Library of Congress Manuscript Reading Room, Washington, D.C. In his advice to Nelson Rockefeller during the mid-1960s, Kissinger expressed pessimism about the war in Vietnam, but he continued to emphasize the need for more American force. See Kissinger to Rockefeller, 29 October 1963, folder 61, box 11, Series 1, Record Group 15, NAR, Gubernatorial, RAC; Kissinger, Recommended Position for Rockefeller on South Vietnam, 1 January 1964, folder 183, box 31, Series J.2, Record Group 4, NAR, Personal, RAC. Kissinger criticized the neutralization of Laos in 1963 as a case of American weakness that would encourage more communist aggression. He advised Rockefeller to embrace a stronger American posture in neighboring Vietnam. Kissinger to Rockefeller, 23 October 1963 and 10 January 1964, ibid.

114. Kissinger to Philip W. Quigg, folder: Kissinger, Henry, 1963–1972, box 39, Armstrong Papers.

115. Henry A. Kissinger, "The Viet Nam Negotiations," *Foreign Affairs* 47 (January 1969), 234.

116. Notes of President Johnson's Meeting with Dean Rusk, Robert McNamara, Nicholas Katzenbach, Walt Rostow, Henry Kissinger, Abe Fortas, Maxwell Taylor, and Clark Clifford, 18 October 1967, *FRUS,* 1964–1968, vol. 5, doc. 357; History of "Pennsylvania" Discussions, folder: Pennsylvania, box 140, National Security File, Country File: Vietnam, Lyndon Baines Johnson Presidential Library, Austin, Texas. For more on the "Marigold" and "Pennsylvania" negotiating initiatives in 1966–67, see Robert K. Brigham and George C. Herring, "The Pennsylvania Peace Initiative, June–October 1967"; and James G. Hershberg, "'A Half-Hearted Overture': Czechoslovakia, Kissinger, and Vietnam, Autumn 1966," both in Lloyd C. Gardner and Ted Gittinger, eds., *The Search for Peace in Vietnam, 1964–1968* (College Station: Texas A&M University Press, 2004), 59–72, 292–320.

117. Instructions for Henry Kissinger on prospective negotiations with North Vietnam, undated (ca. 11 August 1967), *FRUS*, 1964–1968, vol. 5, doc. 277; Kissinger to Henry Cabot Lodge, 7 June 1966; Memorandum of Conversation between W. Averell Harriman and Kissinger, 25 October 1966, folder: Kissinger, Henry, box FCL-13, Papers of W. Averell Harriman, Library of Congress Manuscript Reading Room, Washington D.C.; Memorandum of Conversation with Harriman, Kissinger, et al., 2 August 1966, *FRUS*, 1964–1968, vol. 4, doc. 196.

118. See John Prados, "The Shape of the Table: Nguyen Van Thieu and Negotiations to End the Conflict," in Gardner and Gittinger, *The Search for Peace in Vietnam*, 355–360; Robert Schulzinger, *A Time for War: The United States and Vietnam, 1945–1975* (New York: Oxford University Press, 1997), 267–273.

119. Averell Harriman handwritten letter to George Ball, ca. September–October 1968, folder: Paris Peace Talks, Chronological File, December 1968–January 1969, box 558, Harriman Papers. See also Harriman Notes on Secure Telephone Conversation with Ben Read, 4 September 1968, ibid; Gareth Porter, *A Peace Denied: The United States, Vietnam, and the Paris Agreement* (Bloomington: Indiana University Press, 1975), 70–79; Robert Dallek, *Flawed Giant: Lyndon Johnson and His Times, 1961–1973* (New York: Oxford University Press, 1998), 564–584.

120. Seymour M. Hersh, *The Price of Power: Kissinger in the Nixon White House* (New York: Summit Books, 1983), 12–22. See also Clark Clifford, *Counsel to the President: A Memoir* (New York: Random House, 1991), 574, 581–584; Marilyn B. Young, *The Vietnam Wars, 1945–1990* (New York: Harper Collins, 1991), 232–234. For a more cautious account of the Nixon campaign's actions and Kissinger's role, see Herbert Y. Schandler, "The Pentagon and Peace Negotiations after March 31, 1968," in Gardner and Gittinger, *The Search for Peace in Vietnam*, 321–354. For an account that gives less attention to Kissinger, see Dallek, *Flawed Giant*, 584–592.

121. For Kissinger's account of this period, see Henry Kissinger, *Ending the Vietnam War: A History of America's Involvement in Extraction from the Vietnam War* (New York: Simon and Schuster, 2003), 52–54, 585 n. 2.

122. On the role of nonstate actors in the Vietnam War, see Robert K. Brigham, *Guerrilla Diplomacy: The NLF's Foreign Relations and the Viet Nam War* (Ithaca: Cornell University Press, 1999); Mark Bradley, *Inventing Vietnam and America: The Making of Postcolonial Vietnam, 1919–1950* (Chapel Hill: University of North Carolina Press, 2000), esp. 10–44, 107–145.

123. For Kissinger's discussion of how great leaders, particularly Metternich and Bismarck, failed to prepare their successors, see *A World Restored*, 321–324; and "The White Revolutionary," 918–922.

124. "Superstar Statecraft: How Henry Does It," *Time*, 1 April 1974; Marvin Kalb and Bernard Kalb, *Kissinger* (Boston: Little, Brown, 1974), 3–13; Blumenfeld, *Henry Kissinger*, 148–161, 208–228; Isaacson, *Kissinger*, 355–370.

125. For Kissinger's reflections on the challenges of international complexity for the statesman, see *A World Restored,* 315–332; idem, "The Conservative Dilemma," 1027–30; idem, "The White Revolutionary," 913–922. For an insightful analysis of how international complexity undermined the grand strategy of one of early modern Europe's most impressive statesman, Philip II, see Geoffrey Parker, *The Grand Strategy of Philip II* (New Haven: Yale University Press, 1998). For accounts of Kissinger's ignorance about the effects of his policies, especially outside Europe, see Hanhimäki, *Flawed Architect,* esp. 399–426; Odd Arne Westad, *The Global Cold War: Third World Interventions and the Making of Our Times* (Cambridge: Cambridge University Press, 2005), esp. 207–249; Piero Gleijeses, *Conflicting Missions: Havana, Washington, and Africa, 1959–1976* (Chapel Hill: University of North Carolina Press, 2002).

126. Many historians have made the same basic point, especially regarding the Vietnam War, from different methodological perspectives. For a sample of this enormous literature, see Kuklick, *Blind Oracles;* Lloyd Gardner, *Pay Any Price: Lyndon Johnson and the Wars for Vietnam* (Chicago: Ivan R. Dee, 1995); Fredrik Logevall, *Choosing War: The Lost Chance for Peace and the Escalation of War in Vietnam* (Berkeley: University of California Press, 1999); Bradley, *Inventing Vietnam and America;* Robert D. Dean, *Imperial Brotherhood: Gender and the Making of Cold War Foreign Policy* (Amherst: University of Massachusetts Press, 2001); Robert J. McMahon, *The Limits of Empire: the United States and Southeast Asia since World War II* (New York: Columbia University Press, 1999).

127. See note 1 above. Kissinger offered the same critique of Metternich; *A World Restored,* 322–324. Kissinger sought to formulate a grand strategy that embodied the wisdom of prior experiences, but he failed to learn all the necessary lessons of statesmanship. In an ironic twist of history, he recreated the "smug self-satisfaction" that he criticized in Metternich. Also like Metternich, he overestimated his own capabilities. Kissinger's grand strategy suffered from the hubris of its predecessors.

5. A Statesman's Revolution

1. For analysis of the origins and nature of global revolution in the 1960s, see Jeremi Suri, *Power and Protest: Global Revolution and the Rise of Détente* (Cambridge, Mass.: Harvard University Press, 2003); idem, *The Global Revolutions of 1968* (New York: W. W. Norton, 2007), x–xxiii.

2. Michael Stewart, handwritten diary, 17 April 1968, STWT 8/1/5, Churchill Archives Center, Churchill College, Cambridge University.

3. Notes on conversation between Hamilton Fish Armstrong and Henry

Kissinger, 30 March 1972, folder: Kissinger, Henry A., 1963–1972, box 39, Armstrong Papers.

4. Handwritten letter from Henry Kissinger to Nelson Rockefeller, 30 December 1968, folder 245, box 10, Series P: Ann C. Whitman—Politics, Record Group 4, NAR, Personal, RAC; Kissinger to Rockefeller, 20 August 1968, folder 110, box 7, Series 35, Record Group 15, NAR, Gubernatorial, RAC.

5. Henry Kissinger, "Central Issues of American Foreign Policy," in Kermit Gordon, ed., *Agenda for the Nation* (Washington, D.C.: Brookings Institution, 1968), 614.

6. See Randall B. Woods, *LBJ: Architect of American Ambition* (New York: Free Press, 2006), esp. 138–157, 440–482, 649–671; Robert Dallek, *Flawed Giant: Lyndon Johnson and His Times, 1961–1973* (New York: Oxford University Press, 1998), esp. 54–121.

7. For a thoughtful engagement with the shortcomings of liberal democracy in a time of social and political stress, see Jeffrey C. Isaac, *Democracy in Dark Times* (Ithaca: Cornell University Press, 1998). Isaac draws extensively on the writings of Hannah Arendt.

8. See Henry Kissinger, *A World Restored: Metternich, Castlereagh, and the Problems of Peace, 1812–1822* (1957; reprint, London: Phoenix, 2000), esp. 144–174; idem, "The White Revolutionary: Reflections on Bismarck," *Daedalus* 97 (Summer 1968), 888–924; idem, *Diplomacy* (New York: Simon and Schuster, 1994), esp. 394–445.

9. Idem, "Central Issues of American Foreign Policy," 602. Kissinger rejected the programs advocated by "New Left" and "New Right" radicals, but he sympathized with the protestors' criticisms of containment, liberal politics, and Cold War policies in general. See Kissinger to Rockefeller, 31 May 1968, folder 91, box 5, Series 35, Record Group 15, NAR, Gubernatorial, RAC; Kissinger draft article to be published under Rockefeller's name, 1967, folder 246, box 10, Series P, Record Group 4, NAR, Personal, RAC. This draft was the basis for Nelson A. Rockefeller, "Policy and the People," *Foreign Affairs* 46 (January 1968), 231–241.

10. Memorandum of Conversation between Henry Kissinger and a group of Fellows from the Harvard Center for International Affairs, 7 December 1971, NSA (accessed 26 July 2006).

11. Notes from Conversation between Michael Palliser and Henry Kissinger, 19 December 1968, PREM 13/2097, Public Records Office, Kew, London. The term "statesman's revolution" is my own, not Kissinger's.

12. Kissinger to Rockefeller, 30 December 1968.

13. Rockefeller to Kissinger, 17 January 1969, folder 111, box 7, Series 35, Record Group 15, NAR, Gubernatorial, RAC.

14. Henry Kissinger to William Elliott, 12 May 1955, with attached letter to Vice President Richard Nixon, 12 May 1955, folder: International Seminar, Harvard, 1951–1959, box 2, Elliott Papers; Kissinger to Rockefeller, 20 August 1968; Henry Kissinger to Ernst Van der Beugel, 14 August 1968, Papers of Ernst Hans Van der Beugel, National Archive, The Hague. See also Henry Kissinger, *White House Years* (Boston: Little, Brown, 1979), 9–10.

15. Author's interview with Henry Kissinger, 27 July 2004; Henry Kissinger, *Years of Renewal* (New York: Simon and Schuster, 1999), 54–63.

16. William F. Buckley Jr. to Henry Kissinger, August 1969, folder: White House (1969)—Kissinger, Henry A., box 67; handwritten notes of telephone conversation between Buckley and Kissinger, August 1968, folder: Kissinger, Henry A., box 51, both in Buckley Papers. In his notes regarding this telephone conversation, Buckley wrote of his "introducing K[issinger] to Nixon via Frank Shakespeare." For some earlier communications between Buckley and Kissinger regarding the prospective Nixon administration, see Buckley to Kissinger, 12 August 1968; Kissinger to Buckley, 14 August 1968, both in folder: Kissinger, Henry A., box 51, Buckley Papers. Buckley's association with sociologist and Democrat Daniel Patrick Moynihan reflected a similar mission to protect social order against growing tides of violence and disruption. See Moynihan's speech, "Politics as the Art of the Impossible," 1 June 1969, folder: White House (1969)—Moynihan, Daniel P., box 67, Buckley Papers. Buckley helped bring Moynihan, as well as Kissinger, into the Nixon administration. See Buckley's list of suggested cabinet appointees in his handwritten notes of a telephone conversation with Kissinger, August 1968, folder: Kissinger, Henry A., box 51, Buckley Papers. For Schlesinger's quote, see Ralph Blumenfeld and the staff and editors of the *New York Post, Henry Kissinger: The Private and Public Story* (New York: Signet, 1974), 170. See also Robert Schulzinger, *Henry Kissinger: Doctor of Diplomacy* (New York: Columbia University Press, 1989), 23; Walter Isaacson, *Kissinger: A Biography* (New York: Simon and Schuster, 1992), 134–139.

17. Transcript of audio recording of President Nixon's conversation with John Dean, 14 March 1973; transcript of audio recording of Nixon's conversation with H. R. Haldeman and John Ehrlichman, 3 August 1972; transcript of audio recording of Nixon's conversation with Henry Kissinger, 29 August 1973, all in Stanley I. Kutler, ed., *Abuse of Power: The New Nixon Tapes* (New York: Free Press, 1997), 229, 113, 373–374.

18. Transcript of audio recording of Nixon's conversation with Haldeman and Kissinger, 1 July 1971; transcript of audio recording of Nixon's conversation with Haldeman and Ehrlichman, 3 August 1972, both in ibid., 9, 113–115.

19. Kissinger, *White House Years,* 299.

20. Schulzinger, *Henry Kissinger,* 23–28; David Rothkopf, *Running the World:*

The Inside Story of the National Security Council and the Architects of American Power (New York: Public Affairs, 2005), 108–156.

21. William Safire, *Before the Fall: An Inside View of the Pre-Watergate White House* (Garden City, N.Y.: Doubleday, 1975), 164–165.

22. Henry Kissinger, *Years of Upheaval* (Boston: Little, Brown, 1982), 73–74, 1182.

23. Transcript of audio recording of Nixon's telephone conversation with Kissinger, 17–18 April 1973, in Kutler, *Abuse of Power*, 321–322.

24. Transcript of audio recording of Nixon's meeting with Haldeman, 20 October 1972; transcript of audio recording of Nixon's meeting with John Ehrlichman, 29 March 1973; transcript of audio recording of Nixon's meeting with Ehrlichman, 13 August 1972, all in Kutler, *Abuse of Power*, 172, 288–289, 129. See also Stanley I. Kutler, *The Wars of Watergate: The Last Crisis of Richard Nixon* (New York: Alfred A. Knopf, 1990), 324–325. Richard Reeves documents Nixon's recurring anti-Semitic comments—including the use of epithets like "kike"—throughout his time in office. See *President Nixon: Alone in the White House* (New York: Simon and Schuster, 2001), esp. 170–171, 263–264, 343–344, 369–370, 377–379.

25. Transcript of audio recording of Nixon's meeting with Charles Colson, 1 January 1973, in Kutler, *Abuse of Power*, 191. For more on Kissinger's "background" briefings for the press, see Isaacson, *Kissinger*, 573–586.

26. Transcript of Kissinger's telephone conversation with Nixon, 16 October 1973, State FOIA (accessed 31 July 2006). For Kissinger's incomplete published version of this transcript, see *Crisis: The Anatomy of Two Major Foreign Policy Crises* (New York: Simon and Schuster, 2003), 268.

27. C. L. Sulzberger's diary entries for his 26 February 1970 and 8 March 1971 meetings with Kissinger, reprinted in idem, *An Age of Mediocrity: Memoirs and Diaries, 1963–1972* (New York: Macmillan, 1973), 613, 714. I thank Salim Yaqub for drawing my attention to these diary entries.

28. Leonard Garment, *Crazy Rhythm: My Journey from Brooklyn, Jazz, and Wall Street to Nixon's White House, Watergate, and Beyond . . .* (New York: Random House, 1997), 186–187. Before serving in the White House, Garment was Nixon's law partner in New York. Garment's account of the anti-Semitism in the Nixon administration is particularly credible because he expresses a generally favorable judgment of Nixon; he is not recounting the anti-Semitism of the Nixon White House to condemn the president.

29. Transcript of Kissinger's telephone conversation with David Abshire, 3 October 1973, State FOIA (accessed 31 July 2006). The term "WASP" was an acronym for members of the white Anglo-Saxon Protestant establishment. In this conversation, Kissinger was mistaken in his assumption that Joseph Sisco was Jewish. Sisco was the child of Italian immigrants, from a non-Jewish background. See his

obituary in the *Washington Post,* 24 November 2004, B7. I thank John Tortorice for his insights about Sisco's biography.

30. Transcript of Kissinger's telephone conversation with Secretary of Transportation William Coleman, 3 August 1976, State FOIA (accessed 31 July 2006). It is not clear that the Nixon administration hired more African American Foreign Service personnel than its predecessor. Kissinger made frequent references to his Jewish background in his telephone conversations, especially when he anticipated attacks on his character. See, for example, transcript of Kissinger's telephone conversation with Nixon, 23 September 1973; transcript of Kissinger's telephone conversation with Kenneth Jameson, 2 November 1973; transcript of Kissinger's telephone conversation with David Landes, 2 November 1973, State FOIA (accessed 31 July 2006).

31. On Kissinger's confrontation with presumptions of Jewish disloyalty to the United States during the Nixon presidency, see Garment, *Crazy Rhythm,* 187. On the emergence of ethnic politics, the transformation of the American political landscape, and Nixon's appeals to the anti-Semitic and racist attitudes of the "silent majority," see Dan T. Carter, *The Politics of Rage: George Wallace, the Origins of the New Conservatism, and the Transformation of American Politics,* 2d ed. (Baton Rouge: Louisiana State University Press, 2000), esp. 324–414; Bruce J. Schulman, *The Seventies: The Great Shift in American Culture, Society, and Politics* (New York: Free Press, 2001), esp. 23–117; Michael W. Flamm, *Law and Order: Street Crime, Civil Unrest, and the Crisis of Liberalism in the 1960s* (New York: Columbia University Press, 2005), 162–178; Melvin Small, *The Presidency of Richard Nixon* (Lawrence: University Press of Kansas, 1999), 153–183.

32. On the "war at home," see Michael Sherry, *In the Shadow of War: The United States since the 1930s* (New Haven: Yale University Press, 1995), 292–336; Tom Wicker, *One of Us: Richard Nixon and the American Dream* (New York: Random House, 1991), esp. 569–648.

33. This is one of the central insights of Stanley Kutler's seminal book, *The Wars of Watergate,* esp. 77–184. For the most influential discussion of the imperial presidency, written against the backdrop of the Vietnam War and Nixon's first term in office, see Arthur Schlesinger Jr., *The Imperial Presidency* (Boston: Houghton Mifflin, 1973).

34. Kissinger, *White House Years,* 226–227. On the improving military situation for the United States in Vietnam, see Special National Intelligence Estimate, SNIE 14–69, 16 January 1969; Memorandum from Chairman of the Joint Chiefs of Staff Earle Wheeler to Secretary of Defense Melvin Laird, 21 July 1969, both in *FRUS,* 1969–1976, vol. 6, docs. 1 and 100; Lewis Sorley, *A Better War: The Unexamined Victories and Final Tragedy of America's Last Years in Vietnam* (Orlando, Fla.: Harcourt, 1999).

35. Henry Kissinger to Henry Cabot Lodge, U.S. Ambassador to South Vietnam, 7 September 1965, reel 20, part 5, Lodge Papers. For the same argument, see Kissinger, "Central Issues of American Foreign Policy," 585–614; idem, "The Viet Nam Negotiations," *Foreign Affairs* 47 (January 1969), 211–234.

36. See Kissinger to Nixon, undated (ca. late March 1969), *FRUS,* 1969–1976, vol. 6, doc. 46.

37. President Lyndon Johnson's Telephone Conversation with Ambassador Adlai Stevenson, 27 May 1964, 10:50 A.M., citation 3518, tape WH6405.10, Recordings of Telephone Conversations, White House Series, Lyndon Baines Johnson Presidential Library, Austin, Texas. Stevenson died in 1965, so we do not know what his position on the Vietnam War would have been in 1968. Like most other mainstream Democratic critics, including Hubert Humphrey and even Robert Kennedy, we can assume that he would have opposed the war in 1968, but that he also would have felt compelled to support America's general Cold War posture of anticommunist containment. For Humphrey's support of Nixon's attempt to use escalation to end the Vietnam War in 1969, see Notes of Telephone Conversation between Nixon and Kissinger, 10 October 1969, *FRUS,* 1969–1976, vol. 6, doc. 135.

38. Kissinger, *White House Years,* 227–228. For more on the depth of American liberal commitments in Vietnam, see Michael E. Latham, *Modernization as Ideology: American Social Science and "Nation-Building" in the Kennedy Era* (Chapel Hill: University of North Carolina Press, 2000), esp. 69–108; Lloyd C. Gardner, *Pay Any Price: Lyndon Johnson and the Wars for Vietnam* (Chicago: Ivan R. Dee, 1995), esp. 40–64; Suri, *Power and Protest,* 131–163. For more on American public opinion regarding the Vietnam War, see John E. Mueller, *War, Presidents and Public Opinion* (New York: John Wiley and Sons, 1973), 42–167; Robert Schulzinger, *A Time for War: The United States and Vietnam, 1941–1975* (New York: Oxford University Press, 1997), 280–283; Melvin Small, *Johnson, Nixon, and the Doves* (New Brunswick, N.J.: Rutgers University Press, 1988), esp. 162–224.

39. For an excellent discussion of "credibility" and American foreign policy, see Robert J. McMahon, "Credibility and World Power," *Diplomatic History* 15 (Fall 1991), 455–472.

40. Thomas C. Schelling, *Arms and Influence* (New Haven: Yale University Press, 1966), 124–125. Like Kissinger, Schelling generally supported American actions in Vietnam during the 1960s. After the American invasion of Cambodia in 1970, however, Schelling strongly opposed Nixon's and Kissinger's policies. See the accounts of the infamous meeting of Harvard faculty, including Schelling, with Kissinger on 8 May 1970: Mike Kinsley, "I Think We Have a Very Unhappy Colleague-on-Leave Tonight," *Harvard Crimson,* 19 May 1970; Bruce Kuklick, *Blind Oracles: Intellectuals and War from Kennan to Kissinger* (Princeton: Princeton University Press, 2006), 201–202.

41. Kissinger to Nixon, 8 March 1969; transcript of telephone conversation between Nixon and Kissinger, 5 April 1969, both in *FRUS*, 1969–1976, vol. 6, docs. 34 and 55.

42. Nixon to Kissinger, 9 May 1972, folder: Memos, May 1972, box 4, President's Personal File, White House Special Files, Nixon Papers.

43. For Kissinger's clear articulation of this strategy for Vietnam, see Kissinger to Nixon, 3 April 1969, *FRUS*, 1969–1976, vol. 6, doc. 52; handwritten notes on Kissinger's conversations with Ambassador Henry Cabot Lodge, 28 February 1969 and August 1969, reel 9, part 1, Lodge Papers. See also Jussi Hanhimäki, *The Flawed Architect: Henry Kissinger and American Foreign Policy* (New York: Oxford University Press, 2004), 46–48.

44. On Nixon's "madman" ideas and their influence on the administration's foreign policy, see Jeffrey Kimball, *Nixon's Vietnam War* (Lawrence: University Press of Kansas, 1998), 63–86; idem, ed., *The Vietnam War Files: Uncovering the Secret History of Nixon-Era Strategy* (Lawrence: University Press of Kansas, 2004), 11–24, 53–120; William Burr and Jeffrey Kimball, "Nixon's Secret Nuclear Alert: Vietnam War Diplomacy and the Joint Chiefs of Staff Readiness Test, October 1969," *Cold War History* 3 (January 2003), 113–156; Scott D. Sagan and Jeremi Suri, "The Madman Nuclear Alert: Secrecy, Signaling, and Safety in October 1969," *International Security* 27 (Spring 2003), 150–183.

45. Kissinger to Nixon, undated (ca. early October 1969), with attached paper "The Modern World: A Single 'Strategic Theater,'" by Kissinger's old mentor Fritz Kraemer, 29 September 1969, folder: Kraemer, Fritz G., box 822, NSC Files, Nixon Papers. For Nixon's thinking about the "big play," see Safire, *Before the Fall*, 97–106. For Kissinger's emphasis on a "conceptual" shift, and the influence of Thomas Schelling and others on his thinking, see Chapter 4.

46. Kissinger to Nixon, 16 March 1969; Nixon to Kissinger, 22 April 1970; Kissinger to Nixon, undated (ca. 23 April 1970); National Security Council Decision Memorandum 57, 26 April 1970, all in *FRUS*, 1969–1976, vol. 6, docs. 40, 245, 253, 260; Kissinger, *White House Years*, 489–499. The literature on the U.S. attacks on Cambodia during the Vietnam War and their tragic effects is enormous. The most moving account remains William Shawcross, *Sideshow: Kissinger, Nixon and the Destruction of Cambodia* (New York: Simon and Schuster, 1979). See also David P. Chandler, *The Tragedy of Cambodian History: Politics, War, and Revolution since 1945* (New Haven: Yale University Press, 1991); Schulzinger, *A Time for War*, 284–287; Marilyn B. Young, *The Vietnam Wars, 1945–1990* (New York: Harper Collins, 1991), 236–251; Small, *The Presidency of Richard Nixon*, 77–81; Kimball, *Nixon's Vietnam War*, 131–145, 197–212.

47. Kissinger recounts that he first brought the idea of a nuclear alert to Nixon. The president was making threats about the need to end the war in Viet-

nam soon, and something had to be done. Kissinger reiterates that the alert was meant to be seen by the Soviets, but not threatening. This was a warning, not a provocation for war. Author's interview with Kissinger, 27 July 2004. See also Memorandum of Conversation between Henry Kissinger and Anatoly Dobrynin, 27 September 1969, folder: Dobrynin/Kissinger 1969 (Part 1), box 489, Henry Kissinger Office Files, NSC Files, Nixon Papers; Kissinger to Nixon, 16 March 1969, *FRUS,* 1969–1976, vol. 6, doc. 40; Sagan and Suri, "The Madman Nuclear Alert"; Burr and Kimball, "Nixon's Secret Nuclear Alert." My analysis in this section draws on these two articles and on the broader collaborative work that went into the Sagan and Suri article. I thank Scott Sagan for sharing his expertise and insights with me. Sagan also acquired a number of crucial documents, particularly from the military. For Schelling's influence on Kissinger's manipulation of risk and uncertainty, see Thomas C. Schelling, *The Strategy of Conflict* (Cambridge, Mass.: Harvard University Press, 1960), 187–203. Describing the "threat that leaves something to chance," Schelling famously explained: "it may make sense to try to keep the enemy guessing as long as we are not trying to keep him guessing about our own motivation. If the outcome is partly determined by events and processes that are manifestly somewhat beyond our comprehension and control, we create *genuine* risk for him" (201). See also idem, *Arms and Influence,* 92–125. Daniel Ellsberg offered a similar analysis in the late 1950s. See Ellsberg, "The Theory and Practice of Blackmail," RAND P-3883, July 1968 (originally delivered as a lecture at the Lowell Institute at the Boston Public Library, March 1959), available at http://www.rand.org/pubs/papers/2005/P3883.pdf (accessed 10 September 2006); Tom Wells, *Wild Man: The Life and Times of Daniel Ellsberg* (New York: Palgrave, 2001), 126–128.

48. Alexander Haig to Kissinger, 14 October 1969, folder: Haig Chron., 1–15 October 1969 (1 of 2), box 958, NSC Files, Nixon Papers. The account of Kissinger's 6 October 1969 telephone conversation with Laird comes from William Burr and Jeffrey Kimball, "New Evidence on the Secret Nuclear Alert of October 1969: The Henry A. Kissinger Telcons," *Passport: The Newsletter of the Society for Historians of American Foreign Relations,* April 2005.

49. Lieutenant General Robert Pursley to Haig, 9 October 1969, folder: Items to Discuss with President, 8/13/69–12/30/69, box 334, NSC Files, Nixon Papers; Pursley telephone interview with Scott Sagan, 4 November 2002.

50. Kissinger to Nixon, 9 October 1969, folder: Schedule of Significant Military Exercises, vol. 1, box 352, NSC Files, Nixon Papers; Haig to Kissinger, 9 October 1969, folder: Items to Discuss with President, 8/13/69–12/30/69, box 334, ibid.

51. Haig to Kissinger, 17 October 1969, folder: Items to Discuss with President, 8/13/69–12/30/69, box 334, NSC files, Nixon Papers.

52. History of the 92nd Strategic Aerospace Wing (Heavy) and 92nd Com-

bat Support Group, 14 September–31 December 1969, KWG-92-HI, AFHRC, Maxwell Air Force Base; Strategic Air Command to Eielson, March, and Fairchild Air Force Bases, 21 October 1969, Freedom of Information Act release; Sagan and Suri, "The Madman Nuclear Alert," 173–179. The risk that Moscow might misconstrue an alert or exercise as the start of war was real. In 1983 Soviet leaders apparently misconstrued a NATO nuclear exercise—"Able Archer 83"—as a possible initiation of nuclear war. The KGB began to prepare for imminent conflict. See Benjamin B. Fischer, "A Cold War Conundrum," History Staff of the Center for the Study of Intelligence, CIA, 1997, https://www.cia.gov/csi/monograph/coldwar/source.htm (accessed 18 August 2006); Christopher Andrew and Oleg Gordievsky, *KGB: The Inside Story* (New York: Harper Collins, 1990), 583–605; Jeremi Suri, "Explaining the End of the Cold War: A New Historical Consensus?" *Journal of Cold War Studies* 4 (Fall 2002), 69–70.

53. Kissinger confirms that to his knowledge the Soviet Union never reacted to the October 1969 U.S. nuclear alert: "They must have seen it, but what were they going to do?" Kissinger recounts that he never discussed the nuclear alert with Soviet officials. He does not, however, reject the logic behind using nuclear maneuvers to signal and intimidate adversaries. Author's interview with Kissinger, 27 July 2004.

54. Henry Kissinger, Memorandum to Arthur Schlesinger Jr., 8 December 1954, folder: Kissinger, Henry A., 1954–1957, box 39, Armstrong Papers. On the 1973 nuclear alert, see Chapter 6; Kissinger, *Years of Upheaval,* 575–599. On Kissinger's attempts to create new limited-nuclear-strike options for diplomatic leverage, see Willliam Burr, "The Nixon Administration, the 'Horror Strategy,' and the Search for Limited Nuclear Options, 1969–1972," *Journal of Cold War Studies* 7 (Summer 2005), 34–78; Terry Terriff, *The Nixon Administration and the Making of U.S. Nuclear Strategy* (Ithaca: Cornell University Press, 1995), esp. 51–96, 159–203.

55. Kissinger, *White House Years,* 228–229.

56. For more on the isolation of foreign policy from popular interference and accountability in this period, see Suri, *Power and Protest,* 213–259.

57. Quotations from author's interview with William A. Rusher, 20 April 2004. Abraham Sofaer made similar comments about Kissinger's charm and personal effectiveness in an interview with the author, 16 September 2003. See also Ernst Hans Van der Beugel oral history, chap. 7, Archive Location 2.21.183.08, Inventory 60–65, National Archive, The Hague.

58. Kissinger to Nixon, 15 February 1969; Memorandum of Conversation between Nixon, Soviet Ambassador Anatoly Dobrynin, Kissinger, and Malcolm Tune (Acting Deputy Assistant Secretary of State for European Affairs), 17 February 1969, folder: USSR, Memcons, Dobrynin/President, 2/17/69, box 340, NSC Files, Nixon Papers.

59. For an excellent analysis of the secret back channels between U.S. President John Kennedy and Soviet Premier Nikita Khrushchev during the Cuban Missile Crisis of October 1962, see Aleksandr Fursenko and Timothy Naftali, *"One Hell of a Gamble": The Secret History of the Cuban Missile Crisis* (New York: W. W. Norton, 1997).

60. Kissinger to Nixon, 15 February 1969, NSA (accessed 7 August 2006).

61. Anatoly Dobrynin, *In Confidence: Moscow's Ambassador to America's Six Cold War Presidents* (New York: Random House, 1995), 199; Kissinger to Nixon, 6 March 1969, NSA (accessed 7 August 2006). Nixon's description of the proposed back channel to Dobrynin does not appear in the summary of their 17 February 1969 meeting. Nixon made these remarks to Dobrynin after Malcolm Toon, the representative from the State Department and the note-taker at the meeting, left the room. On this last point, see Kissinger, *White House Years,* 141.

62. Memorandum of Conversation between Leonid Brezhnev, Anatoly Dobrynin, Henry Kissinger, et al., Moscow, 24 October 1974, 11:00 A.M.–2:00 P.M.; Memorandum of Conversation between Leonid Brezhnev, Anatoly Dobrynin, Henry Kissinger, et al., Moscow, 26 October 1974, 7:10 P.M.–10:20 P.M., both in folder: 11/74, Japan, Korea, USSR, box A6, Kissinger-Scowcroft Files, Gerald Ford Presidential Library, Ann Arbor, Michigan. These two documents are reprinted in William Burr, ed., *The Kissinger Transcripts* (New York: New Press, 1998), 327–355.

63. See Suri, *Power and Protest,* 213–259; Raymond Garthoff, *Détente and Confrontation: American-Soviet Relations from Nixon to Reagan,* rev. ed. (Washington, D.C.: Brookings Institution, 1994), esp. 77–122; John Lewis Gaddis, *Strategies of Containment: A Critical Appraisal of Postwar American National Security Policy* (New York: Oxford University Press, 1982), 274–344; Keith L. Nelson, *The Making of Détente: Soviet-American Relations in the Shadow of Vietnam* (Baltimore: Johns Hopkins University Press, 1995).

64. Kissinger to Secretary of State William Rogers, 31 January 1969, *FRUS,* 1969–1976, vol. 6, doc. 14. Kissinger's secret French contacts with North Vietnam in late 1968, as well as in earlier years, were Raymond Aubrac and Jean Sainteny, two men with deep personal connections to the leadership in Hanoi.

65. See Jeffrey Kimball, "The Case of the 'Decent Interval': Do we Now Have a Smoking Gun?" *Passport: The Newsletter of the Society for Historians of American Foreign Relations,* September 2001; idem, *The Vietnam War Files,* 24–28; Jussi Hanhimäki, "Some More 'Smoking Guns'? The Vietnam War and Kissinger's Summitry with Moscow and Beijing, 1971–73," *Passport: The Newsletter of the Society for Historians of American Foreign Relations,* December 2001. For evidence that Kissinger recognized "Vietnamization" would not create a viable South Vietnamese government, see Summary of Kissinger's conversation with Henry Cabot Lodge Jr., 29 December 1969; Lodge to Kissinger, 23 January 1970, both on reel 9,

part 1, Lodge Papers; Memorandum of Kissinger's conversation with Jean Sainteny, 27 September 1970, NSA (accessed 11 August 2006). For Kissinger's doubts about "Vietnamization" as a general strategy, see Kissinger to Nixon, 10 September 1969, folder: Lake, Misc. Material, Sept. 1969–Jan. 1970, box 1047, NSC Files, Nixon Papers.

66. Kissinger quoted in Pierre Asselin, *A Bitter Peace: Washington, Hanoi, and the Making of the Paris Agreement* (Chapel Hill: University of North Carolina Press, 2002), 19.

67. Memorandum of Conversation between Le Duc Tho, Kissinger, et al., 21 February 1970, 4:10 P.M., *FRUS,* 1969–1976, vol. 6, doc. 190.

68. Ibid. See also Memorandum of Conversation between Le Duc Tho, Kissinger, et al., 16 March 1970; Memorandum of Conversation between Le Duc Tho, Kissinger, et al., 4 April 1970, both in ibid., docs. 201 and 222.

69. Memorandum of Conversation between Le Duc Tho, Kissinger, et al., 21 February 1970, 4:10 P.M.

70. Kissinger to Anatoly Dobrynin, 6 January 1973, with attached excerpted transcript from Kissinger's 9 December 1972 meeting with Le Duc Tho, NSA (accessed 17 August 2006). My reading of the transcripts from the Kissinger negotiations with Le Duc Tho agrees on basic matters, but differs in interpretation from Larry Berman's excellent study, *No Peace, No Honor: Nixon, Kissinger, and Betrayal in Vietnam* (New York: Free Press, 2001), esp. 61–81. Berman discounts Kissinger's ability to influence Le Duc Tho and his other interlocutors.

71. See Asselin, *A Bitter Peace,* esp. 31–77.

72. Le Duan quoted in ibid., 180; Kissinger to Nixon, 28 September 1972, NSA (accessed 10 August 2006); Schulzinger, *A Time for War,* 297–300. This paragraph draws on the research in Vietnamese sources by Robert Brigham, *Guerrilla Diplomacy: The NLF's Foreign Relations and the Viet Nam War* (Ithaca: Cornell University Press, 1999), 94–112; Asselin, *A Bitter Peace,* 79–180.

73. Brigham, *Guerrilla Diplomacy,* 105–112; Schulzinger, *A Time for War,* 300–304.

74. Larry Berman argues that all the signatories to the Paris Agreements, particularly the United States and North Vietnam, intended to violate them. The agreements were, in Berman's analysis, political cover for a withdrawal of American troops but a continuation of the war, including U.S. air support for South Vietnam; *No Peace, No Honor,* 8–10, 240–263. For a searing account of the final American evacuation, see Frank Snepp, *Decent Interval: An Insider's Account of Saigon's Indecent End* (New York: Random House, 1977), esp. 473–562.

75. Ford quoted in Schulzinger, *A Time for War,* 325; Mrs. Aase Lionaes, Chairwoman of the Nobel Committee of the Norwegian Storting, Nobel Peace Prize Presentation Speech, 1973, available at http://nobelprize.org/nobel_prizes/

peace/laureates/1973/press.html (accessed 10 August 2006); Lodge to Kissinger, 9 July 1974; Lodge handwritten notes, undated (ca. early 1974), both on reel 9, part 1, Lodge Papers; Rockefeller to Kissinger, 16 November 1973, folder 245, box 10, Series P, Record Group 4, NAR, Personal, RAC; *Time,* 1 April 1974.

76. Snepp, *Decent Interval,* 579. See also Berman, *No Peace, No Honor,* 221–273.

77. See Odd Arne Westad, *The Global Cold War: Third World Interventions and the Making of Our Times* (Cambridge: Cambridge University Press, 2005), esp. 202–206.

78. Kissinger, *White House Years,* 78. Although she is more critical of American diplomacy, Margaret Macmillan confirms Kissinger's judgment about the transformative and exceptional nature of the China opening in 1972. See Margaret Macmillan, *Nixon in China: The Week That Changed the World* (Toronto: Viking Canada, 2006).

79. Memorandum of Conversation between Kissinger, Raymond Aubrac, and Winston Lord, 14 September 1971, NSA (accessed 11 August 2006.)

80. Kissinger, *Diplomacy,* 726. Edward Friedman writes that Kissinger, like many other Western observers, uncritically accepted Chinese myths about their historic regional role as a peace-loving society. Friedman questions the accuracy of this image of China, both in history and in contemporary affairs. See Edward Friedman, "China's Rise, Asia's Future," *Journal of East Asian Studies* 6 (2006) 294–295.

81. Memorandum of Conversation between Kissinger, Raymond Aubrac, and Winston Lord, 14 September 1971. Many historians, and Kissinger himself, have described the elaborate secret communications between Washington and Beijing through Pakistan and various figures, particularly the journalist Edgar Snow. The archival record is filled with numerous other secret overtures to Beijing initiated by Kissinger, including communications through French, Dutch, and papal intermediaries. Kissinger was clearly anxious to open a back channel with China from his first days in office. President Nixon and other officials shared a desire for improved relations with the People's Republic, but Kissinger took the initiative behind the scenes to open communications, often without consulting others in the administration about his maneuvers. For examples of the numerous secret overtures to China, see Memorandum of Conversation between Kissinger and Sainteny, 27 September 1970; Memorandum of Conversation between Kissinger, Monsieur and Madame Sainteny, Alexander Haig, W. Richard Smyser, and Winston Lord, 25 May 1971, NSA (accessed 11 August 2006); Henry Cabot Lodge Jr. to Kissinger, undated (ca. January 1970); Lodge to Kissinger, 3 February 1970; Lodge to Kissinger, 11 August 1971, all on reel 9, part 1, Lodge Papers. See also Kissinger, *White House Years,* 698–732; Hanhimäki, *Flawed Architect,* 105–109, 116–124; Schulzinger, *Henry Kissinger,* 75–90; Suri, *Power and Protest,* 232–241.

82. Kissinger, "Central Issues of American Foreign Policy," 612, 614. See also Kissinger's first article published in *Foreign Affairs*, "Military Policy and Defense of the 'Grey Areas,'" *Foreign Affairs* 33 (April 1955), 416–428. Kissinger uses the same term—"gray area"—in his memoirs; *White House Years*, 223.

83. Richard Nixon, Informal Remarks in Guam with Newsmen, 25 July 1969, in *Public Papers of the Presidents: Richard Nixon, 1969*, 548, 554. For a fuller statement of the "Nixon Doctrine" see Richard Nixon, Annual Foreign Policy Report, 18 February 1970, ibid., *1970*, 118–119. See also Kissinger, *White House Years*, 222–225; Gaddis, *Strategies of Containment*, 298–299.

84. Notes from Secretary of State Kissinger's Staff Meeting, 23 December 1974, *FRUS*, 1969–1973, vol. E-6, doc. 22; Kissinger to Ford, Briefing paper for Meeting of National Security Council, 27 June 1975, NSA (accessed 14 August 2006). For the beginning of Kissinger's cooperative approach toward the South African government, see NSC Interdepartmental Group for Africa, Study in Response to National Security Study Memorandum 39: Southern Africa, 9 December 1969, NSA (accessed 14 August 2006).

85. Notes from Secretary of State Kissinger's Staff Meeting, 23 December 1974; Response to National Security Study Memorandum 224, United States Policy toward Angola, 13 June 1975, NSA (accessed 14 August 2006); "A Brief Chronicle of Events in Angola" and "Discussion of Soviet Involvement in Angola," undated (ca. early 1976), NSA (accessed 14 August 2006). See also Hanhimäki, *Flawed Architect*, 399–426; Thomas Borstelmann, *The Cold War and the Color Line: American Race Relations in the Global Arena* (Cambridge, Mass.: Harvard University Press, 2001), 233–242; Piero Gleijeses, *Conflicting Missions: Havana, Washington, and Africa, 1959–1976* (Chapel Hill: University of North Carolina Press, 2002), 273–299; Westad, *The Global Cold War*, 228–241.

86. Charles Meyer to Ambassador Johnson, 15 December 1969; Kissinger to Ambassador Edward Korry, 7 October 1970, U.S. Department of State Chile Declassification Project Tranche III (1968–1972), both at State FOIA (accessed 13 August 2006); NSC Meeting with Nixon, Kissinger, et al., 6 November 1970, reprinted in Peter Kornbluh, *The Pinochet File: A Declassified Dossier on Atrocity and Accountability* (New York: New Press, 2003), 119. For a critical analysis of Kissinger's support for militaristic regimes in Latin America, see Kathryn Sikkink, *Mixed Signals: U.S. Human Rights Policy in Latin America* (Ithaca: Cornell University Press, 2004), 106–120.

87. NSC Meeting with Nixon, Kissinger, et al., 6 November 1970. See also Kornbluh, *The Pinochet File*, 1–152; Seymour M. Hersh, *The Price of Power: Kissinger in the Nixon White House* (New York: Summit Books, 1983), 258–296. Kissinger spoke in public of his expectation that Allende "will establish over a period of years some sort of Communist government. In that case you would have one not on an

island off the coast which has not a traditional relationship and impact on Latin America, but in a major Latin American country you would have a Communist government, joining, for example, Argentina, which is already deeply divided, along a long frontier, joining Peru, which has already been heading in directions that have been difficult to deal with, and joining Bolivia, which has also gone in a more leftist, anti-U.S. direction, even without any of these developments." Background Briefing at the White House with Kissinger and Assistant Secretary of State Joseph Sisco, 16 September 1970, reprinted in Hearings before the Subcommittee on Multinational Corporations of the Committee on Foreign Relations, U.S. Senate, 93rd Cong., 20 March–2 April 1973 (Washington, D.C.: U.S. Government Printing Office, 1973), 543.

88. Minutes of the Meeting of the 40 Committee, including Kissinger et al., 19 November 1970 (document dated 10 December 1970); Colby to Kissinger, 13 September 1973, both in Kornbluh, *The Pinochet File,* 126–129, 150–152. Both of these documents remain heavily redacted. The Colby memorandum includes a cover sheet indicating: "You may also recall discussion of a Track Two in late 1970—which has *not* been included in this summary." "Track Two" refers to the covert American cooperation with the Chilean military that Colby excluded from his memorandum. See also Jonathan Haslam, *The Nixon Administration and the Death of Allende's Chile: A Case of Assisted Suicide* (London: Verso, 2005), esp. 158–230.

89. Memorandum of Conversation between Kissinger, Guzzetti, et al., 6 June 1976 (the document is incorrectly dated: the meeting took place on 10 June 1976), National Security Archive Electronic Briefing Book 133, http://www.gwu.edu/~nsarchiv/NSAEBB/NSAEBB133/index.htm (accessed 13 August 2006). For evidence that Kissinger received information indicating that the Argentine government's domestic security forces were "totally out of control" and responsible for "daily waves of murders," see Notes on Secretary of State Kissinger's meeting with Harry Shlaudeman et al., 9 July 1976, ibid. On the "dirty war" conducted by the U.S.-supported Argentine government against its own citizens, and potential opponents throughout Latin America, the United States, and even Europe, see John Dinges, *The Condor Years: How Pinochet and His Allies Brought Terrorism to Three Continents* (New York: New Press, 2004), esp. 63–81, 135–155.

90. Memorandum of Conversation between Kissinger, Guzzetti, et al., 6 June 1976.

91. Quotations from Kissinger in Westad, *The Global Cold War,* 212, 246. For these quotations and his overall analysis of the links between the United States and South Africa in the 1970s, Westad draws on documentary materials from the South African Department of Foreign Affairs Archives. See also ibid., 207–249; Gleijeses, *Conflicting Missions,* 273–372.

92. Steve J. Stern, *Remembering Pinochet's Chile: On the Eve of London 1998*

(Durham, N.C.: Duke University Press, 2004), xxi. For the parallel (and perhaps higher) figures for "disappearances" in Argentina, see Dinges, *The Condor Years,* 139.

93. Memorandum of Conversation between Kissinger, Pinochet, et al., 8 June 1976, reprinted in Kornbluh, *The Pinochet File,* 257.

94. This paragraph draws on the interviews and analysis in the pioneering study by Margaret E. Keck and Kathryn Sikkink, *Activists beyond Borders: Advocacy Networks in International Politics* (Ithaca: Cornell University Press, 1998), esp. 89–92. Paul Heath Hoeffel and Peter Kornbluh quote similar statements from Eldridge in their article "The War at Home: Chile's Legacy in the United States," *NACLA Report on the Americas* 17 (September–October 1983), 31. See also Kathryn Sikkink, "The Emergence, Evolution, and Effectiveness of the Latin American Human Rights Network," in Elizabeth Jelin and Eric Hershberg, eds., *Constructing Democracy: Human Rights, Citizenship, and Society in Latin America* (New York: Westview, 1996), 59–84; Stern, *Remembering Pinochet's Chile,* xxiv–xxv; Vanessa Walker, "The Paradoxes of Human Rights Diplomacy: The Institute for Policy Studies and U.S.-Latin American Relations in the Carter Administration" (Master's thesis, University of Wisconsin–Madison, 2004).

95. Hoeffel and Kornbluh, "The War at Home," 27–39; quotation on 39; Lars Schoultz, *Human Rights and United States Policy toward Latin America* (Princeton: Princeton University Press, 1981), 80–82.

96. See Robert G. Kaufman, *Henry M. Jackson: A Life in Politics* (Seattle: University of Washington Press, 2000), esp. 242–260. Charles Vanik, the cosponsor of the "Jackson-Vanik Amendment," was a Democratic member of the House of Representatives from Ohio.

97. See *Covert Action in Chile,* Staff Report of the Select Committee to Study Government Operations with Respect to Intelligence Activities, U.S. Senate (Washington, D.C.: U.S. Government Printing Office, 1975); *Alleged Assassination Plots Involving Foreign Leaders,* Interim Report of the Select Committee to Study Government Operations with Respect to Intelligence Activities, U.S. Senate (Washington, D.C.: U.S. Government Printing Office, 1975); Sikkink, *Mixed Signals,* 48–76; Schoultz, *Human Rights and United States Policy,* 74–108.

98. Kissinger, "Building an Enduring Foreign Policy," speech delivered in Detroit, 24 November 1975, reprinted in *Department of State Bulletin* 73 (15 December 1975), 848–850; Kissinger, *Years of Renewal,* 34. Kissinger recounts that he devoted extensive time to work on the "heartland speeches." He believes they offer an important statement of his policy aims. Author's interview with Henry Kissinger, 12 September 2006.

99. Kissinger, *Years of Renewal,* 1070. In his memoirs, Kissinger refers to his

"minority view" that "America's historic idealism had to be leavened with an assessment of national interest." See ibid., 48. For some of the press coverage of Kissinger's speeches see *Minnesota Tribune,* 16 July 1975; *Detroit News,* 25 November 1975; *San Francisco Chronicle,* 4 February 1976; *Chicago Tribune,* 7 July 1976. See also Hanhimäki, *Flawed Architect,* 427–438. For an excellent analysis of Kissinger's "heartland speeches," see John Lewis Gaddis, "Rescuing Choice from Circumstance: The Statecraft of Henry Kissinger," in Gordon A. Craig and Francis L. Loewenheim, eds., *The Diplomats, 1939–1979* (Princeton: Princeton University Press, 1994), 564–592. I thank Julie Lane for her help with research on Kissinger's "heartland speeches." My understanding of these speeches and of their public reception is influenced by her work.

100. On the influence of the human rights provisions ("basket three") in the Helsinki Accords, and Kissinger's initial opposition, see Jussi Hanhimäki, "'They can Write It in Swahili': Kissinger, the Soviets, and the Helsinki Accords, 1973–75," *Journal of Transatlantic Studies* 1 (2003), 37–58; Daniel C. Thomas, *The Helsinki Effect: International Norms, Human Rights, and the Demise of Communism* (Princeton: Princeton University Press, 2001); Michael D. J. Morgan, "North America, Atlanticism, and the Helsinki Process"; and Jeremi Suri, "Henry Kissinger and the Reconceptualization of European Security, 1969–1975," both in Andreas Wenger, Vojtech Mastny, and Christian Nünlist, eds., *At the Roots of European Security: The Early Helsinki Process Revisited, 1965–1975* (London: Routledge, 2007). Ironically, the human rights provisions in the Helsinki Accords strengthened Washington's relative power because they most directly undermined Soviet legitimacy and empowered Eastern bloc dissidents. On this point, see Thomas, *The Helsinki Effect.*

101. On the emergence of "rights talk" centered on global human rights, see Mark Philip Bradley, "The Ambiguities of Sovereignty: The United States and the Global Human Rights Cases of the 1940s and 1950s," in Douglas Howland and Luise White, eds., *The Art of the State: Sovereignty Past and Present* (Bloomington: Indiana University Press, 2007); Elizabeth Borgwardt, *A New Deal for the World: America's Vision for Human Rights* (Cambridge, Mass.: Harvard University Press, 2005); Carol Anderson, *Eyes off the Prize: The United Nations and the African American Struggle for Human Rights, 1944–1955* (New York: Cambridge University Press, 2003).

102. For the most explicit accusation that Kissinger is a war criminal, see Christopher Hitchens, *The Trial of Henry Kissinger* (New York: Verso, 2001).

103. James Reston, "Kissinger Sees the World on Verge of Historic Era," *New York Times,* 13 October 1974.

104. Handwritten notes from Henry Cabot Lodge's conversation with Kissinger, 6 July 1974, reel 9, part 1, Lodge Papers.

6. From Germany to Jerusalem

1. Henry Kissinger, *Years of Upheaval* (Boston: Little, Brown, 1982), 416.

2. Quotations from David Binder, "Kissinger Sworn, Praised by Nixon," *New York Times*, 23 September 1973, 11; Kissinger, *Years of Upheaval*, 432.

3. Kissinger, *Years of Upheaval*, 431.

4. Transcript of Henry Kissinger's telephone conversation with Richard Nixon, 23 September 1973, State FOIA (accessed 31 July 2006).

5. Ibid.

6. Transcript of Henry Kissinger's telephone conversation with Richard Nixon, 25 October 1973, 3:05 P.M., State FOIA.

7. Quoted in Kissinger, *Years of Upheaval*, 125–126.

8. Henry Kissinger, *White House Years* (Boston: Little, Brown, 1979), 341.

9. Ibid., 347–348; transcript of Kissinger's telephone conversation with Richard Nixon, 25 October 1973, 7:15 P.M.; transcript of Kissinger's telephone conversation with Alexander Haig, 25 October 1973, 7:19 P.M., both at State FOIA. See also William B. Quandt, *Peace Process: American Diplomacy and the Arab-Israeli Conflict since 1967*, 3d ed. (Washington, D.C.: Brookings Institution Press, 2005), 57; Leonard Garment, *Crazy Rhythm: My Journey from Brooklyn, Jazz, and Wall Street to Nixon's White House, Watergate, and Beyond . . .* (New York: Random House, 1997), 184–188.

10. Kissinger, *Years of Upheaval*, 203–204.

11. Yitzhak Rabin with the assistance of Eithan Haber, *Yitzhak Rabin mesocheach im manhigim ve-rashey medinot* (Yitzhak Rabin Converses with Leaders and Heads of State) (Giva'atayim: Revivim, 1984). My research assistant Gil Ribak translated these passages from the Hebrew original.

12. Memorandum of conversation between Kissinger, Ismail Fahmy, Abdallah El-Erian, and Joseph Sisco, Washington, D.C., 30 October 1973, NSA (accessed 10 August 2006).

13. Transcript of Kissinger's telephone conversation with Brent Scowcroft, 18 October 1973, State FOIA.

14. See Jussi Hanhimäki, *The Flawed Architect: Henry Kissinger and American Foreign Policy* (New York: Oxford University Press, 2004), 330–331; Quandt, *Peace Process*, 172–173.

15. Transcript of Kissinger's telephone conversation with Alexander Haig, 6 October 1973, 8:35 A.M.; transcript of Kissinger's telephone conversation with Richard Nixon, 7 October 1973, 2:07 P.M., both at State FOIA. See also "Indications of Arab Intentions to Initiate Hostilities" (ca. summer 1973), folder: Rabin/Kissinger (Dinitz) 1973, January–July (2 of 3), box 135, Henry Kissinger Office Files, NSC Files, Nixon Papers.

16. Abraham Rabinovich, *The Yom Kippur War: The Epic Encounter That Transformed the Middle East* (New York: Schocken Books, 2004), esp. 65–100; quotation on 89. See also Avi Shlaim, *The Iron Wall: Israel and the Arab World* (New York: W. W. Norton, 2000), 318–320.

17. Dayan quoted in Rabinovich, *The Yom Kippur War,* 219. Rabinovich reports that, after hearing Dayan's remarks, Prime Minister Golda Meir contemplated suicide; ibid., 219–220.

18. Transcript of Kissinger's telephone conversation with Nixon, 6 October 1973, 9:25 A.M., State FOIA.

19. Ibid.; transcript of Kissinger's telephone conversation with Anatoly Dobrynin, 6 October 1973, State FOIA.

20. Transcript of Kissinger's telephone conversation with Haig, 6 October 1973, 12:45 P.M., State FOIA; Douglas Little, *American Orientalism: The United States and the Middle East since 1945* (Chapel Hill: University of North Carolina Press, 2002), 106; Hanhimäki, *The Flawed Architect,* 307–308; Kissinger, *Years of Upheaval,* 507–515.

21. Transcript of Kissinger's telephone conversation with Nixon, 16 October 1973, State FOIA.

22. Memorandum of conversation between Kissinger, James Schlesinger, William Colby, Admiral Thomas Moorer, and Brent Scowcroft, 19 October 1973, NSA. See also Kissinger's briefing at the secretary of state's staff meeting, 23 October 1973, National Security Archive Electronic Briefing Book 98, doc. 63, available at http://www.gwu.edu/~nsarchiv/NSAEBB/NSAEBB98/ (accessed 2 October 2006).

23. Memorandum of conversation between Kissinger, Rabin, and Peter Rodman, 24 January 1973, folder: Rabin/Dinitz, Sensitive Memcons, 1973 (2 of 2), box 135, Kissinger Office Files, Nixon Papers.

24. On the night of 24 October 1973, as Kissinger prepared to raise the American nuclear alert to "Defcon III" in response to Soviet threats in the Middle East, he told Alexander Haig: "You cannot be sure how much of this is due to our domestic crisis. . . . I don't think they would have taken on a functioning president." Kissinger and Haig then discussed whether they should awake Nixon for the decision about raising the nuclear alert. In the end, the president did not attend the White House Situation Room meeting that decided on this extraordinary course of action. See transcript of telephone conversation between Kissinger and Haig, 24 October 1973, 10:20 P.M., State FOIA; Kissinger, *Years of Upheaval,* 585–588. On 25 October 1973 Kissinger and Haig discussed the alert and its aftermath with the clear understanding that they, not the president, had made the key decisions: Kissinger: "you and I were the only ones for it. These other guys were wailing all over the place this morning." Haig: "You're telling me. Last night it seemed like

someone had taken their shoes away from them. You really handled that thing magnificently." Kissinger: "I think I did some good for the President." Haig: "More than you know." Kissinger then called Nixon, who was evidently preoccupied with Watergate. See transcript of telephone conversation between Kissinger and Haig, 25 October 1973, 2:35 P.M.; transcript of telephone conversation between Kissinger and Nixon, 25 October 1973, 3:05 P.M., both at State FOIA.

25. Quoted in Kissinger, *Years of Upheaval,* 594–595.

26. Memorandum of conversation between Anwar Sadat, Ismail Fahmy, Henry Kissinger, Hermann Eilts, and Peter Rodman, Cairo, 30 May 1974, NSA.

27. Kissinger, *Years of Upheaval,* 636.

28. Memorandum of conversation between Anwar Sadat, Hosni Mubarak, Ismail Fahmy, Richard Nixon, Henry Kissinger, and Joseph Sisco, 1 June 1975, NSA.

29. Memorandum of conversation between Kissinger, Nixon, Brent Scowcroft, and bipartisan congressional delegation, 31 May 1974, NSA.

30. Kissinger, *Years of Upheaval,* 647, 638.

31. Anwar el-Sadat, *In Search of Identity: An Autobiography* (New York: Harper and Row, 1978), 291; Memorandum of Conversation between Sadat, Mubarak, Fahmy, Ford, Kissinger, and Sisco, 1 June 1975, NSA.

32. Memorandum of Conversation between Sadat, Mubarak, Fahmy, Ford, Kissinger, Sisco, 1 June 1975, NSA; Memorandum of Conversation between Sadat, Fahmy, Kissinger, Eilts, and Rodman, 30 May 1974, NSA.

33. Memorandum of Conversation between Sadat, Fahmy, Kissinger, Eilts, and Rodman, 30 May 1974, NSA; Sadat, *In Search of Identity,* 291. Edward R. F. Sheehan argues that the leaders of Saudi Arabia similarly believed that Kissinger had powerful personal leverage over Israel; *The Arabs, Israelis, and Kissinger: A Secret History of American Diplomacy in the Middle East* (New York: Reader's Digest Press, 1976), 75.

34. Memorandum of Conversation between Sadat, Fahmy, Kissinger, Eilts, and Rodman, 30 May 1974, NSA.

35. Transcript of Kissinger's telephone conversation with Brent Scowcroft, 18 October 1973, 10:45 P.M.; transcript of Kissinger's telephone conversation with Mr. Jameson, 2 November 1973, both at State FOIA.

36. Menachem Begin's 13 November 1973 speech in the Israeli Knesset, quoted in the Israeli newspaper *Ha'aretz,* 16 November 1973, 5. After the Yom Kippur War, vituperative criticisms of Kissinger saturated the Israeli press. Critics focused on Kissinger's alleged deference to the Arabs. See *Ha'aretz,* 2 November 1973, 7–8; 6 November 1973, 4; 7 November 1973, 6; 22 November 1973, 5; 6 December 1973, 7; *Ma'ariv,* 29 October 1973, 2; 2 November 1973, 13; 16 November 1973, 17; *Yediot akhronot,* 2 November 1973, 8; 8 November 1973, 24. A group of Israeli right-wing

extremists allegedly hired one or more foreign hit men to assassinate Kissinger. See "Bare Plot to Kill Kissinger," *Chicago Tribune,* 14 January 1977, 1. I thank my research assistant Gil Ribak for helping to find and translate these materials.

37. Quotations from Ralph Blumenfeld and the staff and editors of the *New York Post, Henry Kissinger: The Private and Public Story* (New York: Signet, 1974), 254; Memorandum of Conversation between Kissinger and American Jewish Intellectuals, 6 December 1973, NSA. See also Blumenfeld, *Henry Kissinger,* 248–261; Joseph Kraft, "Secretary Henry," *New York Times Magazine,* 28 October 1973.

38. See Rabin, *Yitzhak Rabin mesocheach im manhigim ve-rashey medinot.*

39. Author's interview with Henry Rosovsky, 7 July 2006; Rabbi Alexander Schindler's remarks at the Conference of Presidents of Major American Jewish Organizations, Hotel Pierre, New York City, 11 January 1977, quoted in *Washington Post,* 12 January 1977, A16.

40. Memorandum of Conversation between Kissinger and American Jewish Intellectuals, 6 December 1973, NSA.

41. Memorandum of Conversation between Yitzhak Rabin, Henry Kissinger, et al., 11 September 1974, NSA. Between 1969 and 1973 Kissinger frequently met with Rabin in Washington, D.C. The two men had an intense, frank, and trusting relationship. See the accounts of their meetings in boxes 134–35, Henry Kissinger Office Files, NSC Files, Nixon Papers.

42. Memorandum of Conversation between Rabin, Kissinger, et al., 11 September 1974, NSA. Between 1973 and 1974 annual U.S. assistance to Israel increased from $492 million to $2.6 billion. See the Congressional Research Service report, "Israel: U.S. Foreign Assistance," updated 26 April 2005, available at http://www.fas.org/sgp/crs/mideast/IB85066.pdf#search=%22us%20foreign%20aid%20israel%201973%22 (accessed 4 October 2006).

43. Yigal Allon quoted in Richard Valeriani, *Travels with Henry* (Boston: Houghton Mifflin, 1979), 208.

44. Kissinger's address to the Conference of Presidents of Major American Jewish Organizations, 11 January 1977, *Department of State Bulletin* 76 (31 January 1977), 90. See also "Kissinger Is Honored by U.S. Jewish Group," *New York Times,* 12 January 1977, A3; "An Emotional Kissinger Affirms Support of Israel," *Washington Post,* 12 January 1977, A16; "Kissinger Says 'Shalom' to Jewish Leaders," *Daily News* (New York), 12 January 1977, 13.

45. Kissinger's address to the Conference of Presidents of Major American Jewish Organizations, 11 January 1977, 91; emphasis added.

46. On the Iranian Revolution and the hostage crisis, see David Farber, *Taken Hostage: The Iran Hostage Crisis and America's First Encounter with Radical Islam* (Princeton: Princeton University Press, 2004).

47. Author's interview with Henry Kissinger, 26 October 2005.

48. George W. Bush, Second Inaugural Address, 20 January 2005, http://www.whitehouse.gov/news/releases/2005/01/20050120–1.html (accessed 6 September 2006).

49. Numerous journalists have published insightful accounts that make this point. See, for example, George Packer, *The Assassins' Gate: America in Iraq* (New York: Farrar, Straus and Giroux, 2005); Thomas E. Ricks, *Fiasco: The American Military Adventure in Iraq* (New York: Penguin, 2006); Rajiv Chandrasekaran, *Imperial Life in the Emerald City: Inside Iraq's Green Zone* (New York: Alfred A. Knopf, 2006).

50. Henry A. Kissinger, "Democratic Values and U.S. Policy in Iraq," *Wall Street Journal,* 11 April 2004. See also idem, "Realists vs. Idealists," *International Herald Tribune,* 12 May 2005.

51. On Kissinger's access and advice to George W. Bush's administration, see Bob Woodward, *State of Denial: Bush at War, Part III* (New York: Simon and Schuster, 2006), 406–410. See also James Mann, "For Bush, Realpolitik Is No Longer a Dirty Word," *New York Times,* 11 April 2004, 5.

Acknowledgments

This book began as a study of Henry Kissinger, and it quickly grew into much more. It became an examination of deeper, sometimes troubling, issues related to democracy, power, and identity in the contemporary world. Along the way, I became entangled in questions about my own views of democracy, my own anxieties about power, and my own mixed background. I have generally kept these issues out of the book, but they are part of the way in which this project—and Henry Kissinger himself—has become a part of my life.

This is more than a throwaway line. Fortuitous circumstances brought Henry Kissinger and me together in Fürth, Germany, and various New York area venues. Becoming acquainted with this larger-than-life figure has, quite honestly, been a thrill. Talking with him has been enlightening and frustrating. Understanding him has been an ordeal.

The story does not begin or end with Kissinger. Hundreds—perhaps thousands—of other people have become a part of my life during this project. Armies of archivists, crowds of students, and scores of friends have helped me with acquiring, reading, and interpreting various materials. Many have listened patiently to my analyses of this or that issue. Many have pointed me in directions that greatly improved my research and writing. In particular, I owe deep gratitude to Barton Bernstein, Elizabeth Borgwardt, Lawrence Dickey, Carolyn Eisenberg, Jeffrey Engel, Michaela Fröhlich, David Holloway, David M. Kennedy, Danielle Kleijwegt, Stanley Kutler, Melvyn Leffler, Fredrik Logevall, Thomas McCormick, Alfred McCoy, Michael McManus, Clark Miller, Norman Naimark, Jack Rakove,

Thomas Schwartz, Steve J. Stern, Jeremy Varon, Amir Weiner, Salim Yaqub, and Peter Zinke.

A number of students assisted me with specific parts of the project—including background research on various topics, source identification, archival photocopies, and fact-checking. They all helped me to think through the materials they had found and to ask new questions about materials I had already digested. I want to thank Shauna Fitzmahan, Trudy Fredericks, Sean Gillen, Justin King, Lukas Klessig, Floris Kunert, Jeremy Kuzmarov, Julie Lane, Deborah Meiners, Sonja Mekel, Shawn Peters, Gil Ribak, David Rodriguez, Lauren Roth, Gabriel Kou Solomon, and Vanessa Walker.

I also want to thank the many colleagues and friends who commented on the manuscript, in part or as a whole. Their reactions varied, but their wisdom and generosity were constant. Their insights greatly improved the book. I am indebted to Daniel Abrams, Harvey Black, Clea Bunch, John Milton Cooper Jr., Susan Ferber, John Lewis Gaddis, Frank Gavin, Jussi Hanhimäki, Francine Hirsch, Holger Klitzing, Jim Kurtz, David McDonald, Tony Michels, William Reese, Mary Louise Roberts, David Sorkin, and Odd Arne Westad.

I like to brag that I have the best editor in the business. Kathleen McDermott not only worked through every line of the manuscript; she also helped me to conceptualize, write, and rewrite the book. Her guidance was invaluable every step along the way. This is the second book we have done together, and I cannot imagine this process without her. My agent, Andrew Wylie, also played a crucial role in formulating this project and bringing it to fruition. I am in awe of his knowledge about the book industry, and glad he is on my side. Rose Ann Miller and Kathleen Drummy at Harvard University Press helped in crucial ways. I am honored to have worked with this dream team for a second time.

My gratitude to all of these people is sincere, but it pales in comparison to what I feel for my immediate family. They have sustained me through this project. They have offered me love when I am grumpy and preoccupied. They have inspired me when I am down. They have given my life its deepest and everlasting meaning. Thank you, Alison, Natalie, and Zachary.

Index